RAILS THAT CLIMB

DEDICATION
**To The Moffat Railroaders and the many others
who recognized the value of history as it was being made.**

SMOKING AROUND THE BEND by Howard Fogg—A freight running wide open rounds Yankee Doodle Lake on the 4% grade up Rollins Pass. The original of this painting was donated to the Denver Public Library, Western History Department by the Rocky Mountain Railroad Club in memory of longtime Moffat railroader Bert Fullman—*Used by Permission of DPL; color work courtesy Leanin' Tree Publishing Co.*

RAILS THAT CLIMB

A NARRATIVE HISTORY OF THE MOFFAT ROAD

by
EDWARD T. BOLLINGER

Edited by
William C. Jones

Indexed by
A. D. Mastrogiuseppe

COLORADO RAILROAD MUSEUM
GOLDEN, COLORADO

ACKNOWLEDGMENTS

It is difficult to know where to begin and to end our acknowledgments because so many people helped to make this book possible. Every effort has been made to include a credit for each photo and thus the repetition of listing each photo contributor will be avoided here. However, certain institutions and individuals are to be accorded recognition for their unusual or considerable contributions including the staff of the Western History Department of the Denver Public Library; the staff of the Documentary Resources Department of the State Historical Society of Colorado; the Engineering, Executive and Operating Departments of the Denver & Rio Grande Western Railroad; Bob Munshower, the Mobile Post Office Society and the authors of *Colorado Postal History,* William H. Bauer, James L. Ozment and John H. Willard, for the use of historic post marks; Chuck Weart for information on the Moffat rotary plows; Wally Maxwell, Robert W. Richardson and Hol Wagner for their generous assistance; John Maxwell for his historic color photography; Robert E. Jensen for his painting done especially for this book; Howard Fogg for his fine painting which is made available through the courtesy of Edward Trumble of Leanin' Tree Publishing Company; the late Wilfred Stedman for the especially made drawings used on most of the chapter headings; and John Buvinger for the Moffat Road map researched and drawn for this book.

Finally the author and editor must express their thanks for endless patience and willing help from their wives, Alice Bollinger and Bettyann Jones.

For convenience in identifying the sources of photos, those from two major collections are identified with the following abbreviations:
DPL — Denver Public Library, Western History Department
CRRM — Colorado Railroad Museum

Dust jacket painting — PLOW TRAIN AT RANCH CREEK by Robert E. Jensen. (See page 210 for complete data on this painting.)

Endpaper — Train No. 1 in South Boulder Cañon — *Otto Perry, DPL*
Half Title Page — Engine 302 hurries west near Plainview on Dec. 7, 1941; Pearl Harbor Day — *Richard H. Kindig, CRRM*

Colorado Railroad Historical Foundation, Inc.

The Foundation is a non-profit Colorado institution organized to operate and perpetuate the Colorado Railroad Museum. The Museum was established in 1958 by Robert Richardson and Cornelius Hauck, for the preservation of Colorado's unique railroad heritage. Your support in the work of the Foundation and Museum is earnestly solicited; and inquiry will bring membership information.

©Copyright 1979
by the
Colorado Railroad Historical Foundation
P.O. Box 10, Golden, Colorado, 80401

Printed in the United States of America
by Johnson Publishing Company
Boulder, Colorado

Typography by New Morning Composition
Boulder, Colorado

Color Separations by Spectrum Inc.
Denver, Colorado

Library of Congress Cataloging in Publication Data
Bollinger, Edward Taylor, 1907-
 Rails that climb.
 Reprint of the 1950 ed. published by Rydal Press, Santa Fe.
 Bibliography: p.
 Includes index.
 1. Denver and Salt Lake Railroad—History. 2. Moffat, David Halliday, 1839-1911. 3. Capitalists and financiers—United States—Biography. I. Jones, William C., 1937- II. Title.
HE2791.D4432 1979   385′.09788   79-14634
ISBN 0-918654-29-7

PREFACE

This book has been designed to take you back in time for a number of visits. You will learn to know a few men, and greet others in passing. I warn you that your ears will be frosted if you do not keep them covered, you will pant in the thin air and choke in the snow shed gas, for this is the story of the *Rails that Climb*.

The selection of the men who you meet most frequently was determined by the accidents of time that brought Barnes to the Moffat after years of railroad experience and Culbertson likewise. Even earlier Nels Johnson and L. J. Daly, husky kids of sixteen, were at work in the construction of the line. We hear of H. A. Sumner in almost every chapter because of the importance of a chief engineer in the building of a railroad in such a country and also because of the very lustre of his character. But Sumner would have been lost in the dust of men's memories had not his letters been carefully preserved in letter presses. In contrast we have none of the general manager's letters and only two diaries remain giving a day to day account. Some men you hear about because they were my neighbors or friendships were formed through incidents of no importance. But these men do give you, as we follow them or pass them, an idea of how the rails climbed.

Over the thirty years since the first edition of *Rails that Climb* was being prepared, much new research has unearthed both factual material and collections of pictures, found after determined hunting. Erksel Deakins and his Moffat men on the west end filled many gaps and there were located the fine photographs of engineer Glenn Spaulding, the late Joe Preiss and Colonel George Pappas. The determined research of Leda Reed answered many questions and there were others, many others who gave assistance to fill the gaps in history.

Over this same span of years the demand for energy reopened the great coal resources in Moffat and Routt Counties. Rio Grande President Gus Aydelott shared the Moffat idea — dig into your pockets but don't go to the government. His vision was that the line from Denver to Craig must be made immediately one of the most modern and he was backed by his Board of Directors. The line now handles more than a score of trains each day and when that number soon doubles there will be no need to have work trains tying up the line. Aydelott's determination and vision is second only to that of David Moffat and W. G. Evans who were seventy-five years ahead of their time.

Edward T. Bollinger

EDITOR'S FOREWORD

When Ed Bollinger offered the Colorado Railroad Museum the opportunity to publish a new edition of his work *Rails that Climb*, we at the Museum saw this as an opportunity to produce a book which would combine his text history with an excellent collection of photographs that had not been available when the book was first published. We have endeavored to bring these two mediums together into what we believe is an interesting and accurate history of a mountain railroad; the men who built and operated it under sometimes hopeless conditions, and the people and country it served.

A highlight of this undertaking has been the endless enthusiasm put forth by Mr. Bollinger for his subject. The original text has been basically retained but greatly expanded and updated. The volume of new photos and data have caused the project to expand from what was first planned as a mere reprint, to a final product which is in fact an entirely new book. We only hope that you will experience some of the same satisfaction in reading this history as we had in its production.

William C. Jones

Denver & Salt Lake Railroad

Sight-Seeing Excursions to the Snow Banks on the Crest of the Continent

TOP O' THE WORLD

"THE MOFFAT ROAD"

CAFE-PARLOR CAR ———————————— VESTIBULED TRAIN
Leaves Denver Daily 9:00 A. M.   Returning, Arrives Daily 5:00 P. M.

City Passenger Office, 719 Seventeenth Street
Moffat Depot, 15th and Bassett Sts.

SMITH-BROOKS PRINTING CO.

Poster circa 1920 — *CRRM*

TABLE OF CONTENTS

DAVID HALLIDAY MOFFAT
July 22, 1839 — March 18, 1911

1

A Great Man Dreams

This is primarily the story of David Moffat and a railroad; but it is also the story of some very stubborn mountains and some very rugged men.

In 1860 Denver was a sprawling town something like a noisy boy with unkempt hair and pockets filled with fishing worms. Here, where the streets were churned dusty by heavy wagons, the seekers for gold rested after they had crossed the prairie. The man who had made a strike of precious metals celebrated his return to civilization, as he picked up more tools and helpers.

Ever to the West the mountains kept watch over the ambitious village and reminded all who dared to climb the battlements that nowhere in the Rocky Mountain West was there so high or so rugged a wall as this one which said, "You can come this far, but no farther. You can go south two hundred miles through Raton Pass, or you can go north a hundred miles through a friendly grade in Wyoming. But you can not scale my heights with wagon or train, for I have made an alliance with Old Man Winter to dump out of the skies snow and more snow from October to June. I have called on the North Wind and the East Wind and the West Wind to defend my battlements with sub-zero blizzards."

The mountains, however, were kind to those who dug in their icy stream beds, so that the demand for food, goods, and machinery was great. Denver's business men found wagons far too expensive and slow to bring freight to these men. Denver clamored for a railroad, the only road in that day, that was a road.

So rugged was this wall of mountains that America's first transcontinental railroad had spurned Andrew Rogers' survey for a route in the James Peak area. Denver seemed threatened to remain a cross-roads mudhole, for some of her enterprising merchants were closing shop and moving to Cheyenne, Wyoming, on the route of the Union Pacific. But there was gold and silver in "them thar hills." Cities like Central City needed roads to develop them. But it takes men with tenacity to build in the Rockies.

Such were the affairs of Denver in 1860 when David H. Moffat, Jr., a lad as tall and thin as a lodge pole pine, opened a stationery store. Like a modern drug store, David Moffat's store adapted itself to the demands of these miners. Many of them had a taste for the good things the East had taught them to love, but which the West denied them. When his wagons from St. Joseph, Missouri, arrived ahead of the mail, he put the newspapers under his arm and peddled them to his regular customers for twenty-five cents apiece.

Dave had an eye for business and a kindly consideration for his friends that matured into greatness.

For seven years he had been away from home. Washingtonville, New York, had given him a good grade school education and the stories of the Bible's great men. His high school had been a New York bank and his lessons, the work of a messenger. From this school he ran away to far-off Iowa to be with his brother who had preceded him. Messenger, teller, cashier was the story of higher education in three words. He raced west to Omaha ahead of the proposed Pacific Railroad to make and lose a fortune in real estate before he was of age. Just twenty, but in the eyes of the West every inch of his bean-pole height a man, he formed a partnership with C.C. Woolworth of St. Joseph, Missouri. Alone, David went to Denver to open the new store.

With only the intention of making a stake and returning East, he dug into the business problems of early Denver. One year later he brought his boyhood sweetheart west to make his house a home. Lace curtains went up in the windows; Indian males flattened their noses on the panes, peering within to see just what kind of house-keeping job this pale-face squaw did; or perchance to see if it were true that the pale-skinned male did some of the work!

In this house and not in the gambling dens of Denver was born the Moffat Railroad. The mountains had won David Moffat's heart, for here was the Empire of Governor John Evans' vision. Here was more than gold, silver and lead. Here were iron, oil, wool, timber, and far more precious metals than man had yet learned.

In 1864, four years after the Scotch-Irish youth had come west, Territorial Governor John Evans appointed David Moffat Adjutant General, an important post during the Civil War. In 1867 he became Cashier of the First National Bank of Denver where his financing would soon touch railroading.

The Union Pacific turned down the Colorado route for the easier grades of southern Wyoming and soon people were moving to Cheyenne. Denver could become a dusty ghost town without a future. When the city's business leaders stood up and were counted, the Denver Pacific was organized and built from Cheyenne to Denver. The first locomotive was named after the kindly, loyal man they trusted as their treasurer — David Moffat.

That construction engine was inadvertently symbolic of the friendly man who became treasurer of the Boulder Valley Railroad and whose signature would be seen among the original incorporators and directors of the Denver, Utah and Pacific which organized on December 11, 1880, with Moffat as the Treasurer. Edgar C. McMechen states in *The Moffat Tunnel of Colorado* that this was Moffat's first effort toward his idea of a railroad running directly west.

Moffat was by necessity a 'railroader'! Industry could not be built by hauling mining machinery in lumbering wagons on the little improved trails. Cities like Central City and Leadville were to be reached by narrow gauged railroads, which cut down the overhead incurred by costly wagon transportation.

Moffat, having heavy financial interests in one hundred mines, was technically a miner; but he was essentially a builder. So it was in that day when some men made money selling Taos Lightning to Indians, Moffat began developing the Rocky Mountain Empire.

If the narrow gauge branch lines converging in Denver could be tied up with a direct western outlet, Denver would become a great city. The Rio Grande had been beaten in its race to Raton Pass in New Mexico, but its intentions had been Mexico, not the West Coast. When the Rio Grande, however, won the Royal Gorge battle, many people in Denver were enthusiastic. But the route west would be as far south of Denver (over a hundred miles to Pueblo) as the Union Pacific was north. Not only was Pueblo south and a little east of Denver, but Salt Lake City was even north of Denver. The Rio Grande was thus a very indirect route.

General Palmer had built his steel mill by organizing the Colorado Fuel and Iron Company, June 23, 1880. Pueblo could become a steel city like Pittsburgh, but this plant, like the woolen mill and the cotton mill in Denver, was to have a rough road against the competitors in the East. They would control the railroad rates so that it would be cheaper to ship to the West Coast from Pittsburgh or even from the New England states than from Pueblo.

Moffat realized that the real enemy of Colorado expansion was not the Indian, but the freight rates discriminating against the Colorado manufacturer; and he, instead of being filled with murderous thoughts about the Indians, hoped to get a road west that would be financially controlled by Colorado men. In 1885, when he became president of the Rio Grande Railroad, he began surveys to find a shorter route west.

The weary and aging General Palmer turned to the much younger David Moffat, asking him to become president of the Rio Grande. Two things were needed to compete with the newest threat in the building of the standard gauge Colorado Midland; to standard gauge the Rio Grande and find a direct route west. Moffat immediately complied.

During his presidency he spent $106,374 for surveys. He found for example, that a rise and fall of

2

4,000 feet to Pueblo (which landed a train further east than it had been to start with), was not sound railroading. But with Eastern directors not seeing eye to eye on the great expense of a new line, Moffat turned to improving the existing line, making it broad gauge, thus correcting the narrow gauge mistake. Where a few hundred feet could be saved in relocation, the line was relocated; where a branch would develop a good mine, a branch was advocated. Sometimes Moffat himself financed and built branches which the board turned down, such as the Creede Branch which the Rio Grande later was happy to take over.

Moffat had come a long way since he had peddled papers; yet not so far but that he still had troubles. The board of directors wanted him to fire Syl Smith, general manager, for staying with the bottle and for old age inefficiency. Moffat refused, for he stood by his men when he had once accepted them. For such as this he was fired in 1891. Moffat still owned the Florence and Cripple Creek line and later he was to help with building the Denver and New Orleans. The Mining King of the state might have been considered past the age of adventuring further but Denver was still off any transcontinental railroad.

By the close of the century Moffat still bore the hurt of his departure from the Rio Grande, and it was deepest because the dream of a road west never matured. He was now involved in the challenge of electric power in use for streetcars and interurbans. He was deeply moved by the statement of J. J. Hill when he pushed his Great Northern line over the Rockies, that the answer was just power.

Moffat was sixty-three years old when he attempted the most daring scheme of his life. If he were successful, the Burlington and the Rock Island would have a route west of Denver. At that time the Eastern owners of the Rio Grande looked with great disfavor on the scheme, though today the Rio Grande, the Burlington and Western Pacific use the Moffat to save 175 miles on a transcontinental route.

Moffat was no longer a lanky lad with a stationery store. He was now the financial wizard of the state with the lessons of forty-two years in Colorado's mining and railroad business deep in his mind. But above all else he kept the vision that saw a way through the Front Range (Continental Divide at this spot) to the Northwest of Colorado where fabulous resources lay undeveloped and where further west lay the route of the transcontinental road Denver needed. Spurred by a great dream this great man laid his plans.

Edward H. Harriman reacted with great anger. As president of the Union Pacific, the smallest threat to his railroad caused him to act like a wounded animal.

An enlightening description of Harriman is provided in the biography of his financial associate Otto Kuhn.

> Harriman was physically the most unprepossessing of men. His enemies sneered, called him "the little bookkeeper." He had always suffered poor health. He was small, frail, and retiring. He spoke in a low voice and wore thick-lensed, steel-rimmed glasses.
>
> In a cogent essay on Harriman, Kuhn characterized him as ineloquent and incapable of tact or diplomacy. No one ever heard Harriman tell a joke. He rarely smiled.
>
> His genius, Kuhn said, "was the genius of the conqueror, his dominion was based on rugged strength, iron will, irresistible determination, indomitable courage and . . . upon those qualities of character which command men's trust and confidence. He was constitutionally unable either to cajole or to dissemble. He was stiff-necked to a fault. It would have saved him much opposition, many enemies, many misunderstandings, if he had possessed the gift of suavity . . . I ventured to plead with him that the results he sought could just as surely be obtained by less combative, more gentle methods, while at the same time avoiding bad blood and ill feeling. . .
>
> Within one year Harriman had turned the line toward success. He became the ruling spirit and the genius of the board, which by 1899 conceded leadership to him.*

*Matz, Mary Jane, *The Many Lives of Otto Kuhn.* MacMillan Publishing Co. New York. 1963. Reprinted with permission.

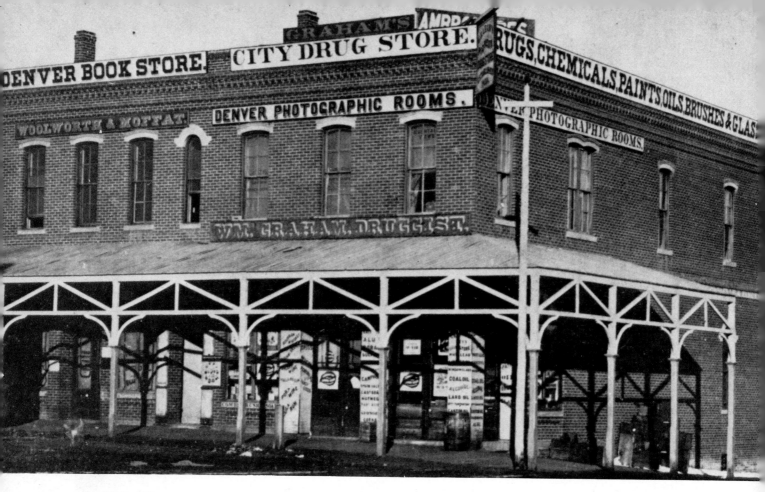

In this building at the southwest corner of 15th and Larimer Streets, the partners of Woolworth and Moffat opened their book and stationery store in 1860. The photo was taken about 1866, shortly before Moffat left the business. —*DPL*

4

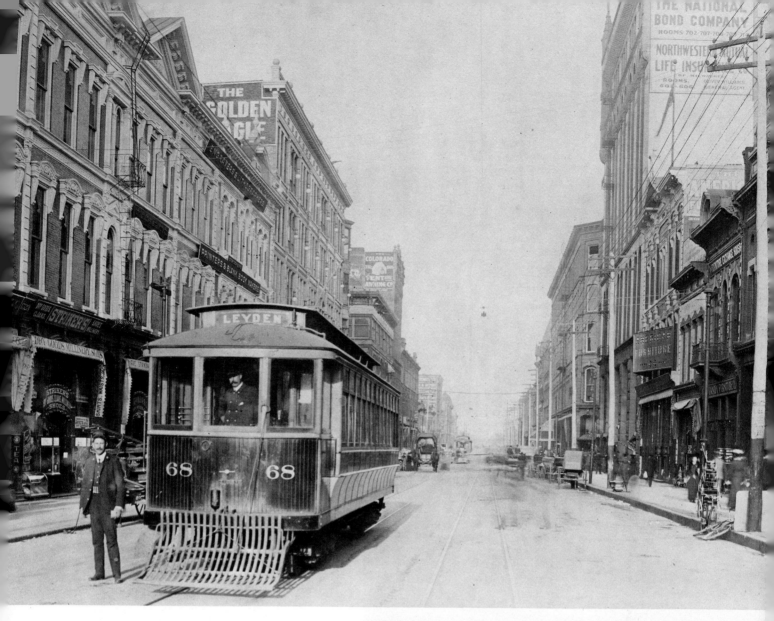

The First National Bank is seen (left) under construction at 15th and Blake Streets in 1865. Moffat became cashier of the new bank in 1867 and president in 1880, a position he held until his death. The interior view of the bank (right) provides a glimpse of his office. During the winter of 1875-76 the Colorado Constitutional Convention was held in this building but following an arsonist's fire its future is in doubt.

Two of Moffat's business ventures are seen (above) as a Leyden electric car of the Denver & Northwestern Ry. poses in front of the Moffat and Kassler Building at the left in the photo taken on Lawrence Street between 15th and 16th Streets about 1904. — *above, Wm. Jones coll.; others State Historical Soc. of Colorado.*

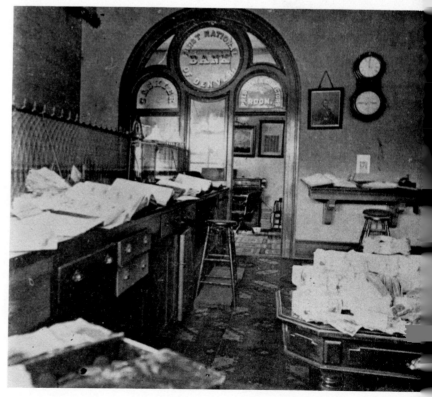

The plains spread to the horizon in this view from Tunnel No. 8. The roadway below is a remnant of grading by the Denver, Utah & Pacific in 1881. That early attempt to build a railroad west from Denver failed but to H. A. Sumner, a young locator on the job, it provided invaluable experience for the task he now faced in locating the Moffat Road. Eventually this grade was used by the Denver Water Board in building their system to bring water to Denver through the Moffat Tunnel. The resort town of Eldorado Springs lies along the creek near the center of the picture. — *L. C. McClure, DPL*

No one photo can depict the fortress that nature placed in the path of the Moffat Road but in this view is seen the panorama of the Front Range looking east from near the summit of Rollins Pass. — *L. C. McClure, DPL*

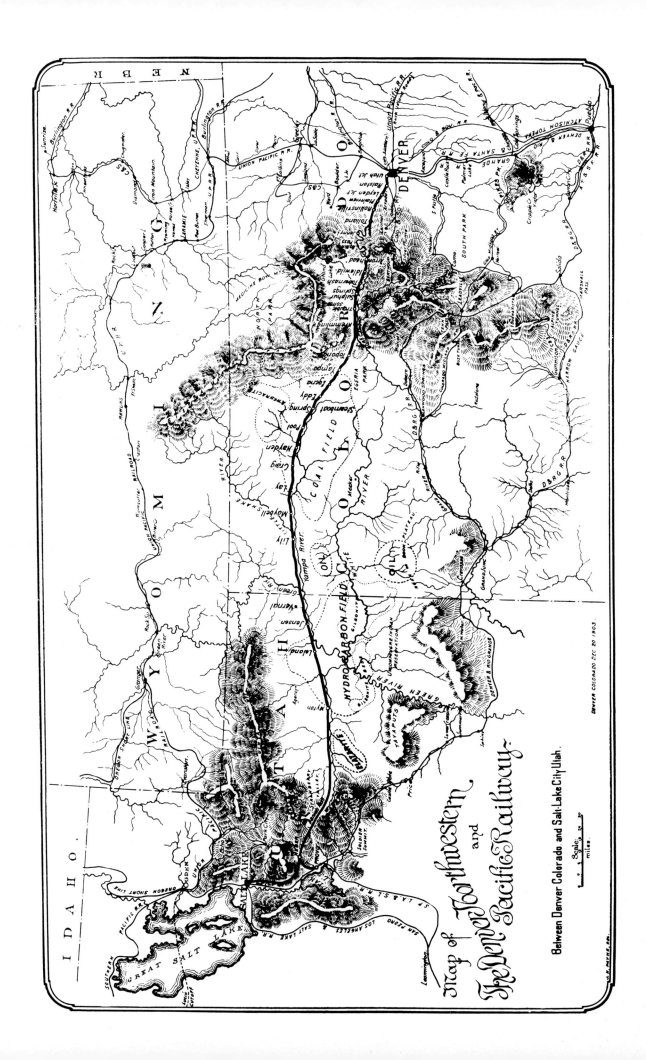

Map of Northwestern and The Denver Pacific Railway.

Between Denver Colorado and Salt Lake City Utah.

This 1903 map was used to promote the railroad before the first train had been dispatched. It is interesting to note that the proposed 2.6 mile tunnel is included along with the Rollins Pass line. — *Western History Coll., Univ. of Colorado*

2

Men and Mountains

The date is July 18, 1902. The place is Coal Creek Cañon seventeen miles west of Denver in the foothills of the Divide.

It is about noon. A husky young man swings himself over a rock with the aid of his surveyor's rod. "Hey, what do you think you are doing? Pole vaulting at a track meet?" growls R. Bruce Parker, whose transit is being planted in the sage brush to make another reading.

"Naw, I'm just trying to spike a chipmunk so that we have enough meat for dinner. Say, Bruce, just because you have a girl back in Kansas, don't start acting as if you are married, have kids, and grandchildren."

"Art, you're not dry behind the ears, even though you are only a year or two younger than me. Watch it, for Blauvelt is out here some place trying to find a grade that does not exist for Old Man Milner."

Another youthful kid by the name of Herb Reno comes up with a bag of stakes. "If you tenderfoots think I am going to carry stakes all day and try driving them in this rock infested mountain, you're mistaken. I was on this job a month before you showed up with your pranks and hungry looks."

Bruce Parker grins in his mild way and points to a little dust down the road where a spring wagon — an apt name for a wagon with no springs except two directly under the seat — is bouncing over the ruts and rocks. "It's Ed Milner looking for Blauvelt."

Milner calls out, "Say, where is Blauvelt? I've got to find him. All hell has broke loose. You ought to see the morning paper."

Art Weston vaults back over the same rock and catches the reins of the perspiring horse and says, "Hold everything and tell the news. We don't print the Post or the News out here. We just print menus of hunger and starvation."

"Let go! Let go! I've got to find Blauvelt. This is not a game of cowboys and Indians. You kids ought to be back home tied to your maw's apron strings."

By this time Herb Reno had parked in front of the horse that was content to breathe a bit, and Parker, having no rebuke but a mischievous look, burst forth laughing, "Now, Ed Milner, you know you are just dying to tell us something. Has the old man found a mistake in our last line or was it a gold mine some one stole, leaving the hole and no pay dirt?"

"Come now, we care not for news. Did you bring the cook a quarter of beef? I'm starved," barked Art Weston.

"I brought your beef and the cook stole the morning paper which reads, 'DAVID MOFFAT TO BUILD STEAM ROAD TO SALT LAKE'."

Herb sputters, "Hold everything! You mean I've been carrying stakes for a steam road instead of a narrow gauge juice line? Those stakes are too skinny for a standard gauge steam road."

"Pipe down, little fellow. Who said anything about a standard gauge road? Ed said a steam road."

"I don't care what I said. It's steam and standard gauge and the Old Man has been left out, and a man by the name of Sumner is chief engineer.''

The field engineer, Blauvelt, has all the while been slipping down the hillside on his horse and has heard it all, so he is able to interrupt, ''What's this about Sumner?''

''Hey, you fellows! Sumner, Moffat, T. J. Milner or what not, it's ten past noon, and I'm starved. Let's find the eats.''

As the men rode back to camp, uppermost in everybody's mind was the fact that T. J. ''Ed'' Milner was not to be chief on the new job. The interurban line, known as the Denver & Northwestern Railway, would be completed as far as Leyden in 1903 and a branch from Arvada to Golden by 1904. That would be the extent of the line although a standard gauge third rail was laid along with the 42 inch gauge trolley line to allow an interchange of coal between the electric line and the Moffat at Leyden Junction and with the Colorado & Southern in Arvada. Moffat took advantage of the interurban route and build the new steam road parallel for the six miles from Arvada to Leyden Junction. The electric line soon passed into the hands of the Denver Tramway and continued to operate until 1950.

As the food disappeared inside the cook tent, Art Weston was filled to capacity. The noon hour lasted two hours, for Blauvelt had taken off towards Denver to get back to the office and learn what was not printed. The boys realized their jobs were good for more than a summer. They laughed to think how they had been surveying for a steam railroad. They still heard the echo of Blauvelt's statement that Sumner had been on the 1890 survey over this route for the Colorado Railway. Some of the other boys had started the remark that it was unfair for T. J. Milner to lose out, but they all seemed to think David Moffat had a reason, for Moffat was a great man, one to be respected. Above all else they asked, ''Would Harriman let this move of Moffat's go unchallenged?'' They knew this would be no ordinary battle between rival railroads, for Moffat was going to build the finest road West.

On the other side of the Divide, in fact not too far over the top, another survey party blistered in the two-mile high rare air. These boys would not learn the news until the next day.

That fall this party continued its search for the narrowest point of the Divide where a tunnel could pierce the Front Range to best advantage.

The autumnal equinox has dumped tons of snow above timberline. A dozen young men start plung-

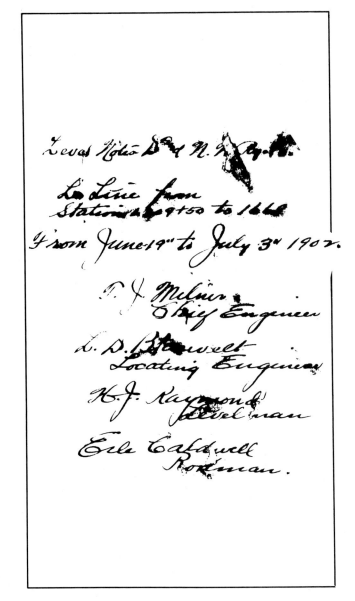

The title page from T. J. Milner's ''Level Notes — D. and N.W. Ry. Co.'' reminds of this man's heartache. As the well respected chief engineer of the electric line he surely expected to be included in Moffat's plans for the Denver, Northwestern & Pacific. Instead H. A. Sumner was given the assignment because of his greater experience. The stock certificate for the D&NW RY was issued May 1, 1902, only weeks before announcement of the steam road. Years later famed railroad photographer Otto Perry took this unusual photo (right) from the Coal Creek bridge looking west along the 3% grade T. J. Milner had planned for the electric line. Perry's Plymouth sits in the foreground. — *right, DPL; above-right, Wm. Jones coll.; above, Western History Coll., Univ. of Colorado.*

10

THE
DENVER AND NORTHWESTERN
RAILWAY COMPANY.

No 3091   WHOLE ISSUE $6,000,000.   No 3091

FIRST AND COLLATERAL MORTGAGE THIRTY-YEAR FIVE PER CENT GOLD BOND

PRINCIPAL PAYABLE MAY 1, 1932

For value received, The Denver and Northwestern Railway Company promises to pay to the bearer, either at its office in Denver, Colorado, or at its Financial Agency in the City of New York, at the holder's option, on the first day of May, 1932. **One Thousand Dollars ($1000)** in United States gold coin, of or equal to the present standard of weight and fineness, with interest thereon at **FIVE** per centum per

WILLIAM G. EVANS

Evans urged Moffat to build his railroad and stood unflinchingly behind him, becoming president at Moffat's death. Gerald Hughes, another close Moffat associate, writes (right) of his relationship and comments on the electric line. For many years coal from Leyden was interchanged with the Moffat at Leyden Jct. using trains such as seen (below) at Leyden in 1903. — *below, Gene McKeever coll; others DPL*

GERALD HUGHES
INTERNATIONAL TRUST BUILDING
DENVER, COLORADO

April 16, 1947

Rev. Edward T. Bollinger
308 South Third Street
Raton, New Mexico

Dear Sir:

Your letter of March 17, 1947, concerning your forthcoming book, and Mr. Moffat and the Moffat Road, was duly received, and the delay in answering was not through neglect, but my desire to see if I could obtain some of the information which you wanted.

It would be impossible by letter to express to you my high and affectionate regard for Mr. Moffat. The qualities to which you refer were all genuine and consistent, and too much credit cannot be given to him as a man, as well as a financier. On this subject, however, I could only suggest that if you are some time in Denver I will be very glad to talk with you, when personal reminiscences might be of help to you.

I recall the trip to Steam Shovel Cut, but I have no copy of the photograph to which you refer, nor any picture of Mr. H. A. Sumner, whom I also recall so well. I can, however, answer your question about the Electric Line, and it is in the negative. The "Electric Line," so called, was an independent thought which preceded any thought of the Steam Line, and while it was in process, Mr. Moffat changed his mind and definitely notified Mr. Evans and myself, who were in New York, to drop the Electric Line financing and return to Denver, as he had decided to try and build the steam road through to Salt Lake.

If I can be of assistance to you, I will be only too glad to do so, but I believe the personal interview which I have referred to would be much more satisfactory to you.

Yours truly,

Gerald Hughes

GH:W

ing off the Divide in the blinding sun after the storm. They are in single file. W. I. Hoklas, a tall youth of twenty-five, is in the lead breaking trail. You cannot see that he has on high-top shoes and wool socks, for he is sinking in far above them time and again. Those legs, that once had stood on the deck of a Rio Grande engine cab gaining sinews of steel as he fired, give out and he drops to the side for the next fellow, Spencer, to break trail.

Their idea is to get down to their regular camp from this fly camp. But there is no end of going up and down in this rugged high line country above 11,000 feet. It is a good thing no new men are in the party. Spencer drops to the side. The next man is Meredith, the location engineer. He stops. It's time the boys get their breath. Again they are on their way. Meredith is soon replaced by Dick Holmes, a six-foot-six giant. J. J. Argo, the transitman, growls about the need for snow shoes, some one snorts about how easy it must be in the Denver office; one lad grimly reflects how early in the summer he had marveled at the beauty of this country, and now it all seems so painful. They are all wet, even though the snow is dry.

Camp is reached. Supper is served. Smitten with sudden snow blindness, they grope for their food at the table. Strong words are heard.

That night the one-time Rio Grande fireman, Hoklas, rubs a slice of raw potato over his eyes. Since there is not a drug store within two days from this isolated spot, the men try anything for relief. Hoklas, exhausted by the day, reaches under the tent from his cot for snow to cool his eyes as he tries to sleep. In the morning he tries painting around his eyes with charcoal.

As autumn continues and their eyes again see the golden aspen leaves around camp, their spirits are warmed by the balmy days, revelling in the glory of Indian summer in the Rockies.

The evening camp sing is heard again. The cook is busy in his tent; his helper is washing dishes as the lad with the fiddle signals the fellowship of song. "There'll Be a Hot Time in the Old Town Tonight" is the tune that comes from around the crackling fire. Some one arrives with a mouthharp, and Dick Holmes' deep bass voice booms as he throws some more wood on the fire and calls for a Spanish-American war song. This giant can well be respected, for he placed the flag above Manila.

As the song dies out, it is evident that the orchestra is incomplete, for some of the players are doing chores or are in conference. Meredith lets the mandolin player go from his tent, while he and J. J. Argo go over the notes for the day by the kerosene lamp light.

Some one tells a story that smells worse than a skunk. There is a roll of laughter, and the boy with the jew's harp appears. The "Jacks" (pack mules) are now cared for, and he and the axeman join the sing.

The evening air is chilly. Some one remarks that the moon looks like snow. And what are these dainty little flakes now dropping out of a mist above? Some one swears and as though his words were heard, the flakes thin out. "Merrily We Roll Along," "Old Kentucky Home," "Swanee River" and, above all, "Strolling Down the Shady Lane With Gurley (Gurley transit)" are sung.

J. J. Argo now joins them, as does Meredith before long. The snow flakes begin to spit in the fire again and some one says, "Now just remember it is not snowing." Argo suggests they sing "When the Mists Have Rolled Away," using the words "when the snow has melted away."

Meredith wanted to sing, "Heidelberg," but he is deserted as the flakes increase and the fire dies low. The fiddle player is gone, a prank upsets the man with the jew's harp, as he stumbles to his tent. The evening concert is over. The outcasts have taken to their "Bull Pen," so named because the occupants are too lazy to clean out their tent or see that sufficient wood is at hand for a snowy or cold morning.

But within the other sixteen-foot square tent Dick Holmes is still singing as he undresses. W. I. Hoklas has turned to his books, for he is determined to utilize the long winter evenings for an engineering course under International Correspondence School guidance. On his suitcase, ingeniously opened as a writing table, he is figuring the problems of the course. He has an extra sweater, for in this tent men are considerate of one another. He would no more roast out his bunkmates with more heat from the Sibley stove than they would think of refusing their turn at sweeping the dirt floor. Old "Aunty" Spencer, the stake cutter, has sprinkled down the dirt floor more than once, for he can do this from his nearby job during the day. He also furnishes the shavings from his work to catch a blaze in the hot coals on early morning rising.

This Sibley stove was an inverted light sheet metal funnel set on the dirt floor and fed dry wood from the pine and aspen stock. It was stoked well late at night with green wood to hold the fire in the chill wee hours of the morning.

As Hoklas dropped off to sleep at 1:00 a.m., the other lads already were dreaming of home, the gal, or another camp fire when they would sing, "Good Night Ladies," some classics, and a hymn, for the latter was not uncommon on Sunday night.

So the winter went with the boys not so high in the mountains but with memories of how they had climbed, behind head chainman Hoklas, to build a monument on top of the Divide where a tunnel was proposed. From this monument Mitton could tie in his party's work on the East side with Meredith's work on the West. Some days they all were down in the Fraser Valley hastily making a right-of-way through Fraser Cañon lest some one beat them to it and file claims for a competitor to hole them up.

Strange men were wandering through the timber. If Mitton or Argo knew who they were, they did not say, and the stories of an enemy's engineers were allowed to grow.

Monthly reports from the engineer's tent included maps made on the field with topography carefully shown. Every ridge was to be run for elevations, and every ravine marked with its depth, so that in the Denver office the entire mountain could be seen by the locating eye of their chief, H. A. Sumner.

Spring came, bringing another summer and its work. Rails were starting to climb on paper and rails were climbing by promotion. Meredith was field chief west of the Divide, and J. J. Argo was head of his own party.

Argo was keeping his own diary now. In a good hand he had written:

"D.N.W. & P. Ry. Co.
Diary
Beginning November 1st, 1903
J. J. Argo
Loc. Engineer"

Now he was recording in a few words the day's activities:

"Sunday, November 1, 1903
"Camp on Deer Creek about 10,300-foot elevation
"Fine clear day
"No field work as usual on Sunday
"Made up reports and bills for October."

A leaf still clinging to the aspen trees told of the Indian summer that was past and the winter that was at hand. The Lodge Pole Pines and Engleman Spruce would stand watch in deep green throughout the winter.

It's Sunday; a few boys have been hunting,

others reading, and some have ridden the "Jacks" down to Idlewild where the saloon and stage station are located.

Argo's party has twenty men including teamsters, axemen, cook, and the survey crew. Argo is worried about the snowshoe order that has not been heard from. He remembers the shortage of the winter before. Only four pair of snowshoes would mean plenty of trouble again. He had better write Meredith once more. Meredith had been through the winter. He would understand. On second thought he remembered that their chief, H. A. Sumner had been all over this country twenty or more years before when the "Q" — the nickname for the Chicago, Burlington and Quincy Railroad — was working on its survey.

Argo's pen had ceased to write. He was dreaming, gazing off into space past the pearl-handled pistol hanging underneath the fishing pole. The topographer was at work at a table. He made a slighting remark about canned food, cans of food, army stuff.

Argo may have heard but he did not answer. He was thinking about that man Sumner. He had a way with men. He recalled Parker's telling how, when they were riding along, Sumner dropped pertinent remarks and hints that Parker later realized were almost an advanced course in engineering.

He contrasted the wild antics and spirit of the boys with the reserved quiet manner of this great location engineer. He had noted that after the "Chief" had been in camp, the boys invariably settled down. There were even signs that gentlemen might grow out of the Bull Pen.

Argo remembered the Sunday monring he had last been in Denver; it was such a joy to be with his wife and five children. But he had felt he must get down to the office, for there the chief would be and he might get some help.

The office engineer who was in said, "The Chief may be in this afternoon, but if you have to see him you go up to . . ." then pausing as though trying to recall the name, "that church up . . . yes, it's Congregational. . . . What in the deuce is its name? Plymouth, that's it!"

It was better working under such a chief, for no one could say he confined his religion to one hour in church . . . . The dream faded; the pen that had been writing reports dipped again in the ink and resumed its work.

The late December snows and the lack of snowshoes had made the work difficult. Sumner thought it wise that Meredith call his men out of the high country. So on Wednesday, December 23, Argo's men began moving camp. In five feet of snow the sled was unsteady. It overturned once and everyone was concerned about —- of all things! —- the fiddle.

It was a painful trek moving tents and stoves and bunks down to Idlewild. It was only a few miles, but what miles. Some one growled, "Still only four pair of snowshoes." Someone swore that the shoes must be coming from China, not Maine. Someone else sputtered that they ought to shave off Sumner's mustache and make a snowshoe out of it; but that remark did not set well.

The sun had set when they reached Idlewild. Too tired to set up camp, the men slept on the floor of Ed Evans' saloon. Now whether Ed removed all his precious bottles, we do not know, but likely the boys warmed their stomachs with drink as well as food.

In the morning, one last great effort by the twenty-two men and Bob Throckmorton's teamsters brought down the last pieces of camp equipment. The day wore on and the last load overturned. The air was filled with anything but Christmas carols.

By stage time in the afternoon, most of the boys had taken off over Berthoud Pass behind the careful driving of Bill Proctor, whose stage brought a warm glow to hearts homeward-bound on Christmas Eve. Bob Throckmorton returned to Coulter and his family.

J. J. Argo and the few remaining boys spent Christmas Day in Idlewild. It is doubtful if any of them took particular note of the stately Engleman Spruce or the Fraser River playing hide and seek under the ice and snow. They were still working on setting up camp, drying out things that had been soaked by the snow.

It was Christmas evening. Argo had helped the cook get a great dinner for the lads. "Ed Evans has a Christmas tree with candles," Argo grinned and added, "Did you see all the cotton on our Christmas tree?"

"Don't you insult cotton with this frozen water that goes through nature's cotton gin and comes out snow," laughed Dick Holmes, who began humming a Christmas carol.

Argo thought of his five kiddies as he looked at his men around the table. Yes, he knew by now almost all the secrets of their lives. The girl who missed her date for tonight; the mother who had mailed out a fruit cake to her son.

Good! the packages had come in! It was Christmas evening. The snow fell softly so as not to bring distraction as the boys sang "Silent Night, Holy Night." The fiddle was there, but no one knew how to play it. The mandolin had gone home, but the boys could sing Christmas hymns. Someone knocked on the tent door. It was Ed Evans from the stage station. "My wife made a cake. I thought you boys might enjoy it." So they spent Christmas evening in a beautiful spot nestling below towering peaks that kept the stormy blasts of winter from drifting the snow.

"Looks like Bill Proctor will have to give up the stage for the winter pretty soon. But we usually get the mail even if they have to walk out on snowshoes for it," remarked the local stage boss.

"I'm expecting E. A. Meredith, our field engineer, for this side on Sunday," Argo announced.

Ed Evans, who by now was enjoying a cigar one of the boys had offered him said, "Great fellow. I hear that he walked against the world's champion doing one hundred miles in twenty-four hours."

Argo answered, "Yes, he was an all-round athlete at Yale; can talk on any subject with intelligence. He is a six-foot giant."

"Did you say 'giant,' Mister Argo?" came the mocking quiet words of Dick Holmes. Everyone roared, for Dick was six-six.

"But I tell you, Mister Evans, I never saw a man like him. He works after the sun is set and can see through that transit when I can't see the stones on the trail. If he is one or ten miles from camp, it makes no difference. He just stretches his legs and goes like no man's business."

Everyone laughed, with Dick Holmes leading the laughter. After a pause, Evans turned to Argo and questioned him about the construction work on the eastern side of the Divide.

Argo replied in this fashion, "Let me tell you a story that Art Weston relates about an incident that happened nearly a year ago when contractors came out into South Boulder cañon to look over the proposed route. It was evening in the mess tent of the survey camp. The dinner had been served them and these men were reflecting on the problems involved.

"One eastern contractor remarked that he did not see how they were expected to build through such rough terrain! It was just impossible to get steam shovels onto the work. William Crook (of the firm Orman and Crook of Pueblo) quietly replied that he could get a mule and a cart anywhere he had seen.

"It was a little more than a year ago, in fact it was December 18th, 1902, that the contracts were let to Orman and Crook and George S. Good and Company of Lock Haven, Pennsylvania. They had twenty-eight tunnels to build. They were of every length and most of them had curves in them. Old Mother Earth did not seem too friendly about Moffat's idea of cutting holes through her ribs in South Boulder Cañon, for she wrinkled her sides as though tickled and began shaking the walls of some of the tunnels with tremendous pressure.

"The chief was greatly distressed over the slowness of the contractors moving in. It was February before the Pennsylvania contractor was doing much. You know this country. Where you need roads, there are trails! and where you need trails there are cañons; and where there are no cañons, there are dense forests making it necessary to cut trees down to sight a line.

"In fact, getting over or even through this Divide is a second rate problem compared to getting up South Boulder Cañon."

Evans agreed and added, "When you get up that cañon and over the Divide, you have Fraser Cañon to tease you, and Byers Cañon to annoy you, and Gore Cañon to make you swear. What's on west, I have never seen. . . . Well, good night, boys. A merry Christmas to you all."

Back in the engineering offices in the Majestic Building in Denver, H. A. Sumner continues to weave the pattern of things to come, ahead of the construction men. He must keep the surveyors continuing their work and eye the progress of his contractors so that no bottlenecks develop.

He was born and educated in Massachusetts where he secured his first position as a rodman on the Old Colony Railroad in 1865. In following years he rose to become locating engineer on the Burlington and from 1886 to 1888 was locator on the Colorado Railway, a Burlington subsidiary which had planned to follow much the same route as eventually taken by the Moffat Road. Sumner held the position of Colorado State Engineer from 1895 to 1897 and during his sixty year career became known as one of the great locating engineers in western history. As a man he endeared himself to his associates by his kindness, gentleness and humility. The experience working for the Colorado Railway proved invaluable during his years as chief engineer for the Moffat.

As Sumner tackles the problems of engineering, chief among them will be the construction of the main range tunnel, which is being considered at the 9,930 foot location. Such a tunnel which is to be 2.6 miles long, if constructed after common practices, would be higher in the center than at either end to afford drainage of water during construction. This apex in the center would leave a smoke pocket in the tunnel. A fan would be needed to ventilate the tunnel. Inquiries are sent out to firms for such a fan. Concern is also felt regarding the kind of rock formations that will be discovered. Geologists are asked for advice.

The second major concern is over the snow conditions that will have to be battled over the Divide via the temporary branch line. The chief writes to railroads that the enemy, Harriman, controls, "If consistent, will you send us plans of double track snow sheds. . . ?"

One would suppose that the work of chief engineer would consist of directing the surveys, pouring over the reports sent in to select the most practical route, and the supervision of contractors, when construction had been authorized. His letters as chief engineer, however, reveal that Sumner wove into his work, day after day, other threads, many of which took much of his time and indeed burdened him greatly by keeping him away from the things he was really supposed to do. He also had to take care of all the general correspondence for the railroad.

In fact, until one learns the heavy load of detail that Sumner carried, one may for a moment miss the great stature of this man. Yet some of the world's greatest men handled such detail. This habit paid a rich dividend in loyalty on the part of his field men who suffered no small privations, for if a small screw was lost from a transit, an entire party would be snagged. These men were miles beyond the last wagon road.

We can see this for ourselves if we ask the elevator operator to let us off on the seventh floor. We find Sumner happily coming to the end of some disagreeable small dark threads. There was the twenty-five-cent telephone call that some surveyor refused to pay and over which there was considerable heated argument before it was settled. Whether the company acknowledged the bill as wrong or whether the lad or his party chief paid for it, we do not know. But one less pebble is in the Chief Engineer's shoe.

But the matter of the warehouse broom is not settled. Sumner's lecture on searching thoroughly before yelling for missing items has produced a search that proves the warehouse broom has not arrived. Days have gone, in which some remotely located survey party has lived in dirt, unable to sweep it out. We can hear the remarks of the men as to "what Sumner might know about sweeping anyway. There is probably a maid who uses the broom at his house." Sumner now must turn the heat on the supply clerk.

As field engineer in charge of the parties this side of the Divide, Blauvelt phoned in his reports of the work every evening. Incidentally the men took pride in this telephone line as being the first use made of the wire for construction purposes. H. A. Sumner would listen to the reports, while A. C. Ridgway would listen in on the line and the next morning give Sumner the third degree just to prove that he was doing his work.

Another inquiry has come to the office, about a man weighing one hundred eighty pounds and thirty-four years old. This writer recognized the fact that he might be under an assumed name. The pathos of mistakes, loneliness, and crime is woven with heartache into the day's work. Spoiling beef is a problem with the men; a satisfactory solution of this summer problem is thrown back to the chief engineer again. The question of personnel comes up and the suggestion goes out to an engineer that he shift his topographer to terrain and terrain to topography and see if that will not be more satisfactory. Contractors have not learned to respect the property owner. The telephone line through Arvada has hurt trees and the legal department had to work out a settlement to those grievances.

Thus, if an irritation or two are ended, the chief, however, has new ones. The relocation of the state wagon road through Byers Cañon over the mountain north of the cañon had been agreed upon by the commissioners of Grand County, August 11, 1903. The contract for construction was ready to be let after an estimate of $8,165.00 was made of the cost. But Pettingell sends in a bill for his services to the railroad — $57. Ridgeway or someone thinks the bill too high. Sumner writes August 12, "It should be allowed. As he worked hard, and has been of more influence than any man of Grand County to get the road through the cañon." Pettingell perhaps would never have been judge of Grand County if Sumner's letter could have been brought out at election time unless the shop men at Tabernash could have elected him. But it was the cost of progress, justified as Grand County's part in that which developed her resources — the railroad. (A law suit would have condemned the right-of-way in favor of the railroad since it held the first filing of the Colorado Railway.) It is in-

teresting to read a letter of Sumner brushing aside the suggestion of one person that the county commissioners be "salted." "The Chief" only knew one way, and that was one of straight forward honesty, which pointed out the merit of the railroad having the right-of-way.

The railroad had her right-of-way, but for half a century people would be talking about the terrible Switzerland trail that twisted over the mountain drifting full of snow. At great expense a highway was carved on the south wall of the cañon which slipping rocks blocked every once in a while. Before this road was built, push-cars on the railroad pulled by a horse were used to bring people on occasion from Parshall and the valley to the south up to Hot Sulphur Springs. Even a corpse had been brought this way when the early impractical routing of this road was snowed under.

Through the letters of Sumner we read his character. One man had been hired for a certain work, and as he was not needed, he was given work in a lower pay brakcet. Complaint was made by the engineer. "Considering his connections, we had better make out a check for the difference." So he got his $100 a month instead of $80.

About this time an engineer was told to take better care of his stove pipe for his range, and he would not need to be writing in for new pipe so often. Another engineer is admonished to keep an eye on a wasteful cook. Please do not forget that these locating engineers were men of rare ability, who as they looked at a cañon or mountain could see a two per cent grade or a one per cent grade. Yet these men, who were good enough to save the running of dozens of trail lines were told to watch out for wasteful cooks and take better care of the stove pipe, while the story would get around that one man got $20 a month more than his work justified because he had "connections."

Now we come to a smile, Bob Olge of Bridge and Building writes in "Why should a driver of a four-horse team get double that of a two-horse team?" He agreed to pay for the horses, but not the driver.

A bill for $30.00 has come into the office for the use of a saddle and horse. Patiently Sumner asks for the details to be written up as previously instructed. "The boss's" two characteristic expressions when seeking advice from other railroads were "If not inconsistent. . ." and "I beg to reply."

"If not inconsistent . . ." he writes the Northern Pacific and Great Northern, "would you advise what kind of switch to use in high altitude subject to heavy snow storms and wind?"

The Rollins Pass branch is under consideration. Sumner has toyed with the idea of building a turntable at Rollins Pass to turn his engines. The logic would be that it would take less snow shed to cover a turntable than a wye. Ridgway had advised stub switches to be installed on the branch. They would be cheaper but, may we add, dead-sure derailment, if run through way up on top of the world.

Tunnel Thirty-three will be ready on this branch for timbering October 1. As this is a branch not expected to be used longer than the time to construct the main-range tunnel, native timber is considered and bids put out. This "Loop Tunnel" project is to cause the men in the office to curse when the bids for the timber come in. To them they are out of reason but not to the men wading around hewing in the deep snow. The price Middle Park timbermen want is $22 a thousand board feet for the timber hewed.

That locating engineers are a species now extinct in America is not questioned. Such men as Meredith were more than locating engineers. A letter of his contains this sentence suggesting "that the R. R. Company stock Fraser and Jim Creeks, as they are fished out, so that streams will be popular when trains start running."

We have a priceless picture of what the men in the field can expect. Engineers are being pushed further West into Utah. "A new party is being formed," their locating engineer writes.

"Kindly advise the men you send that we will undoubtedly have a hard trip at best, and unless they think they can stand it, they had better not come out. We will be one hundred miles from a railroad and from ten to seventy miles from a post office, and as far from any base of supplies. . . .

"I shall do everything possible to make as comfortable and pleasant as possible the party. I have no doubt but what at times it will be necessary to put up with inconveniences, which would not occur were we nearer civilization."

At this time Paul Blunt's party consisted of ten men, an axeman, and a teamster. Mention was not made of a cook, which would have raised the number to thirteen. Parties working in timbered lands would have three axemen to cut the timber away so that lines could be sighted. Some sport! (Once indulged in by the writer with a bush hook.)

The list of accidents mounts. Sumner is considerably disturbed about reading these reports in the paper rather than hearing from the field over the telephone. August 27 we read a man was killed, another badly injured about the head. August 31 another man is killed by a missed shot. One man received a dislocated shoulder and left arm broken above elbow. An axeman was injured.

The month of September was little better. A man is killed by drilling into a missed shot. A few days later five were injured severely and one slightly in a similar accident. October 13 E. A. Meredith reports that one of his men was killed by a mule that kicked him in the head.

It is to be regretted that we do not read letters from the office urging every effort be taken to teach men safety and insist on safety. The office can roar and ask the board of directors to help enforce the fulfilling of contracts, but not one word is written about safety.

As to how much the Moffat road was interested in safety compared to other lines in that day would make only a fair study, but this is not the purpose of this book. The character of Moffat and Sumner would lead us to believe they were above the average in concern for the welfare of their men.

Secrecy surrounds the movement of the reconnaissance parties in Western Colorado. Every precaution is being made to outwit the enemy. One party has a reconnaissance transit that is to be sent to Paul Blount at Maybell. No one is to know that Blount is sent there. The transit is left at the post office with a tag on it so that Paul can secure it when he arrives.

The immediate problem most perplexing to the office in August had been the bottleneck at Steam Shovel Cut seventeen miles west of Denver. As the shovel ate into the swell of the rolling prairie ground, gypsum and lime were discovered. These airslacked and caused the walls of the cut to slip. The shovel continued on a double shift in an effort to remove this added 10,000 cubic feet of earth so that rails could be laid through.

Twenty-one teams had been working during August at one tunnel site. Tunnel Ten had experienced trouble in the work there because of the failure of the electric power plant that was handling the electric drills. Tunnel Sixteen had the problem of rotten or fractured granite, so that the timber was holding only the west end with difficulty. Tunnel Seventeen had been delayed in construction by a slide, which had carried away one portal.

At Tunnel Eighteen, where they had air drills presumably receiving their pressure from an engine and steam boiler, a delay had occurred due to the difficulty of lifting water to the point of operations. Eighteen shifts had been lost. When it was not lack of water, it was lack of muckers or lack in quality of the muckers.

Around Gato (present Pine Cliff or just Cliff) a channel change was effected by forty Japanese who were moving seven and three-tenths yards of dirt a day per man in wheel barrows. The branch line had been under construction by Streeter and Lusk, who had moved in on August 15 starting construction of roads and camps.

Late September found a new problem at Tunnels Nine and Seventeen where the ground was slipping. Sumner urged abandoning both tunnels and opening them as cuts. The top of the timbering was bending one to two inches. Tunnel Seventeen seemed to have a pressure on one side but further in the tunnel, the pressure came from the other side.

Work had begun in Fraser Cañon. Three thousand dollars a month was allocated, but the engineering office urged $8,000 to $10,000. Finally permission was cleared to push the work at $8,000.

The first of October and again the fifteenth found terrible storms sweeping the Divide miles above, demoralizing the newly begun construction work where one hundred sixteen men struggled through snow to their tents and bunk houses on the west side of the branch over the mountain pass. This pass had been officially named Rogers Pass by the Board of Directors of the road and appropriate action taken to see that all maps would bear that name. We find a letter of H. A. Sumner dated September 1st, issuing such instructions.

> Subject 13 Rogers Pass Action. After due consideration, it was unanimously agreed that the pass over the main range near where our main line passes be officially designated as 'Rogers Pass' and the name indicated upon the maps.

Andrew N. Rogers had been the first man to consider a main range tunnel in the James Peak area. He had forwarded surveys to the Union Pacific, when it had built west urging the hogback to be pierced by a 3,000-to-4,000-foot tunnel a little above 10,000 feet elevation. Andrew Rogers had operated the Bob Tail Gold and Mining Co. in Gilpin County. He was honored by being appointed to the commission to settle the Rio Grande-Santa Fe dispute over the Royal Gorge. Judge Hallet in 1870 said, "Mr. Rogers was undoubtedly the finest engineer in Colorado of his time, experienced beyond all his contemporaries."

It matters little what a pass is named unless people use the name. Men had called the pass Rollins for a long time, so it remained Rollins Pass. There is, south of the pass on some maps, another pass with the name of Rogers. Andrew N. Rogers, friend of David Moffat, died in 1890, never living to see the first train over the pass or the Moffat Tunnel opened.

Not so far south from the road at Coal Creek is the School of Mines at Golden. The professors took advantage of this gigantic undertaking and asked permission for their students to make an excursion. H. A. Sumner was proud of the opportunity and sent them passes to be honored by all contractors so that the future engineers could see the trestle and tunnel work, in which he presumed they would be most interested. They might have noticed the shoo-fly track that was thrown around Tunnel Nine that had given trouble because of a shifting in the rock formation which developed tremendous pressure. Tunnel Seventeen was also temporarily abandoned with a track around it. Tunnel Nine, however, would not be shoveled out until the late '30's, when the big 3600 of the Rio Grande would be authorized to come over the track, as well as the stiff high stepping 1700 and 1800 Northern type passenger giants.

A party on the west side of the range was high up in the early snows crying for eight paris of snow shoes. If these could be secured, Argo would have twelve pairs for his crew.

A party on the east side wanted the telephone line extended from a construction camp two miles up to Yankee Doodle Lake. But more important decisions were being weighed, like the building of a branch line from North Park over Willow Creek Pass to a point nearest on their rail line near Willows (midway between Granby and Sulphur).

The office engineer is smarting over the removal of the awnings from the Majestic Building windows and the resulting glare on their eyes all day long. Sumner types a letter on the typewriter to the vice-president asking for the awnings to be replaced immediately to save their eyes.

Sumner comes awake and wonders if it is too late to send out a warning to contractors to preserve the natural beauty of nature around the station grounds.

"The Chief" is away a day and comes back to find some pictures of his father that W. Z. Cozens, who had a ranch between Idlewild and Fraser, had left. Sumner writes "I had known him for many years and always admired his sterling qualities, knowing as I did what he had done for the state during his life."

The building of the railroad was a maze of detail, minor yet pressing which had to be handled together with great battles. I presume the detail and minor incidents wore the heavier on the men in responsibility.

"A policy will have to be established by the new road regarding injured men," Sumner writes the general manager, A. C. Ridgway. "It is usually customary to carry men on roll when sick or injured and they remain in camp. In this case a doctor's attention was necessary, and I will ask what steps had better be taken in view of this."

The General Manager has inquired about what consideration they have made for fire protection of the tunnel timbering. Twice in the road's history Ridgway could have seen the fires roaring in Tunnels Ten, Sixteen and Twenty.

Indian summer is long since passed. The latter part of November finds the weather bad on the east side of Rollins Pass, where the snow had to be shoveled out of the cuts after each storm. Three hundred and seven men were employed at this high altitude work above 9,000 feet, where men puffed when they attempted even a little exercise. On the west side the Sunnyside Basin work has been abandoned. But below in the valley Wm. Cozen reports there is less snow in Middle Park than at any time in thirty years.

Further down the weather is favorable. Nelligan is hauling slag, the yard foreman at Utah Junction needs only to employ six laborers, a watchman, and a pumper as the road is not in business yet. December weather is similar. Permanent log buildings were being pushed on the "hill", as the pass was called. Only 130 men are employed now instead of the 350 needed. But who wants to work at 10,000 feet in such weather? Is $2.00 or $2.25 a day sufficient under such conditions? On the west side the Sunnyside Basin work is considered abandoned until June 1. The Loop Tunnel not only has a blanket of snow five to eight feet deep, but friction between the contractors. Cold weather in Fraser Cañon freezes the Fraser River, making a natural highway, so that 100 men working there can really make headway. But don't forget that on normal nights the temperature would be 20° to 30° below in good December weather there.

In January the weather roughens up in the higher altitude because of high winds which drift the snow. The wages on the hill are now $3.43 a day for two hundred men working there. In Fraser Cañon when the wages are lowered from $2.00 down to $1.75, the Italians leave the job.

Accidents continue to fall upon the construction workers. One man has an arm amputated, another suffers a broken leg; a third man loses both eyes; a fourth man is killed for disregarding a warning when he built a fire in a cut, where rock, when the frost began to thaw, had loosened and crushed him.

From the grief and agony which accidents bring, we turn to the main battle front where the effort is to out-maneuver the enemy. Paul Blount, who is in Rio Blanco County, is given this warning, "I have been a little suspicious that we may have some interference in our plans should it be known that we are contemplating the use of Yampa Cañon. I want you to lose no opportunity to quietly . . . start knocking your line. I have written W. H. Clark today at Meeker for his opinion of the country South of the cañon and have inferred that you are running the cañon line at your suggestion and rather against my best judgment. All of which you will understand, when it comes to you second hand." Then he offers him the suggestion, "You can easily change your views of the country."

January 13, H. A. Sumner wrote W. H. Clark of Meeker a letter to mislead him, so a rumor would spread that he is unfavorable to Paul Blount's line in Yampa Cañon. "The grade is good but torturous nature of the stream — little bottom land — many tunnels, and bridges involved. Always impressed with land south, what do you know?"

The famous Pat's Hole Country comes up for scrutiny. As cattlemen looked there for their stolen beef, so Sumner searches for a hidden route West, "Do you think it advisable to send a man through Pat's Hole at mouth of Yampa to reconnoiter?" Our interest is aroused, for if someone goes through this country he will meet the Hermit of Pat's Hole. The sun shines in this spot only six months a year because of the height of the walls. Blue horses were rumored to be running in this country, and the hermit was some man to see.

Sumner was in possession of a letter about Pat Lynch, the hermit, and this country. It had been sent to him from the files of the Burlington and Missouri River in Lincoln, when they had surveyors in this country in 1889. M. W. Ensign writes from Salt Lake City September 12, 1889, "At last the impossible has been accomplished by my making a trip through the Bear and Yampa River Cañon on foot and at no time being over forty feet above the present water level. Altogether it was necessary to wade the river eighteen times from the head of the cañon just below the mouth of Disappointment Creek to the junction with Green River. Upon reaching Green

River, we found an old duffer by the name of Pat Lynch, who told us it would be impossible to wade the river or follow one side to Island Park, but that it would be perfectly safe to go on a raft to transport us through.

"On Saturday, the tenth, we made the trip after eight hours hard work and a thorough soaking to the waist. We being obliged to lift the raft off the rocks at nearly every rapid. Fortunately our raft proved built well, standing the numerous hard knocks without breaking or upsetting. The only man thrown overboard was our French friend mentioned above, whom we engaged as our pilot. As it is certain most of his body had not felt water in years before, the risk of a cold was great, still he survived and at noon today was all right."

S. P. Weeks, then chief engineer of the Burlington & Missouri River, must have roared when this letter arrived. Pat did not take a fatal cold, for Paul Blount's party found him O.K. fifteen years later in the winter of 1904, when they camped near his cabin, which the cowboys had built for him. Edgar McMechen, in Charles Leckenby's book *The Tread of Pioneers,* describes how Paul Blount's men had been making the trip on the river ice when the spring break-up came. Pat Lynch told the boys about the mountain lion he had tamed and how he could call the lion by a plaintive cry. The lion would "scream and answer to his yell" and old Pat would say, "That sound is sweeter than any Jennie Lind ever sang." Pat was found to be reading the New York World, Colliers Weekly, and the Literary Digest to which he subscribed. The cowboys would tell how he had jerky (jerked meat) stored in holes all over the country. So it was, Paul Blount's men had many a tall tale to tell from his harmless gentle old man, who had seen plenty of cattle thieves come down the upper end of the cañon with their beef on the famous horse thief trail to Hole-in-the-Wall, Wyoming. But since Pat never talked about what he saw, he lived to a ripe old age and did not float down the river.

As he was lost in the wilds, Paul Blount was slow to hear that the Interior Department gave the road permission to construct the line through Gore Cañon. But to Argo's survey crew above Idlewild on the branch line survey came much better news than the Interior Department order, that eight pairs of snowshoes had come from Maine after a sixty-day delay! These men, working near the proposed Main Range Tunnel entrance high up the Divide south of the Loop Tunnel entrance operations, must have floundered around hopelessly with only four pairs of shoes.

The office could not feel that these delays were entirely lost time, for it constituted a warning of what they would battle in another winter. They determined, therefore, to have a report of the snow depth by these North Pole explorers.

The report reads about some places blown clean of snow. In others the cuts filled four feet deep for some two hundred feet; other cuts filled level (ten to fifteen feet). Around the loop only the tops of carts were standing, in the lowest places six to eight feet deep. C. F. Womeldorf signed his letter at Baltimore Camp with the news that the snow was as deep as eighteen or twenty feet at the worst on the Loop. But in February the winter snow had not begun. Meredith's report made in April told that snow at Rifle Sight Notch was forty to fifty feet deep. This was the route the branch line would be using for two years, while the tunnel was under construction, to haul freight and passengers over the top. After all, A. C. Ridgway was wise in having George Barnes and his snow experience ready to operate the first regular trains on this line.

The engineering department had been busy sending out letters to other roads, "If not inconsistent . . . will you send us a copy of double track snow shed blue prints." When summer arrived the construction of snow sheds had to be rushed, for the summer is past before it has begun at 10,000 feet. And at 11,660 feet the summer is but a beautiful dream in the daytime with winter holding forth throughout the nights all year round. A decision was also reached that Rollins Pass was to have a wye instead of a turntable, as it was considered cheaper. Eighteen stub end switches and three split switches were already on order.

H. A. Sumner was, however, concerned about more than construction work and plans. When it was brought to his attention that Streeter and Lusk had allowed fifty men to sleep out in the open for three nights, he immediately warned the contractor that when such news would get around, the adverse advertising would be disastrous. Sleep out in the open for three nights in May! What intestinal fortitude men had who needed a job and desired to work; how tragic that the contractor was doing such a poor job of supervision when he needed men who would stick with him to finish the hill.

On the fifteenth of May George Barnes pulled his construction train almost into Mammoth, which later became known as Tolland, named after Tolland, England, for English friends. The news of the progress of the construction train, which was using the Roberts track laying machine, was blown across the Divide to Fraser Valley, where cattlemen desired a date set for the construction of the line to Arrowhead so they could plan the fall shipping of cattle. Sumner thought they might make it by September or October. Meredith over in that country received the 25,000 fish that he had asked for and planted them in Vasquez and Jim Creeks so that the fishermen would have plenty of trout by the time fishermen-specials were run.

Meredith now had another idea. It would be advisable to construct a wagon road from Arrowhead down to the wagon road which came down Berthoud through Idlewild and on west. This road would enable the cattlemen and shippers to reach Arrowhead, which would be the end of the line for year 1904.

It seemed unbelievable that the railroad would be able to pick up a little revenue traffic in a few months. Yet A. C. Ridgway was already working on Time Card Number One, which they expected to put out the latter part of June. The issue of this card would be a fitting celebration for the months of hard work. Sumner could report that ten to fifteen large parties had been in their field since 1902.

Modern motive power had arrived in March, two heavy consolidation freight engines Nos. 100 and 101, having been delivered for the price of $21,493.00. Their little fifty-seven inch drive wheels would really develop power on the heavy grades. With the vast amount of material being hauled, the great amount of slag for ballast required heavier power than the six-wheeled switch engines 20 and 21 could provide. But the real proof of the road's moving out of the construction stage was the arrival, in late April, of engine number 300, a mountain passenger engine, a ten-wheeler type having sixty-three-inch drive wheels.

The weather was so beautiful in Utah Junction late in May that everyone expected the handicaps of winter to be past and fewer problems to appear. Surely April was past with the three feet of snow that had fallen in the Rollinsville yard and the bad storms of Rollins Pass. April had been a fearful month to try to hold men on the job anywhere, yet the month of May was worse. On the Rollins Pass branch it had taken men three weeks to shovel enough snow away from around the loop in the west side to get the job moving. Now three more feet of snow had fallen. Then with the bright sun in the clear air, so much snow had melted that the wagon road from Idlewild to the Loop was almost impassable except at night when the ground was frozen and then passable only if you could stay out of the deep ruts.

Still with June approaching, even though spring had never come to the Rockies, Sumner could smile. Why, he even included section foremen on his list of employees. There was John Callaghan, John Mathews, F. M. Osborne, and John McGrath. These men could hunt out the wet spots developing on the right-of-way and tamp up the slag under the ties. My, what numerous things had been left incomplete. They could take care of fence and a rock that slid down into a cut and loosened bolts in rails. What would a road do without "gandy dancers" anyway? When someone is needed to do something that no one else can do, call on the gandy dancer. Who shoveled the snow and swept the switches at Rollinsville the day three feet of snow fell? The gandy dancer!

The calendar said June the first, but eight feet of snow fell at Jenny Lake high up on the mountain side. There the newly-blown cuts slipped and boulders rolled in, making the men wish for hip boots as they tried to shovel out the melting snow and water. June in the Rockies. What next?

H. A. SUMNER
As chief eingineer Sumner was assigned to locate a railroad through some of the most difficult country in America. The line's continued success is witness to his skill. — *DPL*

Denver, Utah and Pacific Railroad.

The Denver, Utah & Pacific RR was incorporated on Dec. 11, 1880, to construct a line from Denver to Salt Lake over generally the same route as the Moffat Road. Among the incorporators were Horace Tabor, James Archer, Charles Hallack, W. B. Daniels and David Moffat. The line's history is one of the most obscure of Colorado's many railroad ventures. By 1884 it was controlled by the Burlington and while it did build north to Lyons, no track was ever laid on the route to Salt Lake. However, much grading was done of which evidence can still be clearly seen (see photo on p. 6) and work was begun on two tunnels. One tunnel can be seen at Yankee Doodle Lake and near the mouth of the other, just north of Rollins Pass, Ed Bollinger found these three foot gauge wheels (right) from a construction cart abandoned in King Lake near the portal. Left to right, Bill Jones, Ed Bollinger and Augi Mastrogiuseppe inspect the wheels now at the Colorado State Museum. In 1959, Bob Richardson and Jim Ozment located a pile of rail on the D.U.&P. grade near Eldorado Springs; the rail was dated 1881 and thus indicates work had progressed almost to the point of track laying.

The D.U.&P. surveys and records were sold to the Colorado Railway, another Burlington subsidiary and eventually to the Moffat Road where they proved very useful to H. A. Sumner in his office on the seventh floor of the Majestic Building (below). This fine structure at 16th & Broadway was torn down in 1976.—*Right, Augi Mastrogiuseppe, below, L. C. McClure, DPL*

Atlanta & Southern Ry. Co.

Report of New Side Track Built at *Marshall Smith Leg of Y*

Gauge 4' 8½"

Extended		Feet.	Name or Number of Track
Constructed	590	Feet.	Spur or Passing Track *Spur*
Total Length	710	Feet.	Side of Main Track *South Side*

To be used *Addg Material for new Road DVN 91 + Y*

Date Begun *Dec 26th 1902*   Date Authorized *Dec 24th 1902*   Date Completed *Dec 29th 1902*

Estimated Cost

DRAW A ROUGH SKETCH BELOW OF TRACK AND SURROUNDINGS.

QUANTITY OF MATERIAL		DESCRIPTION	PRICE	AMOUNT
NEW	OLD			
180 ft		Steel Rail 70 Lbs. per yard		
30 ft		" 75 for Guard rails		
1240 ft		Iron Rail 56 Lbs. per yard		
1		Split Switch Complete		
1		Spring Frog 65# – Left –		
1		Axle Rod		
6 Pr		Angle Bars – 65# –		
	42 Pr	Fish plates		
200 lbs		Track Bolts		
700 "	600	" Spikes		
303		1st Class Pine Ties		
1		Head Block		
	1	Switch Stand		

Duplicate

Cost Labor Laying and Surf.	$50.75	
Cost Labor Grading	47.00	$97.75
Owner of R. of W.		
Owner of Material		
Agreement Number		

_____ Roadmaster.

NOTE This Report should be made in duplicate, to cover all side tracks laid, extended or changed in any manner, and forwarded to General Superintendent on completion of track.

Dec 30th 1902

The winter of 1902-03 found this crew with only four pairs of snowshoes, the rest having been lost in transit from Maine. Turtleneck sweaters were then in style and would enjoy a revival in popularity half a century later.

As preparations were made to start work on the tunnels there was the need for a supply delivery point. Marshall, on the Colorado & Southern, just south of Boulder, was found to be the closest point and as the bill (left) indicates a siding was completed in the last days of 1902. — *left, CRRM; above, Art Weston, DPL*

These photos of a Moffat Road survey team were taken near Idlewild in 1903 and provide much insight as to the lifestyle of these men. J. J. Argo's office tent (above) provides a wealth of information. A long barreled pistol and a fishing rod tell of the wild nature of the land. To the left of the lamps are the diaries he is writing while on the right are engineering manuals. There are five colors of ink and a spare bottle of black since supplies are days away. Line maps will be drawn on the paper rolls. The Indian blanket was bought when Argo was surveying in Mexico. Outside the tent (right) the men display their arms and are obviously ready for timber wolves, bears, mountain lions or hopefully occasional ducks or rabbits for dinner. "Cookie" pauses in serving dinner so Art Weston can take this photo (above-right) as the men enjoy the wholesome meals needed to keep up morale. — *all, Art Weston, DPL*

THE DENVER, NORTHWESTERN AND PACIFIC RAILWAY COMPANY

GENERAL OFFICES: MAJESTIC BUILDING
DENVER, COLORADO

Fortune Colo Jany 6" 1904

Mr H. A. Sumner.

Chief Engineer.

Denver Colo.

Dr Sir

In return herewith the blueprints of the Alignment Notes of the Rollins Pass Branch East. As you will see we have checked them all through, and found an error of 2°–18' in one of the angles. Carrying this correction up to the tangent, from Sta. 339+83.6 to 344+35 we make the course N 29° 04' E where Mr Ringer has it N 29° 12' E

Our Solar observation of Jany 2" 04 on the tangent from Sta. 394+99.7 to 80?+?? makes this course S 57°–03' W, as we have corrected this course we make it S 57°–02' W.

Yours very respectfully

M. H. Rendorf.

Work continued without interruption through the winter of 1903-04. The letter (right) informs Chief Engineer Sumner of progress in checking the alignments for the Rollins Pass Branch, as the line was then known, reflecting the belief that the "hill line" was only temporary while work progressed on the 2.6 mile tunnel. Travel from Middle Park to Denver was difficult at best in winter. On March 30, 1904, H. A. Sumner stopped to take this photo (below) as the men shoveled and bucked snow on Berthoud Pass. — *right, CRRM; below, DPL*

Hauling Out! Rail was laid into the tunnels to permit the use of small rail cars and thus speed the work of removal. The men on either side are surveyors responsible for checking the work. — *Art Weston, DPL*

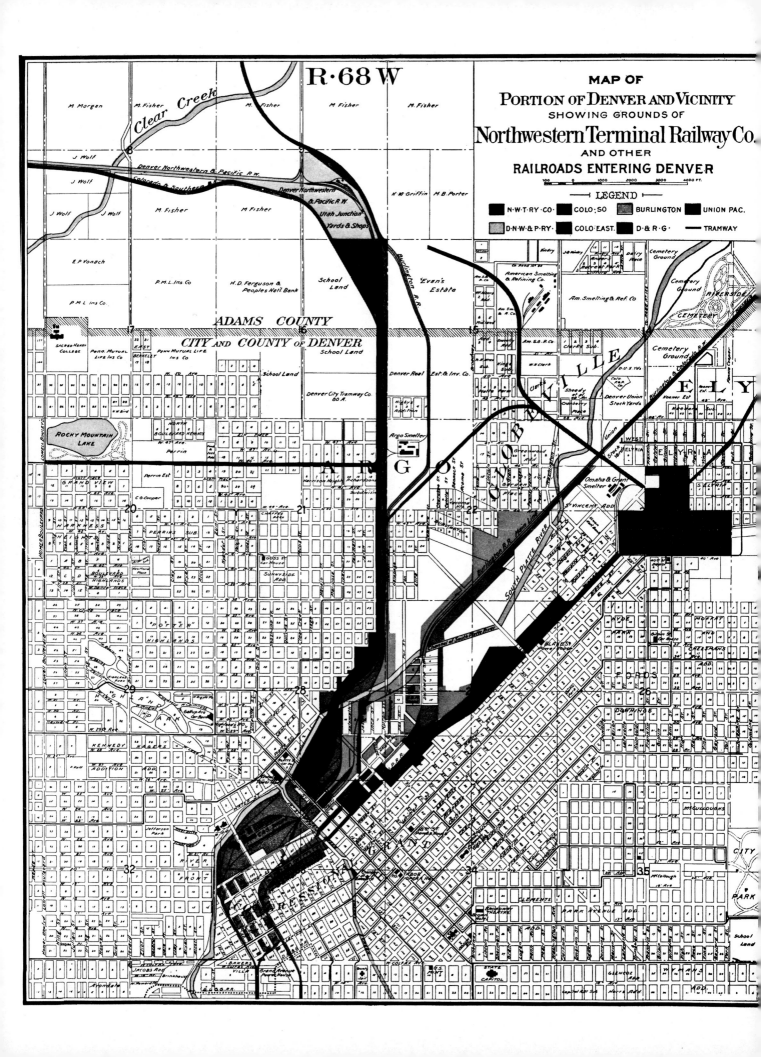

The Moffat Road was denied access to Denver Union Depot by the influence of Harriman and Gould. The Northwest Terminal Railway was organized to provide a line into the city and it acquired a large parcel of land from west of Union Depot to the Platte River and to 15th Street with the Moffat Depot built at 15th and Bassett Streets. The area is seen (above) with the one-time amusement park at the Walker Castle, later to be used by the Moffat. Stock certificate No. 1 was issued to David Moffat in 1906, but was actually a replacement for a temporary certificate issued on August 1, 1904. — *below, CRRM; others, DPL*

The ruggedness of Gore Cañon required that foot bridges be hung from the sheer walls. W. I. Hoklas is seen at the extreme right bringing a load of survey stakes while next to him a young man carries a case holding the transit. Above his head can be seen a steel pin driven into the rocks to hold the bridge, suspended just above the flood swollen Grand River — today known as the Colorado River. — *W. J. Hoklas coll., DPL*

3

Gore Cañon — Intrigue and Squirrels

In telling the story of the Moffat, it is not easy to keep out the intrigue of forces working against construction of the road. The Moffat faced one of its most critical challenges in the struggle for control of Gore Cañon.

H. A. Sumner was hired only as a chief engineer but he, more than anyone else, carried the weight of it all. From Sumner's letters we gather that the hand of the enemy showed itself in January, 1903, when the first construction work was begun. Sumner seemed not to be surprised, for he had been schooled in railroad building in a day when the giants caused many a much needed road to be still-born.

E. U. Spring of Kremmling had brought the news which caused Sumner on February 2, 1903, to write to David Moffat who was in New York City.

Dear Sir,

Some time ago a Denver firm styling themselves 'The Hydro-Electric Power Plant Company' made a preliminary survey in Gore Cañon. They are on the ground, declaring they intend to dam the Gore Cañon and form a great lake containing 20,000 acres of land . . . .

Nowhere could the enemy strike at a more vulnerable spot. Gore Cañon had been selected by the two predecessors roads. The Denver, Utah and Pacific Railroad between 1880 and 1882, surveyed a line over Rollins Pass, began heading a line for South Boulder Cañon and also started work on a tunnel near Yankee Doodle Lake. In 1883, the Colorado Railway, a subsidiary of the Burlington, purchased the D.U.&P. and work resumed until a strike of locomotive engineers on the Burlington in

1887, forced a suspension of all work. In addition, both the Rio Grande and the Union Pacific had shown interest in Gore Cañon as Art Weston writes:

The Burlington and the Union Pacific became involved in a fight over the right-of-way through Gore Cañon in 1886. They did a little grading in the upper end of the Gore, about three miles below Kremmling, but both abandoned the project. The reason for this is said to have been a general strike that year by the Brotherhood of Railroad Trainmen, which stopped all construction work on western lines for a time. There is also a cut along a hillside south of the river just a little above the beginning of the cañon. This was done as early as 1894 by the Rio Grande Railroad.

At this time the Rio Grande was building the Blue River Branch from Leadville to Dillon and they had some intention of building down the Blue to Kremmling, thence up Muddy Creek over the Muddy Pass, and thence down the North Fork of the Platte River to the Fort Steele plains on the Union Pacific. Whether they had an intention to build through Gore Cañon or were only trying to prevent the other companies from obtaining a right-of-way in the cañon I am unable to say. They had done some grading along the Muddy just north of Kremmling.

In 1909 I located a preliminary line for the Laramie, Hahn's Peak and Pacific up the North Platte River in North Park as far as Coalmont, which is the present terminus of that road (now a branch line owned by the Union Pacific). On a sage brush flat about due west from Walden we found some old stakes set by the Rio Grande survey party in 1886. I had with my party at that time old Aron Weatherby, as cook, and he had been with the Rio Grande party which made the survey in 1886.

In October of 1902 the Hydro-Electric Company had filed rights in the Glenwood Springs land office to locate a pipe line down the cañon to supply the power company with water. This filing in no way interfered with the railroad but may have made Sumner feel a little uneasy. This discovery showed their true intentions because on the twenty-first of January they had changed their filings to include the reservoir.

The case was complicated by the fact that on January 27 the incorporation papers for the New Century Power Company were filed in Grand County's court house, proving that H. A. Sumner was not aware, when he wrote David Moffat, that there were two distinct companies: one, a power company and another, a reservoir company. Art Weston was in Gore the summer of 1903, and adds some interesting notes:

> I was with the survey party under Wm. Dietrick. We spent about one month in a camp near the beginning of Gore Cañon below Kremmling. The power company was doing some drilling in the cañon, prospecting for a suitable dam site. An interesting fact developed by this drilling was that the stream bed had once been some 90 feet lower. They drilled through a log 90 feet below the existing stream bed. This may seem somewhat afield from our subject, but it had a tie-in with the case. The ranchmen, who had sold some options to right-of-way to the power company, were familiar with the fact that the flat hay meadows between Kremmling and the cañon were underlain with mud to a great depth and used the argument that a railroad grade could not be constructed across this "bottomless" mud. The subsequent experience of the railroad indicated that it was not impossible. Some fills in this locality had a habit of sinking out of sight in the mud overnight. Eventually these were built up to where they became stable.

The actual battle against intrigue was a legal battle, which was magnificent, directed by Charles J. Hughes, Jr., the attorney for the railroad.

The question foremost in the minds of Moffat men was "Who is behind the trouble?" Could it be possible that some of these firms were legitimate companies started up, now that the railroad had promised to open up the country? Or were they efforts to extract fancy prices for rights-of-way? Or worse yet, was this the hand of the giant Harriman with his millions and millions of dollars ready to wear down by delay and expense the very idea of building or investing in the Moffat Railroad?

The New Century Power Company started immediately buying up all the land around Kremmling it could. It paid fabulous prices of $35.00 to $50.00 an acre for land, much of which, because of its unsuitable location was not good for irrigation and therefore not worth in that day better than $2.50 an acre. Ranchers owning the land were greatly impressed by these options for ninety days and immediately held the reservoir in the highest regard. C. J. Hughes, Jr., attorney for the railroad, directed Sumner to get construction work going on the right-of-way through the cañon. The Colorado Railway had begun this work in 1886 or '87 through a Chicago contractor by the name of D. D. Streeter. Inasmuch as the Denver Northwestern and Pacific had bought up the filings and construction work, it was important to establish an early date of construction, so that the New Century Power Company could not argue that the Denver Northwestern and Pacific was not in a position to finance it, or that it never held any idea of building here and was only doing this to make them buy out the right-of-way from the Moffat at a high cost.

Locating Engineer Meredith was racing around on horseback, meanwhile, getting Contractor Dumphy and Nelson busy in the Gore. Some tools were known to exist in the microscopically small town of Kremmling. Sixteen men were finally rounded up to begin work with wheelbarrows, picks, and shovels.

H. A. Sumner did not wait for the tri-weekly mail service. He dispatched orders to Meredith by special messengers on horseback, and he told Meredith to do likewise. Sumner sent his own son to Sulphur with an "instrument" to be recorded, for he would not trust others at this critical moment.

The air was tense, the opening moves of a death battle being prepared in great haste.

At this time Sam Adams from Steamboat Springs came to Denver. Sam Adams was the man who knew the most about the northwestern part of Colorado and its economic possibilities in minerals, oil, iron, and coal. For the rest of his lifetime he sought capital to open up this territory and was foiled by wars and depression every time the capital was secured.

Adams had come into Denver at his own expense, a long route by stage and roundabout railroad line, to warn H. A. Sumner that the intrigue was showing its hand further west. He was all excited and worried. It seems Sumner had not paid too much attention to him previously in his warnings to the locating engineers, but by April 2 Sumner was convinced of the seriousness of the matter. In fact, all hell seemed to have broken loose.

Sumner wrote to David Moffat saying:

"On March 31st Sam Adams called to inform me that parties in the interest of the Union Pacific were contemplating filing reservoir sites in Yampa River Cañon between Steamboat and Hayden. . . ."

Sumner suspected former Chief Engineer Milner to have made the moves in filing these reservoir sites. This may have been Sumner's own suspicion for possibly bitterness had developed between the two men. After his discharge, Milner had, of course, the right to accept employment from anyone.

Sumner sought advice from his superiors, Ridgway and Vice-President Smith, as to whether it would not be wise to get some friends of the Denver Northwestern and Pacific to file reservoir sites in six possible locations such as east of Toponas, Egeria Cañon, Yampa Cañon, and in Snake River territory to beat the enemy at his own game. The cost of surveying these and filing the locations was expected to be around $300.00 a piece.

F. N. Briggs at Sulphur, meanwhile, was building up good will for the railroad by circulating a petition against the power company.

One week after his first Denver trip, Sam Adams was back in Denver again with news of trouble around Poole. Sumner immediately dispatched C. L. Adams to make a survey for a line through this location and file it. He was to go on horseback, making as little commotion as possible in his trip, and to take some pictures of the cañon, whenever he could get to it.

March 18 a court injunction was secured against the Moffat, stopping it from working its own right-of-way in Gore Cañon at the spot where the dam was proposed. Thirty or forty men appeared and began work for the New Century Power Company, which was building a wagon road to the dam site. This court action prevented any convenient access to the Gore Cañon right-of-way below the dam site and greatly handicapped the men working on the railroad right-of-way.

C. J. Hughes secured the removal of the court action to Grand County and filed a counter suit against the New Century Power Company, which prohibited them from working on the right-of-way of the railroad.

With this victory for the railroad excitement increased, particularly when W. R. Dietrick, the locating engineer at the cañon, wrote that the injunction was being disregarded by the power company.

H. A. Sumner tried to calm Dietrick enough to get out of him the actual place this was happening. Dietrick was so excited about this violation, which would prove a good case against the power company, that he was incoherent and forced Sumner to ask, "Where?" Sumner also asked for witnesses and pictures.

So complaints began to come into the courts about the movements of the power company men, who seemed never to be able to find the railroad right-of-way and to stay off of it.

In June the Hydro-Electric Power Plant Company sold out its interest to the New Century Power Company for $60,000. It was supposed that the Hydro-Electric Company was a legitimate company, but Moffat men felt the New Century Company was nothing less than a blind for the hand of Harriman.

In time the New Century Company proposed that they and the railroad, get together to talk the matter over. J. C. Hughes, Jr., accepted the opportunity which turned out to be simply another delay. The longer the right-of-way was being blocked, the longer capital would be discouraged from investing in the Moffat.

At this time some one discovered that the Denver Northwestern and Pacific filings for right-of-way had never reached Washington.

Sumner immediately called in Hughes to investigate the Denver Land Office. The discovery was made by a man sent to Glenwood Springs at that time, that the Denver Northwestern and Pacific filings had been lost in the files of the Glenwood Springs office. It was peculiar how so many reservoirs were being proposed all of a sudden along only one proposed railroad, and how people involved in filing the right-of-ways in the Land Office were getting so careless.

The newspapers began to scream headlines like this: "SCANDAL IN GORE CAÑON."

Who blames Dietrick for getting excited? With the New Century Power Company having thirty or forty men getting ugly and Dietrick having only sixteen men at work, one never knew what would happen next, for pitched battles had happened before. H. A. Sumner was understanding in his letters and managed to get Dietrick calmed down.

When the discovery of the tie-in of the Gore Cañon survey proved inaccurate Sumner was on the spot for a moment. But he had a good comeback for the railroad attorney, C. J. Hughes, Jr., who used it with telling effect in the court case and this was that the government maps were frequently off as much as two miles. H. A. Sumner could furnish the data, which Hughes used with machine gun fire. It seems that Aulls was the man who made the discovery of the imperfect tie some time between February 2 and 11, 1903.

Art Weston was on the spot as draftsman, for Dietrick and tells the story as follows:

Well, the power company obtained an injunction to prevent us from trespassing on their right-of-way and we got a similar injunction. We had Dumphy and Nelson, grading contractors, doing a little grading just above the cañon. Now the Moffat people had made a survey through the cañon the previous year, with Mr. Scott as the locating engineer. A filing map had been made and the railroad thought they had a valid claim to their filing on a right-of-way through the cañon, as the map had been accepted by the U.S. Land Office. There was, however, a serious slip-up.

The U.S. requires that the line of survey be connected to the section corners of the public land surveys for the lands it crosses. In showing connections to section corners Mr. Scott had used a corner near Kremmling and then had not found another until he reached the open country below the cañon about ten miles below the corner. Now it had developed that the corner near Kremmling was incorrectly marked (marked for the corner diagonally across the section) and this showed the line of survey as being nearly one mile north of the cañon and we were in somewhat of a predicament. The case came to trial in court at the county seat of Hot Sulphur Springs.

I think Mr. Dietrick and Mr. Meredith, who was division engineer, testified as to the incorrectness of the markings on the corner stone. The other side put a ranchman on the stand and he claimed to have known the corner for many years and to know that it was correctly marked. On cross examination, it developed, however, that he not only did not know how corners were marked but that he could not tell how it was marked. Then we introduced pictures taken of the corner with Mr. Meredith standing beside it and finally won the case. This is interesting because it in a way parallels the other right-of-way fight between the Union Pacific and Burlington roads in 1886. It indicates the importance of the Gore Cañon to any company seeking a direct westerly route from Denver.

But the entire lid blew off and Gore mountain turned into a volcano when the Interior Department announced that it was taking steps to make a dam at Kremmling.

The months went by with efforts being made to withdraw the land around McCoy from the public domain. The Los Angeles Chamber of Commerce all of a sudden discovered that if the railroad Moffat was building was to prevent the Interior Department dam, Los Angeles would not be assured sufficient water. Harriman had his hand in the Southern Pacific.

Now the battle became one to prove that the Gore Cañon was not the place for such a reclamation dam, which was built years later at Boulder Dam. The Interior Department said there was no place nearly as favorable. H. A. Sumner sent men out to prove there were better locations with more than the trickle of water, which he told Hughes would never fill the proposed reservoir. Paul Blount and the locating engineer were sent down the Green River to do this work.

T. J. Milner came in the picture at this time making an embarassing statement to the press. He said that the Board of Directors had taken such issue with him over his insistence that the road go through Gore Cañon instead of over Gore Pass, that he was dismissed. As the first chief engineer, this statement carried great weight to prove that the railroad did not need the cañon. And it is true. Subsequent operation of the road through the cañon has given so much trouble that this line, with its additional climb in elevation over the pass would have been far better. For the Moffat was not planning on building down Gore Cañon and the Grand River Valley to Glenwood Springs. Or was it?

The cutoff had always been known as a possibility. Sumner argued in his letters to accept this route, that it would give an opportunity to build a branch down to the Rio Grande for immediate shipment of coal west. Moffat, being squeezed for finances, knew that if he went down the Gore, he could sell his road to the Rio Grande if he could not finish it with his own funds. Otherwise, the route over Gore Pass would have been better, as surveys made at that time and filed away show.

But this is not what the public heard. They heard it was much too expensive to build over the Gore. The lawyers argued in court it would cost $60,000 a mile, while we find in H. A. Sumner's own estimates that it would cost $50,000 a mile. But who holds this stretching of the truth against Sumner? That happens in most business deals when bargains are to be made.

Meanwhile, H. A. Sumner had the rat trapped!

Friends in Grand County had been doing some sleuthing for the Moffat. Mr. Alvinzo F. Slippery,

Sr., told that he had been in partnership with Mr. Munn of the New Century Light and Power Company. He claimed R. G. Munn had misrepresented stock with a confidence game in the Mid-West. He was known, in fact, to have been crooked enough to deserve a long term in the penitentiary. Slippery advised that an investigation should be made of Munn in Flint, Michigan.

Mr. Frank S. Byers, the founder of Hot Sulphur Springs, was the detective who had gotten the information out of Munn. H. A. Sumner must have had a long conference with Hughes when this information arrived. Munn swindled a Mr. Cook of Forrestville, Michigan. Munn ruined Old Man Knickerbocker of Flint. "In fact, D. Traxler of Port Huron will give the name of stockholders, if his name is kept quiet."

With this information, Hughes hired a private detective to dig up the record of this swindler, who was behind the New Century Power Company.

But more good news for the Moffat side of the case came, when H. A. Sumner was permitted opportunity to look at the blue prints of the proposed dam. There was no place on the entire blue prints for water to be drawn from the dam to connect with the power plant. With this discovery the defense for the railroad cried, "This is a plain fraud. This company is illegitimate!" The embarassed attorney for the power company sputtered around that the water was to be drawn about twenty feet from the top of the dam.

While the Interior Department case was being fought in the Washington office, it was discovered that photographs had been taken at such an angle to make it appear that there was a natural ledge of rock high up the wall of the cañon, on which the railroad could be built. If anyone can find this ledge today, they are better than good.

During these early years there was plenty of hard going in the battle of the Moffat.

The road had not made much progress in getting into Union Station in Denver, as a newspaper article described.

"It is said that Hawley has determined Moffat shall never get into the Union Depot, and, if possible will keep Moffat terminal at Utah Junction. The Rio Grande, Colorado and Southern and Union Pacific control Denver Union Depot."

Also about this time in Utah steam was gotten up for the building of a reservoir to be known as Strawberry Reservoir right across the right-of-way of the proposed road.

By this time, however, another telling discovery was made to help the case against the power company. The cañon had been bored one hundred feet deep and no bed rock could be found. Another bore was tried. This one went down one hundred ten feet with no bed rock found. No great dam could be built in such a location.

Then out of almost a clear sky, Teddy Roosevelt summoned the contesting parties to the Capital. There was no question as to who was running the Interior Department's hearing. When men rose to speak, they were introduced by the President with such expressions, "Oh, yes, you represent the power companies and the opposition railroads."

Carl Ewald, whom Teddy Roosevelt could trust, had investigated the controversy for him. The die was cast. Gore Cañon was open to David Moffat. Number One could parade through as today the *Rio Grande Zephyr* and countless freights still wind through the depths of Gore Cañon.

The railroad should have at least attempted to rename Gore Cañon — Teddy Roosevelt Cañon. The honors for this battle go to Hughes who had just begun his faithful work for the Moffat Road.

The blustery winter was passed. Ties and rails were being laid west of Arrowhead. The locating engineer, J. J. Argo, was moving to the far western end of Grand County to tackle the third great problem of the Moffat, the location of a road at the upper end of Gore Cañon.

J. J. Argo's second diary, that fortunately has been preserved, is inscribed "Beginning May 21, 1905." It is the story of the camp at the upper end of Gore Cañon.

The only way to by-pass this cañon was to go over Gore Range. Numerous surveys were run and satisfactory grades were developed in routes that went up the Troublesome before reaching Kremmling and on over to the Gore and down to Toponas. H. A. Sumner advised against these routes as the rise in elevation was twice that which occurred by going down the Gore and climbing Conger Mesa and Egeria Cañon.

An even more important reason H. A. Sumner gave against these routes was that going down the Gore would make possible the building of a cutoff to the Rio Grande. The choice of going through Gore was dictated to Moffat that early day that Harriman declared war on him.

Rock slides in the Gore made this route one of continual problems. Efforts were made to move the railroad far away enough from the wall so that rocks could drop on that space and not on the right-of-way. Today electric fences stand ready to signal any rock slides which may fall onto the track.

To survey the Gore was a problem. Hoklas understood that the first survey in 1884 was run by use of boats with one man losing his life near Burns.

T. J. Milner must have run a preliminary survey in the winter of 1901-02. He speaks of sending men down on the ice and securing a map with ten foot contours by use of ropes held by men on top of the cliffs, while the surveyor with the end of the rope around him walked the face of the cliff.

Some idea of the paraphernalia with which survey parties were equipped is found in this list of things sent to Charles Mitton.

1 hand level
¼ box pencil eraser
2 dozen assorted No. 3 and No. 5 H. Kohenoor Pencils
1 Pt. bottle writing fluid
1 box thumb tacks (likely more than a dozen in the box)
1 doz. level books
½ roll plate B. tracing paper
1 doz. pay roll blanks
1 time book
Gurley level and rod

J. J. Argo faced a tremendous task in making an accurate survey with the spring flood waters filling the cañon from bank to bank. The canon is from one to two hundred feet wide near the bottom. Argo described it thus: "The sides of the cañon are in some places rugged granite bluffs rising to the height of 3,000 feet and in other places it is coarse slide rock."

At places there was only one way to get down the cañon and that was to build bridges on the side of the cliffs. The work had been carefully planned months before.

Sixteen-inch machined steel pins had been made. A man was swung over the face of the cliff by a rope. He drove these pins into the crevices of the bluff. Then logs that were six to ten inches in diameter and sixteen feet long were floated down to the spot. These logs were tied over ropes that were held by men on the top of the cliff. One end of the log would be hoisted to the proper height and a rope five-eighths of an inch in diameter would fasten this log to the pin. Then the man would climb out on the log and drive another pin. Because pins might occasionally slip out, extra pins were driven in. On occa-

sion holes had to be drilled in the solid granite as the men worked over the face of the cliffs on these foot bridges. We see this in the picture. Strong winds made it difficult to hold a transit steady.

Argo's diary for June 6 reads, "Built foot bridges in afternoon along bluffs. Hoklas fell in river and narrowly escaped drowning."

W. I. Hoklas tells the story in more detail. "Yes, a rope from above hitched to a log, which was being brought to place on a cliff in Gore Cañon and on which I had walked out, slipped off a rock or a loop slackened and let down the end of the log on which I was standing. I had learned to swim in swift water as a school boy, very much to the disgust of my father. By the kindness of the Lord I swam to shore and climbed up on a ledge, from which Argo helped me back to the replaced log.

"We then walked back to the slide rock. Argo rubbed his hands and although it was about 3:00 o'clock said, 'I guess we will go to camp.' So the men were called off the cliff and we plodded home. It was only about a mile and a half or two miles, but this took about an hour's time. The cliff was about 3,000 feet high." Very significant are the words out of Argo's diary, "As usual we got wet."

The next day the transit party continued to build foot bridges. Ladders, built in the cañon out of slim lodge pole pines that had been peeled of their bark, were used to scale many places. Trees growing on the high-water line of the Colorado River afforded handy logs or slim poles as needed for this work.

Among the visitors to this spectacular survey was T. J. Milner, chief engineer of Denver Tramways. His heart was still on this job. He felt welcome with J. J. Argo and Meredith, who were fast friends. Milner told the boys how he had begged Moffat to start the Main Range Tunnel, but Moffat did not feel this necessary. He considered the tunnel at that time a refinement that could be made when the road became a paying business. To Moffat, according to Gerald Hughes, Rollins Pass was simply a matter of power. Did not the Rio Grande scale such heights? James J. Hill seems to have been consulted and agreed to this idea. With such choice gossip coming from the tent of J. J. Argo it was worth all the hard work to survey the cañon and endure the mosquitoes.

Another week Sumner with his retiring manner and his sparkle of humor came to see "Argo's squirrels." On this trip were Blauvelt, Meredith, and Deuel. Deuel's nature was so winsome and magnetic that men were becoming greatly attached to this man whose manner made him a little Moffat.

Down in the Gore the June weather was beautiful. At night the campfires burned brightly and songs were in keeping with the brilliant light of the moon. These moments the boys never forgot. The week-old newspapers had been read before sunset or by campfire-light. As to how the boys felt in regard to the continual harping that Moffat had sold the road, we conjecture that there were hot debates. For there is a certain obstinate quality in man that insists on taking the opposite view point.

Headlines like "Union Pacific May Soon Control or Buy Moffat Line. Seven million said to be paid for the short line, fully compensating Mr. Moffat for his investments," seemed to verify the rumors.

To add to confusion the next day the boys read, "The Line to be rushed to completion by Senator Clark and Rock Island Syndicate." Then came the announcement that Moffat was back from New York and was too tired to talk. And in a competitor's paper they read, "Not sold. But it's for sale."

After pay day the poker games would pick up. Albert Peck, later an assistant engineer for the Rio Grande, tells how a teamster and Clyde Mitton, brother of locating engineer C. L., played all one night keeping others awake. They fought awhile and then worked awhile throughout the following day. Dick Holmes, the six-foot-six-inch Spanish-American War veteran threatened to throw the one who tried foul play into the Grand River.

But none of this bothered the mountain sheep grazing near by.

Sunday October 22, J. J. Argo wrote in his diary that Lyn Doane, Sexton, and Will Uzzel had been hunting and killed two bears.

The boys talked about the bear hunt for weeks. The only thing that stopped this story was a better story of a gent among them who jammed Albert Peck's gun full of shot and blew the gun up, stole a suit of clothes of Will Uzzel, and an overcoat of Jack Scanlon. When the story ended, this gent was in the "big house."

When it came to moving camp, the nearby contractors were not always able to furnish the teams needed. Argo used as high as three teams on such jobs. Among the moving troubles were such things as sleds breaking down, forcing part of the load to be left where the breakdown occurred. It was not flat tires in those days, but it was trouble, nevertheless.

When the party was moved to a location near McCoy, the men had the McCoy's Hotel where they could entertain their families when they visited the men in the field. Peck tells that men were charged according to their finances. From the frequency with which J. J. Argo entertained at the hotel we have every reason to believe that this historic old stopping place was maintaining its tradition for serving the best meals.

The nearest railroad to McCoy, was the Rio Grande, reached by a wagon road through State Bridge and over the hill to Wolcott. We gather the condition of this road was not good in spring weather, from this note of Argo: "I returned from Wolcott with Mrs. Argo and the children. Weather fair, roads very bad."

Leckenby tells of the stagecoach days and the trials of the stage drivers in the spring thaw. This stage line, which begun operations in 1888, first used McCoy as an overnight stop to rest the passengers going to Steamboat. It had as high as 100 horses in use, when Whipple and Shaw operated it.

We read that "Mrs. Argo and myself went down to McCoy to dinner with Mrs. Meredith." Mrs. Meredith loved society life but could not do much entertaining out here. And since her husband insisted on being a locating engineer, the tension was aggravated with his prolonged absences from home.

The annual Yampa pioneer day celebration of 1906 was turned into a premature celebration for the coming of the railroad on June 21st and 22nd. Art Weston remembers the occasion vividly:

"We located the route northwestward to Yampa and Steamboat. While we were near Yampa, there was a three-day celebration, given principally in honor of the coming of the railroad. A baseball team from Hayden played a game with the Yampa boys who proved no match for the Hayden team. So a team selected from the engineering parties (there were several in the vicinity) took the field and beat the Hayden boys very nicely. But the Hayden team, not having anything to celebrate, went to bed and got plenty of sleep. On the other hand the engineers celebrated most of the night. (There were plenty of saloons at that time.) So the next day the Hayden team beat the surveyors badly."

In these days when we are endeavoring to establish security in year-round guaranteed wages by industry, we see the contrast in which the party members found themselves in those days. Winter came and men would be laid off until spring. Men would hunt the country over for jobs that would help pay back their college education. Art Weston tells of his case:

"There did not seem to be much doing on the Moffat in the winter of 1905. I went with some other Colorado men to a job in western Arkansas. This was a branch line subsidiary to the Missouri Pacific Railroad. There I caught malaria and was sent to the company hospital in St. Louis. When I recovered, I returned to Denver and about April 1, 1906, Mr. Sumner sent me to the party under J. J. Argo, then camped near McCoy."

Twice that summer Art suffered attacks from his malaria and had to be hospitalized in Yampa. Running true to the form of the brotherhood established in these parties, Argo writes, "Myself and family went to visit Mr. Weston." That afternoon the entire party went to Yampa to play ball. We judge they must have won the game this time, and all came tramping in afterward to see Art.

Gore Cañon and westward the line was located, while back in Fraser Valley the rails followed.

W. I. Hoklas saved this poem, a product of a surveyor. It was popular among the boys in camp and is representative of the age:

IF

If you can swing an axe, or yield a brush hook,
    Or drive a stake, or drag a chain all day,
If you can scribble "figgers" in a note book,
    Or shoot a range pole half a mile away—
If you can sight a transit, or a level,
    Or move a target up and down a rod—
If you fear neither man or devil,
    And know yourself, and trust the living God—

If you can wade a swamp, or swim a river,
    Nor fear the deep, nor yet the dizzy heights
If you can stand the cold without a shiver,
    And take the Higgins ink to bed o'nights—
If you can turn a thumbscrew with your fingers,
    When every digit's like a frozen thumb—
If you can work as long as daylight lingers,
    And not complain, nor think you're going some—

If you can sight thru tropic heats reflection,
    Or toil all day beneath a blistering sun—
If you can find a sort of satisfaction,
    In knowing that you've got a job well done—
If you can be an Eskimo and nigger,
    And try to be a gentleman to boot—
If you can use a "guessin' stick" to figure,
    And know a coefficient from a root—

If your calculus and descriptive are forgotten,
    And your Algebra "just serves you fairly well—
If your drafting and your lettering are rotten,
    And your Trautweine' always handy by, to tell—
If you can close a traverse without fudgin',
    Or check a line of levels by a foot—
If you can set a slope stake just by judgin'
    And never kick the tripod with your foot—

If you can climb a stoll and not feel lowly
    Nor have your head turned by an office chair—
If you can reach your judgments slowly,
    And make your rulings always just and fair—
If you can give yourself and all that's in you,
    And make others give their own best too—
If you can handle men of brawn and sinew,
    And like the men and make them like you too—
If you can run a line where you are told,
    And make it stay somewhere upon the map—
If you can read your notes when they are cold,
    And know that contours mustn't ever lap—
If you can line a truss or tap a rivet,
    Or make a surly foreman come across—
If you can take an order, well as give it,
    And not have secret pity for the boss—

If you can't boast a college education,
    Or, if you've got a sheepskin, can forget,
If you can meet with trimph and disaster,
    And treat them without favor, nor with fear—
You'll be a man and your own master,
    But—what is more—you'll be an ENGINEER.

    By Robert Isham Randolph, with apologies
        to Rudyard Kipling.

Bollinger Collection, DPL

No one was allowed to join these survey teams unless all agreed because each man's life was dependent on the clear thinking and steel nerves of his teammates. Herb Eno captured on film these scenes of the men at work deep in Gore Cañon under J. J. Argo in the spring of 1905. One brave lad (left) is lowering himself down the cañon wall and will place steel pins to anchor the heavy ropes such as being carried (below) to support the walkways. It was vital that a bit of humor occasionally break the tension of such risky work; such as provided by W. I. Hoklas (below-left) when he drew his "Humble (?) Surveyor's Opinion of the Party Chief". — *all, DPL*

TEDDY ROOSEVELT AND THE BATTLE FOR GORE CAÑON

The struggle by the Moffat Road to retain its right-of-way through Gore Cañon is skillfully chronicled by Robert C. Black, III in his history of Grand County, *Island in the Rockies*. The following is reprinted with permission of the author and the Grand County Pioneer Society, its publisher.

The intervention in its early stages was quiet. At the beginning of April, 1904, Professor E. H. Newell, chief engineer of the Reclamation Service, was approached by "six consulting engineers" with the suggestion that the Kremmling basin was especially well adapted for the impounding of water. Two weeks later the Director of the United States Geological Survey (Walcott) requested Secretary of the Interior Hitchcock to withdraw from entry the public lands within and above Gore Cañon, citing the necessity of water storage for irrigation in Arizona and California. The matter was referred for comment to Assistant Attorney General Campbell (who had been the author of the February opinion against the New Century company); this time, however, Campbell suggested that a provisional withdrawal order, for the benefit of a *government* project, would be permissable. There followed a ground investigation by A. L. Fellows, resident hydrographer of the Geological Survey at Denver, and there occurred a suspicious delay in the processing of certain pertinent Moffat filings. And on May 18 an Interior Department order "segregated" twenty-eight sections of land within the area of the proposed reservoir.

The Denver, Northwestern and Pacific first learned of this development in an emergency telegram, dispatched on May 24 by C. C. Clements, the company's attorney in Washington. Moffat and his associates were, of course, appalled. A confrontation with Mr. Fellows produced the bland assurance that a two-hundred-foot dam should in no way inconvenience the railway, and on June 9 the Acting Land Office Commissioner rejected "certain maps" which the D.N.W.&P. had filed. It furthermore became known that Reclamation engineers were examining additional sites — especially at Windy Gap, Potato Hill, and Byers Cañon — most of which lay athwart the Moffat road's alignment. Moreover, the Service was offering the same attractive terms which the New Century company had tendered, and representative landowners like Willis C. Call, Tracy Tyler, and William H. Martin were openly shunning the railroad representatives.

The Moffat interest wasted no time with invective; it even kept up a polite correspondence with Fellows. But formal protests were lodged with the Land Office, and early in July the D.N.W.&P. requested another hearing before the Interior Department. Private appeals were also circulated among suitable personages, of which the most effective was to Philip Bathell Stewart, a utility and mining executive of Colorado Springs. Mr. Stewart was by normal standards a man of moderate influence, but he was currently of supreme consequence as a "straight, clean" hunting companion of President Theodore Roosevelt.

The struggle was, nevertheless, lengthy. The proceedings before the Interior Department were several times postponed, and a further reconnaissance by Mr. Fellows was followed by the creation of an impressively elaborate government camp, complete with barracks and shop buildings, at the head of Gore Cañon. But in December Mr. Harriman suffered a personal falling out with Mr. Roosevelt (a misfortune never to be taken lightly), and in the spring of 1905 the President, surrounded by orbiting politicians and in close communion with "straight, clean" Stewart, spent a fortnight in the White River country in search of game. There the atmosphere was heavily pro-Moffat; moreover, Stewart, as soon as the hunt was over, wrote at length to William Loeb, Roosevelt's confidential secretary, suggesting that the Reclamation Service was permitting itself to be used, not only by Harriman, but by the even less savory George Gould of the Denver & Rio Grande.

Roosevelt declared afterward that he at once took steps to set things right. Nonetheless, the Reclamation Service applied late in the summer to Judge Moses Hallett of the U.S. District Court for the District of Colorado, asking that the Denver, Northwestern and Pacific be enjoined from building into the disputed area. Following a conspicuously able argument for the railroad by Charles J. Hughes, Jr., the injunction was denied, on grounds that the reservoir was as yet unnecessary and therefore a contrivance. The government lawyers promptly announced they would appeal. At this point, however, the President did intervene. On October 9 he instructed Attorney General William H. Moody to bring the contestants together informally. Meanwhile he dispatched to Colorado a highly regarded engineer named Carl Ewald Grunsky to make an independent study. The upshot was a half-forgotten conclave, probably on November 15, in the Presidential presence, wherein the Reclamation Service was given a crisp dressing down and the Secretary of the Interior was directed to drop all further proceedings. Moffat's victory was clear, though Roosevelt characteristically confused certain of the particulars when he came to give the story to the press.

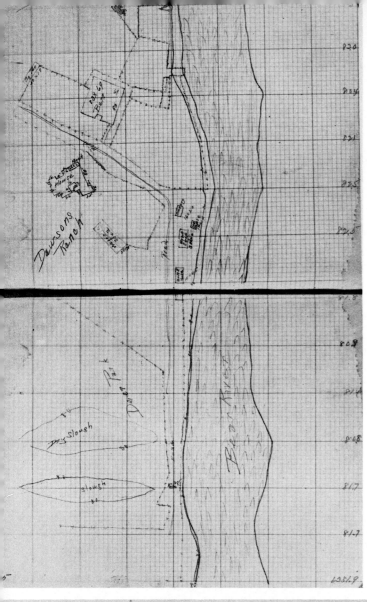

From Gore Cañon the survey teams continued west. J. J. Argo's team is seen (below) on the move near Oak Creek. A page from Art Weston's topography book (left) made in this area in 1906, shows the Bear River. The name would soon be changed to Yampa River as it is known today. — *left, DPL; below; State Historical Society of Colorado*

WHERE THE MOFFAT ROAD BEGAN! Utah Junction was far out beyond the city when in the winter of 1903-04 this historic photo was taken. The scene is looking southeast with the main line of the Colorado & Southern Ry. at the extreme left. Engine 20 has recently been delivered and is being kept busy moving construction supplies. On the right sit the passenger cars recently delivered from the Chesapeake Beach Railroad and beyond the construction tents is the station from which Joe Culbertson would soon be dispatching the first trains. — *CRRM*

4

If a Man Have Faith

"If a man have faith he can say unto the mountains, be thou removed into the sea." Some of the mountain barriers, the ribs of South Boulder Cañon, got removed into the sea as the men shot and shoveled the debris over the mountain side for the melting snow water to carry on to the sea.

It was winter, February of 1903, when the sixteen-year-old husky Swede by the name of Nels P. Johnson arrived in a gulch below the site of Tunnel Twenty-three. He had come with ten other men, one of whom had a tent that the eleven of them could sleep in for the next two weeks. Sleep in a tent in a climate so cool in summer that it has become America's vacation land!

Nels Johnson writes, "In the sleeping tents we had a regular tent stove in the form of an inverted funnel made from the same sheet iron that stove pipe is made from flared at the base to about three feet in diameter. You would dig a hole under the rim for draft and a place to spit, there being a fire door up on the side of the stove. These stoves came in crates of a dozen or so weighing about fifty pounds per dozen.

"The first day we walked up to the tunnel, no trail was established from camp below the tunnel, as the camp was built to serve Tunnel Twenty-one. Later a fair trail was worn up to the bigger camp on top of the tunnel where about one hundred men serving both ends of the tunnel were employed for a year."

"The first day we started with the twelve men, two drilling crews of three men each, and six with picks and shovels."

Nels Johnson, who weighed words and spoke deliberately, spent that sunny day with two other campanions drilling fourteen-foot holes, which were placed about three feet below the grade-line, for the floor of the tunnel had to be shot clean. After the holes had been hand-drilled by the slow process of swinging on a drill (long chisel), these holes would be sprung by placing three sticks of sixty per cent dynamite in them and hammering three feet of clay on top of them. They would not only be sprung once but three times, building up the charges to seven sticks the second time and a dozen sticks the third time. The sprung hole was now large enough to pack seventy-five pounds of black powder in them and was ready to be shot. By evening, however, these lads were only ready for the first charge of dynamite, which was to be shot by electricity. As the third hole failed to explode, the boys began clearing the clay out with a fourteen foot drill. All of a sudden the dynamite let go, driving the drill through Nels Johnson's partner and shooting Nels' eyes full of dirt. As Nels rolled over the bank, he found he could not see. His third companion, who had suffered only a sprained wrist, announced to Nels the death of the first fellow, while Nels was led away to a little log hospital on the wall of the cañon above.

The sun had set in the mountains and darkness had come as though a great light had been doused out. Supper was ready in the contractor's cook tent above the tunnel. One man was dead, another had been led away to the hospital unable to see. Thus ended the first day at the east portal of Tunnel Twenty-three.

After supper the men stepped carefully down the trail among the scrub pines and over the rocks to their sleeping tents below in the gulch. The air was chilly and they knew life was rugged with "x" marking the spot where a man had died, just as they could die in any ill-fated accident. They gathered wood and chopped it for the night. They hung up their damp stockings within the tent, passed the Copenhagen snuff around, and spat in the hole made for draft under the stove, sometimes spitting near the hole, other times on the stove. They debated among one another, if Nels would see again. They considered the death of their companion, probably sensing it was the death of a man whose name would be forgotten despite the sacrifice he had not been asked to make. Some of them wished that they had a bottle to forget with. Such was life. One man's life had ended; no more struggle, no more hope of the future enjoyment of abundant living. That age, as all ages, considered his life another boulder rolled aside for the sake of progress.

Next morning ninety-nine men continued their work. One drill crew was almost wiped out. Three wheelbarrows were on hand to mechanize the job. The men got to talking about deer. They did not see any, had not seen signs of any. Probably man's invasion with all the blasting had driven them back. More likely the close proximity to Denver had thinned them out years before.

Three days Nels rested with his eyes burning. But for three days only could this Swedish buck be kept from work. At times he might fumble from his smarting eyes as he worked for the next three months, but to swing on the pick, to scoop with the shovel was his determination.

This tunnel, like other tunnels less than a thousand feet in length, had been sub-contracted by Swedes from such contractors as Good and Company. The boys could rent a horse or mule for four bits a day, the same price being charged for a cart. Usually the contractor furnished an outfit car for cooking or even the cook and all so that the food was usually good.

To us it would seem a slow process — drilling 14-foot holes by hand, springing them three times, pouring powder, and then blowing out a piece of tunnel which had to be carted away. And it was!

H.A. Sumner was able to report that 1,187 men were at work during February. If any of these men had ambitions to become an engineer on the great railroad they were building, we do not know. But we do know that Nels Johnson did sometime later.

Art Weston, who was in the party assigned to assist the contractors, tells the story from another survey angle. "When grading began," he said, "the contractors wanted to take out the portal cuts on the numerous tunnels near the lower end of South Boulder Cañon. Mr. Rodgers had Herbert Reno and myself stake out these portal cuts. The side slopes were so steep that we worked with two wye levels, one near the upper edge and one near the lower edge of the cuts. We used our wits and derived the middle cut from the profile, without mentioning this bit of finagling to the boss. This enabled the contractors to begin on these tunnel portal cuts early and follow by starting underground in the tunnels, a slow process. All drilling in rock both in open cuts and in tunnels was done by hand and the muck removed in carts drawn by mules. Instead of being driven, the mules were led by a man on foot. This practice was known in the construction camp jargon as "leading a mule by his whiskers," and the men who did this were looked down upon by "mule skinners," that is, mule drivers, especially by those experts who could drive four mules on the narrow, winding mountain roads. The supreme test of a mule skinner's skill was the ability to drive four mules down the "trough road," this being the old wagon road that ran down the south side of Gore Cañon. (The present auto road down this route is still a trifle nerve-wracking to those driving it for the first time.)

"Drilling in hard rock was an art, requiring a strong back and not a little skill. (It is still regarded as a notable accomplishment by "hard rock miners.") I recall that we used to say that only a curly-haired Swede could drill blue granite, and none of us had ever seen a curly-haired Swede." As the men crawled all over the mountainside eating out the right-of-way for the new railroad, the cooks battled with the problems of butter melting in the day time and potatoes freezing at night. It was winter in the Rockies. Some days the sun shone and the boys went to work in their shirt sleeves; other days the winds blew and blizzards kept them in at cards. But with the thought "no work, no pay" they kicked around the snow and were happy as the tunnel dug in. After all, the eastern slope of the Divide has beautiful winters. The men could look above to the fresh snow on the Divide and wonder what it would be like when they started going over the top. But with the continual blasting, wild life disappeared, wondering what war was being fought over this hitherto little disputed habitat. The pack-rat welcomed their arrival, as did the camp-robbers (birds) whose steel-gray feathers kept slick under the crumbs they stole from lunches.

The sub-contractors of these less than 1,000 feet tunnels would be the envy of builders today, for men with a rented fifty-cents-a-day horse and a like-priced cart moved earth for fifteen cents a yard, loose rock for thirty-five cents a yard, and hard rock for sixty-eight cents a yard. Using modern machinery, the building of this railroad would be many times more expensive today. In that day, gun powder had more to do with building the railroad that any one factor. The line was literally blown out, and the cans the powder came in are still rusting along the right-of-way.

The long tunnels, however, were dug with the use of machinery. At Tunnel Ten five electric Gardner drills were in use. At Tunnel Sixteen Legner air drills were used. At Tunnel Thirty a donkey "up-right boiler" steam plant and steam drills were busy. As the internal combustion engine had not been very well developed, almost all of these plants depended on a steam plant either to make electricity or to compress the air. Inasmuch as these tunnels were high up on the south wall of the cañon, water had to be pumped up great distances, for in few places was there sufficient water to keep the boilers going. We can read the monthly reports with the list of shifts lost because of water failure. In that day when an electric motor got out of order, the entire tunnel job reverted to hand drilling until the motor was hauled by the slow speed of a cart to the interurban and then into the city to be overhauled. Muckers and other men losing six or seven shifts would become restless, for their wages barely took care of a man's own needs outside of a family. Many men would move to another job, and by the time the contractor was able to work again, he was phoning the contractor for more help. If a mucker was to make headway, he had to be skilled. No common laborer was a mucker. By the time a laborer was broken in, more time was lost. The surveyors were ever at hand checking up and keeping the work within the specifications of the railroad. (George Berry was one of these lads.)

The toll of accidents was heavy because of the very dangerous nature of the work. Inasmuch as the line was literally constructed by gun powder, several mysterious explosions occurred. Most of them came from exploded powder, which the mucker set off by sparks from his shoveling.

After Tunnel Nineteen was completed, pipes were laid in the tunnels to pump out the gas and smoke from blasting. One day J.N. Farman went in with his foreman, after a round of shots had been fired, to connect the air hoses to the pipe. A loosened rock struck and crushed his arm. Neither of the men knew whether the rock slipped from the roof or from the sides.

There was danger in springing the holes so that more powder could be put in for the final blast. The men discovered that by filling these sprung holes with water any spraks could be arrested. But when more was packed in and the clay tamped on top, two little rocks might be tamped together, making a spark which would let go an explosion causing lacerations in the faces of the working men. On one occasion five men were injured in this manner.

If you can hear the explosion of powder echo and re-echo through the hills and cañon walls, if you can smell the aroma of pine needles, if you know what it is to be dog-tired, if you have slept in a bunkhouse where dirty socks are hung to dry out for the next day, then you have some idea about the construction of this railroad.

Tired at night, as tired as only strong men can be, you have to go out for some more wood. It's your turn tonight. Loud voices of men turning to a bottle, the dice on the floor as men try to make better wages with Lady Luck — it all speaks of the slaves men have been.

Leaking roofs on bunk houses as the snow piles high on the roof and the ice forms; a new cook who is not so good; a delayed wagon bringing supplies and the monotony of the same beans; the smell of cheap coffee; the heartache of being away from home and loved ones — these all are a part of building a railroad. (Youth's thrill of the romance of being away from home is gone!) The arguments of men who can't get along with themselves or anyone else, the piercing night air, the cold, the days you are sick and not at work that feeling of longing, the continual grind of working harder to keep up — all make a motion picture that no plush-seat recliner can ever understand.

No dollars ever measure the building of a railroad, though we can say something about dollars and cents. This tunnel section from Leyden Junction to Mammoth (Tolland) was the most expensive contract let by the road. It cost three times what the branch line cost over Rollins Pass, including the mile of easy grading above Gato (Pine Cliff). It was contracted for a total of $78,323 a mile, which in 1903 was very expensive. Only in Rock Creek Cañon were there two miles of more expensive building $200,000.00 a mile. The cost was four times what normal railway construction was contracted for in that day.

This was but the first cost, for trestles had been allowed to stand rather than costly fills made. This was standard practice in construction based on the idea that when the road started hauling revenue freight, it could better afford to make improvements like replacing of trestles with fills.

The story of construction now moves down to Denver, where we must meet Dave Moffat's boys who will lay the rails and man the construction trains.

Denver was proud of her million dollar Tabor Opera house and her Windsor Hotel on Larimer Street, where the best guests of the city were amazed at the rich old-world furnishings. Those were the days when women would not be served at the bar, even though one day a gal would come in and shoot the ceiling full of bullets for refusal of service.

But the Denver Northwestern and Pacific had no such important offices as those modern buildings like the Brown Palace Hotel suggested. The Railroad had two box cars set off the track at Utah Junction. There was a short piece of main line track and the scale switch when George Barnes, the most loved character of the Moffat, went to work under General Manager Ridgway, supervising the unloading of ties. Ridgway knew him well, for Barnes had worked up to trainmaster on the Rio Grande under A.C. Ridgway's father, R.M. Ridgway, who was Superintendent of the Third Division.

Born in Illinois, Barnes was the son of a Civil War volunteer who had been shot through the chest at Chickamauga Creek, dying thirteen days later. As a child, Barnes discovered that his community was kind to war widows. His mother was given a job teaching school, so that she could pay her husband's debts. George was ten when they moved to Galena, Illinois. Although his mother had ambition to give him an education, he did not take to the teachers. His mother then sent him to the German Normal School, where they also taught English. Every minute of his spare time he spent in the telegraph office, where he was put to work doing odd jobs and janitor's work for the crippled day operator, who in turn taught him telegraphy.

In 1876 or '77 George left school and became night operator at Scales Mound, where he was a "sound operator," being able to take the messages by sound rather than having to decipher the punches in the paper tape, as most men did in that day. His wages were $40 a month. He bounced around working on several roads including a nar-row gauge the North Western had taken over. As a conductor on this road he was fired for having protected his engineer, who was under the influence of alcohol. This man had gone to work in this condition (unknown to Barnes). Barnes had been fired once before for working another man's trick as telegraph operator. "I deserved to be fired each time," was Barnes' comment. But the third time he was fired from the Rio Grande.

He had gone West to visit his brother J.E. Barnes, division traveling engineer, at Salida. Stopping over in Denver, he had seen a very happy St. Patrick's Day parade that was plenty rough. When he arrived at Salida, his brother wanted him to work for the Rio Grande. George at first refused. Men, however, frequently change their minds, George Barnes later became a Rio Grande switchman, and in time a yardmaster. The double order system was introduced to the Rio Grande at this time. When Barnes was examined for this change, it was discovered that he knew more than his examiners. One of the examiners on the three-man board was very happy to drop off and to let Barnes take his place.

Mr. R.M. Ridgway, the division superintendent, was known by all the boys as "Old Tige." Only two or three men, of course, ever called him that to his face.

At that time "Old Tige" had at his disposal a two-car train for use over the very busy narrow-gauge lines. George Barnes was assigned as his conductor. For some time "Old Tige" would not trust Barnes with his orders for he had run his own train for years. Later, he found Barnes so capable and trustworthy that Barnes was not only handling his orders but acting as a clerk at night, answering many of "Old Tige's" messages rather than waking him.

After seven years on the Rio Grande, Barnes became trainmaster with 1,000 miles of track under him. When Division Two was added to "Old Tige's" territory, the mileage was almost doubled. Both Marshall and Tennessee Passes were under Barnes who had to train his men to operate on three and four per cent grades.

The blizzards that attacked these passes are world famous. As trainmaster for almost thirteen years, Barnes learned the ABC's of snow fighting. One winter he was away from home from December to March, standing by a rotary snowplow trying to keep transportation running once in a while into the great mining center of Leadville.

One summer when George had business over Marshall Pass, the master mechanic asked him to look over the 210 which was used as a helper engine. All trains that this engine was pushing were falling down on their time. George observed that the engineer was working the engine perfectly, and the fireman had the steam gauge right on the mark. Barnes climbed ahead over the cars to see where the slack began between the cars to ascertain how many cars the engine was actually pushing. There he discovered she was not holding her own. Saying nothing, Barnes mulled the subject over in his mind but could not think of any reason for the 210 falling down. When they approached Montrose, he had an inspiration. The steam gauge might be registering too low! So he wired A.W. Jones, the master mechanic "Suggest another steam gauge." When tested, the old gauge was twenty pounds off!

Barnes' superintendent, "Old Tige," had trained his oldest son, A.C. Ridgway as his clerk. In time A.C. Ridgway became assistant superintendent over Barnes. Neither of these men realized they would later work together under David Moffat, who would be president, not of the Rio Grande, but of the Denver Northwestern and Pacific. Although "Old Tige" and his son were often referred to in that time as "Old Tige and his Pup," they did not always hit it off in harmony. Age and youth see differently. After one of these explosions, A.C. Ridgway parted company with the Rio Grande and was received by Moffat over on the Florence and Cripple Creek.

Since Moffat was no longer with the Rio Grande to protect his loyal men, the day came when all of the management was fired from the general manager on down to men like George Barnes. In their place came the superintendent and all of his foreman from an Oklahoma railroad. The superintendent was well experienced in the plains country, but within six months, the three and four per cent grades on the passes, the sharp curves, and the blizzards caused the new management to fly the white flag.

Meanwhile, George Barnes worked for the Colorado Midland as coal inspector. When the job was abolished, he was offered the position of chief dispatcher. Barnes declined this offer and sought work on the El Paso North-Eastern, where he became trainmaster. This leaky boiler road was not to his liking, but he did notice one day the name of J.B. Trull signed to a way bill for feeding stock. When he investigated, he found the man to be his former boss on the North-Western, who had re-hired him every time Trull's son-in-law had fired him. Trull cried and showed Barnes the watch that he, together with the other boys, had bought him

when he left the North-Western.

When the Moffat Line was conceived, Barnes hit for Denver and began his work supervising the unloading of ties and materials. Ridgway next sent Barnes to the southern part of the state to inspect piling and posts that the railroad had contracted. On his return to Denver he was sent to Omaha to the office of G.M. Holdridge of the Burlington and Missouri River Road to purchase some obsolete box cars, which were needed for outfit cars. Ridgway and Holdridge had agreed on the sale price of $100 a car delivered, before Barnes had been sent out. A minor official at Lincoln was the man Barnes had to deal with, a man impressed by his own great importance. The first day he put Barnes off. Barnes, having been an official, was greatly disturbed at this official snubbing. The second day that he was "too busy," Barnes' steam pressure skyrocketed. "I'm going back to Holdridge and tell him what a courteous gentleman you are," exploded Barnes.

Needless to say Barnes did not have to go to Holdridge. The cars were located and arrangements made for their delivery. Barnes went back to Denver to wait for these cars that were to become outfit cars. When they arrived, the first ones were immediately equipped as kitchen and dining cars for the National Hotel Company, which had been feeding the men in tents.

J. E. Markel of Omaha was president of this company. His nephew was Chancey De Puy, who was in charge of feeding the men at Utah Junction. Chancey was to grow up with the Moffat Railroad working for various firms until 1935 when he bought out the eating concessions and went into business for himself.

Ridgway found plenty to keep Barnes busy. He asked him to install the first switch. When it was installed, Barnes told Ridgway, "You sent me a right hand stand instead of a left hand stand." Other switches were placed, before Bob Olge, the bridge and building foreman, saw the work and took some men over to re-line the switches. To Barnes' disgust they were not "one sixteenth of an inch any different when he had gotten done shoving them around.

While Bob Olge was making up his mind to disagree on anything Barnes attempted, H. A. Sumner had a new problem. A complaint came in from Rollinsville that on May 23 a sub-contractor, Mr. McClure, had put off a shot of powder at Rollinsville which knocked a hole in the school house, injuring the school teacher and partly demolishing the front of two or three buildings.

But who wanted to read the letter Sumner wrote reminding the contractor that he was entirely responsible for any accidents, when the news got around that the first engine would puff over the Moffat Rails the next morning?

It was July 7, another one of those days when you are sure "it is a privilege to live in Colorado." The Denver Northwestern and Pacific had two engines on order which had not arrived, so they leased the Burlington and Missouri River engine Number 265, a little freight locomotive. George Barnes stopped putting in switches and was skipper and A. F. Norbury, who would continue to pull Barnes' train for eighteen years, was the engineer. Lee Fuller was the fireman, and so good a fireman that he later became the Denver general agent for Westinghouse Air Brake, eloquent evidence of his own ability to handle the air on a mountain.

The engine crew went over to the Burlington and Missouri River roundhouse, ran the 265 over to Utah Junction, which then consisted of two box cars for offices, a water tank without a roof, and a well that was not down to water as yet. The scale track switch had been the first switch put in, but this day there were several switches. In fact, all the future roundhouse lead switches had been built. The engine crew picked up their skipper, George Barnes, and the work train was made up. The rail-bending machine was located where the shop later stood. Indeed this road was preparing to bend its rails. Such treatment would strengthen the rails for the strain on the sharp curves in the mountains. That day the men were very proud of the progressive methods of their infant road. The rails were bent so far under pressure, then allowed to straighten. This procedure was kept up until they gained sufficient strength for the pounding of engines on the sharp curves, a practice continued on the Moffat down to its last day.

On this July 7 run Barnes and Norbury looked over their new route as they climbed the rails, noting points to teach other men who would later run over it.

The road lengthened day by day, for the practice was to assemble a mile of track alignment each day. However, track was laid with the iron car only until July 16, for from that afternoon on, the leased Robert's track laying machine was used. George Barnes' train would pull this construction train one day. The next day would be spent loading materials, while the trackmen surfaced the track laid the day before. The construction train consisted of a pioneer car, the Robert's track laying machine, which was followed by ten flat cars on which had been constructed a tramway from car to car. This carried rails on one side of each car and ties on the other side on ahead to the track laying machine. Power for the little tramway was furnished by a steam engine using steam from the locomotive in the construction train, which was behind the first ten flat cars. Normally two locomotives were coupled together here. The Irishmen laying the rails were paid $2.00 a day and did a wonderful job. Perhaps their good eats had something to do with it.

As the train tied up for the noon lunch hour, Barnes would get to talking about how he and Ridgway had spent the greater part of the night going over the various surveys. Barnes had fought any thought of a grade over two per cent.

Ridgway said, "George you are surely against any grade over two per cent." George had tried to shove trains every day for thirteen years as trainmaster on the Rio Grande over Marshall Pass. He was the operating man who knew the problem of his day. He had argued with the general manager, and he would continue to argue down the years with the wisdom of operating experience and practical insight.

The noon hour was over. The construction trainmen had "their good grub." George pulled out his watch, and the construction train was on the move again. They sky was blue overhead — the Rocky mountain clear deep blue — that "you never see back East."

On beyond the last rail and the steamshovel the the contractors hitched four horses to the fresnoes that were capable of carrying two-thirds yard of dirt, and the two-horse pignose that carried less.

A breakdown occurred in the tramway built on the construction train. George Barnes got to talking about the two locomotives in his construction train.

Engines 20 and 21 had arrived in July, being delivered for $12,996.50 and $13,501.61 respectively. Why their cost differed is lost from the memories of every one. They were supposedly built exactly alike. Little six wheelers, these engines were built for yard and construction work and sold directly to the Utah Construction Company as well as all the first equipment.

As the Moffat line shops were not ready, they were delivered to the Burlington and Missouri River shops. Their delivery had necessitated the hiring of two more men, Bob Bishop, who worked as fireman for Norbury on Number 20, and Fuller, who fired for Chester Foltz, on Number 21. On the days the construction train was being loaded, these engines pulled trains of slag to ballast the new track, which had been spiked and gauged but would be surfaced as the slag was scattered over it. One place, east of Tunnel One, the road bed settled so much that 3,335 loads of slag was dumped in before the fill held without further settling.

That evening as the construction train slipped back into Denver, George Barnes noticed a seventeen-year-old water boy standing at the side of Clear Creek trestle looking up enviously at the skipper of the train. George had seen him before. In fact, he had worked the year before when the tramline to the coal mine was under construction. Leclaire Daly was a nervy lad with intestinal fortitude, who would later handle a construction gang and handle it well before he reached his eighteenth birthday. He would keep looking at trainmen, until he went braking with a boost from Engineer Louie Larsen on whose engine step he would some day sit while watching his men work. He would later battle storms over the Divide, become trainmaster and finally assistant to the general superintendent of the Moffat. Daly had been working on the Moffat, even before that May day Barnes had gone to work, but not so early as Nels Johnson had driven his pick in Tunnel Twenty-three. Little did any of these three men realize the role they would play down the forty-three years of the Moffat.

There is a fourth one of Dave Moffat's boys we have yet to meet, Joe Culbertson, who was working as dispatcher over at the Burlington and Missouri River's office issuing orders for the construction trains on the Moffat.

Joe had begun his railroading as a boy operator nine years before on the Burlington and Missouri River road. Before working in Denver, he had worked at McCook as dispatcher. It would be June of the next year before Joe would sign his initials of JBC as chief dispatcher on the Moffat Road. Forty-two years later the same initials would speak of the grand little man who trained operators and dispatchers so carefully that never was a passenger's life lost.

Joe was beginning to feel the thrill of the 3,800 men who crawled over the cañon side with two-wheeled carts hauling dirt away from the mouth of tunnels. One contractor alone had a thousand men working up ahead of the rails.

Engines Number 20 and 21 were not very impressive but other engines were on order. The men were talking how the Burlington would be running through sleepers over this road to Salt Lake. Joe was not saying much, but he was fighting in his mind with an idea that when the chance came, he was going to bet on Dave Moffat's new road.

So on September 28 when the first special train of inspection was to be run over the Moffat, Joe Culbertson was wishing for a chance to become one of Dave Moffat's boys. The special was to run nineteen miles to the end of the track, which was then in the center of the big S at Little Ten Curve, as the boys called it between Arena and Fire Clay. This was to be one of the few Moffat trains ever to leave Union Station.

Engine Number 21 pulled the special which left Union Station at 10 a.m. A. C. Ridgway and David Moffat were the hosts to the following guests: H. A. Sumner, Charles Hughes, Gerald Huges, W. A. Deuel, superintendent of the Union Pacific, G. Vallery of the Burlington, F. Harris, assistant superintendent of Burlington, J. W. Gilluly, treasurer of the Rio Grande, W. F. Jones, auditor of Colorado Construction Company, and W. C. Thomas, assistant cashier of the First National Bank. Naturally George Barnes was skipper. The "Rocky Mountain Mines" was deeply impressed with the construction work. "It is one of the best pieces of road in the country as far as constructed." David Moffat was not being kidded by visiting railway men when the Number 21 was called a "most powerful mogul." The little stout construction engine had her day of great honor. She had pushed the flat car ahead of her on which chairs had been nailed to the floor for the distinguished passengers.

As a result of the very impressive thorough construction, Walter Cheesman withdrew his support for fear David H. Moffat, who was the mining king of the state, would become the railroad king of Colorado. Years later he told Edgar C. McMechen, "I just burned up with jealousy." This was told to the author and can now be said since Cheesman requested it to be kept confidential until after both of their deaths.

Walter Chessman had always had the help of Moffat on his railroad and mining enterprises. He was the second most wealthy man in the state and his withdrawal meant Moffat did not have the resources to build the 2.6 miles long Main Range Tunnel that H. A. Sumner planned. Cheesman's support could have allowed the railroad to reach the coal fields immediately. This was the first tragic blow to David H. Moffat.

On their way back the guests were interested in seeing the coal mines at Leyden. George Barnes was instructed to get permission at

Leyden Junction. He telephoned the tramway dispatcher. After permission and clearance were secured the little 21 shoved the flat car with guests to the mines. Three rail tracks ran here; otherwise, the standard guage Moffat train never could have made this move.

Number 21 pulled her train back to Union Station at 1:30 p.m. Union Pacific and Rio Grande men felt the road would surely stop short of its goal. But Burlington hoped she would get through and offer a western gateway. On the other hand, some of the officials kept in mind that it would be smart to get in on the ground floor of this railroad, if it could be financed.

After this memorable day, Moffat men had only several more miles of rail to lay to the location of the great steel trestle which was to be built over Coal Creek.

Four days before the steel had been shipped from Leavenworth, Kansas. Orders had been put out to hold the steel in the Utah Junction yard until the steel company erection foreman was at hand to lay the steel. Olge's big day as the bridge and building foreman was at hand. On October first the track had reached the Coal Creek bridge site.

But on that same October first and on the fifteenth following, which we mentioned before, those terrible storms swept the Divide for miles, playing havoc with the new work on the branch line over the Pass. This terrific storm was the major subject of conversation as Norbury shoved the construction train with the $18,600 bridge steel up to Coal Creek bridge site.

George Barnes signaled his engineer to ease the construction train with the steel to the bridge site. Lynn Holliday, who later became the conductor and even west end superintendent, was brakeman for George Barnes that day. An Indian, one of our real Americans who was not allowed to vote, was in charge of the erection crane which could handle twelve tons. But the girder weighed twenty-eight tons. The Redskin eased the girder slowly off the flat car until it was half way clear, then with a crash the girder swept to the bottom of the fill. A chain had broken and a link struck Lynn Holliday's hat brim. Lynn was standing by the flat car, as any good brakemen would have been. He was so scared that he jumped to the bottom of the fill presumably fearing Gabriel would reach down and take him to the pearly gates.

Another day when they were delayed at Coal Creek Cañon after the bridge was completed, Lynn lay down on some pine ties that were properly inclined for a snooze in the friendly sunny air of Colorado. Mischieveous George Barnes saw him. Lynn slept with a good conscience, while the impish nature of George let go in roping him to the ties. Then George went ahead to Engineer Norbury, who always sat in his engine, and asked for the bell to be rung. His dreams abruptly ended, Lynn attempted to jump to his feet for fear he would miss his train. Then Conductor Barnes lit into him for sleeping on duty.

A good laugh eased the tension of those days, when Gabriel stood leaning over the battlements of heaven, as the men drove piling into the rocky creek beds where high waters chilled them to the bone. Coal Creek Cañon bridge sixty feet high and two hundred fixty-six feet long was to be hit more than once by flash floods converging in the cañon from the gulches draining the mountain watershed. Above Coal Creek the line was one tunnel and then two trestles, and then two tunnels and one great trestle as the men carved their way forward with the short grading between the twenty-seven tunnels in twenty-four miles of that territory. Standard practice on the Moffat Number One and Two passenger trains was to let the train go through the first tunnel without lights. This woke up the brakemen who turned on the lights for the other twenty-eight tunnels on up to Pine Cliff. But in those days it was candle-lit cars. I guess the first passenger trains shot the tunnels in the dark.

With the rails reaching the first tunnels, the men who had completed their work either went ahead with the construction company or found some other job, as did Nels Johnson who became crane operator on a shovel. The steam shovel was at work above Arena on the second level of track in a cut called "Little Ten." Howard Wells was the engineer on the shovel, Nels Johnson operated the crane, and their fireman was Tom Cain. The cut was about sixty feet deep at this place. As they worked away at the slide, Mother Earth became very affectionate and in an unexpected embrace almost buried the shovel. The engineer fortunately had his face against the crane and his one hand was just above the slip of dirt, so he was able to dig his way out. The slide had ripped steam cocks off the boiler, which now was letting steam spurt from broken pipes. Added to his fear of Mother Earth's embrace was the fireman's fear that the boiler would let go. He ran down the meadow and hid in a hay stack. No amount of coaxing could get Tom Cain back on the job. As a memorial of this day's experience the rancher each year keeps a stack of hay or baled hay on the spot where Tom Cain hid.

This was the second close call for the Swede, Nels Johnson.

It is almost unbelievable, but construction work was carried on during the winter of 1903 and '04 on that hill line high above Tolland. After those two terrible storms on the first and fifteenth of October, it was not long until the work at the elevation of 11,600 feet was abandoned, especially on the first mile on the western side of Rollins Pass in what was called Sunnyside Basin.

Sudden changes in weather striking with or without warning could, in fifteen minutes, turn a sunny winter day into the fury of a terrifying blizzard on both sides of the Pass above timberline. All the preceding winter men had shivered as they had looked up to see the storms attack the Pass day after day. Now the contractors and men were on this stretch of excavating and filling in the road bed from an elevation of 9,000 to fairly near 12,000 feet. But the blasting went on; frozen rock could be exploded and carted away, if it was not frozen solid again under heavy snows.

Not many men stayed long on the job. Conditions got serious. H. A. Sumner was ever insisting the work be carried on, for without this temporary branch completed over the hill, the other side of the main range tunnel could not be completed. After all, this railroad was supposed to get to Salt Lake City in three years. This hill line had to be built.

To hold the two hundred men wages were raised from $2.00 a day to $3.43 in January. But even with men making high wages, how much work can a man accomplish in a day at this high elevation? It takes six weeks for a man to get really acclimated to the altitude so that he can work without stopping to puff every few minutes. In lower altitudes a man can get used to the thin air in two weeks, but above timberline it is another story. Every storm meant tons and tons of snow to be shoveled out. Every blizzard meant snow blown back in that had already been shoveled out.

On beautiful days the temperature would drop a degree a minute after sunset until it hung in the twenties to forties below.

No modern bath accommodations were dreamed of. It was just go out and freeze and take a chill at night. Then come back in and warm up on the cherry-red stoves. Potatoes would freeze over night, and teakettles would be frozen on top of the stoves with half an inch of ice by morning, as the cold swept through the cracks of the log cabins under the howling drive of a storm. And if a man got sick, all the company doctor would do was to take care of him there and await some sunshiny day to risk moving him on a wagon down to Tolland. It was still more miles to the construction train.

Frost-bitten faces, and toes, the smell of men who had not taken baths, and the ever-present remedy of whiskey to warm a man up — went into building the railroad above timberline that winter of 1903 and 1904. The men joined out-of-state people in sneering at the Denver Post line, "'Tis a privilege to live in Colorado." But somehow those who had faith hung on. By their faith they were moving mountains even as greater men's faith had worked miracles.

A constant concern of the surveyors was in checking the work of the contractors. George Berry, holding the rod, discusses the progress with two companions. Note the saddle on the ground at left and the two wheel construction cart. —*Art Weston, DPL*

53

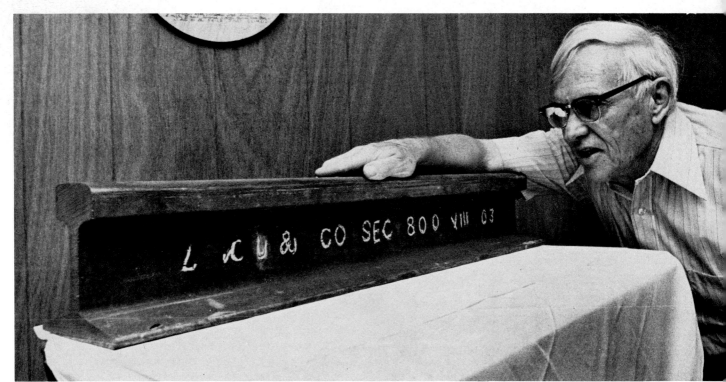

UTAH JUNCTION

Utah Junction became the center of construction activity. In this view (above-left) looking west can be seen ties, timbers and rails stockpiled for the Colorado-Utah Construction Company, the company Moffat organized to actually construct the line for the railroad. Engine 21 (above) is preparing to take a construction train to the end of track and is well equipped for its job. A steampipe has been run from the steam dome down and to the one cylinder construction engine which powers the track laying machine. The suction hose draped over the boiler can be used to pick up water from a creek or other source along the line as needed.

A section of original rail, laid in Utah Junction Yard in August, 1903, was recovered from a scale track by Art Black of the Rio Grande Engineering Department and is inspected (left) by Ed Bollinger. The rail is now displayed at the Colorado Railroad Museum. — *above-left, CRRM; left, Mel Schieltz; above, DPL*

The process of railroad construction is illustrated by this series of photos. The contractors, Streeter and Lusk, sometimes had 2000 or more men at work and two of them (above-left) take a break, perhaps to contemplate the endless wealth of boulders — big and small — as they do finishing work on the grade. The heaviest work was done by teams pulling scrapers (far right) and by the use of plenty of dangerous black powder. As the work reached Mammoth (right) Mrs. Katherine Wolcott Toll came out to view the progress. The Toll family, owners of the townsite, soon changed the name from Mammoth to Tolland in remembrance of Tolland, England.

As grading was completed, construction trains brought up ties and rails. Engine 20 (below) is pushing the Roberts Track Laying Machine and pulling a supply train, assisted by Engine 21 pushing at the rear. The track laying machine (right-below) was fed ties on a roller belt along the left side and rails could move up along either side. — *Left and right, Katherine W. Toll; right-below, W. I. Hoklas; all, DPL*

As the railroad built west, construction camps were established such as Benson, located a few miles from Tolland, where Jenny Lind Gulch joins South Boulder Creek near the wagon road to Baltimore. It was called "slabtown" by some and "ragtown" by others. The main street (left) boasted the usual saloons and shops, a hospital for railroad workers, and rather spartan accomodations (above-left) offering bargain rates for those willing to share their bed.

Work has already begun (above) to bypass what was to have been Tunnel 17. After pressures within the mountain began to cause movement within the bore, it was simply bypassed by a sharp curve. Years later Wilson McCarthy and Al Perlman decided to eliminate the curve by putting through a cut, thereby permitting use of the Rio Grande's large power after opening of the Dotsero Cutoff. —*Above, CRRM; others, Katherine W. Toll, DPL*

59

The winter of 1903-04 left 40 foot snowdrifts at the construction site (left) of Tunnel 33, known as Loop Tunnel. Even with a raise in wages to $3.43 a day, it was difficult to find men willing to work under the harsh mountain conditions. At Bogin Cut (below) work was carried on throughout the winter so as to be ready for track laying the next summer. The line reverses itself here, cutting to the right and climbing above Dixie Lake to Needles Eye Tunnel. — *Both, Katherine W. Toll, DPL*

60

The time was drawing near when regular freight and passenger service would begin. Caboose 10002 was new when in the winter of 1903-04, (left to right) Paul Brown, Frank Spaulding and engineer Bob Bishop stood proudly before the "Conductor's Palace" for this historic photo. The box-like object on top of the copula is a signal light which could be used to communicate with the engineer of an approaching train to warn if the train had not yet cleared the siding or passing track. New power was also being delivered and on a spring morning in 1904, photographer H. H. Buckwalter captured the proud moment when the newly arrived Engine 300 made her test run.—*Both, DPL*

| FORM 19 | THE COLORADO & SOUTHERN RY. CO. | FORM 19 |

Train Order No. ⟍   June 23 1904

To C & E Eng 300 101 and Work E, 20

At **Utah Junct** STATION.   X   Opr.;   M.

Eng 300 and 101 Will run as 1st and
2d No 1 Utah Junct to Mammoth.
1st No 1 Will run 20 Mins late
And 2d No 1 Will run 1 hour
And 20 Mins late Utah Junct
to Mammoth

MME

CONDUCTOR AND ENGINEMAN MUST EACH HAVE A COPY OF THIS ORDER.

Made **Complete** Time **7³⁰ a.M.** **Edgar** Opr.

The orders for the first train scheduled under Timetable No. 1 (right) were written on forms borrowed from the Colorado & Southern; evidently the Moffat Road's forms had not yet been printed. — *above, DPL, right, CRRM*

5

Time Table No. 1

The first fruit stand to appear on a Denver street was established in 1903 by Mr. C. L. Robinson, a man with fifteen years of railroad experience in the East, who had come to Denver for his health. He had not attempted to secure a mountain railroad job fearing it would be too much for him. One evening, a year after he had established the fruit stand, one of his customers came up and said, "You are a railroad operator, aren't you?"

"Yes."

"The Moffat is going to start running trains tomorrow. You get down to the Burlington and Missouri River freight yard by 8 a.m. and ask for Mr. Edgar."

So it came about that on the morning of June 23, 1904, Mr. Robinson could no longer turn down the call of the railroad in his blood. When he found Mr. Edgar, he said, "I understand that you are hiring telegraph operators."

"Yes, I want an operator, but he has to be pretty good."

Mr. Robinson then told him of his experience and gave his references. He had been a Baltimore and Ohio man and had worked on the Cincinnati, Chicago & St. Louis.

Mr. Edgar said, "I believe you will do. When can you go to work?"

"Right now," Robinson answered, producing his grip.

Mr. Edgar smiled, "You must have thought you would get this job."

Mr. Robinson, never having heard of the Moffat before he was tipped off about the job, was not particularly disturbed that the road had no station. He did not know how bitter was the battle that was keeping the Moffat out of Union Station and trying to prevent the road from securing a right-of-way from Utah Junction into the city.

The Colorado and Southern at that time was controlled by Harriman of the Union Pacific. Headlines of this battle, which the Colorado and Southern openly fought, were printed in the Denver papers of the day. In fact 32,000 inches of news print were given in the first fifteen months of operation.

The Moffat had plenty of passengers (three hundred) the first day that Time Card Number One went into effect. The Chamber of Commerce was on hand for the trip.

Robinson took a look at the engine — Number 300. She had very small wheels for a passenger engine, but that meant power in the Rocky Mountains. This ten-wheeler was a good engine for that day. She was, in fact, good enough to haul five Chesapeake Beach coaches on that run without a helper. The 300 was good for forty-two year's service battling storms and the grades of the Moffat.

Moffat had bought out the Chesapeake Beach road in the East and had numbered her coaches the 700-708, and 800.

Time card Number One called for Number One to depart at 8:10 a.m. But the orders that Trainmaster Edgar had written up, acting as dispatcher, called for first Number One to run twenty minutes late. If some important dignitaries were late, we do not know. Or, if some people were expected to arrive late from an outside connection, we do not know. Anyway, George Barnes could not give the high ball for the first train to leave on time.

Billy Rush, who was in the cab of second Number One, was given orders to follow an hour behind the first One. He commented dryly that his orders authorized him to run sixty miles an hour from Ralston to Leyden Junction on new track. Now new track is not like a new concrete paving. For new tracks are oozy in the spots where the joints settle, and all railroad men are cautious about speeding over new track. Billy Rush, being a railroader, expected a restraining order. But Edgar was only a trainmaster. He did not go into the details that Joe Culbertson would go into the next day in making out orders as the first chief dispatcher. Edgar simply counted on Norbury and Rush to handle their trains like they had every day with plenty of common railroad sense. So the engineers laughed about the first order under Time Card Number One, written as you see on the Colorado and Southern train order blanks. We would have expected the use of Burlington and Missouri River order blanks, but not the Colorado and Southern. It all spoke of a certain fraternity that courteously exists between railroad men of all lines, in spite of some of their Wall Street owners' competitive differences.

George Barnes swung a high ball. Norbury cracked his throttle and the first scheduled passenger train began to clear the Burlington and Missouri River yards. Norbury whistled for street crossings and made the stop at Utah Junction. Here everyone on the trip was eager to see what

kind of line Moffat had built.

Colorado had seen plenty of narrow gauge mistakes surveyed and constructed. Uncle Dave had straightened out one such mistake — the Rio Grande. In fact, his entire management of the Rio Grande had set a good pattern for Harriman to follow when he took over the Union Pacific and made it a real railroad.

The first eighteen miles one could know he was in the Rockies only by the heavy exhaust of the 300 which was hammering her stack on the heavy grade, for the country appeared to be prairie land. On the eighteenth mile the bark of the engine had slowed down as the grade became a steady two per cent. Here Dave Moffat was proud to show how his engineers had gained elevation by building a giant S from Arena to Fire Clay. Two or three of the passengers had been out this far, previously, when Moffat had taken some guests on a flat car special. The newspapermen had on that occasion written that this was as fine a piece of road as could be found anywhere. What would the newspapermen be able to write when they continued beyond that point?

In the next several miles they found two beautiful steel trestles, the last one being over Coal Creek. Being on a curve to the right, it allowed the passengers to get a glimpse of Tunnel Number One. The windows were closed as Number One took on water at the Coal Creek tank. The enthusiasm of the passengers was whetted now, for they realized that they were actually in the mountains. What thrill would Dave Moffat give them?

Norbury whistled off and, by dropping his Johnson Bar low, was able to get the 300 with her five coaches moving. The 300 barked her way through the short tunnel and eased to a stop at Plainview just one hour and twelve minutes after she had pulled out of Denver only twenty-five miles away. Plainview speaks for itself. Eastern Colorado looked like a great flat dry lake. Here it was possible to see that they had really been climbing all the way out of Denver.

Norbury had brought the train on its first twenty-five miles to the approval of George Barnes who now gave him the high ball to show what he could do through the tunnel district.

The tunnels started appearing one after another, an even twenty-six of them in the next ten miles. Between the first tunnels (Two, Three, Four and Five) Dave Moffat pointed out to his special guests, Eldorado Springs down in the depths of South Boulder Cañon. He told them they could see the old excavation of the Denver, Utah and

Pacific. Most of his guests politely said, "I see." But it is doubtful if they did get their eyes focused on the right spot, as Norbury hammered his way through one tunnel after another. Only an occasional tunnel was straight. The others would curve to the right or left at the entrance or exit. (Two tunnel locations had been abandoned as a fault appeared in the mountain locations leaving the timbers so twisted under pressure that temporary lines had been build around the sites. From tunnels to trestles the road was spectacular. Trestles would later be replaced with roadbed fills as business developed, an accepted construction method. The line was otherwise one superb piece of costly construction, which told that Dave Moffat was "removing mountains into the midst of the sea" by the waters of the South Boulder Creek.

At Crescent the passengers had their last view of the plains country. They could now see, off to the north on the other side of the far cañon wall, a water flume, which had tunnels of its own. The story of The Pactolus Hydraulic Mining and Milling Company was recited by Barnes as he had heard John Daly and others tell how it had been constructed in the '80's to furnish water for the hydraulic mining below. Mention was made that some of the construction men had helped build this water flume. The steady two per cent grade continued, while the sharper drop of the creek soon found its headwaters just under the track of the line, as they rolled through their last tunnel and into Gato, which later was renamed Pine Cliff.

Among the passengers that day were some men who saw the opportunity to build summer homes along this railway between Crescent and Gato. There was no gold in the hills the line had come through, but there was an air conditioned summer climate that bankers and those with wealth could afford and which was convenient with transportation daily to Denver.

Above Gato the Lodge Pole pines and Engleman Spruce hung close to the laughing frolicking water of the South Boulder Creek which has danced down all through the years to the delight of fishermen. This country was unmarred by man, for even the construction men had been cautioned to preserve nature.

Nature seemed to be kinder to the railroad for the next few miles as she gave it a little valley for the construction men to build through.

Rollinsville was passed by and Mr. Robinson knew he was nearing Mammoth, where he would be the agent operator. What kind of town would he find? The engineer blew the one long whistle calling the mile board for Mammoth. George Barnes began announcing "Mammoth, Mammoth — the end of the line, Mammoth." The valley again broadened out, but Robinson could not see a house anywhere. He climbed down off the high step of the train to find there was no station, only the tent of John Daly, the foreman of the bridge and building gang. The rails were laid a few hundred feet above. Box cars and outfit cars were on the siding. A tent was down on the leg of the wye by the ice pond and a lone cabin. This was Mammoth!

Edgar asked for one of the outfit cars to be brought up for a station. George Barnes relayed the news to Engineer Norbury. Climbing on the step of the tender, Barnes made the pick-up himself — the brakeman being busy elsewhere. John Daly's bridge carpenters were on hand, as the cinders were smoothed away for the outfit car to become the station and bunk house for Robinson. He climbed the nearest telegraph pole and cut the wire which coupled Mammoth with the outside world, home, and civilization.

Second Number One had long since come in. It was after 3:00 o'clock. Time for the train to return to Denver was 3:30 p.m. The passengers and guests of Dave Moffat were climbing aboard the train. Norbury whistled off. The bridge carpenters finished their work. Robinson discovered that he was "the most lonesome boy you ever saw." The mountains seemed to rise higher as the sun went down. This was a new experience as construction line operator. His responsibilities were 'round the clock, but he was given time off, when it was known his services would not be needed.

The sun set, the world was dark. The coyote began to prowl and send up his cry of protest to the steam monsters that were bringing man into his domain. Robinson knew he was in the Rockies. Would he see wild life like deer and elk? Were there bear and mountain lions 'round about? There should be. This was the foot of the great Divide. Last evening at this time he had heard for the first time that there was a Moffat Railroad. Now he was the advanced guardian of communications for a railroad he had heard a great deal about that day, a railroad Moffat was building to Salt Lake. Who was Moffat? It was all new to a former Easterner in the West for his health. Well, anyway he liked John Daly. George Barnes he would see again tomorrow, when Number One pulled in. There seemed to be some real honest-to-goodness friends.

It would not be many months until this town,

named for Mammoth Lake, would be renamed Tolland by the Toll family, owners of the townsite.

Morning came and Mr. Robinson stirred. It was chilly even though the Fourth of July was hardly a week away. In fact, Mr. Robinson saw frost on the roof of his box car depot. John Daly's men had breakfast ready in their tent on the wye. From them Robinson heard of Ragtown, a gambling joint below Mammoth. Men who won high stakes were occasionally slugged on their way out. Bodies of men were found in strange places. There were things to talk and think about.

That day Joe Culbertson went to work as chief dispatcher at $115 a month (good wages in that day). A month later Arthur Durbin was hired to assist Joe, who found that there was no end to delays. He could not understand at first why things did not run as smoothly on this hill as it had on the Burlington, but he was willing to learn from mountain railroaders like Barnes.

Picnickers came up to Mammoth on almost every train. Since the train arrived at 10:32 a.m., there were almost four hours to fish or hike around the meadows and hills. But not only were there picnickers, there was also the constant going and coming of men to the construction work on ahead. The grading on the ladder cut on the mountain to the north was clearly seen. As the rails were laid up this grade the follow-up work progressed to make Mammoth a subdivision point where helpers would be stationed in the near future for the heavier grade ahead.

An eating house was established, but the service was so slow that men were delayed in going to work. Such a thorn in the flesh did this eating house become that H. A. Sumner wrote a letter to correct the matter.

On July 20, Engineer Chester Foltz reported that a rock fell in Tunnel Fourteen and struck his engine, a fact that set the men to talking. It was appearing more and more certain that much of the granite was rotten in these tunnels and that more timbering would have to follow. The civil engineers were never to cease learning new things about the rock formations on their road. Years later the construction of the Moffat and Eisenhower tunnels, as well as the Leadville tunnels which carry water to the Colorado Springs and Aurora water systems, would prove that engineers are not taught the necessity of studying the lessons of engineering history.

George Barnes was honoring passes to such people as Mr. K. W. Toll and Sheriff Solomon Jones of Grand County. In fact, Parlor Car 800 came up one day filled with guests of Mrs. K. W. Toll. In that day the well-to-do entertained in such fashion. The Tolls owned everything around Mammoth and as the picnickers did not leave Tolland looking like a city park, they soon complained to the railroad.

One afternoon young Nels Johnson appeared at Mammoth. He had just walked over the Divide from the other side around what is now Winter Park. He got lost on his way down Mammoth Gulch and went into American City. Nels wanted some tools. He picked them up and started back, climbing from an elevation of 8,869 feet at Mammoth to 12,000 feet where he crossed the Divide. He walked down Jim Creek to Idlewild (Winter Park) before dark. That trip was enough to wear out a man on horse back today, but the brawny Swede hiked it!

At first the engines took water from a hose at Mammoth, but soon Ben Spitler, the water foreman, had a water tank up and a water line laid to supply the railroad and a few other places.

Ben Spitler had a side interest of trying to find Whistling Jack's gold men. Whistling Jack had a cabin on the side of the hill. He and his wife would load up two gunny sacks with groceries and disappear at night, only to re-appear two weeks later with plenty of the precious yellow dust. Ben and one of his friends would try to follow Whistling Jack, who always proved able to throw them off his trail or simply tire them out by going back to his cabin. Neither Ben Spitler nor anyone else was ever able to find that mine.

Ben Spitler was a remarkable man in handling web snowshoes. Later when the line was completed over the top, he could out run the slow passenger trains coming off the hill.

One of the men working for Ben Spitler was Joe Snider, who will tell us the story of Arrowhead. Joe worked on the Union Pacific before coming to the Moffat. Although he looked like a piece of human driftwood, he was a mighty man and preserved in his mind a remarkable memory of many events. Joe recalls the day Dave Moffat came to Mammoth. Dave was not at all uneasy with the most common workmen and seemed to enjoy waving at the boys from the rear of his car.

Operator Robinson recalls this same occasion. Moffat had brought along the builder of the famous Massachusetts Hoosac Tunnel, Mr. Thomas Doane.

In the evening the two men walked back from

the Main Range Tunnel site location. Robinson hastily filled the wash basin and got a clean towel so they could wash the dust and grime off.

What Robinson overheard was of tremendous importance, even to this day for those of us who try to straighten out why the main range tunnel was not immediately constructed.

This famous engineer addressed Moffat saying, "You have a hard proposition, but you will have to have that tunnel. It will likely cost four million."

Moffat answered, "I will have to get help. I have already sold my tramway stock and water stock."

Moffat would push the temporary line over the hill for $440,000.00 hoping to stretch his dollars out to get the line into revenue territory — the cattle country and coal fields.

As to how daring the idea of a 2.6-mile tunnel appeared to western engineers at that time, Arthur Ridgway comments that men did not think of tunnels over a mile long.

With the dirt from great men's hands on his towel the agent-operator of Mammoth began to take a great deal of interest in the newspaper stories he had previously overlooked regarding this "Shortline."

J. F. Galbrath, the president of the Chamber of Commerce of Denver, in his speech that memorable first day Robinson had arrived, had spoken of Mr. Moffat and Mr. Cheesman. But from that day on Cheesman's name seemed conspicuous by its absence from the stories.

Of particular interest to the lonely man at Mammoth was the statement Moffat released to the press: "We do not intend to request bids for the big tunnel for six months and will use the track on the hillside until it is finished."

In the box car station John Daly's bridge carpenters helped discuss the newspaper stories. "Now look here — 'Wall Street Believes Gould Is One of Moffat's Unknown Associates.' " If the boys believed the story, the next day they smiled as they Read "Moffat Is Emphatic — Once More He Denies Gould and He Are Together."

"They are going to build a steel plant," the section boss read as his men tamped the ballast under the new siding. "It's to cost $15,000,000.00 and will be at Utah Junction."

"Yea, and where are they going to get coal and iron?" a drifter asked.

"It says here they will get it in Middle Park."

Had this plant been built it would today pose a serious air pollution problem for Denver.

While the newspapers talked about what was

to happen no end of picnic trains arrived to keep the new agent busy. Grocers had their specials. Denver Dry Goods Store had a Moonlight Excursion, Parson Uzzell took three trains to handle his Sunday crowd to get the inspiration of the Sermon on the Mount. The Woodmen had their day. The First Baptists had a picnic special for orphans. One little fellow wrote on the snow:

"The Hon. David H. Moffat
    Is an awful good man;
And in pleasing children
    He does all he can.
When we grow older,
    And lay by our slate,
We will make him governor
    Of our beautiful state."

The many specials required both coaches and locomotives to be borrowed to handle the welcome surge of business.

The battle of the "Moffat Shortline" to enter Union Station was watched eagerly by the men building the line over the hill. The final showdown came when permission was granted for the sum of $18,000.00 a year which was paid by all other railroads. This was immediately rejected because it didn't take into consideration the present amount of business the new "Shortline" would have. The great builder recognized every effort was being made to bleed his new project to death.

Then followed a series of quick moves which put this road downtown where its own station could be built only to be found inadequate.

Indeed, it was a history-making summer that Robinson spent at Mammoth. Middle Park ranchers, eager to have the new road to ship their cattle on, beheld one rancher who drove his cattle over the pass and down to Mammoth, for the box car agent to write a way bill. This load of cattle was quickly sold in Denver for one cent a pound above the market.

George Barnes tells how one morning, when he got Number One to Mammoth, he found Charlie Clark there with the construction train which was loading rails and ties. Charlie said "Good God, George, you ought to see that track ahead. Marshall Pass on the Rio Grande is a hole in the ground compared to it."

With this as a spur for our curiosity, let us climb aboard the flats and ride the construction train up the hill. We will, of course, have to stay over until tomorrow, as it will take the Italians and Austrians all the rest of the day to load the ties.

We rise early again to see frost on the roofs of outfit cars and the new buildings going up in

Mammoth. The air is filled with the aroma of pines, and though it is past the middle of August, we are enthusiastic about this unique country where almost every morning of the summer there is frost.

Billy Rush has his engine under the water spout and Charlie Clark tells us to load on for the other engine has her water. The Irishmen seemed to be full of pep and songs, and we have good reason to believe they are ready to lay rail.

Billy Rush whistles off and our train of ties and rails starts on west. We look across the valley to the mountain to the north, where we can plainly see "the ladder" which we will climb. The track is straight until we have pulled up the first mile and find the valley suddenly crowding us to the right across a small trestle over South Boulder Creek and then we swing left again to continue a short distance further west. We eat cinders from our two switch engines, which are not laboring hard on the two per cent grade, while we wish we had broad rimmed hats like the cowboys!

The road now reverses the direction completely, as we swing to the north side of the valley, which has narrowed exceedingly. We have no idea, of course, that years later this would be part of the wye for turning helper engines at Moffat Tunnel, which was located straight west rather than higher up on the Divide, as was first planned.

Going east we climb the mountain side and have a wonderful view of the valley and Mammoth. Our train is moving about ten miles an hour as we climb the first rung of the ladder. As we reach a great curve to the left, we realize we are making the loop back to get on the second rung. The Irishmen laugh at us as we exclaim over a tunnel ahead into which the first engine has disappeared.

While the hot cinders pelt us we close our eyes and pull our neckerchief over our mouth, thankful that the second engine is a pusher.

Billy Rush is blowing for Ladora, the first siding, when we come out into the day light again. Charlie Clark climbs over us to point out some things. "I won't have to tell you when we hit the four per cent grade. The boys are making a run for it now. Look there. See on the left is the two per cent grade continuing on the Main Range Tunnel site. Of course they have not graded the line very far."

Art Weston provides us additional information on the Moffat's grades and curves.

"The route on the east side of the Range up to a short distance from the proposed site of the East Portal of the tunnel was located on a 2% grade. That is a rise of two feet in 100 feet. This grade was compensated for by curvature at the rate of .035 per degree, that is, the grade was reduced by that amount. On a ten degree curve the rise was 1.65 feet in 100. The track where sidings were located was reduced to 1.70 per hundred if on a tangent and if on curves the amount of compensation was also deducted. However, the sidings were usually only 1,600 feet long. Most of these have been extended in recent years to about one mile in length.

"The maximum curvature permitted was ten degrees (radius 573 feet) on the early work. However, later, when it became hard to raise money for the construction, the maximum degree of curvature was increased to sixteen (radius 359 feet). Much of the line in Middle Park was built with sixteen degree cruves. However, about 1935 this was reconstructed using light cruves. All curves above two degrees had spirals on the ends. (These are curves that increase in sharpness gradually until they approximate the central arc.) In 1904, while in Middle Park I devised and computed a table for making the computation of semi-tangents for curves with spirals, much faster and simpler than the method then in the books. I also computed a table for spirals connecting the arcs of compound curves. I still have the old note-book containing these and many other tables. In retrospect I can now see that I learned railroad surveying during my first two years on the Moffat. Of course many changes have occurred in engineering practice since those days, but the fundamental principles remain about the same."
— Art Weston.

Both of our engines are laboring on the four per cent grade, which, we hear, is to continue over the top and down the other side to a place called Arrowhead, where the main line will come out of the Main Range Tunnel.

Charlie Clark smiles and says, "I am going to tell you one on Billy Rush. The day we got the track laid this far, his engine had trouble which necessitated it being taken back to Utah Junction for some repair work. They sent out to us the old Chesapeake Beach four spot, a high-wheeled old girl. Her four drive wheels were eighty inches. She probably could pull two or three coaches ninety miles an hour on the level. But when we hit the four per cent grade and I signaled to go ahead over the track we had just laid, well, we hardly moved. Billy whistled and they made another try. He gave an awful jerk and then the Number 20 lost her footing and her wheels spun. They tried it again. I was getting pretty hot with the monkey business and climbed down and started telling Billy off. He defended himself, 'All I can do is give this girl one good jerk and I am done for. I say, she can't pull herself on this four per cent, let along the work train!' "

What Billy Rush said was true. The Chesapeake Beach four spot could not move herself on the four per cent. So she was sent back to the Denver Pullman shops to be rebuilt with fifty-seven inch drive wheels tailored for these grades. She came in mighty handy the next spring running the daily commuter train into Denver, but she was re-numbered the 390 and her sister was re-numbered the 391. These two engines were used until about 1927 or '29.

But riding with Charlie Clark on the four per cent, we try to keep the cinders out of our eyes as we swing back to the right reversing our direction, crossing a good sized trestle, heading east again on the last rung of the ladder, enabling us to see three levels of track below us.

We are in good timber. All along the right of way we find stacks of ties and lumber brought out of the woods. Our construction train is swinging left again and we are headed northwest to Antelope, a gulch where the wagon road winds below in the timber to our right. As we pass through Antelope siding, we are nine miles out of Mammoth. It has taken us over an hour, as we have climbed over a thousand feet. The sky above us is deep blue, the pine trees are deep green. The patches of snow in the shady spots cause us to exclaim, "There is snow, and this is August."

We are at Spruce where we stop. While the engines take water, the train is switched around so that the pioneer car and the twelve flats with the tram built on them are put in ahead of Billy Rush's engine. Considerable time is lost taking water, as the water tank is not finished and the water has to be siphoned into the engine tanks.

We laugh about the surveyors' saying that inas-much as they ran the line northeast a couple of times, they must have had a bad conscience.

By the sharpness of the curve ahead we realize they were not keeping the curves to a gentle ten or twelve degree. This one must be a sixteen degree curve. Charlie Clark comes over to us again as the men scramble back on and Billy Rush whistles off. "It's not far now to the end of rail," he said. "Did you ever see rails laid with a track machine? We have leased the Roberts track machine."

We noticed that the track was plenty rough as all new track is until the tamping is thoroughly done and the line worked over for low spots that de-velop. We continue our slow pull through the pines. It hurts our soul to see a tree cut; yet in the forest are many trees that have died of age and

have fallen in the storms that sweep this high coun-try. As we look above, we can see that we are almost at timberline.

A sheer wall of mountains is rising a half mile ahead of us. We begin to wonder how the locating engineer is going to get around this barrier. But as a little hill stretches its fir-covered brow in front of us, we turn our eyes to the right and through the trees see a little lake. Our spirits rise within us as we crane our necks to see the high mountain lake, just a dew drop of a lake. There is another dew drop ahead of us. We forget for a moment the narrowing of this valley with its wall ahead.

Just then Charlie Clark taps us on the shoulder and says, "Now you're going to see something."

We look ahead of us to the wall rising eight hundred feet and to our left is a lake the beauty of which we have never seen before. One of us cries, "The most beautiful lake in all of Colorado."

"That's Yankee Doodle Lake," Charlie Clark exclaims.

We answer, "As vulgar a name as could be picked for a thing as beautiful as a cathedral."

Charlie Clark answers, "I'd like to see the man who could build a cathedral as beautiful, yes, half as beautiful."

As the construction train stops, for this is the end of the track, we jump off with the Irishmen and stand there as in the presence of the Creator. The granite walls rise etched by the winds of the cen-turies and chiseled into designs by the frost of the ages. Granite that man polishes for his tomb stone lifts our spirits to the top of the wall, which forms a horseshoe. We wonder how the rails get out of this place. Our eye has watched them climb steadily around the lake and go out on the hill side we came in on but, of course, higher.

Charlie Clark again speaks, "What do you think of this? The Denver, Utah and Pacific started that tunnel and made the fill into the lake for they had intentions of going through the causeway here to Middle Boulder Cañon and on up to the Divide where another tunnel would cut through. Now look up there on the wall and see Tunnel Thirty-two, eight hundred feet above us. We will be laying track through there in a few days."

The Irishmen are swinging their spike mauls and we see their reflection in the lake. It is all very beautiful. We determine to climb the causeway while the track is slowly laid ahead. The climbing is difficult. We stop to breathe and look at the scenery time and again. We watch the trout jump in the lake and finally look south to the Divide and we know we are in the timberline lake country.

Half way up the climb we give up for fear we will miss our construction train which is rapidly, according to our climbing speed, moving around the lake. We want to climb on the flat car and rest. We cannot expect anything more beautiful, but we do not wish to miss anything half as beautiful.

By the time we drop ourselves down to the track and catch up with the train, we are tired. The fleecy white clouds roll over the Divide and are reflected in the lake. A trout jumps out of the water for a fly. We are sorry we did not bring our fishing tackle along, but on second thought our guess is that the men doing the grading have already all the easy catch in the lake.

The wall of the mountain rising straight and sheer causes us to imagine that in this high paradise of sheepherders and lumber jacks, Gabriel must lean over the top wall himself wishing to be down with the Irishmen swinging their mauls. These are truly "Rails that Climb." They climb around the lake. Yes, better than 2,000 feet an hour they are laid today.

In this thin air elevation we take to riding rather than walking the mile and a half the train will slowly push ahead during the day. We marvel that the Irishmen can ever get breath enough to swing on those spikes as they do.

We notice high up on the peaks beyond the quaking aspen trees are already in their glory from the frost-bitten air. Charlie Clark says that we are likely to have snow flakes any day now. The engines are in the middle of the train, the Roberts Track Laying machine being in the lead followed by a dozen flats. We drop back to talk to Billy Rush, as he works on the Number 21. He tells us that the contractors excavating ahead in Bogan Cut are making such poor progress that the road is likely to be delayed, as no track can be laid beyond until the cut is finished. Billy ends his talk by saying it looks as if it will be the first of September before they can get a rail into Rollins Pass.

As we ride back that evening and the chill air settles in the mountains, we bear in mind the date of the first of September and hope we can rate a ticket on the first train up to the Pass.

Back in Denver we keep in daily touch with George Barnes. He tells us that the first train will run the second of September. We extend our vacation a few days longer in Denver so that we will not miss that historic run when the first passenger train climbs up to the top of Rollins Pass.

September the second we drop over to Basset Street, where the Moffat station is almost finished. Number One has three cars this morning. We

count ourselves lucky, for Number One is to be run beyond Mammoth as a special the entire way to Rollins Pass. We hear, however, it will be a month or so before the line is finished down to Arrowhead and Time Card Number Two will go into effect with Number One running daily over the Pass.

At 8:10 George Barnes gives the high ball. Norbury cracks his throttle open, and we are off on another historic trip. George Barnes has two brakemen, Charlie E. Wise and McCartney. We hear that Bob Bishop is swinging on the shovel for Norbury. We make Mammoth on time — 10:35 a.m. The water tank is completed so that we do not waste so much time taking on water. Agent C. L. Robinson comes out with our orders. We notice Bishop spring up the steps to Norbury with the pep of youth and the verve of a real athlete, so we are confident that when we hit the four per cent, we will not be stalled for lack of steam.

As we climb the ladder, we notice what a difference a week has made in the aspen trees. The mountains are spotted with gold where little forests of aspen are seen. The track is not too smooth, we notice, and recognize that Norbury will not make the time on this run that he will expect to make six weeks later. At Ladora we hit the four per cent and can in our minds see Bob Bishop swinging on his scoop keeping the 300 hot. We lose speed, but we notice, as we crane our necks out the window on a sharp curve, that there is a plume of steam from the safety valve telling that the 300 has all the steam she can use.

We start talking with the rail fans making this trip, and we get them very excited about the line around Yankee Doodle Lake. Some one reminds us that over that causeway the old Rollins Pass toll road was built and that it was up that causeway the Crawfords (who settled Steamboat Springs, Colorado) climbed a few years after the Civil War. As we reach Yankee Doodle Lake, we observe that we are just about crawling above timberline. We notice on the Great Divide above us a pale green-like mold, which is new snow that has fallen last night on the tundra.

The steady climb of our train has been unbelievable. We are now finishing our horseshoe curve and bid goodbye to Yankee Doodle Lake. Below us is the track on which we had come. We spot the little dew drops of lakes we had seen the other day. We wonder what will be next as the steady climb of the 300 opens new vistas to us each minute.

Norbury is whistling for a station mile board. Some one says that we stop for water there. Yes, we hear them call the siding, Jenny Lake. Just now the hillside on which we have been climbing gives way suddenly and we swing out onto a wind-swept fill to the right of which is Jenny Lake. Barnes tells us the elevation is 10,960.

Since the water tank is not finished here, we lose considerable time siphoning water into the tank of the 300. One of our new friends says, "Who said we were above timberline?" We notice, too, that the trees have crawled up around us, as though trying to hold back the icy hand of the wintry blast that makes vegetation impossible. On the shady side of these trees we see some of the fresh-fallen snow. But the warm sun which we are now enjoying, as we wait for the men to siphon the engine tank full of water, betrays the reign of cold that slips over the mountain at night.

"All aboard," George Barnes calls and his echo comes from the mouths of McCartney and Wise. We can clearly see the hog-back of the mountain rising, as Nature's last defense against those who desire to cross into the land of the setting sun. Yes, that is Tunnel Thirty-two up there, but we are going south about a mile, the road clinging to the base of this hog-back all the way, before we will twist around some more sharp turns and be on the great swing up to Tunnel Thirty-two.

The 300 labors with her three coaches. It is just four miles to Rollins Pass. What a view we hope to see from there. As we plod our way slowly into the sharp turns and then back north again above timberline and the last green shrub, we look down on Jenny Lake. The track is rough, and we seem to crawl at times. The safety valve pops, so we know that Bob Bishop has not given out.

We are climbing and climbing and can see miles back of us. Our breath is taken in ecstasy. The 300 chime whistle blows a long and a short. This must be Tunnel Thirty-two. The windows have already been closed when we feel the train swing to the left in the tunnel. We gasp as we emerge looking eight hundred feet below to Yankee Doodle Lake almost straight down. We cross the Rollins Pass wagon road, which comes up from Boulder, and now we look down into another cañon, Middle Boulder, as we head west for the Pass. We know that it is much more than a thousand feet down. We are very content to have the train crawl on the top edge of this cañon. We see lakes and more lakes and waterfalls. Enough people have crowded to our side of the car to make us fear we are going to tip over. The mile-board has been passed and the whistle has been blown. George Barnes calls out, "Rollins Pass — the Top of the World."

We are the first to get off, and when we reach the engine ahead, we find Norbury out of his cab. Bob Bishop is there. What is this we hear? The front two wheels of the leading pony trucks are on the ground? Bishop tells us that the switch was open and McCartney, frozen to the foot board, refused to jump and run for the switch, while we came to a stop at two miles an hour. The switch has been spiked in but there are no rails beyond. Engine 300 had come to a stop with the first two pony trucks over the end of the last rail.

Well, anyway, this was something with which to remember the day. Barnes decided that for this occasion the pony trucks should come right back on the track, when they backed up. So seeing that no one was in the way, Barnes gave the signal to back up and the pony trucks climbed the ends of the rail, as neatly as they had left them. Then Norbury crawled out of his cab again to get his picture taken.

This is indeed an historic day — Norbury out of his cab twice. A. C. Ridgway explained that they were going to put in an eight-car stock track here at the Pass. He also told us the snow shed would be started immediately so that a part of it would be up before the winter set in. No water was available at the top for the first winter, but two miles down the other side at Sunnyside, they had a little reservoir filled from a spring ten feet above the tracks where engines got water from a hose. The breeze came up out of the valley to the west, for we were in Grand County now, looking down the western slope.

To the west Fraser River Valley was walled in by mountains that seemed as high as the Divide itself. Some one pointed to a place south of us and told us to stretch our imagination and we could see the wagon road going over Berthoud Pass. We understood that Berthoud Pass was 300 feet lower than Rollins Pass — 11,660 feet.

We hiked over north a few hundred feet with the crowd and discovered how badly we needed to stop and get our breath. Ah, here it was. A real view! We looked and looked at the lakes. The more we looked down in the valley, the more lakes we saw. We could hear the waterfalls, as the lakes fed the Middle Boulder Creek with melting snow water from the little banks of snow that will never melt away. Don't say little. They may have been fifty feet deep. We walked out to the east on a bank of snow but were careful not to get too close to the edge. This snow was about as hard as ice. The men dropped down and made snow balls after loosening the snow with their shoes, and everyone joined in a playful snowball fight. We almost wished that

DAY'S CAMP
HIGHEST ON THE LINE
ELEVATION 11760 FT
JUNE 6 04

THE TOP OF THE WORLD! Here at Day's Camp on Rollins Pass, the most hardy men stuck it out with double wages for the entire winter. The photo was taken on June 6, 1904, but it is hard to tell spring has arrived. On sunny winter days the snow melted until sunset when the thermometer might drop sixty degrees in an hour. And those terrible winds! How could this tent remain standing? By August the grade must be ready for ties and rails but the spring thaw meant supply wagons would be sinking axle deep in mud.

One of the first passenger trains (right) posed on the Coal Creek bridge for a publicity photo in the spring of 1904, with the newly delivered engine 300 and freshly repainted coaches from the Chesapeake Beach Line. —*above, Katherine W. Toll, DPL; right, H. H. Buckwalter, State Historical Society of Colorado* the Main Range Tunnel would never get dug, for this was such a thrilling sight.

Rollins Pass had been conquered by a road of steel, a standard gauge railroad. A. C. Ridgway told us, "This is the highest standard gauge railroad in the world, but some fellow may hunt a spot to build a higher one." We all laughed, but the photographers were too busy even to talk.

Joe Culbertson, back in his dispatcher's shanty in Utah Junction, had wished to be there. He would get up there one day, and when he did, he would have a new name for this place. He thought of it in time for Time Card Number Two. The name was Corona — crown of the mountain. Joe was always good at saying things in the least words possible, as dispatchers must. We were going to name the book "Ties That Climb." He said "No, make it 'Rails That Climb.'"

Joe has ever been naming things. He looked at the arrow-like shape of the survey at the place the rails would climb down to that winter, and he came out with the name Arrowhead. As the rails climbed miles ahead, he would do some more naming. Dotsero and Orestod are not names spelled backwards by accident.

But Joe's greatest work came in the years that followed. The vigilant watch he kept on his dispatchers and operators was not easy in later days of bankruptcy, nor was having to take so much help from boomers, who had boomed for good reasons some times. Joe's greatest work was in keeping safe all passengers' lives in the orders that came out for the better part of forty-two years over his signature, "J.B.C."

This honor would be shared with Joe by the engineers, who handled their air on the four per cent, carefully lapping the valve back and forth lest in a matter of two or three seconds' judgment, a train would get out of control. It was shared with George Barnes and the brakemen he and Charlie Clark broke in.

They were men who later became conductors on railroads all over the nation. Men who had learned to set retainers to hold the trains on the heavy grades; men who had learned to be one hundred per cent rule-book men like Pierson. One does not get a safety record of "no passengers seriously hurt" on a railroad with tunnels, rock slides, snow storms and four per cent grades with anything less than devotion by every man from the trackmen on up to the general superintendent, whose special bulletins ever urge the men to safety.

This was first of all, what Rollins Pass meant — the most vigilant care on the part of all railroad men. Second, it meant the tragic years filled with hardships in the great war against blizzards, when brakemen decorated the tops of the cars in sub-zero weather and lost their lives in the blockades — tragedies that would be eliminated with the completion of the Main Range Tunnel. Third, this day spoke of the terrible cost of operation that would bankrupt the road and scare capital away from investing in the enterprise. Last, it spoke of its real purpose, rails that would climb over the Divide with heavy machinery to the West Portal, of — not the 2.6 mile Main Range Tunnel planned to be built a few months later, but of the 6.234-mile Moffat Tunnel built many, many years later.

SCRAMBLE FOR SEATS IN TRAIN FOR MOFFAT ROAD EXCURSION

"Throw him on!"

David H. Moffat poked his head out of the car window and issued the order.

"Throw him on, there—throw him on!" he repeated.

A couple of husky railroad employes grabbed a sparsely built, elderly gentleman carrying a sun umbrella and chucked him into the open door of a passing car.

J. A. Thatcher used his late-to-the-theater gait in going to the formal open- was reached. In order to be sure that all might be comfortable who gained entrance to the cars, Mr. Day stationed assistants at the car doors and allowed none to enter who was without the coveted pasteboard.

Then there was a scramble for tickets, for there were many who failed to buy, expecting to pay on the train. As high as $5 was paid for tickets and yet the supply did not equal the demand.

They Were Repeaters.

But there were other ways of getting a came and returned it many times, but the last fellow that got it went into another car and when the conductor came around Mr. Londoner had to go down in his pocket and pay his fare.

Many tickets were used several times in securing entrance and that is why the cars were crowded beyond the seating capacity.

Mr. Day was inclined to be wrathy when he discovered the trick, and was going to put off all who had no tickets, even though they offered to pay, but

THE CHAMBER OF COMMERCE EXCURSIONISTS READY TO START OVER THE MOFFAT ROAD.

ing of the Moffat road and he found that the performance had begun and no box was reserved for him, and all the standing room he could have claimed was under the Sixteenth street viaduct. But Mr. Moffat's hired men put him aboard.

There were hundreds of others who were disappointed because they could not get aboard the train, either with or without assistance. But there was no room for them, although every piece of rolling stock the new road owns was in service, and the Burlington car accountant reported two coaches missing out of his yards.

Twelve coach loads of Denver's leading citizens went over the new road today at the invitation of the Chamber of Commerce. The excursion was in the nature of a testimonial to Mr. Moffat, and will be recorded as the formal opening of the road.

Tickets were put on sale a day or two ago by a committee of the Chamber of Commerce headed by C. M. Day. At first it was thought that a couple of cars would be all that would be needed, but that idea was soon abandoned and an entire train was ordered. But that was found to be insufficient and a second train was asked for, and when tickets enough to fill it had been sold a third request for more cars was made, but General Manager Ridgway threw up his hands and declared the present limit had been reached, but he did manage to borrow two coaches from the Burlington.

Chairman Day had planned so that each holder of a ticket would have a seat and he stopped selling tickets when the limit ride besides buying a ticket. The man who was securely settled in a comfortable seat by the window and thinking of the pleasures soon to be his could not help feeling sorry for those who paced up and down the platform, unable to get into a coach for love or money.

"Well," said Wolfe Londoner to a friend on the outside, "I'll let you see what a ticket locks like even if you can't have a look-in to the car," and he passed the ticket out of the window.

Then his friend presented the ticket for inspection at the car door and came in and returned it to Mr. Londoner so that the latter could give it to the conductor after his train had started. But other friends borrowed it out of the window and Manager Ridgway interceded and all were allowed to go.

Satriano's band went along and furnished the music.

Mr. Moffat and party occupied the rear coach. With him, among others, were Walter S. Cheesman, William G. Evans, Thomas Keely, S. M. Perry, Irving Hale, Lieutenant Governor and Mrs. Haggott, Mr. and Mrs. S. N. Wood, Mr. and Mrs. Stuart D. Walling, Edwin Van Cise, S. M. Allen, W. A. Smith, F. O. Vaile, W. F. Mills and Lester Brewer.

The first section left the platform at Fifteenth street, where the new station is to be erected, at 8:30 o'clock, and the second section pulled out a little before 10 o'clock.

The official opening of the Moffat Road was an exciting event in Denver and on that June morning it is likely that many more would have liked to come than could crowd aboard the two trains. The Chamber of Commerce, in an obvious show of support for David Moffat, made sure the city's important business and political leaders were along. — *Denver Post, CRRM*

NOTE: See appendix for additional details on opening events.

One sight the Moffat passengers would not be apt to miss was Sphinx Head Rock, seen (above) shortly after the line opened. Original grading of the Denver, Utah & Pacific can be seen running across the foreground of the photo.

On June 9, 1904, the Moffat Road ran a "pre-opening" train to Mammoth for the Colorado State Realty Association, with almost 300 passengers including Genereal Manager Ridgeway and David Moffat. The special is seen (below) at Rollinsville with Engineer Norbury at the throttle. — *both, L.C. McClure, DPL*

The first train arrived in Mammoth (below) on a chilly, miserable day; June 23, 1904, hardly felt like the first week of summer in the Rockies. The passengers have unloaded and the train is backing around the wye to turn for the trip home after the crowd eats lunch. First day passengers witnessed the start of a new town (above-left) as building lots were sold from the town's first building by the Toll family. The railroad established its first station in a box car (above-right) and work had been completed on a steam powered pump house — the building with the tall stack — a water tank, eating house and the usual "out" buildings. — *above, Katherine W. Toll; all-DPL*

Just ten weeks after the line opened to Mammoth, the first train reached the "Top of the World" at Corona, atop Rollins Pass on September 2, 1904. In this historic photo (below) the crew pose in front of the first train — left to right — McCartney, brakeman; A. F. Norbury, engineer; George Barnes, conductor; Bob Bishop, fireman and E. E. Wise, brakeman.

The Tolls soon began work on a fine hotel (above-left) and renamed the town Tolland. Charles Toll (above-right) is enjoying the morning paper just arrived on train Number One and is happy to offer a bunk for the night. — *above, Katherine W. Toll, DPL; below, Culbertson coll., CRRM*

The Burlington and Missouri River has loaned engine 179 to doublehead train Number One up Rollins Pass in this scene taken early in the fall of 1904. The butterfly plow is the only snow fighting equipment available on the Moffat except for a flat car loaded with rocks and with a small plow on the front. Winter is not far behind and the men will be glad to see the arrival of the new rotary plow. — *DPL*

6

The Next Day it Snowed

There was little sense of victory left in the mind of any one the next day. It snowed so hard in contrast to the beauty of the previous day that the bridge carpenters, starting to work on the snow shed, had to give up three times and go inside for protection. Six inches of wet snow lay over the rails at Rollins Pass September the third. The wind bit into men's bones, and the hands of the wind pulled planks out of the hands of the men.

The snow melted below the pass on the western side in a heavy rain and caused the new grade to slip and slough away. Every one had wet feet and wet hands. If one had a half dozen pair of gloves to work in, he would have wanted a half dozen more drying on some stove. The contractors knew they would be losing men. The wages paid weren't so good that men would sneeze and struggle and slip in the mud and fall on the snow and come in at night wet and disgusted forever.

The records show that at the end of this day the rails were one half mile down the other side of the pass. Whether they were laid on the second or third, we are not sure. Billy Rush no longer needed a second engine to help him with the construction train.

Tragedy stalked one day when steel was laid further west. McGuverans was working with a track bar made of steel, or, as some think, with an all steel shovel, when out of the clear sky, lightning struck and killed him. The bolt had blown his shoes off his feet. He was brought immediately on a hand car into the Corona Shed, a small part of which was built. All effort to find relatives was of no avail, so he was buried at the west end of the snow shed, and a wooden marker placed over his grave.

The first snows were to show how ill-advised the placing of a snow fence was at Rollins Pass, for it caused more drifting. It was soon ordered removed. An eight-car stock track was built. If cattle were shipped out on this track in the next few days, we do not know. It would not have been hard to drive the cattle up Ranch Creek to the pass, for cattle had been driven over the pass for years, but it was getting too late in the season to do so now.

Most ranchers were counting on shipping out their cattle from Arrowhead, which was eleven miles down the west side of the Pass. The office had been besieged all summer and even earlier with inquiries as to when the rails would reach Arrowhead. Earlier in the year H. A. Sumner had reasonable expectations of getting to Arrowhead by September fifteenth. This date was in the minds of the people, but the difficulties the contractor met in Bogan Cut had thrown the time back.

There was no doubt that some few men would rejoice whenever Sumner might be wrong, but no one working with the track layers on the Western Slope wished any more delays. The Engleman Spruce might be the envy of Gabriel himself, when it was hanging heavy with fresh snow, but no one envied the job of working in September snow at this elevation. No one would be at ease until the rails were in Arrowhead and most of the essential work completed. For could you ever count on the weather in the Rockies for aught but a surprise? Indian summer would come after some miserable snows that might drive away construction workers.

The rails were steadily laid around Ptarmigan Point and down to Sunnyside, which was to become an emergency water stop and a weather observation point. The little reservoir was constructed on the mountain side above the tracks and the water piped into a house which had a large hose that would water engines. (You can see this spot to this day and drink the water.)

Laying the track was no quick job now, for the grading which had slipped from the melting snows had to be replaced and the next bottleneck would be the Loop Tunnel, which is just below timberline. Here the road bridges (with a trestle) over to a hill standing away from the mountainside like an island.

The grade around this island-like-hill looping back under the trestle by means of a still lower tunnel. The loop was a good mile around. This tunnel, number 33, was not completed until September eighth. John Daly had made short work of the Loop Trestle in a day and night's job, so that the rails were waiting to be laid through the tunnel as soon as daylight came the ninth. That day the rails were laid 2,000 feet west of the Loop Tunnel, this track being directly below the upper track of the Loop.

Men, who had been away from home all summer, were anxious to be back with their wives and children, as school was beginning. The winter before was rough enough to discourage anyone's loafing. The rails were laid north around the peninsula of the mountain and back south to a spot which became known as Ranch Creek, where a water tank was built and a wye later constructed. Here a small trestle was built over Fawn Creek, a tributary to Ranch Creek.

Timber men were busy all through this section. Some men were getting out mining props, others were cutting or hewing ties. Ranch Creek would be the last place engines could get water, for Arrowhead would have no water tank even though it was to be end of the line for the first winter and a helper stop for years.

As the rails approached Arrowhead, it was very evident with curves as sharp as sixteen degrees that this was a branch line. The twenty-three and twenty-five hundredths miles of the branch was constructed at little over $20,000 a mile by elimination of any great excavation and by the necessity of only three short tunnels. This, incidentally was the cheapest piece of track constructed clear to Steamboat Springs. The survey was very remarkable in that it located with an even four per cent grade.

September eighteenth the rails reached the outskirts of Arrowhead. The stockyards had been finished two days before. Since the grading for the wye had to be completed and the switches spiked in, it was the twenty-fourth of September before the rails had been laid past the station into the stock yard. Very apparently the force of men working must have been quite small by now.

Billy Wood (W. R. Wood, Sr.), who became famous as the sawmill operator at Arrowhead and later at Irving Spur, had camped on the site of Arrowhead the year before. He had looked over the entire territory for the possibilities of timber and was wise in locating his first mill near Arrow, so that he could ship out lumber as soon as the line was open to traffic. He claimed to be the first shipper out of Grand County.

But the picture we have of Arrowhead comes from Mr. C. L. Robinson, who had done such a fine job at Mammoth as agent-operator that he was asked to come over to Arrowhead, when Time Card Number Two went into effect October fourth. He found the log station without windows and doors or chinking between the logs. One foot of snow fell the first night. He slept in the office, which fortunately was tight. Snow drifted all through the passenger room and the freight room. The only other building was one up in the woods above what later became the town. All saloons were in tents at that time. The section boss was living in a tent with his wife and two daughters. The first evening Mr. Robinson walked over the hill of Arrow to what would be Pacific Siding and then on to a contractor's mess hall. When he came back, the sun had set and in taking a short cut, he got lost. The author of the book knows that mountain lions live in this spot today; as to what was there then, we will not say.

Four days of such life gave the man, who was not well and had come to Colorado for his health, pneumonia. John Daly went into Denver with him on the train and rode the street car with him to his own door, where he fell. After getting a doctor and helping as he could, John stayed all night with him. This incident brings the tribute Robinson pays the Moffat, "I never found a place where the boys had such a feeling for each other as on the Moffat."

This sickness made Robinson Denver's first Moffat agent, a job he held for eighteen years.

But now that we have Mr. Robinson in good hands recovering from his exposure, we go back.

In fact, we will turn the pages of history back to September 27 and ride with Louie Larsen, who is the throttle artist of a train headed west going up the hill with its destination, Arrowhead. The day is as beautiful as an Indian summer day could be — sky clear with beautiful little fleecy clouds. At

Jenny Lake they took on water. Larsen whistled off, expecting to be through Tunnel Thirty-two and into Rollins Pass in one half hour. Twenty minutes later he had pulled his train up to Tunnel Thirty-two and was hammering his stack off lurching to the left as he came out into a drift that stalled him immediately. The snow soon drifted over his engine. Larson and another man started immediately for Rollins Pass for help and food for the rest of the crew. It was 1:30 p.m., and it was an hour and a half later, before they were in the safety of the snowshed a mile away after a struggle against the howling blizzard.

Three hours later, the storm having abated its fury, they were back to their train. They could find their train at the 6:00 p.m. hour in the starlight only by the smoke rising, as it were, from a hole in the snow. Their gunny sack of groceries was delivered to be cooked on the caboose stove. Charlie Peterson, who later became famous as master mechanic, was with Larsen on this trip.

The next day, September 28, A. C. Ridgway and Joe Culbertson crossed their fingers and took every precaution to get a special made up of motive power and parlor car number "800" over the Pass. They dared not bungle this trip. Perhaps they prayed fervently or perhaps they did not. Be that as it may, the train delivered the important guests safely into Arrowhead, which was only nine days less primitive than Robinson had found it.

The important passengers that alighted from the parlor car in front of the partly completed rustic Arrow station were Mr. C. M. Wicke and daughter, whom David Moffat had encouraged "to come out and look over the wonderland of opportunity" which the Moffat would open. If they were favorably impressed, Moffat would have some much needed financial help.

Two sixty horsepower Stanley machines, having been unloaded from a flat car, awaited them. But let us consider what an automobile was in 1904. The tires were almost as thin as an inner tube and as rough riding as solid rubber. In fact, the automobile had just got out of the horseless carriage era. These cars had only wagon roads to travel. The newspaper story was, "Daring Auto Journey. Miss Wicke, Gotham Heriess, Penetrates Moffat Road Wilds." Indeed it was daring in 1904 to think of attempting to drive one of those new fangled things any distance at all, to say nothing of attempting to drive to Salt Lake City. I imagine Miss Wicke was thrilled at the tents of the construction camps, just as later high school students loved Zane Grey.

The streets of Arrowhead and the Little Chicago road, which stretched down to the Middle Park wagon road were steep enough to scare any man's wife even today in a modern car with good brakes. Two teams were hitched ahead of the car to pull it through the mud holes of Arrow and the bog near "Little Chicago."

We have reasons to believe that General Manager A. C. Ridgway may have come out with them from Denver, as he was making his late inspection trip of the grading before winter set in. If so, he likely accompanied them as far as Fraser in the car. There he would take to the spring wagon, which was the jeep of construction men in that day, while the Wickes continued on their way in the car.

The route of Mr. Wicke and his daughter, roughly speaking, was that of highway U.S. 40 today. Then the road at Fraser went directly west by the Four Bar Four ranch house, which was the regular horse-changing station and beyond Red Dirt Hill. It missed Granby by the Midland trail route over Cottonwood Pass into Hot Sulphur Springs.

The scenery was wonderful, if you had faith enough in the road and the contraption whose engine added vibrations that no osteopath would ever dream of contributing to the health of a lazy liver.

The West must have appeared quite raw to Mr. Wicke. What Middle Park looked like that day with no rich Pennsylvania Dutch farm buildings with their fresh paint, I fear to imagine. From what was the revenue to come to pay his dividends, if he invested?

The thirty-five miles from Arrowhead to Hot Sulphur either exhausted the party or the car, for the party spent the night there. The hot sulphur springs could, of course, be shown and a great tale told about all the miracles the rancid smelling sulphur waters would work. Since there were great resorts in the East and the water here stunk strongly, Mr. Wicke might have been impressed with the potentialities of this as a resort community. The town was growing. A fine new bank building had been started and other buildings were in the blue print stage. One thing is certain: the management of the railroad saw to it that the meals were marvelous.

The next morning the car started down the Sulphur Cañon wagon road, which was promised as the right-of-way. If Mr. Wicke were after thrills, he would be impressed. If he were a timid soul, he would be scared senseless.

A few miles further on they came to Kremmling, where a half dozen buildings represented the community. If Mr. Wicke had asked how many crops of hay were cut off the ranch meadows he had passed, he would have considered his trip a waste of time. But perhaps Mr. Wicke had been born with a silver spoon in his mouth and never knew any better. Surely the little log ranch house and the cattle standing in the open would not be impressive.

Beyond Kremmling their road climbed the general direction of the present U.S. 40, which they had followed from below Arrowhead. The road then went over Gore Pass. It was on their way up this pass that they ran into some greasy red clay left by one of those showers that come miraculously out of a fleecy little cloud of no important proportions. The modern invention on rubber tires got crossways of the road.

So they walked back to the Pinney Ranch to spend the night. It would be thrilling to talk about, if you had the romance of life in your mind's eye, like the poet has who sees such a day and writes a poem that is remembered for generations. But if you did not have eyes that could see, you would conclude that the West was the great American Desert.

The next morning the trip was continued on into the coal regions. The only mines were wagon mines that supplied Steamboat Springs and the surrounding ranch country. If Mr. Wicke were really a business man, he could be impressed by the size of these veins and the quality of the coal. Here were resources that could impress even the hardest-headed businessman, resources that would help to fight two wars.

Whoever officially accompanied these special guests was well prepared to show every prospective mineral and agricultural resource of the country.

Steamboat Springs would be the first community which would impress them with a better-than-cross-roads atmosphere. Here Mr. Wicke was secretly informed by Sam Adams, who was Moffat's right hand man for this area, about the coal, oil, and gilsonite which Moffat had had prospectors and mineral engineers confirm.

On West they went with no car trouble until they got to Maybell. Here the hope for buying more gasoline beyond gave out and a buckboard was substituted, while the car was driven south to Rifle on the Rio Grande and there shipped by rail back to Denver. You have to hand it to Mr. Wicke that he did not back down on the trip from this point.

Two hundred and fifty miles ahead across the great American desert by buckboard. . .!

We leave the Wicke expedition following roughly the survey of the Denver Northwestern & Pacific by spring wagon through Eastern Utah toward Salt Lake City, and we return to the engineer who had pulled the Wickes and Mr. Ridgway into Arrow.

The engineer was Sterling Way, who was waiting for the return of General Manager Ridgway. The time was being spent playing cards in the caboose provided for the crew by his conductor, Charlie Clark.

No one had any idea when Ridgway might return. It was snowing up on the Divide. You could easily see the deepening snow on James Peak from Arrow, even if you had not word over the wire that the plow was busy. But the sun would come out in the day time at Arrow and the boys would know the feverish work the graders would be doing with Ridgway conferring with the bosses in this last rush before winter would settle. But when the sun melted the snows that fell on Ridgway and the men below Fraser, it did not melt the snow 3,000 feet higher up the Divide.

Then came the word that the plow was broken down. The boys joked about staying all winter in Arrow and very shortly Mr. Ridgway appeared. "Boys, have you had your dinner yet?"

"Yes, sir."

"Sterling, do you think you could buck the hill without a helper if we cut the 800 parlor car off and left here here and took only the caboose?" (The helper engine left at Arrow had developed leaky flues.)

Sterling Way answered, "Yes."

The little six-wheeled switch engine was opened up as she charged up the four per cent, the men with the feeling that every minute the snow would be getting deeper on the Divide. They were soon bucking snow three and four feet deep. Then it reached the bottom of the boiler and the wheels spun, just as they got out of the drift on the climb above Ranch Creek.

On the Loop the snow was seven feet deep in drifts. No little engine had ever performed such a stunt. But Sterling Way was a throttle artist. He seemed to sense just how much he could open that throttle without the wheels losing their grip or the engine dying in the drift. He would bounce out backwards and take another run at the drift.

All could see themselves stalled with the general manager to keep them company. Still they crawled up, up through Sunnyside Basin. The snow should have been deeper here, but it was not. They got up enough speed going around Ptarmigan Point to struggle through the deepening snow the last mile into the snow shed. Would they stall just a half mile short of the shed? The conductor was too intent now even to place a bet or suggest what the odds were. The 21 slowed down to a crawl, her wheels spun, but they made the shed! The impossible had been accomplished. Never afterward did any six-wheel engine make such a run. Ridgway knew that he had in Sterling Way a real engineer!

From the time Extra 21 East had left Arrowhead, Joe Culbertson was pacing back and forth in his office in Denver. The operators gave their opinions, and the men wondered how wet or how light the snow might be. But more anxiety was in Ridgway's heart over the impression that the eastern guest had received of the investment possibilities of the railroad. The mail would be watched every day for word from Moffat.

On October second Time Card Number Two went into effect. Number One's run was extended from Mammoth to Arrowhead. Number One left Denver at 8:00 a.m. and climbed to the top of the world, Rollins Pass by 11:32 a.m.

The elevation was a mile above Denver, indeed 1,100 feet more than a mile above Denver. By 12:20 noon Number One had dropped down to Arrowhead. Here was one hour in which you could visit a restaurant and get a good chicken dinner before leaving on the return trip, which George Barnes would again skipper with Norbury at the throttle of the 300. The seventy-six and seventy-seven hundredths-mile trip was made back to Denver in four hours and ten minutes.

It was October 28, 1905, when W. L. York became the agent.

Earlier, on October 17, H. A. Sumner confirmed a conversation down in Denver with A. C. Ridgway, which spoke of the financial freeze Harriman was working. Arrowhead was to have been the end of this temporary line of four per cent grade. For the main range tunnel line was to have swung into the branch just around the curve below Arrow at what became known as Pacific. The main line then would have run on down to Idlewild on a two per cent grade and with curves not over ten degrees. However, A. C. Ridgway wrote this letter:

"In conformity with verbal instruction from you after discussing the situation with Mr. Moffat this morning, we will proceed with the location and construction of the line from Arrowhead West extending the four per cent maximum with sixteen degree curves. . . ."

This would go as far as Idlewild, where the main line two per cent would run on down to Tabernash.

In other words the completion of the road might be made possible by temporary construction from here west as far as the revenue country of the coal fields or the money might give out before. Dave Moffat had no ace in the hole. It was Harriman who had the joker and was set to take the tricks. Or would such a man as Mr. Wicke come to the rescue with financial help which though it might not complete the line, could be of encouragement and help in building a few more miles?

One can read the carbon copies of the letters of Mr. Sumner for hours searching for some word of Mr. Wicke. The first note that we find, written by Sumner, is that Mr. Wicke appeared, to those who accompanied him, "as a characteristic Easterner who considered the West as the great American Desert, while the newspaper accounts printed that the Wickes were favorably impressed."

The press told the final story in this fashion. "Locket Wicke, daughter of C. M. Wicke, New York millionaire, drove an automobile four hundred ninety miles . . . penetrates Moffat Road Wilds."

Unfortunately no research has turned up any more information on the Wickes.

The blizzards of time have a kind way of treating the weary minds of men who have suffered. This is true not only in war but in such a campaign as the years saw fought "on the hill." This chapter is lost in the blizzards of time, just as Number One was lost in the howling snows that whistled over the coaches from the low flying clouds on Rollins Pass. As we shovel the snow out of men's memories, we are not certain which was the first actual blockade.

One day with Norbury as engineer, Number Two got stuck as she came out of Tunnel Thirty-two just below Rollins Pass on the east side. It seems silly for a little train with no more than one car to get stuck going down the much feared four per cent grade. If Norbury had known how deep the snow was on the other side of Tunnel Thirty-two, he might have risked opening up his engine as he went in Tunnel Thirty-two and knocked his way out of the drift. But who with the throttle wide open would want to enter a tunnel that curves sharply to the right and comes out high up on the almost perpendicular wall of a mountain hundreds of feet above the country below? Who would want to be feeding much steam at all on a grade on which it was almost impossible to control a train after it had gained a little speed? Hence, Number Two was stalled here twenty-four hours before she was dug out.

With blizzards breaking through Indian summer, the road was ill prepared to battle a winter on the temporary branch line. For motive power she had two sturdy consolidation engines, numbers 100 and 101, the two switch engines, numbers 20 and 21, the passenger engine number 300, whose low drive wheels would make her of some help, and the two little girls off the Chesapeake Beach, the 390 and 391, which were reconverted to small drive wheels by this time, but of no use in fighting snow. There was no rotary snowplow ordered as yet. A butterfly plow was winter equipment of Engine 21 and a home-made flanger was built onto a flat car which was weighted down with rocks.

There is only one explanation for this lack of preparation. Dave Moffat was taking a long chance on a mild winter in hope that he could conserve every dollar for construction work the next summer. He could always lease engines for a trip or two in a pinch, for the lines coming into Denver were well equipped for the summer wheat rush and fall cattle business. But you could not get a rotary until the other roads were through cleaning out their own lines.

According to Joe Culbertson's memory the first tie up occurred four miles on the western side of Rollins Pass around the Loop. The weather is blustery on the hill, so let us stick around the pot-bellied stove in the office of Joe Culbertson, and let the story come over the wire, as he got it.

Joe's office reminds us of a small town station agent's layout, except for the table with the great rain sheet on it. Several telegraph tickers are queitly ticking away. One is from the Burlington and Missouri River dispatcher's office with the report of an occasional car of materials that will be shuttled over to the Utah Junction yards. The ticker from the hill is turned on loud. The agent at Arrow is reporting Extra 179 east out of Arrow with the home-made flat car flanger. Joe turns to us and fills his pipe with tobacco, possibly from a Blue Lunch box tin popular in that day. He says, "We borrowed the 179 from the B and M. (Burlington and Missouri River)." When railroads borrow something, it is of course on a lease basis for the trip or the day as it may be. Joe continues, "We got to keep snow flanged out so it doesn't drift too deep or we will never handle it. Since Frank Campbell is at the throttle, expect no trouble. But after January sets in, the winter is likely to get rugged."

It is eleven miles from Arrowhead to Rollins Pass. We figure that at the worst Extra 179 East should be reported in the snow shed at the pass in two hours. After a short chat with Joe and a good smell of his tobacco, we take care of our business elsewhere.

Two hours later our curiosity gets the better of us. We see clouds boiling over the Divide, and decide to annoy the young dispatcher by a second visit.

Extra 179 East has not been heard from. We pass away the next hour discussing the probable route the Moffat will adopt through Eastern Utah and discussing the Gore Cañon injunction, which is denying the Moffat a right-of-way through western Grand County.

Meanwhile, Joe has talked with Arrow and Rollins Pass learning nothing of the flanger. We are getting hungry and impatient, thinking that after all we have our business to tend to. Then we see Joe intently listening to his key. We shut up and wait for Joe to break the news. He deftly taps back an answer, which makes us regret never learning the language of the telegraph key.

Between the calling of A. C. Ridgway and the calling of additional crews we learn that the 179 had made the first six miles with little delay, cleaning out both ends of Tunnel Thirty-three where the snow was drifting badly. We recall that the snow piled forty-five feet on top of the west end snow shed last winter in one bad storm. Frank Campbell had gone the mile around the Loop and was gaining some speed for a drift a hundred feet beyond as he crossed the trestle over the Loop. He managed to get through this drift but a little further on the grates fell out of the fire box down into the ash pan. He shut his steam off and made a quick decision to drop down to the Loop siding and there try to put the grates back in. If he failed, the engine would have to be drained, a very difficult proposition in severe weather.

Campbell had no difficulty in dropping the 179 down to Loop Siding. Since his fire was in his ash pan, he dumped the fire under the engine to lessen the heat and eliminate the smoke and gas. Engines are equipped with slash bars and clinker hooks, so that Frank prepared to fish up the grates with one bar, while his fireman would work from the outside up under the ash pan with the clinker hook. Using old gunny sacks soaked in water for a kind of asbestos overshoe, Frank crawled backward through the fire door. The head brakeman handed him his bar, while the fireman was already trying to shove up the first grate. Fire boxes are lined with fire brick. These hold the tremendous heat of the fire box for hours. It would be as hot as blazes in there. Since it was a cold night, the hot flues would form a natural suction to pull the gas up from under the engine into the fire box. Frank worked skillfully getting the grates up. Unfortunately with the shifting of the wind Frank inhaled considerable gas into his lungs. It was a terrible experience to work in the fire box all cramped over. But the grates were finally put in. Soaking the gunny sacks, which were now as dry as tinder, with engine oil and borrowing kindling from the caboose, Frank built a new fire in the engine. No doubt two hours or more were lost by this maneuver, which about wrecked Frank Campbell's breathing apparatus.

This delay made it impossible for the 179 to handle the fast drifting snow. The line was blocked. The material clerk, H. M. Dickson, had come in from his office and could feel the chilled-steel attitude of Joe Culbertson. There was no raving or bellowing or loud cursing. Joe was too busy to waste his effort in that way. He just moved around from phone to telegraph calling men, listening to Ridgway, and giving orders as unobtrusively as the 303 would later quietly pull a light train with limited cut off. Joe's pipe left a trail of smoke around the office like the one the 303 would leave when she had been built and was in operation.

The story does not end with the digging out of the west side. The story ends with the poor lungs Frank Campbell had for the rest of his shortened years. "The gas raised heck with his lungs," Joe tells us. Frank Campbell had to give up making runs over the hill. He went to work as a hostler in the Utah Junction round house, and later even had to give that up. This was the price of devotion beyond one's duty.

Such incidents did not make the work of any of the dispatchers easy. G. A. Durbin and H. A. Griffin carried the burden together with their chief. Joe was trying to foresee the proper amount of motive power for every move. Tie-ups usually occurred, as you will see, from such incidents as Frank Campbell had and as occurred in the next story.

Soon after the above incidents, Joe was handed weather reports off the hill that made him immediately light his pipe and call for more power and men to operate Number One's 8:10 run out of Denver. On short call all they could do was to pick up someone around the shops working at something else. George Clark had come to work that morning, had put his street clothes in the locker, and was wearing just his overalls.

Bob Bishop led the parade out of Moffat station with engine 21 and no fireman, as he was to pick up George Clark at Utah Junction.

I do not know what the residents around Arvada thought as they raked leaves that morning and beheld Number One pulled by four engines with the butterfly plow built over the front end of little Number 21. The crew should have no trouble the first forty-seven miles unless some of the engineers eased on the throttle to let someone else do the work. The passengers might have been comforted by the thought that they surely had sufficient motive power to knock any drift off the right-of-way. As to what was in the Adams express that day or as to what was in the mail bags, we do not know, but Arrowhead and her lumber camps likely had items that were very important to their operations and life that early winter's day. This may have been the train that carried a box addressed to the pastor of the Congregational Church in Hot Sulphur. H. A. Sumner had written the railroad land agent at Hot Sulphur, this explanation:

"The Ladies of Plymouth Congregational Church here have made up a 'box' for the pastor of your church, and I have sent it on my frank by Adams Express to you. If there are any charges on stage from Arrowhead to Hot Sulphur Springs, please send me the bill and I will pay it."

Number One should have arrived a little off schedule at Tolland from her delay in leaving Denver; if not, the time consumed by four engines taking on water at Tolland would surely have been more than the allowed ten minutes.

When the last engine had taken water and Barnes had given up the high ball, Bob Bishop blew his two long blasts, followed by Billy Rush with the more important notes of the 100, and then the whistle of the last two engines echoed and re-echoed across the little valley. Number One's four engines raced the one car, the combination baggage-express-mail and coach, up the two per cent and later the four per cent grade.

It was a long trip above the ladder. The air was filled with expectancy.

If Billy Wood were a passenger that day, he no doubt exhausted the subject of the merits of the Republican party, but surely not the demerits of all other parties. One thing he would be even more certain to say would be that he had a pair of snowshoes right up there in the luggage rack or up in the baggage car.

In later years Billy claimed, with some doubt by the crews, that he never came out of Denver on the

Moffat without a pair of snowshoes.

The section men working along the right-of-way or huddling close to a fire to warm would have seen a grim portent in the passing of this four-engine train with one car. Its passing surely mocked the aspen leaf or willow leaf that persisted in hanging to its tree.

When this show of motive power hit the horse-shoe curve around Yankee Doodle Lake, all firemen had their fires perfect and their safety valves throwing a feather of steam. They were ready for the usual big drive about a thousand feet under Tunnel Thirty-two. The snow always slid down from above so badly here that a snow shed was later built.

Bob Bishop's butterfly plow on his engine Number 21 handled the drift all right with the aid of his three helpers. The snow must have really burst out of that cut with the impact of those engines.

Everyone breathed easier now. All engineers could hook up their Johnson bar nearer the center just as a truck driver can slip into high after coming out of a tight pull. The wind would be howling over the trains, for they were on the high grade at Jenny Lake, where they stopped to fill their tanks with water.

If any passenger had been crabbing about the time he had lost, this would be as good an opportunity as any to take out his watch and compare with the card. He would tell the trainmen what they already knew, "We are twenty-five minutes late."

There was plenty of time to talk about the weather as the train moved an engine's length at a time permitting each engine to take on water. Here at Jenny Lake the wind dropped 1,500 feet off the Divide like a car on a roller coaster sweeping across the lake over the railroad right-of-way with nothing to break its gleeful sweep. The handful of passengers could attempt to out-blow the storm with a story that any Middle Park resident could have matched.

If Grandfather Button had gone over that day, instead of the day he did several weeks earlier, he could have told about crossing Berthoud Pass in '92. His story would have started something like this. . . .

"Well, when the man carrying the mail stopped at our place on Cotton Wood Pass, I told him the weather was too bad for him to go alone into Sulphur. So I went with him. Some time later I decided to go with him over Berthoud Pass to Empire and Georgetown. I took my granddaughter Daisy. She was about seven. We got on the cutter and rode up through Fraser and past Cozen's ranch. It was getting so dark by the time we got to the Old Fritz Ranch at Vasquez (Hideaway Park) we decided to stay over night. When we went into the ranch cabin, the snow was so deep that it was like going down into a cellar to get into the house. Our beds were crudely built bunks on the side of the room.

"Next morning we got on the cutter and started for the Pass. At first the two horses had no trouble pulling us two men and Daisy, but when we got near the top, the storm was so bad we put on our snowshoes and broke trail for the horses leaving little Daisy and the mail on the sled to drive the team. In fact, the blizzard was so terrible on the top we finally covered her up with a blanket and continued breaking trail for the team on across the top.

"We had not gone far on the other side until the weather was different. In fact, when we got down to the great slab pile, we left our sled and borrowed a wagon which we used for the rest of our trip.

"Nope, the mail didn't always get through. Though some people are now holler'n when the train don't get through as though it always had. The men that carried the mail in those days had better sense then to try and get through on some days. They did not want to be found 'frost-killed' as we used to call it. In the spring, sometimes, we would find men frozen to death sittin' on stumps."

By the time this story was told, all four engines should have been able to whistle off and start the challenge of the last four and one-third miles.

Number One plowed through everything that morning as she gaily took all the sharp curves in the next mile and turned herself around a time or two heading in all the drunken directions the surveys had wound up to Tunnel Thirty-two. If there was much snow at the entrance or exit, it mattered little. Number One was rolling on the home stretch, now above Yankee Doodle Lake and far enough away from the edge to have no fear of plunging over the side.

Bob Bishop was triumphantly leading the parade when they came to the old Rollins Pass-Boulder wagon road crossing, which is on a curve to the left. A hard crust of snow and ice had formed across this place so that Bob Bishop's proud little engine, Number 21, which had no pony trucks just bolted off the track and tried to follow the wagon road to the right.

Again there was a tie-up which was not from lack of motive power.

Someone went to Corona to get the bridge car-

In the incompleted Corona snowshed, train Number Two has a meet order with a lone engine that has come up the east side of the pass bucking snow early in the winter of 1904-05. — *Katherine W. Toll, DPL*

penters, who were feverishly working to get part of a snow shed built before the pass snowed in. Twenty-five men walked down to help shovel out around the 21 so she could be pulled back on the track by setting frogs to re-rail her. The mail must get through to Arrow. One of these men stopped to rest on a boulder, as he was out of breath. A man does not work easily at 11,660 feet. One works by resting and getting one's breath. The rest of the men found that the storm set in now with fury, rejoicing in the victory won in sticking Number One so near her victory. The more the men shoveled, the harder the snow fell until the men realized they were making no headway. At length the fight was abandoned as it was getting colder and the wind stronger.

The fires were knocked out of the 21; and George Clark, who was shivering in his one pair of overalls climbed in the empty fire box to get warm before bucking the blast of below zero gale from over the top. The other engines backed their one car down the hill while Bishop disconnected the main drive rods with wooden blocks carried on the rear of her tender for that purpose. For a moment Bishop looked back from this thousand-foot perch and could see clear to Spruce. Then he too crawled into Number 21's fire box to get warm. The men then headed against the wind for the Rollins Pass snow shed.

As they fought the biting wind by holding shovels in front of their faces, they came upon the short bridge carpenter who was still sitting on his boulder. Bishop swung him up on his back and, thanks to his strong physique, was able to carry him to the pump house at Rollins Pass. The man was frozen from his neck up. Some of his fingers were lost and had not Bishop been rugged, the carpenter would have frozen to death.

This is the memory of Bishop, Billy Rush, and Barnes of what may have been the first blockade of that fall. There were not many days that fall and winter that Number One arrived in Arrow on the time card schedule — 12:20 — noon.

The general manager's office diary does not throw light on the subject of the first blockage for it is too brief, missing such important things as the first passenger train to Rollins Pass.

However, October 10, this entry "A.C.R. Enroute East Clear and Cold." Added is a telegram "Mem. From W. M. Edgar, Rollins Pass to Geo. R. Simmons, Denver:

"Engines 179 and 20 are here headed east and coupled together and are just about ready to go to Sunnyside for water and to get McGoverns men at the loop and bring them to pass.

"Engine 101 with stock is standing in the shed. Wind is not bad here but blowing hard at Jenny Lake around Tunnel Thirty-three (this would be T 32). There are long and deep drifts between here and No. 2's train. Soon as engine 179 and 20 get back we will start for blockade with some grub for the passengers. We had to coal both engines 20 and 179. We started ten or fifteen of Dickson's gang on foot with shovels to go to No. 2's train.

"A good many of Mike's men are leaving him and ten of Dickson's gang quit also. It looks very bad and I fear we may not get No. 2's train out before late today, if at all.

"I do not think it advisable to attempt to run No. 1 west of Tolland unless we have to with a way car to bring Tim Kennedy's men and another gang this side of Ladora up to help us out. We will pass on the latter when we see what advance the force here can make."

One thought helped to compensate the Moffat "Rails" for their hard work, The Old Man was a democratic soul. On December 18 when his business associates presented him with an elaborate loving cup with a capacity of seventy-five pints, made out of silver dollars, a policeman took his turn among the great dignitaries in shaking Uncle Dave's hand. The leading banker turned to his associates saying, "That fellow is Mike Horkons. He used to be night watchman at the bank. He is as true as steel."

The difference a few weeks can make in the high country weather is shown by these two photos of the Loop. The sun is shining on a pleasant September day (left) as a construction train is pushed toward Corona for another load of ties and rails, and probably another engine is pulling at the head end. By early winter (below) a heavy blanket of snow already covers the area as a passenger train emerges from the tunnel. The snowshed is not yet finished and soon snow will lay deep over the entire area as in the photo (right-below) taken from Parmigan Point, later that same winter. In the foreground can be seen the cabins used by the construction men from Streeter and Lusk the previous winter.

Back in Denver, friends and business associates of David Moffat gathered on December 18, 1904, to present him (seated at right) a giant silver loving cup in admiration of his great courage and accomplishments for Colorado. Today the cup is preserved in the Colorado State Museum. — *left and below, L. C. McClure, CRRM; right, State Historical Soc. of Colo.; right-below, L. C. McClure, DPL*

This is sprintime in the Rockies as Moffat men found it in 1905. There have been mud slides at Arena and other lower elevations and although pansies are blooming in Denver, there are no pantywaists to be found at this 11,600 foot location. The hope is to reach the snowshed with enough water to go on down to Arrowhead and one question is on every mind. Will April be any better? — *L. C. McClure, CRRM*

7

NINE EXTRAS EAST - LIGHT!

No ranchers in Fraser River Valley turned their field glasses toward the Divide one stormy morning in February to see if the Moffat had any trains moving. All cowhands were busy opening hay stacks, filling their sleds, and driving out into the blizzard to feed the cattle.

In Arrowhead those who were still trying to exist in tents gave up and went to the newly completed saloons to warm up. The blizzard was so bad one could hardly see more than a few feet ahead. The man running Bill Woods' commissary was apprehensive for his supplies of beef, potatoes, plus half a dozen or so items, such as axes, of which he was running short. The railroad agent, Mr. York, assured him that the car of supplies was on the plow train, which had left Tolland that morning coming over the hill. They could get along and operate their sawmill just as every one else in Arrow could find ways to get along without the items they needed most. But who wanted a tie-up on the railroad when a keg of nails would complete another restaurant, or a roof-jack would put a stove pipe out the roof instead of out the window?

John Daly's bridge carpenters were spending most of the winter at Rollins Pass trying to complete a little more of the snowshed. Their outfit cars were parked just outside the shed. The men had no trouble in keeping warm as the cars were completely drifted over in the deep sea of snow which inundated the pass in this storm. John Daly knew now that a half mile more of snowshed would be a great necessity even if the line were to be operated only three years, the length of time it would take to construct the Main Range Tunnel. But the tunnel had not yet been started.

We can easily imagine John Daly, the section boss, the operator, and a few others in the operator's office, discussing the blizzard that morning. There was now no sighing "if we only had a rotary snow plow," for a plow had been delivered the latter part of January. She was described as "all steel, thirty-six feet long, scoop wheel type, and able to make a twelve-foot cut." It had been built by the American Locomotive Works at a delivered price of $22,476. The price proved well worth it for the plow served well, last being used by the Rio Grande in the winter of 1948-49 to keep open their line in Utah during the great blizzard which forced Union Pacific trains to detour over the Rio Grande.

The boys read from the daily papers in the weeks gone by that this monster plow was missing: "Biggest Snow Plow Ever Built Lost in Transit." Another day the story had read that the roads west of Chicago had feared to accept the shipment of the giant west as it was too heavy for the rails. Now, whether Harriman and Gould were annoying, simply trying to wear down the ambitious "Shortline," we do not know. Hill's Burlington must have brought her west. Any way, when she was needed on Rollins Pass, she was lost, but eventually she got to Denver.

General Manager Ridgway, in an interview with reporters on the occasion of the rotary's final arrival, said she had been named "Red Devil," explaining, "We had it painted that way so it could melt any particularly obstinate snow bank it might

91

encounter if it should not buck it out of the way."

Unfortunately the "Red Devil's" first trip proved that the blades should have been painted red. Encountering rocks in a slide her blades were chewed to pieces. So the proud 10200 was immediately shopped and equipped with a much heavier gauge steel.

On this particular morning, February 10, 1905, "The Monster Termite" was coming slowly out of Tolland shoved by engines 20 and 21, pulling at least two cars of merchandise, a tool car and two cabooses. Billy Woodruff was the pilot of the snowplow, and Mike Broderick was in charge of the train with Engineers Fuller and Sterling Way.

Number One's engine, the 300 with her combination-baggage-express-mail-and passenger car, overtook the plow train at Jenny Lake, where orders had been given for the two trains to be coupled together. Experience had proved that above this point the track could drift so quickly that a second train would have only a slight chance of getting through.

Trainmaster Edgar was on Number One with George Barnes as conductor. A. C. Ridgway had made it very clear to Edgar, before they left Denver that morning, that he was to consult George Barnes when they got to Rollins Pass as to the advisability of going down the other side. Barnes had fought snow for thirteen years as trainmaster under Ridgway's father on the Rio Grande. Edgar was an experienced man in the drifting snows of the cuts and prairie lands east of Denver on the Burlington. Though the plains suffer fully as badly from storms as the mountains, several other factors are involved in battling mountain storms.

At Jenny Lake the wind blew as wild as any of them had ever seen it sweep off the Divide. The track was blown clear, as that is the nature of the spot. Engine 300 filled her water tank. The air was tested after the two trains had been coupled together. The plow train had already taken on water, so when the air test came through satisfactorily, they whistled off.

They began to lose time immediately for they ran into deep drifts within a quarter mile, and they had to let the rotary slowly chew her way through them at about four miles per hour. Every one was apprehensive at this loss of time because this struggle meant using water that would be needed to fight their way out of the western side of the Pass. No water had been provided at Rollins Pass that winter, because of the late date the line arrived there. Plans were made to pump water out of a lake below, but such a line could not be com-

pleted at so late a date. The nearest water on the west side was Sunnyside, two and a half miles down, where it could be secured slowly from a siphon hose.

There was only a little over four miles for this train to climb after she had taken water, but it was all four per cent grade plus a second struggle, which she had around Tunnel Thirty-two. The rotary was "tops" as the boys said, but she took plenty of steam cutting the ten and twelve-foot drifts.

The third struggle came the last two hundred feet getting into the abbreviated snow shed at Rollins Pass. Inside, the engines soon filled the shed with smoke and gas. Barnes got his face smoked like a cured ham consulting with the men as they measured the water in their tenders.

Billy Woodruff, the snowplow pilot, said, "We can't make it."

Engineer Fuller shook his head emphatically, "No."

Barnes hearing the other men report the amount of water said to Edgar, "No use to go any further. Haven't enough water."

Perhaps Edgar was insulted when the general manager told him to consult a conductor working under him. If so, it would not be the first time men have given vent to such a jealous impulse. Edgar made his decision and ordered the train to proceed, saying, "We can shovel snow into the tanks, if we run out of water."

With eyes smarting from the smoke and gas in the snowshed, Barnes went back to his combination coach shutting the door behind him quickly to keep the smoke out. Edgar came in. The blasts of the engines whistled off split the ears of every one in the shed. The train felt her way to the west end. The plow had been through this drift of snow yesterday. Although every engineer was blinded by the smoke of the shed, he did not need eyes to see the drift the rotary hit. They felt it and opened up on their throttles, shaking their heads and muttering, "There goes our water and hope of getting down to Arrowhead today."

With the snow way over the top of the outfit cars parked on the siding, we imagine the cut opened up the day before by the plow was ten or twelve feet deep with new snow.

We can hear Mike Broderick and Spaulding cussing out Edgar, as they sat in their caboose cupola. The brakemen were on top bundled in all the clothes they could get on with scarfs over their faces to shelter them from the blizzard sweeping over the Pass. They were carrying out regulations, which demanded they be ready to twist the brakes down, if the air failed. They would be so cumbered with clothing that it is doubtful if they could have twisted with the brake clubs.

Going down the west side of the Pass the train crawled for a mile, gradually picking up speed to about nine miles an hour as the drift lessened. How the wind howled over the cars!

Within the coach a passenger moved away from the right to the left side as the snow was sifting in the apparently tightly closed window. Barnes was very happy that Edgar had not sat down beside him.

The minutes dragged on like hours. The blast coming out of Fraser Valley seemed enough to blow the train back up the Pass. Midst the howl of the wind a whistle blew. One of the engines had whistled to stop.

Edgar's heart sank. He started buttoning his coats, just as George Barnes was doing, only Barnes was muttering something in his mustache.

The train was stopped. When Barnes and Edgar got ahead, they found one engine out of water. Edgar ordered the men to shovel snow into the tanks. They climbed up the tenders and started shoveling, but Edgar had not reckoned with the wind, which blew the snow off the shovels as fast as it was scooped off the snow bank. The snow was tender high at Ptarmigan Point. The engines died right there.

No sooner had the engines gone dead than George Barnes warned his seven passengers that they should "hit the cinders," and make a run for their destination before the storm drifted shut their road.

You see the tragedy of the situation was that the train had gone dead after it had got through the worst of the snow one mile and half out of Corona shed. The right-of-way was not so badly drifted but that the train could have proceeded from this point even without a plow if the engines had not been low on water. But with the velocity of the wind and the increasing storm, their rescue was very unlikely. Barnes sent these seven passengers ahead down the mountain knowing that every foot of the way they would be dropping below the worst part of the storm. It was less than two miles to the Loop where were parked outfit cars in which they could get warm.

Below the Loop there may have been a sawmill cabin. At Ranch Creek there was a sawmill and loggers camp, where two of the men were headed. The other five passengers could warm here and continue on their way to Arrowhead, which was 2,000 feet lower than the stalled train. No one traveled that train in such weather except lumberjacks and ranchers who had walked over the passes in winter on snowshoes or fought to save the lives of their cattle. So Barnes knew what he was doing when he sent such men ahead.

Meanwhile Trainmaster Edgar started back to Rollins Pass in the fast-filling cut. He must call for the two light engines at Tolland to come up and immediately pull the train back into the snowshed. We wonder if his ears rang with Billy Woodruff's words, "We can't make it." We wonder what he thought would be the humor of Mr. Ridgway, who had warned him to consult with Barnes. Ridgway was in the East inspecting the Mallet-Articulated engine of the Baltimore and Ohio at Rockwood, Pennsylvania. But what was the most powerful engine with no water? The pipe line to Corona should have been finished.

Edgar struggled in the wind. The altitude of 11,600 feet made him stop to pant many a time. He finally staggered into the snowshed. He asked the operator to call Tolland and order up two engines, numbers 100 and 101. One engine may have had the butterfly plow on it.

What chance would those two engines have of even making Rollins Pass from the foot of the mountain on the eastern side?

It must have been almost two hours since the plow had been over the line from Tolland. Would the crews for those two engines be able to get underway in less than a half hour? The crews would likely be sleeping; the steam would be low. Those engines might have to be coaled and watered. If those engines could buck the drifts without a plow, how would they be on water when they made that final climb from the last water tank at Jenny Lake?

Before Edgar reached the warmth of the operator's office at Rollins Pass and listened to the hurricane sweep over the sheds, George Barnes succeeded in making contact with Denver. He had climbed a telegraph pole, tied on the wires of his telegraph instrument and from the chilly shelter of his combination coach telegraphed in the news of their plight. "Engines gone dead because of low water and inability to shovel snow in the terrible gale." You recall that Barnes had learned telegraphy as a boy.

Now, even though there were no women operators on the line, the story got out. By the time the press got the story, it made headlines. But since we are going to have to wait for the paper to be printed, we will let some one in Denver read the story and wire us about it.

Evening soon engulfed the stranded train crews. Barnes immediately knew the sandwiches left over from their noon lunch were not sufficient for his men. He turned to conductor Broderick, who had skippered the plow train which had included two cards of merchandise for Arrowhead, to find out what was in those cars. The waybills said, "Provisions for Bill Wood's commissary." There were canned goods, potatoes that had frozen en route, and several quarters of beef. Barnes wrote down every item they took out. But the men had no hunting knives to cut up the quarter of beef. Their lanterns shed light on a box of axes. Out came an axe and they cut up the beef. (Later that winter the road stocked every train with emergency provisions for just such predicaments as this.)

The combination coach was abandoned as the snow was sifting through the smallest cracks around the windows in an unbelievable manner. The men cooked their meals, first thawing their confiscated potatoes on the caboose stoves.

The two cabooses were terribly crowded with the enginemen from three locomotives and the rotary plow, plus the two conductors, at least three brakemen, and perhaps three or four other men, who had been brought along to assist in battling the snow. The men recognized there was not bunk space enough in the two cabooses for so many men. The usual card games started, while they took their turns carrying coal from the engines to keep themselves warm. The usual storytelling and "beefing" continued. It would have been a miracle if they had not roasted Trainmaster Edgar for his stupidity. Undoubtedly he was made to feel like the lowest worm on the face of the earth.

In such a storm, David Moffat paced the floor all night in his Equitable Building office waiting for reports of his men on top of the world.

Barnes, of course, would have related the story of working with the rotary snow plows around Leadville from December to March without getting home. The men all knew here was the man who should have been trainmaster. He would tell how "Old Tige" rode him in those days when he was exhausted. On one occasion he was about ready to resign when the general manager interceded for him, telling "Old Tige" to lay off. Barnes followed up this story with the one about his small daughter. "She had diphtheria. For three days and nights my wife and I swabbed her throat every thirty minutes." Then he added, "Any parent who loves his children wilts when they are at the door of death."

Thoughts of loved ones at home would silence some of the men and cause other fathers to tell of their grim battles against death in their homes. The men would talk about their lodges. Barnes would uphold the respect he had for his Masonic lodge saying, "Well, if anyone will live up to the promises of the Blue Lodge, he will be all right."

After all, railroaders are not another species of animal life. They are human souls with the same hunger for companionship, with the same desires to get ahead in life and provide for their children as all other men. Subject to the same weaknesses as man the world over, these railroaders growled, laughed, and swore, stretched the truth, resented some of their superiors, and hid a prayer deep in their heart for those they loved.

Although the blizzard was still howling, with morning came the discovery that the two light engines had reached Rollins Pass. After a great struggle with the snow in the last mile, they too were left so low on water that they were abandoned in the snow shed. Billy Rush had brought up one of those engines. Edgar left Charlie Peterson to keep those engines warm enough to keep them from freezing solid, while he and the other enginemen started immediately walking down the other side.

Their best bet was to find a rotary plow that some line could lend and with borrowed power open up the line. These men could operate this power. Of course there were section men at Rollins Pass and some men from a bridge carpenters' gang who might be able to shovel enough snow into the tanks of the two engines so that the crews of Barnes' train could attempt their own rescue. But the fury of the storm left little hope of getting water in these engines and of getting the engines, without a plow, down to the helpless train on the west side.

The only other engine the D N-W & P had in service at that time was the wheezy old 390. This small passenger engine was no match for a four per cent grade in a blizzard. It seems her sisten engine the 391 had not been rebuilt for mountain railroading at this date.

At the stalled trains, morning revealed the blizzard still raging with no sun at all, so George Barnes again contacted the outside world over his telegraph wire to learn that the newspaper said that they were all starving and that Bob Bishop had been lost. Barnes told the dispatcher to let his wife know immediately they had plenty of food. Bob

Bishop had been called to run one of the engines that fateful February morning when they had left Denver, but inasmuch as his wife was ill, he had been allowed to stay home.

The second day the men managed to keep the water hot enough in their engines so they would not have to drain the boilers by the painful process of draining every pipe at the unions. The engines were fired enough to keep from boiling water too fast and still keep them from freezing solid. The card games continued and the stories went on, one after another. The second night, as the wind occasionally blew a gust of snow down the caboose stack into the caboose, the men heard a noise on the roof. When an investigation was made, they found that the men in the other caboose were swiping some of the stove pipe to make their chimney higher.

By the third day the little train was almost completely buried by this February blizzard and Barnes concluded, since no relief was immediately in sight and there were too many of them to sleep in the cramped quarters, that they would walk out. The temperature had been below zero, but no one knew how low. Barnes telegraphed in and the nine men started walking out. George had taken the bell rope out of his snow drifted coach. Each man held onto this bell rope, so the strong could help the less robust. The only way Barnes knew where lay the track was by walking with his arm over the telegraph wire. Yes, the snow was that deep.

When the men arrived at the west end of Rollins Pass snowshed, they came on the outfit cars buried under the blizzard. These cars were occupied by John Daly's bridge carpenters. Seven pieces of stove pipe had been added to the cook car, so that the stack was above the snow. The men got down into the cook car through the sky light. The Italian cook baked the men some cannon-ball biscuits. With this fortification the men went on through the shed and found Charlie Peterson starting to chop the snow shed down in his effort to keep the two light engines from freezing.

The storm abated somewhat, so they followed the track over to Tunnel Thirty-two. As they looked six hundred feet down to the frozen-over lake, Sterling Way, who had been one of the engineers, jumped on his scoop shovel and rode to the bottom like a bullet. They say he warmed up the seat of his pants, in fact he burned the seat of his pants off, on that ride and, hitting the lake, he rolled over a dozen times like a ball. The rest of the men were more timid (if men are timid who brave

such a storm) and they walked around the right-of-way, while Sterling nursed his "hot box," which was now subject to frost bite. The other eight men were able to take a short cut or two along the telegraph line.

Arriving at Jenny Lake boxcar office, George Barnes telegraphed in his famous message, "NINE EXTRAS EAST, LIGHT."

The men looked back at Tunnel Thirty-two and thought of Sterling Way's feat and before they went into the Tunnel how easily that they could have slipped almost straight down into Yankee Doodle Lake a thousand feet below. As the men set out down the chilly track Barnes said, "We will strike another outfit at Antelope and eat. From there the going will not be so hard."

Bill Reddin, a young brakeman, who was not so husky said, "We will make a flag station out of it." He did, for he was about all in by the time they arrived. Below Antelope there were only "eight extras east."

Barnes had telegraphed an order to Tolland requesting dinner for Sterling Way and himself that evening with the good section boss Jim Kennedy. The rest of the boys were going to dine at the eating house. When they arrived and had enjoyed a good dinner, the section boss brought them each a glass of whiskey to warm them up. Sterling Way said, "No." Barnes said, "No." But on third thought, Barnes made an exception, which went right to his head and made him very happy! After getting the key, he and Way unlocked Broderick's caboose, swept out the snow, built a fire, and went to bed. In the morning the boys found another foot of snow had sifted through every crack and keyhole. It was so nice to awake with snow on the covers, hunt around for kindling, build a fire, melt snow water to wash one's four-day-old beard, and then, shivering in the below zero morning, hit out for the eating house for breakfast.

Again Barnes noted a change. It was now just "two extras east" — Sterling Way and Barnes. They were following the first crew who were shoveling out(as they went) the center of the cuts so the plow could find a start in these drifted spots. But gradually the men ahead got tired of trenching out the cuts and one by one threw their shovels away. By the time they got to Rollinsville, five miles away, the weather had changed.

Having caught up to Charlie Clark and the warm Colorado sun, they all sat against the side of the hotel bemoaning the fact that they had no way to get home. Charlie Clark had tried to hire some one to drive them over to Black Hawk so they could ride the Colorado and Southern narrow gauge home. But no one would venture out with a team. They thought of the men over the top at Ptarmigan Point where the blizzard still howled above timberline.

As they continued to growl about having to walk clear to Denver and half prepared to stay in the Rollinsville Hotel, the whistle of 390 was heard coming up the cañon with a coach. The boys piled in. The 390 with Bob Bishop cracking the throttle went on up to turn around on the wye. Here they picked up the other men. On down to Denver they slipped on what was almost a spring day, believe it or not!

At Leyden Junction Bob Bishop had orders to pick up twenty-seven cars of coal. This little American four-wheeler passenger engine slipped down to the junction several times to pick up the cars in shifts. Meanwhile, the men heard the trolley car on the narrow gauge singing along the rails. So Barnes and the men hit out for the trolley.

As the car jingled along Barnes determined to get off at Lowell Boulevard, near his home. He followed this thought up, left the car, rang his wife's door bell, and presented such a sight of dirt and unshaved face that she did not at first know who he was. Barnes was too tired to eat. He phoned the dispatcher telling him that the men had come in on the street car and that Bishop was doubling in with the coal.

Number One and the Moffat plow were still at Ptarmigan Point. Among the men Bob Bishop brought back to Denver with his 390 that day were Billy Rush, Sterling Way, Sam Henry, and Ernest Anthony. My, how those men welcomed their own beds and a good night of rest. As to how well General Manager Ridgway slept as he approached Denver that night is not known.

Next day Ridgway took over the relief of the blockade. It was apparent that engines 100 and 101 were useless so this idea was given up and the tired men struggled back home. But to secure the needed rotary plow and power was not easy, for the same storm engulfed the entire Rocky Mountain region and all lines needed every piece of snow fighting equipment they had.

Their only hope was to borrow some power from the Burlington and Missouri River line and see if they could find some road whose rotary plow was not needed for a few days. Edgar was wise in taking the men with him so he would have some one to run the engines when they were secured. Of course there was a slight chance that the men in the bridge carpenter's gang at Corona might be able to

shovel enough snow in the water tanks to steam up the two consolidation engines in the shed. But the extent of the storm and its fury left small hope that engines 100 and 101 could reach the stalled train without a snow plow. Altogether this was a tremendous undertaking.

The Colorado Midland's powerful small rotary was finally secured. Two engines, numbers 250 and 251, from the Colorado and Southern furnished the power. It looked now like the road could be opened.

How far the relief train with its plow got the first day is not remembered. The general manager's diary does record that Ridgway went up the next day on Number One which caught up to the plow train at Antelope which is midway between Tolland and the mountain pass. Ridgway was on hand now to see for himself why the progress was slow. The snow was above the rotary. This powerful little plow could hurl it over the highest cut but the snow had to be shoveled and dynamited down into the cuts. When the drift was lowered enough for its snout to be above the snow, she could then move through the cut. Another day of frost bites, exhausted bodies and tired minds passed, and the approach of sunset on the twenty-third was near when the borrowed engines and plow reached the pass, 3:00 p.m. February 23, 1905.

Water for steam power was and remained the acute problem. The plow train must back down four miles to Jenny Lake tank for more water. How many times this happened that night and next morning no one recalls.

The task was far greater than simply opening up the mile and a half of the track down the western side. The plow train would have to back up to the pass and uncouple the plow. Colorado and Southern engines 250 and 251 would slip down and attempt to drag back up the slippery four per cent grade. The journals of Number One's combination baggage-coach were frozen and her wheels acted like sleds for a little way. When the coach had been dragged to the top, the 300 passenger engine was bumped and jerked until it was loose from the fifteen-day freeze to the rails.

After the 300 had been pulled back to the snowshed and put on the siding beside the Midland's rotary, the cabooses and outfit cars and two freight cars were taken back, perhaps two at a time. It was a tedious job to get the two engines loose, and lastly the rotary would be dragged back.

Now the two Colorado and Southern engines ran back down to Jenny Lake for some water. Having water, they hooked into the Midland rotary and cut on down from Ptarmigan Point to Sunnyside, a mile below, where there was water which could be secured by a hose. Then the Denver Northwestern and Pacific engines were brought down for water, or perhaps they had been taken down to Jenny Lake for water, and coaled from some gondola standing by. Finally, the two box cars and the baggage from the combination car were hooked onto the relief train and taken down to Arrowhead fifteen days late.

We can hear Billy Woods, Grand County's outstanding lumberman, as he welcomed his much needed commissary goods, even though they were lacking some items. Billy would know that they had been used in an emergency and would be replaced. The mail probably had been carried down to Arrow by section men before this.

Grand County people grumbled about the railroad not having won the battle against winter storms, but they did not despair of the road. They had lost battles against storms ever since they had settled in the Park. And besides, it would be different when the Main Range Tunnel was built.

As a picture of their enthusiasm is this article in the Middle Park Times. "The much talked of Georgetown Loop — over which so many people rave — looks like a missed two spot in a deck of cards compared to the Loop of the Moffat Road." The article went on to explain that the Loop was 1.02 miles long and that the elevation was 11,092 with the bridge one hundred fifty feet higher than the tunnel underneath. One was supposed to be able to see Gray's Peak, Specimen Mountain, and Rabbit Ears from this Loop.

In the same weekly paper could be read advertisements such as this one: "Arrowhead Realty Co., Sulphur Springs. Frank N. Briggs, Mgr. Lots $25 to $150. Terminal of the Road."

Back in Denver those behind the scenes of the winter like A. C. Ridgway, did not have the enthusiasm of Grand County newspaper and business men. There was not enough money for another rotary. There was not enough money to start that much talked of two-mile tunnel that would have eliminated this problem. How then could there be enough money to get into the coal fields?

H. A. Sumner in his Majestic Building office had taken in the entire February episode. But what froze him more than anything else was the notice that lands around McCoy, west of the Gore Cañon, had been withdrawn from the public domain by the enemy-infested Interior Department.

Dave Moffat had been in New York and Boston a great deal of the winter. That the news was not good is witnessed by the fact that A. C. Ridgway considered the new railroad a sinking ship and accepted the offer of the Rio Grande Railroad to become its general manager on March 11, 1905. Ridgway had told some of the boys, "The Moffat Road is going to be a graveyard for railroad men, and I am getting out while getting out is good."

G. R. Simmons took over as acting general manager.

The mail deliveries had been so poor that the U.S. Postal Superintendent for the seventh district, S. P. Taft, made an inspection trip over the line to Arrow and then on down to Hot Sulphur.

Moffat's dream railroad might be on the operating table, but H. A. Sumner went on about his work, giving out passes to all officials in Grand County, attending to all the little annoying questions that had not been frozen out by the winter. Sumner would now consider his enlarged new problem of stretching a dollar as a dollar had never been stretched before in railroading history.

Acting General Manager G. R. Simmons looked at the calendar and saw the first days of March went by without any major tie-up. Spring was near. Possibly he would have a break.

The calendar said, "March 21, 1905." The grass was green around the Capitol building in Denver and people sunned themselves on the park benches. Someone sang an old tune, "In the spring a young man's fancy lightly turns to love." But on the hill there was storm and snow.

The second day of spring was even worse as the private secretary of the general manager wrote in the diary for his boss, "Heavy storm on the hill today."

The contrast between Denver and the hill continued with Denver readings way up to sixty-two degrees as late as 5:00 p.m. in the evening, and Corona readings barely up to thirty-two degrees at high noon. Who wanted to leave Denver and pull a throttle on any Moffat teakettle anyway?

Then they enjoyed spring on the hill for several days before the fury of winter broke again, and every one knew that there was a blizzard on the mountain after just one week of spring.

By the first of April the weather was no better. The heavy clouds that had sent but little flurries now dumped two feet of snow at Tolland, so that by the time the rotary chewed the hill open, Number One had lost seven hours and did not return that day from Arrowhead as Number Two. The run had been cancelled.

If on one day only three to six inches of snow

were added, the next day there would be added a heavy fall over the pass. So bad was the storm on April fourth that Number One dared not move above Jenny Lake. By the time the plow had returned from Arrowhead and got stuck in a slide east of Needles Eye Tunnel, it was 9:30 p.m. Everyone was exhausted and in need of rest, so the plow train and Number One tied up for the night. If the night had been clear, the passengers could have seen the stalled plow train 600 feet above them.

But April the fifth held still more trouble for the Moffat. There was so much snow and ice on the track above Rollinsville, a mile and a half east of the remains of the notorious old Ragtown, that four outfit cars and a caboose were derailed.

Night came and the light of another day. Springtime with sixty-eight above in Denver! But on the hills snow and rocks . . . there were tons of them that held the Moffat's rotary tight in the blockade east of Tunnel Thirty-two. For four more days the men shoveled snow, dynamited, fell asleep, dried out their clothes, and blew their noses from a spring cold. That evening, Sunday, the rotary left Denver about the time the sinners were going to the theater and the saints were listening to the evening sermon. It had been a beautiful day in Denver, but not on the hill.

This plow managed to open the blockade to Rollinsville the following day. Passengers were hauled to Arrowhead from Rollins Pass on the plow train in a mixed combination car. Everyone was breathing more easily now that the line was open. There should be rest for everyone. And there would have been; but Engineer Fuller discovered a fire (Tuesday, April eleventh) in Tunnel Twenty. The only consolation the general manager had was that the equipment was nicely divided on both sides of the tunnel with ten days coal supply on the isolated western end.

This, the first, set the pattern for several disastrous tunnel fires. The flames roared out of the west end fed by a slow steady draft a hundred feet in the air. The tunnel timbering gave its turpentine willingly for the gigantic display of fire, smoke, and sparks while officials stood back wondering how long it would take to burn itself out and then cool enough to let men hole the tunnel through again.

Meanwhile, Engine 21 with a flat car picked up passengers who walked around the tunnel and freight that was carried around, for most of the South Boulder Cañon tunnels were through the ugly protruding ribs of the cañon and not through a pass or divide.

The flat car trip from Tunnel Twenty ended at Tolland where passengers and freight were protected further west to Rollins Pass and Arrowhead by the plow train. So the flat car ride became that of a caboose or a combination passenger, baggage and mail car.

After six days of such service west and with the coal supply dwindling, a circular was issued reducing service on the plow train to tri-weekly.

To add variety to the nightmare of Springtime, slides began slipping into cuts; first, in the cut west of Coal Creek and in cuts both east and west of Plainview. But hopes were rising, for on the fourteenth day after the tunnel had caught fire, it looked as though in another day they would be able to hole through and get the badly needed coal west.

However, the storm that was sweeping the pass that day was a mean one. The plow train had left Tolland at 7:00 a.m. and had taken until 4:15 p.m. to reach Rollins Pass. An hour later, after the men had eaten and the engines had been inspected, an attempt was made to continue to Arrowhead. But after going a short distance the effort was given up on account of the severity of the storm. So the train backed into the shed and tied up for the night.

The following morning another effort was made to go down the western side but Chester Foltz's engine found too much ice in the west switch to the liking of her pony truck which derailed. The laborers went out to shovel the knife-like cut of the snow plow wide enough to re-rail Engine 100. Billy Rush, hogger on the second engine, was concerned about low water, so he started his fireman shoveling snow into the tank. The blizzard was continuing severely with no signs of abating, and the snow was being blown back in as fast as it was shoveled out around the derailed wheels. Likewise, the men were freezing, so between going back to the shed to thaw out, little could be accomplished. The coal was getting mighty low; Tunnel Twenty just had to be holed through and some coal secured.

Tunnel Twenty was holed through at 1:50 p.m. and three cars of coal were sent through ten minutes later. The line was open at the tunnel but the spring rains had caused the fill to settle so badly between Tunnel One and Coal Creek trestle that all trains were annulled. It looked like it would take several days to stabilize the fill with car loads of cinders and slag.

Back on the pass things were not going well. The

gandy dancers made another try in the storm. They continued digging around the front of the engine throwing the snow out of the razor thin cut between engine and snow bank. It was too crowded for many to work and in the rare air of 11,600 feet they had to stop frequently to get their breath.

Blocks were carried on all engines. Great blocks of wood that looked like ties had been sawed into rectangular pieces two feet long. These were placed beside the rails so that the wheels could be raised up on a wood block paving and could be directed to run over the rail by the aid of a frog placed at the proper place.

The frog had to be spiked to the ties. The king snipe, or section boss, likely got down on his hands and knees under the engine to spike this in himself. Or, in those days of real gandy dancers, the king snipe put his best man down there to do the work.

Did you ever try to hit a spike on the head? Did you ever get down on your hands and knees under an engine with the hiss of steam in your face and a mountain of steel above your frail little body, with perhaps only six inches to swing the spike maul to drive spikes in ties and your hands freezing in the cold and your body perspiring inside three pairs of overalls?

If you have done that, you are a full-fledged first class gandy dancer, who probably had plenty of advice to follow from the conductor, the king snipe, and the engineer.

The next day the clouds swooped low over the crust of snow and bumped against the cars, causing little whirlwinds to blow the snow and smoke under the engine, where the gandy dancer was on his knees praying for relief to all the gods he feared, the gods of wind, snow, and brass hats.

Lanterns were lit as evening approached and darkness engulfed the Divide. The frogs were set. Everyone got out of the knife-like cut around the front of the engine. The brakeman went back of the train to flag anyone who might get in the way.

The signal was given and the first engine whistled three blasts, which were answered by the second engine's hogger, Billy Rush. It was hard to back up; the wheels spun from the snow that the men had kicked on the rails.

The attempt was given up and an effort was made to sand the rails by hand after the snow had been swept off. The train moved a few feet, sufficient to rerail the pony truck. But as so often happens when conditions are much easier to work

under, the pony truck refused to climb the frog, tearing it loose from the ties.

The king snipe swore the venerable streak of oaths according to the rich tradition of the Moffat at so early a date. He spat his tobacco cud against the snow bank as he crawled into the narrow snow gorge and ordered his men to start shoveling out another spot.

They worked in the darkness by flares, torches, and lanterns until the blizzard drove them back into Rollins Pass shed. It was midnight with a blizzard howling over the pass. In Denver Joe Culbertson shook his head, and other officials shuddered at the thought of what would happen if this kept up.

And it did happen, for it was Springtime in the Rockies. Even as the spirit of revolt shakes schools with new disciplinary problems, Old Man Winter revolted and hurled his deepest snow over the Pass. He made the snow wet. And when he gave men a breathing space of a few hours or so a day, he teased men toiling on top of the world, as a cat teases a mouse he has caught. He sent night when the thermometer saw the mercury try to curl up and sleep in the bulb. Or he would send beautiful days with the sun shining and every one saying, "It is spring." But night again would freeze the melting snow water into ice over the rails.

Suffice it to say that rotary plow Number 10200, the pride of the Moffat and as powerful a plow as had ever been built, was snowed under with no power to push her on down to Arrowhead. The mail had been carried on by section men, who used a horse and a sled part of the way.

March dragged by and the calendar said April. But day after day and week after week every effort to get the plow loose was in vain. Men carried coal in gunnysacks from the Pass down to the engines on improvised sleds made of boards. Hour after hour they shoveled snow into the engine tanks. Men's beards were long, their faces grimy, and their spirits failing with fatigue.

The management could not lease a plow, for both the Colorado and Southern and Colorado Midland were continually busy with their plows, struggling to open up the blockades that engulfed their Rockies in springtime.

The last of April approached. All efforts to clear the trail had been given up until the weather improved. The entire hill was drifted deep with snow. Here and there little avalanches had occurred. On warm days, as small rocks uprooted by frost and loosened by the heat of the sun started to roll, they brought great rocks and trees down with them.

Bob Bishop remembered how earlier in the winter General Manager Ridgway had started to walk with him carrying food to the men up on some blockade at Ptarmigan. He had given out and stayed with the men in an outfit car parked along the right-of-way, while Bishop went on ahead by himself. Every one was sick of the Moffat and cursed the name of spring.

Help arrived in Denver April 29. The Colorado Midland Railway running west from Colorado Springs sent her small rotary.

The last day of April, this rotary chewed her way up the ladder out of Tolland. Above the lake country the snow was drifted above her little snout that heaved out tons of snow. Unable to move ahead any farther, she whistled to back up. Her three blasts were answered, and she was pulled back a hundred feet by the two engines behind her. Men with dynamite cralwed on the snow she had been unable to swallow, and blasted it into the cut she had opened. Then the snow plow pilot whistled two long blasts, and the engines behind moved ahead, until she was stalled again by the depths of the snow that plugged her rotary blades and snout.

The snow pilot whistled "stop" with a long blast. This was followed by the back up signal. Back they would go to wait for the dynamiters to repeat their blasting of the deep snow into the cleaned-out track. After hours spent in this fashion, the deepest cuts were cleared. But the last day

of April the famous little Midland plow was not half way to the pass. She tied up at Antelope.

It was May Day in Denver, children were all excited about May baskets and parties. On the hill, Moffat Engine 101 was still off the track and the relief plow was chewing her way to the rescue. Mr. W. A. Deuel had taken over as general manger. He could rejoice that the line was opened to the pass by 3:40 p.m. "We will run Number One to Jenny Lake or perhaps to the pass tomorrow," he said. Meanwhile cheers were going up as the Colorado Midland plow came out of the shed on the top of the world and moved towards the stranded train. Some railroaders shot a picture, a picture that would carry the cheers of the men to the front page of the papers and to this book. This was May Day on the Moffat, 1905.

But the rescue of the train took the best part of another day. After the rotary had opened the line down to the train, she was pulled back and uncoupled so the two engines could slip down. Taking one car at a time and then one engine at a time the Moffat's plow train was finally brought back to the snowshed. Frozen journals made some wheels slide like sleds. Meanwhile another blizzard had overtaken this hard-fought-over spot. In fact when May the second was over, all that could be said was that the Colorado Midland plow had gotten one mile west. Back in Denver top-coats were forgotten, the temperature read sixty-four degrees.

May third came and the new general manger still had no word by midnight that the plow train had reached Arrowhead.

In the morning the Colorado Midland plow pulled into Arrowhead at 7:45 a.m., just four days and nights after she started out of Denver not more than seventy miles away.

But Snow was still King in the stubborn mountains of the Continental Divide. When the plow train returned to the pass, four cars derailed in the west end of the shed. So Number One could not get through and return to Tolland. Then on the sixth of May, the diary reads, "Number One of yesterday reached Arrowhead 7:00 p.m.; Colorado Midland plow brought to Utah Junction on Number Two."

"O wind, if winter comes, can spring be far behind?" In the Rockies, yes!

Elsewhere events were happening that would determine the future of the railroad. Edgar McMechen provides this description.

During the first year of Divide operation several conferences were held in New York with Harriman or his representatives. The railroad king had let it be known that he would help Moffat, but delayed a meeting until Julius Kruttschnitt, director of maintenance and operation for the Union Pacific and Southern Pacific, should have passed upon the project. Meanwhile, two Union Pacific engineers had made a trip over the road as far as Arrow and are believed to have reported favorably. Kruttschnitt's decision, however is supposed to have been adverse. One of those present at the meeting finally held has given the following version of the conversation when Harriman and Moffat met. Harriman plunged abruptly into the subject, waiving preliminaries.

"Moffat," said the dictator of the greatest railroad system then in existence, "I will help you build the Denver, Northwestern. I will give you fifty per cent interest for what money you have put into the road, and will raise all the funds necessary to take it to Salt Lake. I will take all the bonds and give you fifty per cent of the stock."

"Mr. Harriman," replied Moffat with considerable heat, "do you think I am a fool or a knave? I refuse your proposition. I know you better now than I have ever known you." Thereupon he turned his back and left the conference. It was most unusual for Moffat to show temper, but he realized that Harriman's proposition, if accepted, would give the latter power to stop operations at any point if he saw fit to do so. The actions and words, of course, definitely ended all attempts at compromise.*

*McMechen, Edgar. *The Moffat Tunnel of Colorado*. Wahlgreen Publishing Co., 1927. Denver. Vol. I, pages 117-118.

We see on these pages two more in a series of excellent photos taken by famed Colorado photographer L. C. McClure during the winter of 1904-05. The "World's Most Powerful Plow" is seen (above) at Jenny Lake with a string of flats going to Bogan Cut snowsheds where the men will load snow that has drifted through the cracks in the shed. The same would have to be done at the other sheds and the snow then shoveled off at some convenient point such as Devil's Slide. — *above, CRRM; left, DPL*

D., N-W. & P. Ry. Form 1322--9-04-50M.

TELEGRAM.

Rec'd from	Sent by	Rec'd by	Time Rec'd	Time Filed	Office Sent to	Sent by	Rec'd by	Time Sent
H	Jn	W	3'10 P.M.	248 P.M.				M.

Arrowhead 1/6 _____ 1905

To A C Ridgway

After leaving Rollins Pass we found storm worse than it was east of there wind very high and snowing hard about 2 miles west of pass we were delayed 1 hour acct. left driver box on plow very hot snow too deep and storm to severe to back up from Loop and ev. if conditions would have permitted us doing so we did not have water enough to risk it and its not safe to No 2 go ahead of plow hence we will get out of here soon as possible and let No 2 follow to Pass and perhaps to Jenny Lake

TELEGRAM.

D, N-W. & P.'Ry.
Form 1323-11-04-20

MN G D
 Tollard Jan 6 1905
A C Ridgway

        Between the Pass and Jenny Lake we found 3 to 5 feet
of snow along side hill to side bridges, six feet in second cut
and 4 or 5 in first cut west of Jenny Lake wind very high west
of tunnel 33.   Seemed to be going down at Jenny Lake and clearing
off some.   We tie up here tonight and out in A.M. at 7 A.M.
for Arrowhead ahead of No 1 and extra 100 that leaves Utah Jct
at 5 A.M.

        W M Edgar   8 P.M.

A typical day in the life of a plow crew is described in these two telegrams sent to Mr. Ridgeway back in Denver. The hazards of winter railroading can be seen in this photo (above) where a recently derailed car has yet to be removed. A classic scene of snowfighting on the Moffat that first winter is seen (below) as two 100 class engines pause with rotary 10200, which in its early years was painted bright red "to help melt the drifts." The head brakeman is seen returning to the train, perhaps with orders, and the passing track here at Jenny Lake still waits to be cleared. The shadows of the telegraph poles indicate no telephone wires have been added and thus clearly tell us it is the winter of 1904-05, prior to installation of phone service. This also meant that a good conductor needed to know how to telegraph by hooking his instrument to the wires if his train got into serious trouble. — *below, L. C. McClure, CRRM; others, DPL*

BLOCKADE ON ROLLINS PASS

Rollins Pass lay in a blanket of white in this beautiful scene (below-left) early in 1905. The Moffat plow crews worked literally around the clock (left) to keep the line open but in the face of one of the worse winters in memory, the task became impossible. By late February the rotary and most of the Moffat's engines were snowbound so a call for help was sent to the Colorado Midland which sent a rotary which managed to open the line with the assistance of engines 250 and 251 borrowed from the Colorado & Southern. Just when spring should be coming the line was hit with the winter's worst storm and again the C.M. responded. Finally after four days, on May 1, 1905, the job was nearly completed as the borrowed plow approaches the rear of the stalled Moffat plow train (below) after breaking through drifts as high as a locomotive as evidenced by the men standing at engine roof level (above) as the train nears the stalled Moffat plow. It would be a long time before the men of the Moffat forgot their first winter of snow fighting on Rollins Pass. —*above-left, CRRM; below-left, L. C. McClure, below, Billy Rush, and above, all DPL*

ARROW
AUG
11
P.M.
1908
COLO

The *Arrow Turn* has just arrived from Denver and will be returning shortly but meanwhile passengers and crew are having a good meal in the new Arrowhead eating house. Arrowhead or Arrow — both names were used — already has a community hall and eight saloons including the Elk Saloon where the colorful Indian Tom would soon be the victim of murder. The train is standing on level track at the station while the track dropping off to the left is on a 4% grade, providing a fine visual example of the steepness of the line. Oh, yes, the handy toilet in the foreground became the last building in Arrow, escaping the forestry demolition crew and was found still standing by the author in 1939. — *L. C. McClure, DPL*

8

Arrowhead — Boom Town

No history of a railroad would be complete without an intimate picture of a boom town.

The building of a new railroad always sent men ahead seeking opportunities. W. H. (Bill) Wood was a businessman who realized that the vast timber resources of this forest could be marketed with the coming of the road.

In the fall of 1903 while the very impressive work of Moffat's thorough-going construction was under way in the tunnel section of south Boulder Cañon east of the Divide, W. H. Wood and John Newman rode horseback over the hill and camped on the site of what is now Arrowhead. The ground was black with other camp fires. Bill Wood immediately recognized that this spot would be the end of the railroad the next year and a logical location for a sawmill with ample resources of Engleman Spruce and lodge pole pines.

In the next days Wood and Newman got a taste of the country and found that there were some ugly characters deep in the forest. One day Wood and Newman ventured further into the timber than they realized. Night had come, and they came across a ranch with a substantial log barn. An ugly-tempered dog would not let them on the place, and they were greeted by an unfriendly man who told them to go down to Fraser for the night. Having no humor to walk that far out of the way that night and back again the next day, Bill wanted to know why he could not sleep in the barn over night. This reception was Middle Park hospitality in reverse. After considerable arguing, the rancher

finally took Bill Wood and John Newman over to the cabin. Now Bill prided himself on being a good shot and did not carry his two 38 pistols without reasons, but he did not expect to find eight or ten men heavily armed with 44's in this cabin.

After considerable talk, back and forth, Wood convinced the men that he was out looking for lumber. The rancher then got his wife's and child's sleeping bags and took Wood and Newman to the barn. Bill was awake as usual at the break of day and saw in the barn several beeves hanging up.

His host explained that they were running cattle out of Middle Park for the winter to get green pasture. He also said he had a contract to furnish some of the contractors with beef. This was what became known as the Fergeson ranch. Since Bill was interested in getting beef for his proposed mill as well as hay, he made a deal.

Within a year Mr. Wood's suspicions of these men materialized in the arrest of most of this gang of rustlers, who had stolen horses from the very contractors they were providing with stolen beef.

In such a countryside of timber and native hay meadows, the hill of Arrowhead protruded like a thumb from the mountain side, and here the town of Arrowhead was founded, to be welcomed by the true pioneers and hated by the thieves who saw civilization encroaching on their domain.

In the spring of 1904 tents were set up. Besides the foresighted businessmen, there were the saloon keepers on hand to supply the thirsty lumberjacks and construction workers with liquor.

But here was the rub. Arrowhead was in the forest reserve. No liquor could be sold there. The saloon keepers therefore, just camped, claiming that any beer or spirits they had were private stock when the ranger of inspector came around. But, of course, they never were Scotch in sharing their beverages with friends who dropped in and left the proper donation. Some tents had a sign — "Walk in any time." The saloon keeper was happy to get out of bed to serve customers.

This was all a very risky business, so they determined to incorporate the town.

On December 3, 1904, their representatives filed a petition to incorporate the town at Hot Sulphur the county seat. Proper elections were advertised and held so that the incorporation was actually granted December 29 and recorded December 31. In this way Arrowhead became the fourth incorporated town in the county.

Sheriff Sol Jones was kept busy in the summer of 1904, not so much as a wagon-maker and blacksmith, but as the representative of law and order, which is imperative wherever men gather in construction work.

On one occasion the contractor of the Loop Tunnel sent an "S.O.S." for the sheriff down to Arrow (the final name usage given to Arrowhead), where it was telephoned to Hot Sulphur in post haste. Blackie, a great six-foot "white negro", and some of the Swedes were drinking their wood alcohol straight at the Loop construction camp. Blackie was a man of fire and proceeded to lick all the Swedes who got near him.

Now Sheriff Jones was a little fellow, but he had a way with Blackie, whom he could lead around like an obedient dog.

Jones took Blackie down to Arrowhead, gave him a lecture on the evils of drink and disturbing the peace, and in particular, on licking a whole tribe of Swedes. Then he bought him a drink and went back to his blacksmith shop thirty miles down the valley. Blackie had great respect for the little sheriff who had been time and again assisted by his husky and clean-cut son-in-law, Charles Free.

As the rails dropped down to Arrowhead that winter, H. A. Sumner became concerned about the squatters outside the town limits. He encouraged the railroad land agent to discourage these traders in men's morals and to ask them to move on.

Arrowhead started moving out of tents into log or clap-board buildings early in 1905. Businessmen could finally get going because the road was open and their long delayed building materials were at hand.

Number One began to overflow the combination baggage-mail-coach which had taken care of the winter business. Another coach was added for men seeking work in the timber sawmills and fortunes in the new country.

Among the best eating houses ready to care for the newcomers was Mrs. Lininger's Hotel restaurant where you could get a chicken dinner for forty cents.

We sit down at a table for our dinner and overhear the conversation from an adjacent table. "Right now the snow is just as bad at Yankee Doodle Lake and Jenny Lake as any time during the winter. The surveyors measured it this morning and found it as deep as fourteen feet."

"That was a bad scare on April eleventh when the cordwood above the timbering in that tunnel got on fire."

"Yes, there ought to be some provision to fight those fires. Might have a bad one in some of those tunnels that are longer than thousand feet, and that would tie up the whole railroad."

"Yeah, it was lucky they got the fire out with the fire hose on the engine."

"What do you think of W. A. Deuel's being our new G. M.?"

"Most of the fellows would go to hell for him. He is swell."

At another table a locating engineer was absorbed in his thoughts. H. A. Sumner has just given him a raise so that he now gets $250 a month. Big money, but the big man who is badly needed was E. A. Meredith.

We rent a room and stay for a couple of weeks. At the post office we hear there are about 2,000 people getting their mail in Arrow. That means lumber camps and neighboring construction camps are full. Mr. M. M. Weston goes by the post office, picks up his mail, and continues in a spring wagon on his way down the valley. The town of Granby has been authorized by the railroad and he is going down to see how George Berry is coming along with the survey of lots.

Everyone around Arrowhead wanted and had to have something done immediately to meet the demands of the railroad building and lumber interests. Indeed, that May day opening of the road opened up opportunity for anyone who could work hard and intelligently.

The rails were being laid around the hill on which Arrowhead was built. Since no passing track had been located at Arrowhead because the hill was too cramped to afford one, on the other side of the hill a long passing track was built and named Pacific.

If you are not in too great a hurry, stop and look at the ties that are being unloaded. Most of them are white oak. They are coming from Arkansas. But look, that is no oak tie. That is walnut. We talk to some of the men and they laugh and tell us, "You have ridden on cherry and maple coming down this hill. What's wrong with them? They are plenty tough. They will hold the engines on the sharp curves and heavy grades. A spike will really hold in those boys."

No road like it. That's the Moffat.

As night comes on, the men drop down to Camp Number Six a little below Pacific Siding. Here a commissary had been opened by a sickly Swede. He was told that it was the custom that every man that came through be given, as a matter of Western courtesy, a can of snuff. He agreed to accept this wisdom. But the next day he backed down when he thought of the money he would lose to the dozens of men coming through and so said to the wanderer, "Nope. Nope. Got to pay for the snuff." This gentleman swore at this breaking of hospitality and said, "You can keep all of your x, y, z snuff," and quietly swore revenge.

That night, while the sickly Swede slept in his bed placed in the center of his fortune, his rebuffed friend stole six sticks of dynamite from a nearby cache for construction work. These were placed under the commissary and lit. The explosion lifted the roof off the frail building, but left the proprietor unscratched. The barrels surrounding his bed protected him from the falling timbers. This gentleman left on Number Two that afternoon for civilization. So Joe Snider tells.

The next day's rails are laid half way to the Idlewild Ranger Station. The second day we see the rails reach Irving. A wye is spiked in so that engines can be turned. The plans call for a water tank. Bill Woods soon gets into his head that this is the place for his sawmill and as a result a great deal of sawmill history was written here for forty-two years. His land was leased from the forests for ninety-nine years.

This community was renamed West Portal, when Moffat Tunnel was constructed. We will find a thousand men living here then. That day passes, and Denver pulled strings to get the community renamed Winter Park despite the vote of the citizens to keep it West Portal. Here is the Ed Evans Ranch, which was homesteaded and remains free land out of control of the Arapaho National Forest. The old log hotel is the post office where skiers from all over the country drop their mail in later years.

Through this spot flowed the little stream called the Fraser River. It had water in it those days, for no water was being drained off to go to Denver through the pioneer bore of Moffat Tunnel. Locating Engineer Meredith had seen to it that the railroad had restocked this stream, so let's take the afternoon off and start fishing down the stream. Beautiful Engleman spruce and lodge pole pines furnish shade against the blistering heat of the sun. Little do we dream how this spot will be marred by the Moffat Tunnel dump, the shacks of the workers of the lumber camp and the Moffat Tunnel.

We fish down the stream for a mile towards Vasquez Siding. Here we see the largest tie camp along the railroad.

Joe Snider drops over to chat with us, telling us about a two-story building in the tie camp that burned the other day. Two Austrians were on the second floor at the time the building caught fire. They carried on in the usual humorous way of throwing out the breakable articles such as the china water pitcher. One of the Austrians decided to run for help. No sooner had he gotten fifty feet out of the building than his partner threw out of the window a double barreled shotgun, which proved by its action to be loaded.

With lead in his pants, the first Austrian ran crying, "Fire" all the louder.

It can be said, however, that some squirrels in a rotating cage were carried to safety.

The railroad is being built on a northerly direction here. The bottom land is impossible, as it has beaver dam after beaver dam in it.

Hundreds of gunpowder cans were left above the cuts as memorials of construction methods.

Vasquez Creek was crossed by a trestle at the Fritz Ranch, which later became Hideaway Park. Near the creek bridge on Highway 40 (when the railroad was constructed) the old toll gate still stood. It was a reminder of the original Colonel Berthoud Road and known as Star Station. North of here on the highway at the present location of Griffen Park cabin camp a town called Little Chicago grew up to supply the thirsty and satisfy the hunger of construction men. Seven saloons and two houses with sporting girls were built. The town lasted one season. H. A. Sumner's carbon copy letters prove that the railroad attempted to break up this community, which was sponsored in part by a Denver saloon keeper who was following up his customers.

The community moved away as fast as it appeared. Some of the buildings were quartered and moved on wagons at the price of five dollars and a jug of whiskey. Joe Snider claims that the first buildings in Granby came from Little Chicago.

Characteristic of the community was this incident. In the backroom of Bull Sheet's saloon was four-eyed Johnson, a grocery peddler, who tramped over this country in spite of a four-foot snow. He was pretty well liquored up and began cussing a girl by the name of Nell. He even threatened to shoot her. Unknown to either of them Indian Tom looked on and opened fire. Both of them disappeared in a hurry and were not seen for a day and a half. They had taken refuge in Nell's dug-out near the river.

Another day Blackie Stephens was seated on a keg of beer between two windows in Jack Graham's saloon. Indian Tom came up to him and exchanged a few words. Blackie had a leather, flat-topped hat on. Indian Tom stepped back and fired three times. Blackie fled, but his leather cap remained with three creases in it.

But Indian Tom was not the only good gunman. In this same saloon one day a gunman was being cleaned out by a well-known gambler, who realized, after it was too late, that it pays to be honest. In terror the gambler fled down the wagon road towards Fraser. The first step he had taken, however, caused a silver dollar to pop out of his pocket. With a bullet or two to encourage the jumping of the dollars, the gunman caused the gambler to increase his stride, which increased the certainty of the silver dollars to jump, until sixteen of them had popped out. At last even his Colt revolver joined the parade of jumping dollars.

One other trait of Little Chicago, was its one price system of groceries. A ham was a dollar; a drink thrown in, of course. In fact, everything was sold in quantities justifying the expenditure of a dollar.

Today Little Chicago is unmarked, except by the old stone quarry and a small cafe, and the mark of a little forest fire of recent years.

I imagine the devout members of the Cozens family a half mile north were very happy to see the town disappear.

The railroad swung down the valley holding its grade on the hills to the West. Before the railroad came, Fraser was no more than a post office. Some hoped to name the town Easton after the builder of the first sawmill. The plots were so surveyed, but since neither the railroad or Post Office Department followed suit, the town remained Fraser.

Fraser people were so anxious for the town to be a division point that they furnished material and labor for the one leg of the wye that was built there. W. H. Wood built the first station in Fraser and gives as the reason for Fraser's selection as division point, the support offered the financially embarrassed Moffat.

As the rails were laid down from Arrow, a train would slip back and forth from Arrow to the end of the track. This train carried the new business of the line until the line was completed to Hot Sulphur Springs. Then regular passenger service was established.

The local ranchers had their own ideas as to what an express train should be. They heard all the optimistic dreams the train men spoke regarding the magnificent trains Dave Moffat was going to put on, when the road got through to Salt Lake City. The old timers saw, however, only this train carrying supplies dropping down from Arrow to wherever the end of the rails happened to be. Someone coined the expression "Feeble-Minded." If you wanted to see the temper rise on a trainman, you simply mentioned that name.

Until the new time card came out in the fall extending Number One's run to Hot Sulphur Springs, mail, passengers, and express took the stage from Arrow to Hot Sulphur Springs. The first horse changing station was at the 4 - 4 ranch beyond Fraser, run by Fred Felch and his wife.

Deep in the timber reached by a winding road through the forest was this ranch. The two story log house also took in summer guests. Fresh vegetables packed in crushed ice for Eastern and Denver guests were shipped in barrels from Denver.

Since the ranch needed a cook, a letter was written to an employment agency in Denver which had advertised in Sweden and Norway. Beda Louise Florquist, who had graduated from a business college and was working as bookkeeper and cashier in a Norway restaurant, answered the advertisement. Her doctor said she had tuberculosis and the mountain climate in Colorado would be a good answer.

In due time she arrived in Denver, her passage having been paid by her future husband, Pete Benson. No one could be found at the station who could speak her language. They thought of a section boss, who came in and heard her story. She was put in the Scandinavian Hotel, where she got along very well. The next morning conductor Barnes took a ticket from the young lady who could not speak English. The train climbed up half way to heaven to be sure, but, oh the dust and cinders of all the tunnels were anything but heavenly. They arrived at Arrow where the agent proceeded, with the help of Conductor Barnes, to round up a Swedish blacksmith who went to the phone and called the Evans Ranch to say, "Will you tell the people at the 4 - 4 ranch their mail and cook has arrived." Yes, he would, if he saw them. He surely would.

But having come all the way from Sweden to have to wait so many hours at Arrow seemed foolish, so the girl who could speak Norwegian and a little Danish, as well as her Swedish, caught a ride with a man in a wagon going her way. As the wagon bounced out into the wilderness near Cozen's ranch, the water splashed up from the holes in the corduroy road while the great trees hung over the road. The little lady thought she would never get out of there.

The Little Chicago road ended and the better Middle Park wagon road continued for a part of a mile through the forest of slim lodge pole and balsam pines. A worm fence marked the edges of the hay meadow to the left and something new and strange appeared to the right, sage brush. It had an odor that was quickly noted by the newcomer. Sage grew without irrigation, but hay took carefully tended ditches to bring the water down from the higher levels of the creeks.

Near the Evans' ranch a hurriedly driven spring wagon almost passed them. The manager of the 4 - 4 ranch had received news that his new cook had arrived and he was losing no time in meeting her.

The passenger was transferred and the ride continued up a hill winding between little meadows and drifts of trees. The gal from Sweden beheld new country, still wondering if she would ever get back to Sweden again.

Towering mountains appeared friendly in the sunny afternoon. The road at last turned into a beautiful woods in which was the clearing for a two-story log ranch house and a great log barn, the 4 - 4 ranch.

Miss Florquist's business education was not a direct asset to learning to cook, but it did help her to learn the English language by the help of the Hot Sulphur weekly paper; consequently she could read a cook book and please her boss.

Bill Proctor, who had just driven the last stage over the pass, was the first man for whom she cooked.

The weeks went by. A great dance was thrown at Sulphur. Everyone left this ranch, horse-

changing stop of travelers, and rode in his spring wagon or on horseback. Beda Louise was left alone. Darkness came on. In the clear evening sky and moonlight Beda Louise made her way to the pump, where she was expecting to get a bucket of water. Out of the woods sprang a horseback rider, who cleared the fence with a jingle of spurs. Miss Florquist froze in her tracks. She could not cry or move.

A handsome half-breed Indian dismounted and said, "I scared you, didn't I?"

He wore two silk handkerchiefs, one white and the other some bright color, a jacket, cowboy boots, the usual blue denim pants and chaps. He had a gentlemanly nature. He carried her bucket of water in, later dried the dishes for her, and then sat down on the floor Indian style. This was Beda's informal introduction to the famous Indian Tom, whom every one had heard about because of his shooting ability. He was known to be able to shoot the balls off a routlette wheel at quite a distance. Beda never heard him swear or use rough or vulgar language.

Miss Florquist never forgot the night she met Indian Tom. Yes, she had heard about Indians, but her first one had been a gentleman. One day she married a Swede in Fraser Valley and became Mrs. "Pete" Benson.

While ladies never heard Tom use anything but gentlemanly language, those that were not ladies heard him use another language, particularly when he had been drinking.

He was supposedly a very hard man to handle. But the railroad conductors never had any trouble. George Barnes handled him easily, even when he had been drinking.

Barnes had first seen him working around Coal Creek. He was driving a spring wagon for a contractor carrying rush materials and supplies beyond the end of the line. Indian Tom's ability to shoot and the stories told of him soon made him a character every railroader heard about. He was at this time working around Arrow.

Sometimes Indian Tom was in private business taking care of the horses for some logger or freighter. He was a good foreman and frequently handled eight or nine freighters. He loved horses and he loved whiskey. Bob Throckmorton recalls how Indian Tom taxied him and his bride from the end of the rails at Arrow down the Little Chicago road one slippery, snowy day. His big white horse had four wheel brakes. The road was steep, and when the going got too fast, Indian Tom cried "Haunch." To the amazement of the bride the horse sat down, with his hind legs creating very successful braking power.

She was on her honeymoon with one of Grand County's young county commissioners, who lived at Coulter. "Bob" worked hard to get the Moffat through the county and worked down the years for every worthwhile project.

Indian Tom's real name was Tom Reynolds. As I set the stage for murder, I admit that the stage could be set several ways, for in such occasions several stories have come out during the years. This account follows the court records and the stories of Joe Snider and Mr. Lininger.

The day was in September, 1906. Indian Tom was quarrelsome. Joe Snider heard the night before that one of the sporting house girls had gotten a $20.00 bill away from Indian Tom and hid it behind a picture. Neil Ragland seems to have sided in with the girl. Normally Neil promoted business for this sporting house, while Indian Tom was somewhat of an advance agent for the competing house. As to how Indian Tom got across the line to the competitor is an open question that only dead men can answer.

Bill Woods tells that it was known that some girls of ill fame had been brought in from Denver and a dance was thrown for them on the second floor of the Graham saloon. Hearing this, Indian Tom got on his black and white spotted pinto horse whose beautiful white legs were a sight for all horse loving men and rode this horse right into the saloon. Having ducked his head to get in the double door, Indian Tom then shot a hole through the glass mirror of the back bar. He then made a sieve out of several boards in the ceiling, so that the Denver girls dancing above were greatly frightened. The lights went out in good old Wild West fashion and Indian Tom, the best shot of Middle Park, was gone.

Let it be said again of Indian Tom, that he was as good a man ever known when sober, and the idol of the boys of the town including young Bill (W. R.) Wood. He gave no ends of favors to the boys. Old man Wood never was known to have trouble handling the half-breed even when drunk.

The night passed and a second day dawned with men whose aching heads were still able to figure out that "all hell might break loose."

By evening Indian Tom was threatening people, who were eating their supper in the restaurant in the back room of Jack Graham's Saloon. Neil Ragland, at that time the town constable, was called in. This was a mistake because of the feud that was developing between the two. Indian Tom was

noiser than ever. He told Ragland to get his gun. Ragland left for his gun, which was in the holster in his room. Ragland did not return to the Graham saloon but went to the Elk saloon run by Mark Wolf and there awaited his deadly enemy. Everyone seemed to have felt that the expert shot, Indian Tom, would plug Ragland on sight.

It was dusk. Those inside the Elk saloon unknowingly strained their eyes before oil lamps were lit. At the bar were three drunken men, Joe Snider, Crazy Minn, and Pete Fisher, who were getting ready to put bets on who would get shot.

Mark Wolf, the bartender, had no love for Indian Tom because he was the business agent for his competitors across the alley. No lights were lit in the Elk saloon lest Ragland be seen by Indian Tom.

Just inside the door, which was in the corner of the room, Neil Ragland stood waiting for Indian Tom. It was a warm summer evening with the door open. The drunks at the bar were sobering up under the excitement. The spurs of Indian Tom were heard to jingle as he came down the side of the saloon. From outside, the saloon seemed lost in darkness. Indian Tom turned the corner, crossed in front of the building, and stretched his hand out for the door knob, not knowing that the door was open. Neil Ragland was only three feet away in the darkness. He fired, shooting Tom right through his heart. He was shot so quickly that his body stood balancing for a moment before it crashed to the floor.

The three drunks immediately started out of the saloon, all three of them stumbling over his body as they went. Joe Snider does not know how he got to the tie pile down on the siding by the wye, but he woke up there the next morning.

A telephone call was immediately put in to Sulphur for Solomon Jones, the sheriff, who gave permission to move the body to a slab in the back of the saloon if they had three sober witnesses. In this way the doorway was not obstructed for the business of the evening, as everyone swarmed in to drink and talk.

Mark Wolf, however, left for Denver that night to consult his lawyer, who became Neil Ragland's defense attorney. Ex-Sheriff E. J. Burner became the witness against Ragland, as he was sober and in the saloon at the time, while Mrs. Mark Wolf took the stand in defense of Neil. Ragland was taken to the Sulphur jail.

The next day Lininger came in on Number One to become foreman of the coroner's jury. The jury had no trouble coming to a conclusion that Ragland should be held for murder, except that Bob Ross, the mayor of the town, was afraid Ragland would shoot him for it. Lininger said, "You'll have no trouble handling Ragland if you get a hold of him first." After great deliberation and encouragement the jury came to its verdict, holding Neil (Cornelius) Ragland for murder in the first degree.

But the smart lawyer that Mark Wolf had hired hamstrung the trial in Grand County, quoting the Middle Park Times newspaper clipping of the story as evidence that "no fair trial could be conducted in Grand County."

He quoted the newspaper, ". . .And fired as his man was coming toward him with his head down to all interests ignorant of Ragland's presence."

The trial was moved to Georgetown, where he was tried and declared "not guilty," one year later on a plea of self-defense.

But Ragland's freedom did not make him a changed man. Dago Frank shot him through the stomach on St. Louis Avenue in Fraser, in front of a saloon some years later. He bled like a sieve, but somehow or other came out of it alive. Dago Frank went to the pen threatening to get Neil when he came out.

Ragland went on his way gambling and having trouble meeting his payrolls down to the beginning of the depression, when he operated a shot-gun pay-off mill at Yampa. But one day a man beat him to the draw on pay day, leaving the world minus one trouble maker.

Now we return to Arrow to discover more of what boom town life was like.

Joe Snider said of Arrow that it was "The dirtiest lowdown town in your life." Other men said it did not compare with Grant, Colorado, some years before, when the South Park Railroad was built. We get another picture, however, from the fine men and women who lived there seeing the town's life as they lived it in a wholesome way.

Joe Snider declared that the town marshal, red-faced Danley, and the mayor, Bob Ross, were working a racket in the early springtime of 1905 before the dining room was built north of the station. This spot then was a mud hole where the melting snow ran from the hillside. On top of this hill was Main Street, or Spruce Street as it appeared on the blue prints, with its line of saloons.

If a customer became obnoxious, he was thrown out of the saloon. The bartender saw to it that he was thrown far enough to roll down the hill into the mud puddle, which was later filled in for the foundation of the railroad's own little Fred Harvey House. The unfortunate gentleman found it too slippery to crawl back up to interfere with the bartender.

Marshal Danley made his rounds regularly because the only pay he got was his meals from the saloons and restaurants and what fees he collected. Seeing a man down, he went for his patrol wagon, the same patrol wagon that janitors at New England Universities used to haul the boys back to the dormitories after big dances — wheel barrows. But since the town marshal had not been paid ahead of time to haul these men home, he hauled them to the jail. The jail was a ten by sixteen building built of two by fours nailed together in log cabin fashion.

As it was the privilege of the law to search all men for dangerous weapons, the victims at Arrow were searched and looted, so Joe Snider charges, of almost everything they possessed, such as the much-prized pen knives of that day.

In the morning, the victim was arraigned before the mayor who was justice of the peace. The costs were assessed as well as a fine. Since the unfortunate man usually had been cleaned out before he had been kicked out of the saloon, Mayor Bob Ross and Danley had little to split between them for their troubles.

One of the saloons did not find itself so favorably located as to be able to throw its men out of the front door and over the hill. So this saloon had a pig pen in one corner of the room where the saw dust was regularly changed. As the sawmills had great piles of sawdust, it was not expensive, only the cost of hauling.

One night two girls from the sporting house in the rear accepted a dare. It was a warm spring evening just at dusk. These girls walked out the front door of the saloon on to the sidewalk in the same clothes that Eve wore, until she knew better.

The first winter the gambling ran high. The roulette wheels were just as willing to accept the summer and winter savings of any lumberjack or

Swede, who had dug a tunnel in Fraser River Cañon, as they were willing to accept the big money of the wealthy in other resorts in the country. Men were known to be cleaned out of $1,500 in an evening.

As Arrowhead was a terminal of the railroad and trainmen brought their families along, the demand arose for a community hall, where wholesome amusement could be provided. It was built immediately. Here the storekeeper, hotel operator, sawmill operator took their families to a dance. The ever present fiddler and piano player thumped out the waltz or polka.

One night "the girls" who in larger towns lived on the other side of the railroad tracks, desired to crash the dance. The air of the community hall became tense. Husbands spoke their indignation in low tones in corners of the dance hall. Who was going to leave? These girls or the wives and mothers of Arrowhead? In the gathering that night was a former judge, who was well fortified with whiskey. He immediately began referring to the Constitution of the United States with particular reference to the Bill of Rights and the privileges of every man and woman. He gave an eloquent speech, such as men hear at election time. His six-shooter dangled in its holster, as he threatened to shoot any man who said another word about these worthy ladies.

The dancing went on with only a few people on the floor. The talking stopped. No one would argue with a drunken man and his six-shooter. But this ex-judge was so loud spoken that he did not notice the railroader who stepped up beside the man and stuck him under the ribs with a concealed weapon, which he held in his pocket.

The judge was unable to reach for his six-shooter. He retired from the floor in great disgrace. The floor was again filled with happy husbands and wives. The indispensable girls soon disappeared.

Then a ripple of laughter went over the crowd. The railroader had held up the boisterous defender of women's liberties with his index finger! Yes, the day was at hand, when the rough house gang was not so popular.

Not only was Arrow proud of her little community house but also of her two boulevard lights. One was at the top of the stairway leading from the station up to Spruce Street. The other light was on the corner of Spruce and Aspen Streets. These were modern gasoline boulevard lights that turned on automatically every night by a clock-like arrangement.

A town well had been dug at the north end of Pine Street from funds raised in the community. Previously, Mary Warren's husband had carried water at the price of two bits a pail from a spring west of town down over the hill at Pacific Siding. Mr. Warren had built a yoke for his shoulders, which made it possible for him to carry four buckets at a time.

Mary Warren was brought to Arrowhead on a stretcher for her health. Invigorated by the mountain air she was soon working in the kitchen. Her first nights were so terrifying that she was afraid even to step outside during the day time. Yet she soon learned no woman had ever been attacked. Hardly anyone locked their doors and a spirit of friendliness pervaded the community.

Death took some wayfarer who had no friends. The storekeeper got out his Bible, read some scripture, and the community was respectful enough to give him a funeral.

The little Arrow cemetery (to the northwest of town) soon had a handful of graves. Today the spot is overgrown with a second growth of timber and is hard to find. But to this spot an Austrian was brought one day. He had died of lead poisoning at a mine prop camp near Fawn Creek. Bill Wood's pinto horse pulled the corpse on his specially built sled, which fit in between the rails. Lead poisoning was common in that day before tin cans were perfected.

Joe Snider tells how he returned from freighting to Granby one day and went to sleep on a tie pile. The next morning he heard something on the other side of the pile that sounded like the rustling of tissue paper. It was a very sick man with pneumonia. He was carried to the Chancey De Puy Hotel, where there was a registered nurse. He was kindly cared for. He revived enough before he died to give his name and the name of a lady, whether a sister or daughter they could not determine. They telegraphed her. She acknowledged being a relative, but said no more.

The community buried this prodigal son who was not wanted at home. There was a sincerity and frankness which met men's needs in Arrowhead, that is often missing in cultured communities, where family skeletons are hidden behind respectable brownstone fronts.

Mary Warren, who in later years became postmistress, confirms the story that it was possible for 2,000 people to have gotten their mail in this community, which neighboring dude ranch guides point out to guests as "probably a sawmill site." The lumber camps, construction camps, and the town itself could easily have housed that many people during the summer of 1905.

The sawmill business was a risky business, particularly to men who spent their evenings gambling or drinking. For the risks and losses were great in the lumber business, taking all the sober reflection and hard labor any man could put out. So it was that many sawmills failed because of improper management and found themselves unable to meet the payroll.

Thus came about the joke that some sawmills had three crews: one that had left, one at work, and one being recruited in Denver. All the manager had to do was to go to Denver before pay day and stay there till his foreman informed him most of the men had left. Then he came back with a new crew.

Mr. Lininger tells how difficult it was for an honest, hard-working man without plenty of capital to keep going. The sheriff was forever serving warrants on a car of lumber, loaded and ready for market. To get around this difficulty some operators would have two cars on the siding, one empty and one full. They would deceive the sheriff and have him post the empty car.

But in spite of such sawmill operators some people maintained a good reputation for honest business, like V. H. Lininger and his mother.

For several years a little Sunday School was run in the school house with a dozen and a half children in attendance. Mary Warren can recall an occasional minister preaching there.

There were men of the character of Bill Wood, who would not operate his sawmill on Sunday, would not swear, would not drink, and, we might add, would not work for any party but the Republicans! This jibe speaks of the keen interest in national matters by the leading lumber man of Middle Park.

Bill Wood became popular with engine crews in later years, when the blockades would tie up trains. Men always knew they could drop down to Idlewild, where the Wood's sawmill was located, and find a meal or provisions without any price. Bob Bishop tells how Bill Wood provided him with lumber for his house twice, when he could not hand over the cash. Train crews had the highest regard for Bill. In return they moved freight cars on his siding that the management never heard about, — or if it did, it kept quiet.

Two jokes are told on Bill. One is that when he would get in a cantankerous argument with the railroad over something that they could not agree on, Bill would say, "I will hire a lawyer. I will hire

two lawyers. I will hire all the lawyers." Well, Bill did hire lawyers.

The other joke developed after a dog fight occurred near the Arrowhead station. Bill thought he would stop the fight by shooting to scare them. But Bill's shot glanced on a stone and went into the station. The story ends with Bill's being arrested by the town marshall.

Thousands of ties were stacked along the right-of-way east of Arrow waiting to be loaded for track laying further west. One day as Joe Snider worked at loading ties, he smelt smoke. It was the smoke that every one fears in the forest. Looking around he saw a forest fire fanned by the wind, leaping from tree top to tree top, headed toward the thousands of ties.

Joe called out the extra gang, which was made up of little fellows, Japanese, who were mostly loading ties. These men speedily performed miracles in moving ties.

Lee Cooper who was the first Forest Ranger at Idlewild, a few miles below, was telephoned concerning the fire. He arrived on horseback to direct the fire fighting. The fire was driven towards the right-of-way clearing and confined there. The burnt timber was easily discernible forty years later to those who traveled over the old right-of-way east of Arrow.

The little community bustled with all the excitement any community goes through in the good old pioneer days. The Chamber of Commerce spirit planned a rodeo. It was a big name for an overgrown school picnic, but ambitious little communities have big ideas of the future. The rodeo ground was the only unoccupied ground in Arrow, the ground between the railroad wye. A greased pole was erected, and we imagine the railroad furnished the grease without the official permission of General Manager Deuel who by such moves won his men.

There was, of course, some bucking. But the potato race was the occasion for the snagging of the happy spirit of the day by Neil B. Ragland. He was a not too successful sawmill operator. He could not be, for he spent too much time at the gambling tables. With a shotgun he discharged men before pay day. It helped pay the bills. At the potato race, Ragland fell out with Jack Smith. It was not gun play but potato play. The potatoes were thrown with bullet-like speed, and the rodeo was broken up.

One of the pieces of gossip that was picked up at the rodeo and carried to the boarding houses concerned the gold nuggets that had been found around Rollins Pass during the construction days. Plenty of construction workers had dragged themselves into energy after long hours of work in that day to look for the gold. But no more could be found. This all men knew. The gossip now was about a conductor, Jim Lafie. It was rumored that H. A. Sumner, the chief engineer, General Manager Deuel, and John Daly, the bridge and building foreman, had hired Jim Lafie to prospect for this gold. Today, we know the rumor was true. But Jim Lafie could not find the gold, even though he searched diligently and used all his experience as a former gold prospector. The conclusion accepted for the failure to find the lost gold mine is this. Years before, Rollins Pass was used by miners from Hahns Peak region and others as a route to Denver. It is suggested that miners, taking out their treasure by pack train, stopped to rest or camp. Unable to resist the sight of their finds they took some of the nuggets out of the bags. With a swig of whiskey they may not have been too careful in repacking the nuggets to which they had drunk a toast.

There were plenty of stories to be retold and added to around the bars of Arrowhead. To the lumber operators these bars were an undermining influence. It was hard to keep the men sober. The narrow margin and great risks involved in sawmill operation made drunken men a serious threat. In desperation, W. H. Wood determined to pay no more whiskey bills. Having duly notified the proprietors, he paid his men off one evening with checks and told them he was not paying their drink bills. He suggested they stay away from the bars so as not to lose their money.

They went, of course, to the saloon and told the story. The bartenders wiped their hands on their aprons and had a council of war before the night got old.

The next day Bill Wood was served a notice to appear in court for the debts of his men. Marshall Danley soon found that Bill's ire was stirred exceedingly.

"Danley, I am not going. I'll just kick you out of the door."

The next day, before train time, a man by the name of Smith said, "I'll get Wood." Everyone knew Wood was leaving on the train for Denver and the coast.

A man, who worked at the mill, warned Smith, "Wood is mad today. You had better stay away."

Mr. Wood let it be known that if the District Attorney, Mr. Lebree, said that garnishee was legal, he would come. Wood argued that one day's notice was insufficient.

Smith came back from the telephone, supposedly, saying Lebree at Sulphur had said he should appear.

Smoldering like a volcano Wood went over to the telephone operator and asked, "Did any one call Lebree in Sulphur?"

"Why, no, Mr. Wood."

With this the volcano exploded. "Smith, you lied to me. I am not going." Wearing his two .38's

Wood ended his brief speech. "Smith don't you come near me. I'll open you to the weather."

While Wood returned to his room to dress for the trip to Denver, Smith organized a posse of seven deputies, the hard losing bartenders of Arrow.

Mrs. Lininger begged Wood, "Now don't get in trouble."

Bill put his coat on his arm, ready to handle both .38's, and started through the deep snow for the station, as the Denver train had arrived. Smith, shaking like a leaf, fired his rifle at Bill. Two shots followed Smith, who jumped behind a stack of beer bottle cases. Glass flew in the air and the seven deputies disappeared, while Bill walked down the narrow path of snow to the station. Passengers were racing for cover and H. A. Sumner and Blauvelt, together with Conductor Barnes, worriedly asked, "What's up?"

Replied Wood, "I am going to shoot the whole d--- crowd," and began the explanation.

Sumner replied, "I am glad they ran up against you. One of our section men lost $600.00 last night."

Just then a deputy who appeared around the corner was greatly surprised to see Bill and took to his heels through the deep snow.

The railroad men assured Bill that if he was in trouble they would stand by him no matter what he had done, for "that crowd must be handled or law would never prevail, nor will decent people settle this new country."

By this time the Lininger brothers had appeared on the double quick as the first armed reinforcement for Bill. Incidentally these three men led the clean-up of the town.

The defeated saloon keepers called on Sheriff Sol Jones of Sulphur to get Wood arrested in Denver. Sol Jones replied over the telephone, "You men leave Wood alone."

Mr. Wood went to see his lawyer in Denver and was advised to get back and stand trial, as he had resisted arrest.

The next day a surprised George Barnes saw Bill Wood get on Number One. A U.S. Deputy also got on. Wood had helped him on occasion and he offered to get off at Arrow to be of some help.

Wood said he needed no help, but the deputy got off the rear of the car as Barnes and Wood got off the front of the coach.

The business men of Arrowhead were standing out in front of their establishments sunning themselves in the noon sun and looking down, as usual, to see who had arrived on the train. When the liquor crowd saw Wood, they disappeared.

Wood immediately went up to the justice of peace and told him he was there ready to stand a fair trial. The judge seemed reluctant, but on insistence of Wood, fined him $50, and remitted the fine.

Wood stamped into the saloon, where the boys were in a huddle. "I have stood trial. Now if any of you x, y, z, buzzards want to shoot it out, come out right now."

Since no one challenged Wood, he went off to California on the next train.

The story would normally be over here. When Bill returned from this trip, however, he was arrested for his resistance of arrest and fined $185.

In those days, Bill tells us, he was rolling in money and it meant nothing, for the town was settling down.

SPRINGTIME IN ARROWHEAD — 1904! The log restaurant (left) is still unchinked but ready to welcome the hungry. Mrs. Graham is relaxing with her young son and daughter but will soon be busy in the kitchen. The first train will not arrive until fall by which time the street will be cleared of trees. Billy Woods explored this area in search of a sawmill site in 1903, as the surveyors were placing stakes for the contractors to follow. The more enterprising men put up tents to stay the winter of 1903-04 in order to be early birds in town and one of them (right) is established as the first drug store. *left, CRRM; right, DPL*

An early autumn snow has about melted in this 1904 scene (above) on Aspen Street in Arrowhead. Passengers are waiting for the train, perhaps tourists who rode up on Number One this morning and will be returning to Denver. The operators of Grahams Silver Brick are probably the same family who last spring opened the town's first restaurant in a log cabin and they seem to have expanded to another restaurant and lodging business seen in this Arrow photo taken in the spring of 1905. — *below, L. C. McClure, both, DPL*

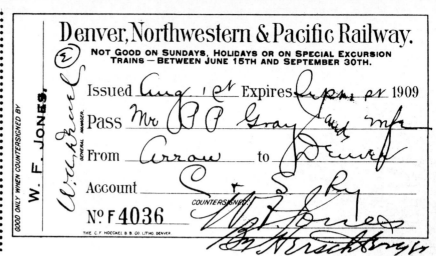

Denver, Northwestern & Pacific Railway.

Pass one way only
in **opposite** direction from
Opposite **accompanying** Ticket

Worthless if detached.

F 4036

PERSONS	FROM	To
2	D	76

Denver, Northwestern & Pacific Railway.

NOT GOOD ON SUNDAYS, HOLIDAYS OR ON SPECIAL EXCURSION
TRAINS — BETWEEN JUNE 15TH AND SEPTEMBER 30TH.

GOOD ONLY WHEN COUNTERSIGNED BY
W. F. JONES,
GENERAL MANAGER

Issued *Aug. 1st* Expires *Sept. pr* 1909

Pass *Mr. R P Gray and wife*

From *Arrow* to *Denver*

Account *C & S Ry*

No. F 4036 COUNTERSIGNED

THE C.F. HOECKEL B.B. CO. LITHO. DENVER

The fine log depot (right) welcomed countless thousands of tourists to Arrow including some lucky enough to have a pass such as issued (above) to Mr. Gray of the Colorado & Southern Ry. When Mr. Robinson, the first station agent arrived, the building was still unchinked and he quickly took pneumonia after sleeping in the drafty structure. During World War I two women telegraph operators were hired to help handle the load at Arrow. The crews were happy to keep the girls entertained as we see (left) with Joe Preiss at the left and a Miss Jones on his right while the other two are unidentified. The women probably roomed with Mrs. Weaver who provided housing also for crews who sometimes laid over at Arrow.

The years brought great change to Arrow as in this scene (below) about 1920. Most of the town has been destroyed by fire and a large coal pocket, or dock, was built by Hewitt Construction in 1918 to help keep the engines fueled during the war years when there was a train movement thru Arrow every half hour. The engine house usually held a mallet and a rotary plow ready to battle the snow. —*right, Judson van Gorder; below, Arthur Hewitt: left Joe Preiss, all DPL*

THE MOFFAT TRIP DAILY REPORTER

CONTAINS DAILY NAMES OF ALL
PASSENGERS MAKING THE MOFFAT TRIP

PUBLISHED DAILY
AT TOLLAND

HARTMAN - SERGEANT CO PUBLISHERS
GENERAL OFFICES - MACK BLDG. DENVER

VOL. 1 NO. 41   AUGUST 23 1906.   TEN CENTS THE COPY

Train Time at the Moffat Station! It is a summer morning in 1909 and the start of a busy day with Number One loading on Track One (on the left) while tourists board a picnic train on Track Four. It will probably run as Second No. One to Tolland or perhaps to Corona or Arrow. On Track Two are the coaches for the morning train of the recently opened Denver, Laramie & Northwestern which for a few years used the Moffat Station and trackage to Utah Junction. The tourists will all want a copy of *The Moffat Daily Reporter* which, as the masthead (above) indicates, will include their names. — *above, L. C. McClure, both DPL*

9

From Summer's Glow to Winter's Snow

Visitors to Denver in the early years of the Moffat were impressed, when they crossed the Sixteenth Street viaduct, by a sign painted on the Moffat station roof which read, "FROM SUMMER'S GLOW TO WINTER'S SNOW IN THREE AND A HALF HOURS." A similar slogan used in news advertisements read "Three Hours Ride From Summer's Heat to Eternal Snow."

If they did not see the sign as they crossed the viaduct, they might have seen people snow-balling in front of the postoffice in mid-July and early August. The snow had been hauled down from Rollins Pass by train and brought to the postoffice by wagon from the stations. It was good advertising, for the weather got warm in Denver some summer mornings. What tourist did not wish to say that he had stood in snow out in Colorado in July or August?

The tourist business was most likely the first revenue business the Moffat had, outside of a barrel or box of groceries shipped up to Mammoth on some of the work trains, before Number One made its first run. Passengers first took the ride to Mammoth for a summer's day picnic. One had from 10:35 a.m. to 3:30 p.m. to hike around, to eat sandwiches, and to ask all kinds of questions about mountain lions and the new railroad that was being built. Even in those days people slept late on Sunday. Consequently the train left Denver an hour later, which unfortunately cut an hour off the vacation outing. As extra cars of tourists swelled the trains on Sundays and special days, the Toll family, as we said before, got out of sorts because of the debris these picnickers left.

With the completion of the road to Rollins Pass and Arrowhead in the fall of 1904, the railroad was all set for a piping good tourist business the next summer.

Among railroad men, Number One's run that summer was called the "ARROW TURN," as the train turned around at Arrow, and went back to Denver after dinner.

It was something to write back East about going through thirty tunnels, for only two or three Easterners knew anything about a certain rat hole division angling into the south with more tunnels than the Moffat had.

The Giant's Ladder — three levels of track above Mammoth — was spectacular. Everyone loved the trees and the dancing streams that leaped over the boulders. Yankee Doodle Lake was beyond description, causing people to exclaim, "I have never seen anything like it." The lake's name caused one Southern woman to insist the South be honored and thus Jenny Lake was eventually renamed Dixie Lake. Everyone commented when the train climbed above timberline and through Tunnel Thirty-two. People gasped as they looked back into Yankee Doodle Lake or down into Middle Boulder Cañon. But best of all was the snow they walked in at Rollins Pass. In June there were great drifts of it, mute testimony of the struggle of the past winter. Then as the train slipped down the other side and the Loop Trestle and tunnel were seen ahead, an argument arose as to which was the more spectacular or beautiful, the Georgetown Loop or the Moffat Loop.

Arrowhead was as good as any town Zane Grey wrote about, for there one played the roulette wheel, had a shot of liquor, or ate a good chicken dinner. This was the Wild West one had read about. If only Indian Tom could have appeared with feathers, everything would have been perfect.

Conductor George Barnes was a gracious host to all his passengers. One day as the train was returning from Arrow to Denver, a man said to him, "Is there a conductor on this road by the name of Barnes?"

Barnes answered, "Yes, I am he."

"I saw your father killed," announced the tourist bluntly.

This went through Barnes like a knife. He immediately knew that the man must be Garret Loop. As people were gathering around to hear the story, Barnes said, "I will come back and talk with you, after I have finished gathering the tickets."

Barnes did. He found a friend of his father's who had gone into battle with him during the Civil War. But George never forgot the knife-thrust those words had put in him.

With the building of the line to Hot Sulphur there came week-end fishing excursions. Locating Engineer Meredith's idea of filling the streams with trout was now paying off handsomely.

When you stop and remember that in the early nineteen-hundreds, the automobile was a risky invention handicapped by wagon roads, which made even good cars in later days impractical except from the thrill that comes from driving something new, you understand why so many people went on the Moffat to go picnicking or to go fishing.

Advertisements for traffic were even run in European papers.

Sundays in the summer saw two and sometimes three sections of these trains, which needed all the Moffat's motive power plus all the coaches they could rent from other railroads, leaving Denver.

The greatest occasion was the time the Moffat landed the Grocer's picnic, August 8, 1905. The Colorado and Southern passenger agent did his best to talk the people out of going on the Moffat, saying that the infant road could not handle the job. But George Barnes handled the job.

He organized enough crews for eleven special trains that Sunday. All engines except Number Two's engine had been run to Denver and several engines had been leased. It was a job getting enough coaches to handle three thousand and eleven persons, but the real problem was to see that there were no break-downs or wrecks. Operators were placed at several passing tracks. They flagged the trains, so that they were kept fifteen minutes apart. Barnes placed a lone engine at Crescent in case any train broke in two or any engine had a failure. Then the emergency could be handled quickly without plugging the entire line. To have a break-down on a two per cent grade is a different problem than on a sea-level route.

According to the prearranged plans the eleven special trains pulled out of Moffat station smoothly. The grocers were high in their praise of Barnes and gave him a real send-off for his management. Some of these trains had one engine, others had two. A shudder went over the passengers of Frank Spaulding's special as it went into an emergency stop in the center of one of those tunnels that has curves. Some smart-aleck kid had pulled the air. The flagman hit the cinders and ran like wild back to flag. How easily a following section could have plowed into the rear if the trains had not been kept carefully apart. When he found out what happened Frank Spaulding got the train moving as fast as he could.

The specials arrived in Tolland without mishap and unloaded their passengers. The Tolland water tank was run dry filling these engines. But the immediate problem was to make provisions for eleven special trains to pass Number Two coming east off the hill. There was room for only three or four of these trains on the sidings at Tolland.

George Barnes sent the specials up the Ladder to pass Number Two sitting on the siding at Ladora. The picnickers counted as many as seven of these specials visible at one time. For some people this alone was a thrill worth coming out that day to see.

George Simmons was the general superintendent at this time and smiled to himself afterward about all the precautions Barnes had taken, some of which he had felt unnecessary. So the day ended without a mishap. The no-injury record to a single passenger was early established and became the pride of the men and officials.

In less than twelve hours, twenty-four passenger trains had been handled on a mountain division with thirty tunnels and no block signals. That record of no mishap and on-time performance was one the Rio Grande could not shoot at even during the war with block signals and diesel power.

The next day Denver's well-liked passenger agent, C. L. Robinson, took $7,000 to bank. This did not include the money from tickets which committee members of the Grocers had sold before the picnic day.

Now, wherever you have tourists, you have to have food. In fact, A. C. Ridgway knew that he had to have food for the construction men. The National Hotel Company began feeding the Moffat men in a tent at Utah Junction in 1903. Chancey De Puy was in charge of this eating tent. He remained down the years with Barnes, Nels Johnson, Culbertson, and Daly. J. E. Markel of Omaha was president of this firm, which specialized in feeding railroad passengers, having seventeen hotels on the Union Pacific at that time.

The first tourists were fed by his news butchers. In 1906 R. R. Burke had the concession for feeding people on the Moffat. In 1909 the Van Noys News Company bought the concession. In 1912 Barkalow Brothers of Omaha fell heir. Through all these years Chancey De Puy continued to be in charge of feeding Moffat's various concession holders. It was only logical that in 1925 President Freeman should turn to De Puy and give him the contract which his years of faithful service deserved.

Mr. De Puy moved from a tent into the Burlington and Missouri Valley box cars Barnes had brought back to be rebuilt into outfit cars and kitchen and dining cars for construction laborers.

The early tourist business necessitated an eating house at Arrowhead. This was built and operated for years. Later there was established an eating house at Corona, as part of a $24,000 hotel with fireplace, great windows, and a few bedrooms for tourists who desired to stay overnight and see the sun rise from the Divide. This hotel did a good restaurant business for the "Scenic" passenger which was run regularly many summers to accommodate tourists from Denver.

Before this hotel was built, however, the railroad men and tourists were fed in a long coach-like frame building, which was reached by a narrow passageway from the snowshed. Most of the snowshed smoke was thus kept from entering this narrow lunch counter room. As you got off the train and left the snowshed by this hallway, you found the lunch room to your right at the end. The first object on the lunch counter was the tall coffee urn, which was heated by gasoline.

The lunch room was in charge of Sam Long, a cousin of Lula Long, the well-known race horse breeder of Kansas City. One day when the gasoline jet burner under the coffee urn went hay-wire, Sam sent a flunkie to the pump house to borrow a wrench.

Sam was squatting down on his haunches studying his problem, when he heard steps of a man coming down the hall. Supposing it was his flunkie returning, Sam extended his hand back of him to get the wrench, when he heard an order, not in the voice of his flunkie, "Put up your hands, you so-and-so." It was a hold-up.

The help was lined up on the stools with their hands on the counter, while one of the robbers sat at the end with a gun ready to plug any man who made the wrong move.

A freight train was coming up the hill. This would mean the watches of three or four engine crews, plus the conductor and brakemen, would be robbed. The haul had not been very profitable so far; only thirty or forty dollars had been taken.

The engineers came in, unsuspecting, one at a time, walking down the hall. Soon stripped of their watches and change, they joined the others on the stools, with their hands on the counter.

When the last unfortunate railroaders had filled their places along the wall, as all seats were now occupied, the desperadoes warned the men that if any one moved for the next ten minutes he would get plugged with lead and be as dead as any so-and-so. The bandits fled down the hall. But the railroad men did not lose one second in getting the news on the wire, feeling that these men had to escape from the top of the world via the railroad, as there were no wagon roads in use any more to Rollins Pass.

A thorough search was made of every car on the train and every train that left, but these hold-up men were never found.

It then occurred that they probably came up through Devil's Thumb Park or Ranch Creek and had tied their horses out back. It was late in the hunting season, when the presence of men with guns would have been taken for granted, as hunters normally used horses.

This was the only successful hold-up on the Moffat road.

It was in this beanery that some famous Boston-baked beans were served by a Mr. Weatherby. He baked the beans in little pots, though a predecessor of his claimed that beans could not be baked at this elevation. Every cook had to adjust his recipes in this high altitude, in fact, in any place in Middle Park. Many a pioneer woman and railroader's bride despaired of baking cakes, until she had found out the cause of the trouble and had decreased the amount of shortening and sugar. Indeed there was a change for every cook who moved from Summer's Glow to Winter's Snow.

However, the men that kept the line to Winter's Snow open in the winter were frequently happy for anything to eat and were not at all particular.

De Puy tells how one morning he accompanied General Superintendent George Simmons in the caboose behind the snowplow, which was called out to get Mike Broderick out of a drift and back on the track in the Loop area. Along the way they picked up section men wherever they could find any, until the caboose was like a can of sardines, with fifteen to twenty men in it.

After Mike Broderick's train had been re-railed, the plow headed for the top. When it got to Needle's Eye (Tunnel Thirty-two), however, it broke down. The men went out into the cold, blustery weather in shifts, working until they were nearly frozen. Then they came in to thaw out, while others took their places.

By 4:00 o'clock they were still struggling against the elements and, inasmuch as all that the men had had for lunch had been their sandwiches, George Simmons asked if De Puy would not take some men and go to Corona for food.

Four men volunteered. De Puy asked the conductor if he had any bell cord, as it was one of the favorite items that was always being appropriated by trainmen from the passenger cars for use in a dozen different emergencies.

Securing the bell cord, the men carefully buckled up their four-buckle overshoes, putting their pants inside the overshoes, but tying their overalls on the outside of the overshoes with string to keep the snow from getting down the tops of their arctics.

There was only way out. You could not go around the tunnel, lest you slip and drop eight hundred feet, as had happened on occasion. So the men went up over the top of the mountain, holding onto the bell rope, with De Puy in the lead. When he had found the telegraph line, he stopped and rested.

In this way the men went from telegraph pole to telegraph pole in the blinding storm. The last man always remained anchored to the last pole until the next pole was found. Sometimes the wind would blow the sky clean of snow so that they could get a glimpse of the next pole. The cutting gale was so biting on the face that men held boards, at times, in front of their faces, to protect them from the wind. When they reached Corona, they walked right up on top of the twenty-foot high snowshed and climbed down through a trap door near the eating house.

While the men rested the sandwiches were pre-

pared, the lunch placed in gunny sacks and the return trip completed in like manner.

But the most famous thing about this story is the unusual coffee De Puy brewed for his men. Herb Chase, the conductor, had a fifty-pound lard can to brew the coffee in, and as De Puy had nothing else to do, he kept adding more coffee and more water, as it was needed, wondering just where these trainmen got all their coffee.

When General Superintendent Simmons came in he discovered that in this outrageously ugly blizzard, the steam from the engine had turned to ice on his coon-skin cap. So he hung his cap over the stove to thaw out.

In the middle of the night Simmons wanted to go out again and see how the men were coming along, but his coon-skin cap was missing. It is a well-known privilege of the general superintendent to ask for his private property in rather demanding terms. Now as to how demanding Simmons was, we do not know. But any of the fifteen or so men that were from time to time crowded in the little caboose could easily have knocked the cap down and stepped on it, or shoved it some place that escaped the eye of the inter-caboose-investigation-committee that hunted without success for the missing cap.

Toward morning, Herb Chase upbraided Chancey De Puy for the abominable coffee, saying that he ought to stop adding coffee and water and make new coffee. As the blizzard abated, Chancey took the fifty-pound lard can out the back door of the caboose and dumped the contents — water, coffee, and coon-skin cap!

Chancey washed the cap very carefully before he made another batch of coffee. The general superintendent was one of the most angry men he ever saw, for the cap had shrunk till it fit not his head, but his fist.

The middle of the following day the train crew got the plow into Corona. But the story was not ended. Years later Mr. George Simmons, who had moved on up the railroad ladder to some larger system in the Texas country, visited Chancey and asked him if he remembered the cap?

"Yes, I do."

"Well, I gave it some time ago to my grand-daughter for her doll." And they had a great laugh about it — then!

Coon-skin caps and twenty-foot snow
Are a part of life that the Moffat boys know.

This chapter has given a picture of the only worthwhile revenue the road had developed beside that of lumber and the hauling of materials used in the construction of the line.

Thus we see that a financial impasse was headed with financial capital dubious of investing more in a project which had already swallowed a fortune and was still unable to pay its operating cost.

The Moffat Road was always willing to try a publicity stunt to lure passengers so on a hot summer day they brought a car of snow down from Rollins Pass and paraded it through downtown Denver to emphasize their slogan "From Summer's Glow to Winter's Snow". Countless groups included the Moffat in their plans as did the Grand Army of the Republic (G.A.R.). The line also welcomed permanent settlers to their rich farming, ranching and mineral lands with booklets (above) describing these resources. —*above, Western History Coll., University of Colo., others DPL*

There was much to see on the way to Rollins Pass including the Hotel Craig, high above Eldorado Springs. It was a popular place to beat the heat and they would gladly haul your suitcases up the hill in a wheelbarrow when you left for your train. About 1915 (below) we find Engine 118, now lettered D. & S. L., paused with a tour train at Pine Cliff. The water tank was supplied by a steam powered pump whose stack is visible near the tank. —*both L. C. McClure, above DPL; below CRRM*

Tolland welcomed tourists with a fine dance pavillion, good restaurants and the first class Toll Inn. Some passengers stayed overnight but those who continued their trip would be treated to a fine view of the town nestled far across Boulder Park as seen (above) from the train as it climbed the Giant's ladder. — *both L. C. McClure, CRRM*

Tolland was a busy stop on the Moffat. We see a doubleheader (opposite-top) paused there about 1906. On one occasion four tourist trains returning from Corona were blocked when the first derailed. Becoming tired of waiting, half the 2400 passengers simply walked to town (opposite-center, right) where they danced and ate the town out of food. The University of Colorado based its Mountain Laboratory for Biology at Tolland and we see a class at Jenny Lake (opposite-center, left) in 1915. The Ossen Photographic Special, sponsored by the Denver photo firm, proceeded past Tolland and held their picnic at Newcomb (below) in 1915. It is at this point that the line starts the climb up the Giant's Ladder.

Perhaps no sight was more breath-taking to tourists than Yankee Doodle Lake. The stately gentleman enjoying the view is Dr. Craig of Central Christian Church in Denver. Despite persistent rumors, no locomotives were lost in this lake. — *opposite-top, CRRM*; **opposite page: center-left,** *David Ramaley*; **center-right,** *Katherine W. Toll coll.*; **bottom;** *above L. C. McClure, all DPL*

"Top of the World"

These two young ladies (left) were among thousands of tourists who posed at this sign after unloading from excursion trains atop Rollins Pass, such as the one (opposite) emerging from the snowshed. On any but the warmest days the shelter of the lunchroom (below) would soon be welcome and besides, where else could you eat in a snowshed? A fine hotel welcomed those who wanted a full meal or to stay overnight at the "Top of the World". Heavy cables can be seen across the roof where they were placed to give protection for winds sometimes rose to 100 miles an hour. After the line was abandoned the bricks from the hotel disappeared into homes in the Fraser River Valley and nothing remains today except some cable anchors and the concrete floor. The vastness of the Pacific slope of the pass (below-right) dwarfs the passenger train in this classic 1904 scene by Mr. McClure. — *bottom-opposite, CRRM; others, DPL*

DR. SUSAN ANDERSON
1870-1960

132

10
Fraser — Home of Doc Susie

Among the summer tourists and lumberjacks on Number One in August of 1907 there was a woman doctor by the name of Susan Anderson, who had graduated from the University of Michigan in 1897. She had been nursing as long as twenty-two hours at a stretch without rest and was "about done up." She got off the train at Fraser for a two weeks' rest from the heat of Denver.

Dr. Anderson had visited Steamboat Springs in 1900 seeking a place to establish a practice. But the community did not appeal to her, for there was no railroad or promise of a railroad.

Doc Susie had a good rest in Fraser. She saw the double rainbows. She marveled how it could sprinkle so frequently from such small clouds. She watched the showers drifting from the west, east to the Divide, and return to dampen the hay that the ranchers were desperately trying to get up before the first snows.

Her vacation over, she returned to Denver. But by December she had so overworked again that she looked around for rest. She feared she had tuberculosis. Not telling her folks, she took Number One again the Fraser, fully expecting to die there. But the busy lumber camps and boom railroad town needed a doctor.

Doc Susie found a suitable room with the Charlie Warner's. The news of her arrival spread. Help was needed at a lumber camp. The railroad's Dr. Harrison was busy and a doctor was a doctor to people so far from help. She was driven to the camp through miles of pine forest.

The men crowded to see how she worked. Her soft spoken orders were carried out. Men, starved for a mother, sister or girl-friend found this most capable physician everything they could desire. They threw a dance for her that night. New life came to the lumber jacks.

The married women of Fraser said she surely must have been chased after by the rest of her class in medical school who were all males.

A call to a timber camp found her snuggling up to the married man who was bringing her home. He made it plain he was married. When she persisted, he gave the powerful shove only a seasoned lumber jack could give. She landed in a snow bank with her medical kit flung in disgust.

It was not long before she found a suitable cabin a block and a half north of the station between the railroad and the county road. There was no highway 40 located there as today.

She had neighbors further north of her, Pete and Beda Louise Benson who had brought several Swedes over to America. Benson's brother had two cows so now Doc Susie appeared at milking time with her glass. She wanted it filled directly from the cow twice a day. She drank it with nature's warmth. Fraser had given her everything she needed. Her heart was happy. There were plenty of males, good food, crisp air and sunshine. She was free of T. B.

She found her man and asked him to put a south door in her cabin. She did not want a window in square with the door but wanted it like a diamond. They quarreled and her love affair was over. As the years passed, she began dreaming about a log house with a fireplace. One day she was offered a log building which was four miles from Fraser, if she would remove it from the property. She found in Tom Smith of Tabernash a man who would build her a fireplace. So she made her plans and took her workmen out to tear down the log building. Doc Susie took a hammer and drove an eight-penny nail in the first log, leaving only the head showing, two nails in the second log, three nails in the third log, and so on. Thus, the builders could easily place each log where it had originally been. They looked at the nail heads and rebuilt the house log for log.

Doc Susie had an eye and appreciation for the cultural, little of which was to be had in a rough lumber town. So she bought from an art glass company several neat little leaded glass windows with art glass roses. Doc Susie cut some glass from a wrecked automobile for the windows in her door.

A beautiful stone fireplace was built in her living room by Tom Smith. Engineers and firemen said that the chimney would need something to break the draft, so they advised putting pieces of sheet metal to hold the draft back. She accepted the suggestion, which worked.

Old cardboard boxes were used to insulate the walls against the wintry draft. Doc was determined to have a house that was warm. Most of the houses in Fraser started out to be summer shacks for log men. Then as the green lumber dried and winter came, efforts were made to make them warm.

Snow lay heavy not only on the railroad, but on the house roofs. Thirty inches to three feet of snow were not uncommon at times. Doc Susie was determined that her house was going to have a real roof. One "rail" said, "I'm not afraid to run my engine on your roof, Doc. That is a real roof."

Doc's practice kept her busy. In fact, she never got her house entirely completed. One Sunday evening a sled came from a logging camp up the East Saint Louis Creek. A man in the Stockholm Camp needed some stitches in his lip. The surgery completed, her presence was celebrated with a dance. "Of course, the Swedes were full of their Sunday night cheer," Doc tells. In time she noted "the very nice waltz the fiddlers were playing started me hunting through my mental register to determine what the tune was that they were playing. It dawned on me that I had heard that tune when I saw four hearses abreast — Chopin's Funeral March. Now, just think of that! On a Sunday night, dancing (this story was told to a member of the cloth) with drunken Swedes to the tune of Chopin's Funeral March. I asked the fiddlers where they had learned the tune. Without a smile, they said, 'in the old country.' And when I told

them what it was, they did not see anything funny about it."

To those of us who knew the graciousness and timely concern for the sick that Doc Susie had, we get a picture of the homesick Swedish lads, who had come to a strange, rough country to build a new empire, a land of opportunity. There seemed no God in this wild west and land of big money. It was a strange world. But there was a woman doctor whose interest was first — and above all else — her patients. Money was needed, but the patients' need was unquestionably primary.

On later occasions Doc Susie would walk back from these camps, her six-shooter by her side. The tall lodge pole pines stretched above, the moonlight shone through the great arms of the trees and the coyote's call haunted men and mountain with its weird cry. But no one was going to touch Doc Susie, when she walked home. That six shooter was under her pillow every night, loaded!

Once, in the middle of the night, a knock came at the door. Doc dressed as hurriedly as she could, surely not taking time to put on the customary half dozen petticoats. Doc had already called out, "Who's there?" The man said that he was a fireman with his engineer who was very sick.

These night calls were hard on Doc, because outside the thermometer was generally below zero, perhaps thirty-five, forty-five, and even once in a while, fifty. Since Doc always thought more of her patients than herself, she seldom took time to dress warmly.

The engineer was brought into her office. The fire in the little coal stove was stirred up and Doc's hands washed clean. The man's sick stomach was relieved of its pain and anguish, but being a very sick man whose heart was acting up, he was in very bad condition. The fireman surveyed the room — an operating table, a desk piled high with medicines and bandages, a combination book case and old fashioned writing desk, open, displaying some letters, a well-worn Bible, and disorder, three class-room chairs with one arm on which one would write, and an old-fashioned chair whose back could be lowered for the patient's comfort. The oil lamp illuminated the room, with great shadows covering the details, which the fireman had little time to scan. For he was a new man. He had never been over the road before. The time was running short which his orders gave him to get to Tabernash, four miles down the hill. If he stayed much longer, he would "be on the law," a term used by railroaders who were under the law of train orders and timetables which spelled out clearly when they had to be at the next station or meeting point.

Doc Susie was more concerned about her patient than about "being on the law." She knew railroading, but thought that the fireman was capable of handling that. Otherwise, she would have told him that there was a telephone in the Fraser station, which he could use to phone the dispatcher to get more time on his orders. Perhaps the fireman did not want the dispatcher to know too much about this. For it was questionable, if this were stomach trouble or Rule G! (Rule G forbids intoxication or drinking on the job).

The sick man was dragged back to the locomotive a half block away and helped up the locomotive ladder to the cab. He was set on the fireman's seat, where Doc Susie held him upright. The fireman took over the running of the engine, left off the air, and opened a little on the throttle to get the engine to Tabernash, down the less than two per cent grade.

No sooner had the engine begun to move than Doc saw something white following them. She asked for the engine to be stopped, and who could deny Doc Susie's request? It was her white Spitz dog which she had forgotten to shut up at home. So Doc climbed down the engine steps, picked up her dog, and handed him to the fireman. Doc climbed back up, picking up a little more that sooty grime for which railroads are famous, locomotives in particular.

The brakes were released, the throttle opened, and the engine dropped down the two per cent. As they reached Tabernash, the fireman stopped, climbed out of the cab, ran ahead, opened the switch, ran back and hurriedly climbed up the ladder, stepped quickly across the cab, and eased the engine through the switch. He then quickly left the cab, ran back, shut the switch, and looked at his watch. They were just "inside the law."

The fireman called for help. Doc Susie gave a carefully detailed lecture on how to make a stretcher and how to lift an injured man out of the cab of an engine. For Doc had in mind other occasions, when she hoped these boys would have presence of memory to recall her teachings. The man was taken to his hotel room and there cared for.

About this time, Doc remembered her little white dog. "Why, he is still on the engine," she exclaimed. "If anyone tries to get him off, he will surely bite him." Refusing to wait a moment for someone to accompany her with a lantern, now that her first care was disposed of, she moved in

haste to take care of her dog and eliminate any danger that someone might receive from his little teeth.

There were no sidewalks in Tabernash, no street lights — just black night and a little fog. The haze of steam hung low around the busy engine house, where many engines were being fired for helping heavy trains over a mountain. When Doc approached the round house, she approached it from the tracks. She saw men standing at both sides of the great round house door, so she walked (in the haze) between the men, plunging immediately into the engine pit. Engine pits are sunk between the rails running the length of the engine so that men can crawl under the locomotives to work on them.

The hiss of steam and confusion that busy round houses generate kept anyone from hearing her fall. The men were looking in the pit, where they were rescuing the white Spitz, who had jumped into the pit from the engine cab. They had first mistaken the white dog for a coyote. The next thing to appear out of the gloom and semi-darkness of that pit was Doc Susie with her grey hair. She was climbing up on the hot steam pipes that were installed to heat the pit. She had broken some ribs and could not call for help. The nearest man said afterward, "I will never be more scared when I see the dead come out of the grave, than when I saw you come out of that pit."

Now these men, who had been carefully lectured and had listened very respectfully to Doc's lecture of how to lift an injured person, quickly lifted her under the arms and stretched her broken ribs further apart.

I asked Doc Susie, "What did you do for your broken ribs?"

Her answer was, "I borrowed a woman's corset and had it laced tight. But you don't want that for the story?" This was too good to keep. Doc felt better and we appreciate hearing of her ingenuity. For those who met Doc Susie will never forget her gentle ways and her radiant character that is representative of all that is good.

Now you have heard Doc Susie's version of how she fell into the engine pit. Some railroaders knew she had taken a great liking to a certain rail and said she had run after him.

As springtime came and Fraser was still lost in the weekly and semi-weekly deep, wet snows, Doc received a call. It came, of course, in the middle of the night. The message was by long distance telephone to the effect that she was wanted back of Parshall — "a baby case." A sled was hitched up and "a pretty good-sized fellow

named Briggs drove me to Tabernash where a freight, a long one, was ready to go west through Parshall. In those days I could stop any engine, anywhere, and get on, so I was welcomed in the caboose." It was twenty-six miles through cañons and meadows to Parshall. In those days the only road opened in the dead of winter and the quickest of all ways in the spring time was a railroad.

Two months before Pearl Harbor, a double headed troop train with navy radio technicians hammered her way to Moffat Tunnel. A lad from New York City, Roger R. Richards, was in a vestibule taking a picture. With a sudden lurch of the train, his arm went through the vestibule door window. It was a terrible cut and the blood was pumping out in great spurts. A tourniquet was applied and his arm folded up. A message was dropped off that a doctor was needed as soon as possible.

The nearest doctor was Doc Susan Anderson. Chris Lomax, the station agent, sent a section hand to "look Doc up" for if she was not at home, someone was certain to have seen her somewhere. Once found, she gathered dressings, needles and thread and all that was needed, and waited in the station.

The long train of Pullmans dropped off the two per cent. The engineer whistled that he going to stop. Doc stood up. She and the agent went out. The train ground to a stop. The first snow of Indian Summer had fallen. The navy lads burst out of the train, the first liberty they had had in days. They scampered around, throwing snow balls. They bought the town out of candy, pop, beer, and cookies. They ran wild.

Doc, meanwhile, took the bandage off the injured arm. When the arm was straightened, the blood spurted out. Doc hurriedly took stitches, telling the lad to "cuss" if he liked, as that was the only pain killer that she could give him. She kept no sedatives like opium because she did not want to be burglarized. Someone kidded her about being nervous. She fired back, in her gentle way, "Who wouldn't be — holding up the navy and the entire Rio Grande Railroad with a special stopped on the main?"

Weeks later she heard from the lad in the Hawaiian Islands. At Christmas time there came a beautiful blanket from the lad's mother in Brooklyn.

The years came and went. The aristocratic Rio Grande had come along, and Doc no longer was able to "flag down a train." But Doc, aged in years, remained young in spirit. She was always on call, though she prayed not to be disturbed at night. The chill air was too much for her. She always found a welcome, noon and night, for turkey dinners at Thanksgiving time. She knew a half dozen homes where she was welcome any day to walk in at meal time. Her Bible was worn thin. Her bi-yearly trips to a lower altitude came and went.

Twice she had moved away from Fraser to a lower and warmer altitude, but each time she found the communities so changed that she was unhappy, so back to Fraser she came. The last time she had grown too weary to finish her unpacking, some one always needed her, so her home was clogged with wooden boxes whose lids had been pried open to get out just what she needed.

One magazine had photographed her and made fun of her strewn house. She complained to the minister as she showed him her sewing machine in her northwest bedroom. "See, everything is neat here. This is where I live. Here and in my office."

When one gets to the time of life she no longer has youth's energy, she can just give up. But at any time of night when she was called on — now over seventy years old — Doc Susie hastily dressed and raced down the highway knowing that seconds counted. She risked colds and worse time and again. Then came the day she took sick. A friend took her to Colorado General Hospital. Later the fine doctors put her in their Good Samaritan Nursing home where they could keep an eye on her. Her friends from over the years with whom she had walked to pick strawberries for preserves were up on the hill or in Denver. Her money had run out. She had lived too long. The poor and the heavy drinkers had been her later patients.

A friend or two in Denver visited her. Her mind was sharp. One day at ninety she took "Train Thirty" over the Great Divide.

When Doc Susie first rode the Moffat in the summer of 1907, Number One would have looked about as in this photo (above-left) with Engine 300 racing down from Rollins Pass on what is believed to be the first train into Fraser. W. I. Hoklas took this view (below) of nearby Little Chicago about 1904, but the town was already fading when Doc Susie arrived. Bill Wood's saw mill (top) at Irving Spur, now Winter Park, became a familiar spot to Doc Susie as she made frequent visits to aid the sick and injured at the mill. Clay Blough visited Mile Evans' cabin (above) on July 16, 1902, taking this photo when only a handful of hardy souls lived in the entire Fraser Valley. Present day Fraser is less than a mile from this cabin site. Yes, this was a rugged area to which the young woman doctor came. — *all, DPL*

138

We see Fraser (left) decked out to celebrate Independence Day, July 4, 1907, with the Cozens and Lemmon store on the left, where Doc Susie would pick up her mail and buy groceries. The town had a brief time of excitement when Hollywood came to film *The Cattle Rustler,* a silent era western and we see a shot opposite from the movie hanging. Doc Susie, weary with the years of struggle and mostly unpaid fees, poses outside her cabin at age 70. It was about this time that Rev. Ed Bollinger came to know Doc and she joined him for Thanksgiving dinner in 1939 at the Presbyterian Church (above) built in 1911. Doc Susie gained a bit of fame when after the Fraser Valley people were refused the right to walk through the Moffat Tunnel for the opening celebration on the east side, she organized a protest and displayed this sign for all to see as the opening day specials emerged from West Portal. Doc is hiding behind the sign which refers to the Denver Post; the protesters felt the paper gave too little credit to the people of the western slope. —*all, DPL*

Doc Susie

THE DENVER, NORTHWESTERN AND PACIFIC RAILWAY COMPANY.

Utah Jct. 10/28—1906

Mr. Steve Pappas,
    Troublesome Colo.,

Dear Sir;

    Enclosed please find Roadway time book. Allow the men from material yard $1.60 per day while working on Section

Yours truly,
D. J. Sullivan
R. M.

11
Fraser to Yarmony

When the railroad reached Hot Sulphur, August 20, 1905, sufficient motive power was on hand to operate. Another passenger engine, the 301, had arrived in June and in May another stocky consolidation, the 102. The road had, by this time, fifty box cars, fifty flat cars, ten passenger cars and three cabooses. There were, of course, the fifty obsolete outfit cars that George Barnes had purchased from the Burlington and Missouri River. The road had one rotary plow, the 10200, but no wrecker.

Denver, Northwestern & Pacific Railway

ISSUED *Oct. 30* 190*5*

PASS *Steve Pappas*

FROM *Denver* TO *Sulphur Spgs*

OCCUPATION *Extra Gang*

COUNTERSIGNED:

No. H 773

GEN'L MANAGER

GOOD ONLY WHEN COUNTERSIGNED BY H. A. SUMNER.

By the summer of 1905, the Moffat Road was nearing Hot Sulphur Springs and over the next two years would be pushed west to Kremmling and on through Gore Cañon. Young Steve Pappas was put in charge of an extra gang and is seen with them, sitting on the rail in his fancy bib overalls. The gang, complete with an official — in the suit — a waterboy and mascot dog, have been at work on the newly laid 90 lb. rail. According to the letter (above-left) the rate for these men is $1.60 per day.
— *Colonel George S. Pappas, CRRM*

For years Moffat had known he would have to sacrifice securities in mines he owned if the rails were to be laid west of Hot Sulphur Springs. But to men who saw Dave Moffat wave to them from the back of his private car, he had already accomplished the impossible. Most men felt that in time they would be running trains into Salt Lake City.

On Sunday, September 3, 1905, Time Table Number 4 went into use giving Hot Sulphur Springs passenger and freight service. The date of September 15th was then set for Railroad Day in Hot Sulphur.

Previously one crew and train could operate daily as Number One and Two using Arrow as a turn around. But with the extension of passenger service into Hot Sulphur two crews were needed as well as two trains. Conductor Charlie Clark bid in for conductor on the second train. When both trains were on time, they passed at their scheduled meeting place, Pacific Siding at 1:15 p.m. Conductors Clark and Barnes waved greetings to one another according to railroad rules. The mileage at this time over the hill to Hot Sulphur was 109.36 miles. The schedule gave Number One authority to leave Denver at 8:00 a.m. and arrive at Hot Sulphur at 3:15 p.m. Number Two left Sulphur at 11:15 a.m. and arrived in Denver at 6:30 p.m., Arrow being the meal stop for both trains.

W. I. Hoklas tells of one lone passenger standing on the platform to greet the first passenger train when it rolled in. "On the platform stood Ute Bill Thompson, looking at it (the train) as happy as a boy with a pair of new boots. Ute Bill Thompson owned land at the upper end of that little valley, a narrow strip of meadow on the north side, which he prized very highly. Since Ute Bill and locating engineer Meredith were very good friends, Meredith had the first survey run well into the slide rock to avoid the strip of meadow, leaving the sad part to be done by the construction crews that followed. This crew made the location as it is now, and old Ute was on the war path. In some manner, however, the peace pipe was smoked and as I stated, old Ute was very happy that it was all over with.''

Either that morning or the next morning J. J. Argo's survey gang boarded Number Two at Hot Sulphur Springs. They had finished the survey of the much disputed Gore Cañon and were headed back to Arrow to run the final line for the Main Range Tunnel. W. I. Hoklas tells that they had about a freight car load of equipment to load. We can bet that J. J. Argo would get his boys to Sulphur for Railroad Day.

The next day nature had no more respect for the brass hats of the engineering department than for the boys setting up camp, for it rained. H. A. Sumner, chief of staff, had taken both resident engineers, Blauvelt of the east side and Meredith of the west wide, with him up to the 9,930 foot Main Range Tunnel site for a conference on strategy. J. J. Argo reports his dampened feelings of that conference with these words, ''Heavy rain.'' Returning to Denver that evening on Number Two, Argo loaded up with equipment and maps that were needed for his work.

The next day he went back to the site with one man and made a tie-in with existing surveys for the tunnel location, while on the west side the boys were cutting a trail through the timber to the west end location. There were so many things to do in this Indian summer weather, which was not living up to its past reputation, that grave concern was felt for the winter.

Thus H. A. Sumner was courageously carrying on his work in spite of the darkest outlook for the future. The new general manager, Deuel, had asked him if the road should not seek for an agreement for a western outlet beyond Salt Lake. Sumner agreed that they needed an outlet to some place on the Pacific Coast like Puget Sound. It is a wonder that Sumner did not pull out as Ridgway had.

But these things were not felt by the boys who were regularly receiving their pay checks. They were ignorant of problems considered in the ''Holy of Holy places.''

J. J. Argo, therefore, saw most of his crew board Number One at Fawn Creek Friday morning, September 15, with all the enthusiasm of youth to enjoy the festivities of Railroad Day in Hot Sulphur Springs. By the time their train arrived, it was mid-afternoon. But that which they had missed on Friday, they saw and enjoyed on Saturday, a repetition of the first day.

The program began with a band concert at 10:00 a.m., followed by a barbecue, horse racing, bucking contests, and small sports. Each day ended with a Grand Ball at night. Grand County residents, who came in their spring wagons, would get home in time to do the morning chores.

The special train, with nine hundred paid fares, that brought Denver residents looked like a great transcontinental limited, which the Moffat hoped to be running daily in a short time.

Middle Park old timers enjoyed recounting events of the old days so that newspaper reporters had a field day taking pictures and recording stories.

Chief among the stories was the subject of Frank S. Byers who had founded the community in 1874. How he had crossed Rollins Pass in 1877 was retold. It had taken him four days to get his wagon pulled by four mules over the Pass and into Sulphur. He had paid a man $10.00 for double heading his wagon with a team of horses. When they reached Yankee Doodle Lake, a snow storm had overtaken them on that eleventh day of September. The wagon was abandoned and the goods placed on the horses' and mules' backs. Three trips were made to timberline with these goods. Then they went back to the lake and picked up the wagon, which they were able to get to the Pass without its load. He landed at the Springs on the thirteenth and considered that his lucky day.

Another story recounted at the barbecue that beautiful Indian summer day was the story of the founding of Cozens Post Office in 1876 near Fraser. Then followed the story of the building of Berthoud Pass road in '74 and '75, Captain L.D. C. Gaskill was one of the men who not only worked on the construction but stayed to pioneer. For eight years he resided at the summit in what became known as the ''summit house.'' The story was told how, when guests came one winter's night, he told them to put their team in the barn. His guests laughed saying, ''Our team is standing on top of your barn now.'' Barns were not three-story buildings and the snow was deep. Later Mr. Gaskill moved down to his ranch at Fraser, which in later years was owned by Frank Carlson.

A very prominent figure at the Railroad Day celebration was Sol Jones, whose advertisement in the weekly paper read, ''Blacksmith, wagon maker, and horseshoer.'' How much of this work he got done when Arrow became incorporated is not known, for he made plenty of trips there to preserve order as Mr. Jones was sheriff of the county.

Grandfather Button told his friends how he had seen through his telescope the smoke of the first construction train dropping down the west side of Rollins Pass from his ranch on Cottonwood Pass twenty-five miles away. He had carried mail with McQueeny over Berthoud after seven sacks had been left in a snow bank and a change was rightly in order. Any one who was so close to the heart of the stage business naturally ran into good drivers like Charlie Free who had battled the stage through one of the worst winters of history between Dillon and Kremmling. And when the fine young stage and freight driver met the daughter of the sheriff, there came wedding bells. So the old pioneer tradition of honesty and a word being better than a bond was passed on to a son-in-law who lived to be president of the first bank in Granby forty-five years later. So Sol Jones was proud on Railroad Day and could tell plenty of stories of the past.

One of the arguments that occurred that day was regarding the sage brush flat known as Granby. A siding had been built there to accommodate Grand Lake business. Some one had dared to suggest that Granby would become a town. This was booed down. No matter how people booed Granby, it became the largest town in the county many years later. Mr. and Mrs. C. H. Nuckolls, who had run a hotel in Arrow opened the Mountain View Hotel. Mrs. Nuckolls became the one most sought for counsel for many years. In fact how she felt about an idea buried it or carried it. But who could see all this on Railroad Day in Sulphur?

Thus passed the summer on the Moffat's new line. H. A. Sumner had seen the rails head to Hot Sulphur and now his work in planning the line was about completed and dependent on cash with which to build.

But the advent of the railroad was the ending of an era. Somethings which were good were lost, one being the hospitality that left one's house open to whomever came through. Perhaps the guest left money for the food eaten. They surely would fill the wood box with chopped wood. No longer, however, would Grandpa Gardner at Fraser snowshoe over the mountain thirty-six miles to Georgetown for a pound of tea when he was tired of nothing to eat but elk and deer during the winter.

No one any longer thought of canning small trout in a brine to make them taste like sardines, as the Cozens had done when they first homesteaded. Now people bought their sardines, shipped with the rest of their groceries on the Moffat.

J. J. Argo's boys returned to Fawn Creek on Number Two on Sunday. Only Hoklas and R. M. Smith had stayed with Argo working around the West Portal site of the Main Range Tunnel. That evening a snow storm set in which found four inches of snow over the hill Monday morning. This day, September 18, Mr. and Mrs. Hoklas quit J. J. Argo's party to join a survey party of the Denver Yellowstone and Pacific Railway Co.

By November 16, 1905, traffic had become so thin that freight business was given to trains One and Two. They ran on a slower schedule which gave them ten hours to make the trip out from Denver.

In January 1906, nine year old Laura Throckmorton, and her mother decided to take the mixed train Number 2 from Hot Sulphur into Denver. When they got to Arrow, the eighteen freight cars were put on a siding and the engine and two passenger cars were returned with the passengers to Hot Sulphur because the line was blocked.

The next noon Laura and her mother boarded the same train arriving at Pacific Siding (just below Arrow) at 2:55 p.m. There was no Number 1 to pass because she was held at Tolland on account of the blockade at Tunnel 32. Five minutes later at Arrow it was learned that the line had not been opened and Number 2 was again returned to Hot Sulphur.

On the third morning word was received in Hot Sulphur that by the time the train reached Arrow, the line was expected to be opened. However, for the third time Number 2 was returned from Arrow.

On the fourth day passengers were assured that the line would be opened and it was. The train picked up the eighteen cars at Arrow and had no difficulty getting to Corona, although considerably off schedule. By this time a new blizzard was raging and the engine stalled in a drift beyond Devil's Slide. When there was a lull in the storm, the passengers discovered their cars were still on the trestle. The rotary was called up and though it was going only 4 m.p.h. it collided with the engine of the passenger train.

Laura and her mother with all the other passengers were stranded there for two days without heat in the coaches. Being pioneers they had brought sufficient clothing along to keep fairly warm. They knew from experience to carry a three day food supply when they travelled. They arrived in Denver six days late.

By May 15, 1906, the schedule was reduced to tri-weekly service, for there was no financial reserve to operate unprofitable trains.

So restless had some of the stockholders become that the management had to assure them that on a certain day construction of the road further west into Byers Cañon would begin. So an order was issued to the section boss to lay enough ties to lay two rails. This was done to fulfill the promise. Both Milner's and Sumner's hope had been to have the rails into Salt Lake City in three years. Two of those years were passed and the end of the line was less than 110 miles out of Denver.

The winter of 1905 and 1906 was one in which chills went up and down the spines of investors in the Denver, Northwestern and Pacific. They did not lack faith in the enterprise, but they did fear that others would not join them, leaving the road without sufficient capital to reach its destination and revenue business. Only two rails had been laid that winter.

During the winter this North Pole Railroad was a great problem to Water Superintendent Spitter. With temperatures running from twenty to forty degrees below zero in the winter and freezing every night in the summer on Rollins Pass, it was almost a superhuman battle to supply water for locomotives. Water tanks were well insulated with saw dust. The large pipe lines were lost in great boxes of saw dust. At Fawn Creek (Ranch Creek) on the west side beavers insisted on building dams every other night, preventing the water from running down the ditch that fed the main from an intake higher up on Fawn Creek.

Ben Spitter, as water superintendent, could run all over the mountain in almost any weather. He did not need trains. In bad weather, when he would have to leave Rollins Pass for Tolland to take care of any emergency, he was known to have snowshoed down in one hour — better time than the Number Two struggling through snow slides and drifts.

At Rollins Pass a pump house was built below on the most accessible lake and a line laid to the snow sheds. A water tank was to have been built here, but as yet it was not completed. This winter engines took water at Rollins Pass only if the water in their tenders, or tanks as the men called them, was below sixteen inches. Then they would telegraph down to Joe Snider, who would start his steam driven pumps going and pump water into the engines.

It was most likely during this winter of '05 and '06 that the snowshed took fire from sparks on one of the helper engines on the wye in the snow shed. The gale howling over the top of the world carried the fire through the shed faster than the engine watcher could run to warn the engine crews and section men.

Joe Snider must have been telegraphed to start the water pumps down on the lake for the fire was put out, after it burned the log station and a small part of the shed. The men fought desperately, suffering first from the heat and burns, then later from frost bite and exposure to the cold blast of wind that swept through the snowshed.

Everyone had gotten out with track bars to straighten the kinks out of the rails as the track cooled. The fire had struck so fast that the operator's office burned before he could tell Denver what was happening.

The operator was nicknamed "Bull." His last name has been lost in the years of many memories. Having no contact with Denver and seeing the need for help, Joe Snider went down to the pump house and brought up his ancient telegraph instrument, which he had received previously as a gift from one of his men.

A wire was strung into a clothes closet of a partly burned room in a shack. "Bull" was wrapped in a mattress and blankets and set a box to hammer out the news of the emergency and the need of a relief train to come to their rescue.

Another springtime approached the Rockies with everyone aware of the nature of spring, the one-day length of summer, and the eternal winter.

Over in Yampa the editor of the weekly "Pioneer" wrote two sentences that completely described the hundreds of articles the Post had screamed in red and black headlines.

"The Denver Post is still engaged in building the Moffat Road. It built it to the coast four times last month, but strange to say, nobody has yet seen it go past Hot Sulphur where they are at present."

Summer came. The grading had been finished through Byers Cañon. On down the valley the grading was pushed around hills and around draws where a trestle or fill could have been placed, for the road was now being completed the cheapest way possible. The rails were laid and spiked to the ties but with no rush of a large crew, for they would not be stretched very far out of the dwindling fortune of David Moffat.

It was July the first before a shuttle train could be run eighteen miles beyond Hot Sulphur Springs to the noisy railroad construction town of Kremmling. Although the pulse beat of the Denver

Northwestern and Pacific was very slow and weak, Kremmling was nevertheless excited and thrilled for the greatest advantage to come to her in her lifetime was a reality. It naturally followed that a great celebration was planned for the fourth, fifth, and sixth of July.

The contractor firm for Gore Cañon was Dumphy and Nelson. It was a grand combination, Irishman and Swede. These men were known for treating their men well. "Pat" Dumphy had a slogan, "It don't pay to pay freight on water," meaning poor canned goods for his men to eat.

In contrast to some other contractors who had one gang quitting the job, one gang at work, and another gang being recruited by the employment agents in Denver, Dumphy and Nelson had and held good men with well arranged tents, plenty of wholesome food, and considerate treatment.

Recalling the difficulties involved in surveying the line through the cañon, one can easily understand the expense involved in constructing it. Thirty thousand dollars was spent in building trails and roads to reach the worst spot in the cañon before one cubic yard of rock was removed for the right-of-way.

At what was known as Brown's Cut in the worst part of the cañon a sub-contractor lost or seriously injured a dozen men through powder explosions, rock slides, and the falling of drunks in the swirling waters of the Grand (Colorado) River.

The surveyors had not lost a life doing a more dangerous work. But the "Squirrels of Argo" had formed a closely knit fraternity that ran off the job any man who did not have or who lost his nerve. This would not be expected of the large gang a contractor would hire.

In 1907 the unhappy Meredith died from overexposure. H. A. Sumner had come out to the location, where work was progressing in Gore Cañon. John Daly, bridge and building foreman, and Pat Dumphy, the contractor, and Blauvelt were in the party. When they went on this trip, Meredith had a severe cold. Knowing Meredith, one realizes he was not the kind that could be kept in bed on such occasions. Meredith appears to be the kind of athlete that cannot be left behind, even when it was for his own good. Anyway, on this trip during the spring flood season when the water was icy cold, a gust of wind blew off his hat. As he fished around for his hat with a stick he slipped off the icy rocks and fell in. He was pulled out, but the damage was done. Pneumonia set in and they rushed him to the end of track nearby, awaiting an engine to take him to Denver. He died somewhere near Arrow.

It was 1907, over a year after Railroad Day in Kremmling, before the rails were laid far enough so that the first train could carry David Moffat and his guests through the cañon. In November the track was nineteen miles west of Kremmling at Yarmony with trainservice established this far for the winter. The Sheephorn ranchers were happy, but the Moffat was still forty-eight miles from the nearest coal mine and any hope of revenue that could make the road pay.

David Moffat could build no further. A mysterious run on the First National Bank was laid to the action of those men (Harriman and Gould cliques), who wanted the Moffat road to fail. Now he would have to send out an "S. O. S."

Steve Pappas, a fine strong youth of Greek ancestry hired on to an extra gang and soon became interpreter for the many Greek laborers. It was not long until he was given his own section gang and we see him (at left) with his faithful dog. The watch in his pocket will save him and his men from being caught by trains and he carries his time book and pencil in the other pocket. We must not underestimate the knowledge and skill of a section boss and thus we dedicate this chapter to Steve Pappas and his son Colonel George Pappas who preserved these photos. — *Col. George Pappas, Coll. CRRM*

145

Logging was and remains an important business in Middle Park as evidenced by this log pile at the Feltch Mill in Fraser. Its founders must have had big plans but the Colorado, Utah and Southwestern Ry. managed only to build a short logging line southwest from a connection with the Moffat in Fraser. Its one Climax locomotive was lettered for the Middle Park Lumber Co. which it served and carried the puzzling number of 684. — *both, Clay Blough, DPL*

Sometimes dangerous incidents appeared humorous as when (left) the engineer's tent was filled with great holes made by rocks flung thru the air when the Swedes misjudged their blasting in Fraser River Cañon.

Tabernash became a division point and is seen (above) in 1924, near the L. C. Hinds general store and (below) on a cold day in 1918 when the thermometer might drop to −60°. The Moffat shops are seen in the distance from George Schryer's house.

The agent at the new Granby depot posed for this humorous photo (right) soon after it opened. — *above, Grand County Museum; right, CRRM; below, Joe Preiss and left, both DPL*

The Rocky Mountain Railway

The Rocky Mountain Railway began construction in 1907 from a connection with the Moffat about one-half mile west of Granby, northeast to Monarch Lake, about 14 miles. It was hoped the line would provide the Moffat with lumber traffic and perhaps eventually extend its line to Grand Lake for the resort passenger business. The Moffat Road provided assistance with surveying the line and leased engine 391 (below) to handle the construction train, shown along side the construction tents at the junction point. One of the first runs (right) took a group of passengers on a tour in open-air cars; perhaps they were stockholders. An engine and caboose are seen (opposite-below) a few years later but unfortunately traffic never developed as anticipated and the line was abandoned in 1917 and completely removed the next year. — *opposite-below, DPL; others Charles Wolcott, Western History Coll., University of Colorado.*

149

As the track laying progressed to each town it brought with it great excitement and in this midsummer scene the ladies have brought along their sun umbrellas to protect their complexions. The men always are seen wearing shirts for protection from the blistering sun at this high altitude. The Moffat offered good paying jobs and men of many ethnic groups could be found working here, especially many Swedes and Greeks. In this photo (right) we see a fine group of men, neatly dressed for their photo. One fellow is ready to play his accordian and the fellow in front is probably pouring Ouzo, the Greek national drink. Steve Pappas, section boss, is third from the right.

Hot Sulphur Springs presents a chilly scene (above) but there is plenty of soothing hot water in the bath house which taps the hot springs with steam visible from the roof ventilators. Many years later Ed Bollinger would serve as pastor in the Congregational Church just left of the two story courthouse. — *above, L. C. McClure; others, Col. George Pappas coll., all CRRM*

A passenger train, possibly the first to run through Byers Cañon, is captured forever by photographer McClure in this scene in the summer of 1907. — *DPL*

The railroad reached Kremmling on July 1st, 1906, and a great celebration was held on Independence Day, July 4th. Steve Pappas poses beside his hand car with two others and his faithful dog. The well dressed man is probably the station agent. The town is seen (above) in the spring of 1908, while the Grand River (now the Colorado) is at flood stage, perfect for assuring a good hay crop this summer. The most prominent structure in town is the two story town hall, built with tax revenue from liquor sales to the construction crews working in Gore Cañon. To the left the long roofed building is the Masonic Temple where many Moffat men attended lodge. — *both, Col. George Pappas coll., CRRM*

Using cant hooks this crew prepares to move these giant timbers which will soon find their way into one of many new trestles. Steve Pappas, in old country decorum, wears a white shirt as befits the boss. Indeed he proved a capable man in his position.

After the track laying machine has passed the section gang (below) must follow to complete the work and make a constant inspection. — *both, Col. Pappas coll., CRRM*

The grading is nearly complete (above) and soon the track laying will begin. Steve Pappas (above-right) is now a foreman and stands with his hands on his hips as he inspects the track work. Locomotive 21 and steam shovel 10100 (right) are hard at work in the cañon as the railroad moves forward during the summer of 1907. — *above, L. C. McClure, DPL; others Col. George Pappas coll., CRRM*

Gore Cañon Conquered!

In this remarkable photo (left) the operation of the rail laying train can be clearly seen. The ties move up on the left side to be set in place as the rails are lifted into position. As summer ended the work was completed and at last shining rails had conquered Gore Cañon. On September 14, 1907, the first passenger train ran through the cañon with David Moffat playing host to railroad officials, businessmen and friends. He poses (right) with the first train behind him. He has exhausted his finances but has managed to push the line to Yarmony. Now he stands alone! L. C. McClure in another of his spectacular photographs has caught the emergence of a passenger train from the west end of Gore Cañon shortly after the line opened in 1907. — *left, Col. George Pappas coll., and below, CRRM; right, State Historical Society of Colorado*

A weary David Moffat relaxes after a bank hold-up when he had been threatened with colored water representing nitro-glycerine. He paid the robber so no one would be hurt, called the police and then sat down to pose for this photo. — *L. C. McClure, DPL*

12

Uncle Dave's Last Stand

Moffat sent out an "S.O.S." which was answered by seventy-year-old Colonel D. C. Dodge, formerly of the Rio Grande. His wife wrote of this pioneer railroad builder: "The parties that bought the Rio Grande made it a provision that General W. J. Palmer should sign a contract to have nothing to do with building any railroad, but they exacted no such promise from Colonel Dodge. The General was almost as much interested in raising money and building the Moffat road to the mines and Steamboat Springs as Colonel Dodge, though of course he put no money in it."

Colonel Dodge's influence and prestige plus his own finances secured sufficient capital to build the line to Steamboat Springs. He organized in 1907 the Denver and Steamboat Construction Company, which built this stretch of the road. Among other large subscribers were Henry M. Porter, S. M. Perry, Charles J. Hughes, Jr., William G. Evans, John F. Campion, Charles Boettcher, Thomas F. Walsh and Laurence C. Phipps, Sr.

Colonel Dodge was an unusual man. People would see him walking with his right arm grasping his left elbow behind his back. He was known to have cursed only once in his life. That was on the day of the Rio Grande-Santa Fe war, when the U.S. mail men hesitated to put the mail on the Rio Grande train. Dodge in exasperation said, "Go to Hell with your mail," and told the train skipper to give the high ball.

This even-tempered man, who was never pro-

fane, put the zest of his seventieth year behind this work of building the railroad.

Beyond Crater the company had either to build a bridge over Rock Creek Cañon, or detour up this cañon to a place where it would be possible to cross it and return down the other side. To bridge the cañon at its mouth was tremendously expensive. To detour up the cañon necessitated cutting a road bed out of the perpendicular wall of the cañon. The latter was done. Some distance ahead the line was swung across the cañon and reversed by a twenty-nine panel trestle bridge, which was four-hundred-sixty-four feet long, one hundred twenty-six feet above the waters of Rock Creek, and on a twelve degree curve, which continued through a tunnel. The line had now reversed its direction, enabling the track to climb gently up the opposite wall of the cañon. There were several places on this wall so steep, however, that no ledge could be cut out, necessitating bridges across the side of the wall. One mile of Rock Creek Cañon cost $256,000.

A rumor persists that Sumner considered this kink in the line a mistake. But with the finances as limited as they were, men were thinking desperate thoughts which did not always materialize. If the line had been run over the Gore rather than through it, all of this would have been avoided including the costly trestle construction.

As the line continued to climb up the mountain by great, circuitous curves, the passing track named Volcano was reached. From here one can see the most perfect extinct volcano in the country, rising out of Conger Mesa. As the men built the line through another tunnel, the line entered Egeria Cañon, with its elevation so high that the view challenges many that can be seen in the Alps.

In September of 1908 the road reached Yampa, having been built across Toponas Summit, where the Gore Pass route would have come in.

Ahead of the tracklayers was Phillips and Swan, a subcontracting firm from Orman and Crook. An eleven-foot vein of coal had been opened as they graded the right-of-way west of Oak Creek. E. C. Phillips of this firm had as his partner Henry Swan who was to become co-trustee of both the Moffat and Rio Grande during the depression. Mr. Swan with Porter J. Preston had made a study of the water and power resources further west in the year 1905. So together with the discovery of these rich veins of coal during his days on this job he became intimately acquainted with the resources of the area and the importance of this railroad which he administered many years later.

One night Henry Swan found his men coming home to their tents tighter than drums. They had been out to a slab shack where a would be post master and storekeeper near Oak Creek and Yellow Jacket Pass had been bootlegging. Henry Swan shivers, today, when he recalls the bluff he pulled as a fearless young buck. Barging in the post office-general store-slab shack without authority of a warrant or six-shooter, he told the man to get out. The treacherous man refused. Swan proceeded to phone the sheriff, his back a ready target for a knife or bullet. The postmaster fled without harm to Mr. Swan.

By February 13, 1909, the rails had been laid through the Oak Creek coal field on down the beautiful Garden of Eden into Steamboat Springs.

The first train arrived in Steamboat on a Sunday. Churches were closed. Two thousand cigars were given away. The good ladies of the town had baked two hundred pies. There was soda pop for everyone. The only mishap was a runaway, which dragged two residents for fifty feet. And, mind you, a dance was given in the snow.

Dave Moffat was making his last stand. But he made it grandly. George Schryer tells how Moffat dealt with his enginemen. They came to him asking for a new wage scale because of the hardships involved in operating over the hill. The ingenuity of these men has been told, as well as their devotion to the company property and the lives of the passengers.

Moffat met the boys with this statement. "You write your own contracts. I will sign them. I know you will treat me right. I hope the day comes and we make it (meaning Salt Lake), when you will get a one hundred per cent (raise)."

In a letter from Gerald Hughes the story was confirmed as characteristic of the man, who Hughes declares, never harmed anyone. The writer of this book has been unable to run anything down that discredits such methods of Moffat as being untrue. J. B. Culbertson in an interview declares the same to be true admitting one fact that when such labor contracts would be finally written up there might be slight hedging in the details.

More recently an elderly retired engineer was asked about labor problems. His voice broke when Uncle Dave was mentioned and he replied, "He had no labor trouble."

One day a tall, lanky engineer went to the First National Bank to cash his pay check for one hundred and fifty dollars.

The teller said, "You will have to have some one identify you." The Canadian-born engineer gave his railroad pass as identification and, when neither this nor his face was sufficient, he started speaking softly, using the word "Hell."

George Shryer, the lanky engineer, asked, "Is David Moffat in?"

The answer came, "Yes, but he is in conference."

But these railroad men, who had shoveled snow for days and nights to keep their engines from freezing, were not going to be turned aside by a bank teller, in particular any "damn white collar workers." George saw the bank guard and asked him, "Would you please tell Mr. Moffat one of his engineers wishes to see him?"

The guard went into the "holy of holies" where the conference was being held. George followed not too far behind.

The answer the guard received was, "Send him right in."

When the situation was recited, Dave Moffat rose and went to the teller and said, "When any of my boys come in, cash their checks. If anything is lost through bad checks I will make them good."

Uncle Dave's last stand was made while the ugly looking "preacher's kid", Ed Harriman, had become accepted in America as Union Pacific president. Harriman's trial on monopolistic charges had lasted a year. But thanks to Otto Kuhn, the twenty-year-younger mentor of Harriman, he had been cleared. Harriman, who could barely be heard when he spoke, hardly knew if he liked being a hero.

160

His acceptance must have deeply wounded David Moffat. Harriman died in 1909. In the great bank chambers of Kuhn, Loeb and Company Otto Kuhn controlled the Union Pacific's successful future as Harriman had. But Kuhn would talk with anyone, reason with him be patient and hear him out. Would he have listened to David Moffat whom he really did not know? I believe so. He would likely have been willing to help develop northwestern Colorado, build the 2.6 mile lone main range tunnel, extend the line to Craig and then build north to the Union Pacific. He was a man of very keen insight. Denver would have been on a transcontinental line as northwestern Colorado developed and the coal industry would have grown tremendously. This line would certainly have been a great money maker in two world wars.

Moffat and W. G. Evans would not have been broken, the Union Pacific would not have lost the Ogden Gateway, nor would a publicly financed main range tunnel have been necessary. This is the hindsight of an historian; it is easy to see afterward. Indeed Kuhn might have seen what a cut-off could mean but on the other hand he might still have sold Moffat out.

Today Colorado does not have a home owned railroad — just another link in a nationwide "industries" whose good for itself may prove to have disadvantages to the public.

Unfortunately, a well-managed and efficiently-run railroad can not make dividends unless it has traffic. The coal was under the ground, good coal. Weston had written in his prospectus after consulting with engineers that there must be twenty-five billion tons. The coal was not hard to mine. But capital was slow in moving into the territory. The only mine operating was one which used wagons to haul the coal out of its depths. Even as Moffat was caught in a squeeze play by his competitors, so were those interested in opening up the coal mines caught in the fears of their competitors. The possibilities of Routt County were purposely distorted by rumors spread by civil engineers to the effect that the coal either was not of high quality or it possessed unfortunate deficiencies.

If the railroad could be strangeled before the mines were developed, competition would be cut down. Rollins Pass was strangling the railroad fast with its terrible operating costs during the long winter.

Steamboat Springs would give the railroad cattle to ship, but even the ranches had to be built up, now that a lower freight rate was possible, and a long drive north to the Union Pacific eliminated. It all took time and the cattle business definitely was seasonal.

March 15, 1909, Dave Moffat had attempted to get the Weston Brothers of Utah to finish the line to Salt Lake City, taking Moffat road bonds for the pay. Apparently Weston Brothers was unable to furnish enough capital or feared the strangle hold that competitors were working in refusing the Moffat any western connections west of Salt Lake City.

Colonel Dodge was greatly disappointed that the coal business was so slow in developing.

He and others remembered the headlines in the February 3, 1905, Colorado Republican, "BELGIANS MAY INVEST MONEY FOR SYNDICATE IN THE MOFFAT ROAD." W. I. Hoklas, an engineer and long time resident of Steamboat Springs describes these plans and why they did not materialize.

> Prior to 1907 and through 1914 a great Belgian Syndicate was planning to take over practically all the Yampa Valley coal, the anthracite and metal mining interests. Sam Adams was the collector of data here and could name the resources of this country like reading a book. He was also Moffat's right hand man from this area who went with him to New York to speak before financial men. Sam Adams had worked hard on this project and had interests which would make him very wealthy and happy also, for he was a guiding hand in opening this empire.

> War broke in Europe. German marched through Belgium. CURTAINS again and then Sam Adams, none too well, died. It didn't take much more — a broken heart. I wonder if Harriman might have had something to do with the sinking of the Lusitania, Dr. G. S. Pearson who would have completed the Moffat, was on it.

The last note was, of course, said in humor but there was reflected the deep concern of the people for this railroad. In truth, The Moffat was a pioneer opening up the country, and time was eating away at the hearts of investors, who needed some dividends from their capital.

One morning in 1911 Uncle Dave Moffat asked for Bob and Skeeter to be called to run his special into Steamboat. Bob Bishop had come over from the Colorado Springs-Cripple Creek short line with Chester Foltz and Charlie Clark in the early days of the Moffat. Skeeter Myers was the other favorite member of the team that Uncle Dave liked to run his special.

Bob and Skeeter handled the special with the consideration all engineers showed to Moffat, when they were called for such runs. The special was made up of a locomotive and Moffat's private car, the Marcia, which was named after his daughter. Leaving Oak Creek and the wagon coal mine, the special ran through Deer Creek and Sidney. Water was running in the irrigation ditches, the hay meadows were green, the wheat was coming up. The distant mountains along Rabbit Ears Pass stood as a wall guarding this little bit of Heaven on earth. It seemed that the stubborn battles of South Boulder Cañon, the struggle with snow, the irritation of Gore Cañon, the cost of Rock Creek Cañon were past. Moffat always felt as though he were in a new land when he rode through this meadow and wheatland.

Moffat thought of the great loving cup the city of Denver had presented him for building the railroad. The cup was as large as a small man, beautifully engraved. Yet Moffat knew that it took more than loving cups, to finish his line. One man he had respected as friend for years had refused to help him. Petty jealousies stood between them. Moffat had never turned down the call of a bank in distress; he had never refused anyone help. Now in the building of the Moffat Road one name hitherto prominent in Colorado railroad building was missing for the first time — Walter Cheesman!* Moffat had become the mining king of the state and a great railroader. Unfortunately there were those who resented red blood being added to Colorado blue blood.†

Newspaper stories in 1905 charged that in New York Moffat's friendship for the Fifth Avenue Hotel head waiter, Thomas Gay, with whom he played poker, had interfered with his efforts to secure financial backing from blue bloods "who would not do business with someone who played poker with a head waiter." Moffat on several occasions had introduced his friend to Wall Street men as "My Friend Tom Gay of the Fifth Avenue Hotel."

But there were both blue and red bloods who had backed him.

Now Moffat's thoughts turned toward his men. H. A. Sumner had stuck by him through it all. He had not let him down. He had built the road for $236,907.62 less than his own estimates. A. C. Ridgway, his first general manager, was making good on the Rio Grande. Moffat knew that by and large he had better men than most successful enterprises had. These men had not failed him, though Wall Street had cowered before Harriman and his kind.

*From an interview with Edgar C. McMeechen, former curator of the State Museum.
†From an interview with Herbert O. Brayer, former state archivist.

Moffat awakened from his day-dreaming. Bob was blowing for the mile board announcing Steamboat Springs. The train slackened its speed gently and glided down the south bank of the Yampa River, leaving the town on the north bank. The special stopped in front of the beautiful brick and tile-roofed station. Moffat stepped down from his car, walked ahead to his engineer and called up in the cab, "As soon as you turn the engine, George will have dinner ready in my car."

After Bob had turned the engine, and washed up, taking off his dirty overalls, he went to the Marcia. An extra plate was set. That night Dave Moffat dined with the boys who never failed him. This was not the first time an engineer had eaten thick steaks in the Marcia, but it was the last time any of them would be the guest of Dave Moffat in that car.

The lank young athlete, Bob Bishop, enjoyed his meal. It made Uncle Dave feel young again. He thought of the little ranch a few miles away he had given to his friend from the Fifth Avenue Hotel in New York. The thought of Thomas Gay must have been a happy thought.

Uncle Dave had made his last trip to Steamboat.

On his return to Denver he went to New York City and secured the promise of new financing. Unfortunately, in his relief and joy, he indiscretely revealed his good news in the dining room or the bar. The next morning, though Harriman was dead, his bankers and railroad officials received word of Moffat's indiscretion by paid informers. An unconfirmed rumor said that Cheesman brought the news. Whatever the truth is, the general manager's diaries reveal that Moffat had loaned Cheesman his private car time and again to go to Chicago. In this manner Moffat had tried to win Cheesman back.

Dave Moffat died that day. Mrs. Moffat claims she had urged him not to leave the room, as she felt he had pneumonia. The ugly rumor is that he committed suicide.

What were the deepest hurts in Moffat's heart before he died? Was it the treason of Cheesman? The lack of vision from older, well established state builders by whom he had stood through every crisis but who had not gone all out with him?

He knew when he collapsed that his most loyal co-builder, William G. Evans, would now be washed out. Would the First National Bank pull through?

Lyle W. Dorsett in his book *The Queen City* (Pruett Publishing, 1977, pages 194-95) writes of the serious condition of the First National Bank at the time of David Moffat's death and places the fault for this condition on Moffat. "Because the Denver, Northwestern and Pacific railroad was as much a matter of prestige to Moffat as it was a course of personal profit or an asset to the region, the vain old promoter recklessly gambled every resource at his disposal. . . . In 1911, $4 million worth of notes were due on the road's construction company, and much more money was needed to salvage the entire project."

Dorsett describes how "Hughes' sagacity salvaged Moffat's mishandled transportation dream like it rescued the First National Bank. In brief, the senior partner of Hughes and Dorsey saved Denver's wealthiest families from great financial loss."

That Hughes was brilliant in handling these affairs is without question but his feelings and respect for David Moffat were not diminished by his old friend's financial reverses as demonstrated in a letter to Ed Bollinger, a copy of which is included in Chapter One of this book.

On this author's later visit with Gerald Hughes following that letter, there was nothing but the highest praise for David H. Moffat. On another occasion President Judge Wilson McCarthy of the Moffat and the Rio Grande told Bollinger about the board meeting of the D. & S.L. that was stalled for two hours as John Evans spoke with tears streaming down his face of all the good deeds of David Moffat including the rescuing of several of Denver's wealthiest men in a panic in 1893.

Dorsett unfortunately selected out sources that could have prevented this error in his estimation of David H. Moffat. It was Walter Cheesman's jealousy that held back not only his support but discouraged millions of dollars from the enterprise. This money went into all kinds of out of state investments as shown by Edgar C. McMechen in his book *The Moffat Tunnel of Colorado*.

The truth was that Moffat came as a red blood and built the greatest fortune in the history of the state until that day. He built it in a way that shook the conservative, timid investors of Denver.

Moffat never wanted the name of one who took advantage of his employees whether it was in a mine or on one of his railroads. Forest Crossen in Volume X of *Western Yesterdays — David Moffat's Hill Men,* gives the picture of the real David Moffat who treated his men with understanding and inspired them to the finest loyalty. The men that Forest Crossen knew had unexaggerated

memories of a man who breathed pure air into a world of early day turmoils.

Moffat not only protected his men but his fellow investors. On one occasion he and his partners were offered a price to good to pass up by some London investors for a mining property. Rumors later came to the U.S. that the London men had ill feelings toward Moffat and his former partners because the mine had run into difficulties. This did not bother the feelings of the other investors and they called Moffat a fool for being concerned. Nevertheless he went to London, astonishing the investors by asking them what would have been a fair return on the investment. When he heard their figure he bought back the investment at no loss to the men plus their fair return.

Moffat hired a new superintendent for the mine who installed sufficient pumps to get the water out and to sink the shaft deeper. The mine became another bonanza, and Moffat invited his former partners back saying, "No hard feelings".

Edgar C. McMechen tried unsuccessfully to interview Mrs. Moffat after her husband's death to learn the inside story. What were her last years like? She could buy no new clothes and had to sell the mansion and move back to their earlier home.

One day wearing an out-of-date dress and a shawl over her head, she came into the Stark Jewelry store as T. R. Ellis describes. "She left something with one of the clerks and he gave her something. My father asked about the little old woman and was told she came in from time to time and sold a piece of family jewelry or silver in order to have money to live on."

There was one piece of jewelry she never sold — David Moffat's ring. This she gave to Gerald Hughes when the Moffat Tunnel was opened saying, "David said I was to give this to you when you finished the line."

One thing was clear — LABOR HAD NOT BROKEN MOFFAT! His workers were the most loyal group of pioneers behind him. His staff had non-college men who had proven that they could operate a railroad. George Barnes was the one he turned to in emergencies, J. B. Culbertson as dispatcher knew first hand the problems of the line and Charlie Peterson as master mechanic solved impossible problems. There were ranchers and business men along the Moffat Road and west of Steamboat Springs who believed in Moffat's dream, who even offered right-of-way without completed deeds, just to get the line through. THE MOFFAT WAS A CAUSE AND THEY HAD BEEN PART OF IT.

It is May 15, 1907, as the first train arrives at the temporary box car station in McCoy. Two stage-like wagons and an automobile are down to meet the train and probably some of the passengers will transfer to the stages for the ride to Yampa or Steamboat Springs. Workman can be seen on the track ahead and the siding has not yet received ballast.

A passenger train is seen (below) in Yarmony Creek Cañon, probably in the summer of 1908. — *below, L. C. McClure, both CRRM*

Among the most difficult and costly construction on the entire Moffat Road was this section of Rock Creek Cañon with this large trestle bridging the gap between a tunnel on either side. A single mile of this construction cost $256,000 and another over $175,000; great sums for that time. In another fine McClure photo (below) a passenger train is seen ascending Congor Mesa soon after the line was completed through the cañon. Some years later the trestle was completely covered by a huge fill. — *above, DPL; below, CRRM*

Rock Creek Cañon is seen (above) with the Conger Mesa irrigation ditch visible above the railroad on the right. Seepage caused numerous slides and derailments until the railroad took over control of the ditch.

Train No. 2 is about to load passengers at Yampa in this 1912 photo. Conductor Barnes stands waiting and the two men prepare to load express. A local tire dealer should be coming by to pick up the tires stacked by the depot. — *both, L. C. McClure: above, DPL; below, CRRM*

Henry Swan, standing on the right (above) was a sub-contractor for construction of the line in this area. He is conferring at the construction tent with Allan Watson. The line was completed to Steamboat Springs on December 13, 1908. Soon after, McClure caught the passenger train at the fine new Steamboat station where mail would be unloaded bearing a Railway Post Office mark (above) indicating it had been sorted en route aboard the mail car. Mr. McClure also was on hand for "train time" at Oak Creek; the town was first known as Coal Creek but the name changed soon after the railroad reached there. — *above, DPL; others, CRRM; RPO mark, Mobile Post Office Society*

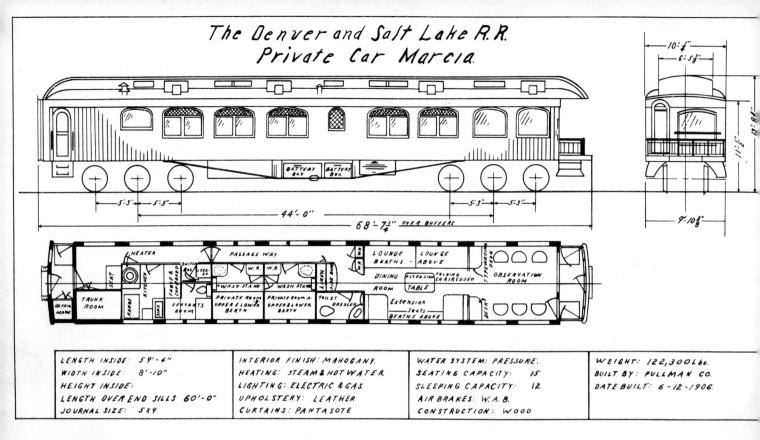

The Denver and Salt Lake R.R.
Private Car Marcia

LENGTH INSIDE: 59'-4"	INTERIOR FINISH: MAHOGANY.	WATER SYSTEM: PRESSURE.	WEIGHT: 122,300 Lbs.
WIDTH INSIDE: 8'-10"	HEATING: STEAM & HOT WATER.	SEATING CAPACITY: 15	BUILT BY: PULLMAN CO.
HEIGHT INSIDE:	LIGHTING: ELECTRIC & GAS.	SLEEPING CAPACITY: 12	DATE BUILT: 6-12-1906.
LENGTH OVER END SILLS 60'-0"	UPHOLSTERY: LEATHER	AIR BRAKES: W.A.B.	
JOURNAL SIZE: 5X9	CURTAINS: PANTASOTE	CONSTRUCTION: WOOD	

Denver, Colo., June 5, 1909.

Mr D. H. Moffat:

5:00 P.M.

No. 1, 7 minutes late at Yampa, handled 31 Reveune, 15 complimentary and 5 Employes deadhead.

No. 2 On time by Plainview, handled 50 Revenue, 1 Complimentary and 4 employes passes.

No. 5 Arrived Arrow on time handled 59-1/2 Arrow, 3 Denver to Corona, 3 Denver to Tolland and 4 passes.

No. 6 On time should have had about same number passengers as No. 5.

Stock extra west with 29 cattle and 1 car emigrants passed Kremmling 5:40 P.M.

Weather on Rollins Pass is fine. Slide at Mile Post 160-1/2 is coming in again, but do not anticipate any delay to stock train. Bear River at Steamboat Springs is getting quite high but has caused us no trouble as yet.

W. A. Deuel,
General Manager.

6:10 P.M.

168

David Moffat's World

David Moffat spent many of his happiest hours aboard his private car Marcia, named for his daughter. The car is beautifully finished as seen in the photo (right) taken looking toward the parlor and observation platform. The car was donated by the Rio Grande to the City of Craig where it now serves as the Chamber of Commerce office. Whether aboard the Marcia or at home in Denver, Moffat kept in close contact with railroad operations by means of reports from his officials such as this one (left-below) from General Manager Deuel. Only a year before his death, the Moffats moved to this mansion at 8th & Grant St. in Denver and we see his wife, Frances, in the library soon after moving in. The fine old home was razed in 1972 after city officials showed no interest in a plan to make it the mayor's official residence. —*below, State Historical Society of Colorado; right and left, D. & R.G.W. R.R.; others, DPL*

Your modern business leader--the man in Class A--is the average man concentrated and consecrated. The employe wh cannot concentrate on his work, and consecrate himself to his work will forever remain in Class B.--*So says Elbert Hubbar*

The Circulation of The Denver Post Last Sunday Was 85,135

THE DENVER POST

PRICE 5 CTS. DENVER, COLORADO, SUNDAY MORNING, MARCH 19, 1911. 62 PAGES.

DAVID H. MOFFAT DIES IN NEW YORK; WHOLE STATE IN MOURNING

Western Empire Builder Lays Down Gigantic Tasks at a Moment's Notice.

BUSINESS ENTERPRISES LONG AGO ENTRUSTED TO TRUSTED ASSOCIATES

Prominent 57 Years in Colorado's History as Banker, Mine Owner and Railroad Constructor.

(By ELIZABETH KELLY.)

In New York city, David Holliday Moffat, Western empire builder, lies dead.

As far from the scene of his life labors as the geography of the country would permit, Mr. Moffat laid down the momentous affairs which had bent his shoulders and walked quietly into the unknown.

That was yesterday morning.

The financial world echoed with the news of the passing of a great financier, but the flurry that comes in the wake of the commercial requiem was strangely absent.

It was David Moffat, the man, who was mourned.

His death meant no revolution in the world of finance.

He had been sitting in the shadow for months, as his intimates knew, and the mental acumen responsible for the acquisition of $20,000,000 or more by David Moffat had been quick to grasp the importance of leaving his business affairs in good condition. There are men, trained by Moffat, to step in where he left off. In fact, much of the detail work connected with what is known as the "Moffat interests" has been passed up to others for several years. As he would have wished, the First National bank, of which he was president, will be open for business Monday and his death will not interfere with its routine.

William G. Evans, president of the Denver City Tramway company, who is closely affiliated with all of the Moffat affairs, will probably assume the active management of Mr. Moffat's business.

It was Mr. Evans who sent broadcast the news of Mr. Moffat's death. The two had been together in New York city for several weeks attending to business connected with the Tramway company and the Denver, Northwestern & Pacific railway.

Mr. Moffat succumbed to heart failure at the Belmont hotel. A complication of diseases was in reality responsible. Grip and pneumonia had weakened the man whose vitality already had been sacrificed in the furthering of a gigantic enterprise. This enterprise had been undertaken when Mr. Moffat had passed an age at which most men retire from the active affairs of life to survey calmly the part they have had in the making of history.

Mr. Moffat came to New York in January with William G. Evans. The two had been closely associated for a quarter of a century in railroad and mining enterprises and their business here was in this connection.

Mr. Moffat got an attack of the grippe and went to bed. Mr. Evans called in Dr. Peter J. Gibbons, the Hotel Belmont physician. Dr. Alexander Lambert was next summoned and the condition of the patient failing to improve, Dr. A. A. Smith was added to the force of consultants. The trouble was diagnosed as a complication of grippe and pneumonia.

Thursday Mr. Moffat had a bad day. Friday night, while in bed, he had a severe chill. This morning he appeared to rally and at 9 a. m. grew cheerful, joked with the doctors and nurses and a friend. The improvement was so encouraging that Mr. Evans left the hotel. At 10:40 a. m. Mr. Moffat beckoned to one of the nurses.

"Please give me a lift," he said. "I think I'll feel beter if I am turned over."

While the nurse was shifting him in his position Mr. Moffat closed his eyes and died.

MUCH TO DO WITH MAKING COLORADO HISTORY.

Mr. Moffat had had much to do with the making of Colorado history.

In fact the story of the progress of this commonwealth is more intimately woven with the life story of David Moffat than of any other one man. For fifty-one years he had been a continuous resident of the state, leaving it only now and then to interest new capital in Colorado's undeveloped resources.

A tardy acknowledgement of the state's debt to David Moffat was the creation of Moffat county by the present legislature.

Mr. Moffat was in his 72d year. Since 1860 he has made Denver his home. Only recently he completed a handsome residence at Eighth avenue and Grant street.

For only ten minutes before the end came was Mr. Moffat unconscious. Dr. Peter M. Gibbons and a nurse were with Mr. Evans in the vigil that preceded the end. Mrs. Mofat, who had been with her husband in New York City, had returned to Denver. The attack of grip which weakened him came after her departure.

Mrs. Moffat was not at home when the news of the death of her husband reached Denver. Those closest to her feared that her first intelligence would come from the shouting of "extras" on the downtown streets. After some time Mrs. Moffat was located at her dressmakers' house on Logan treet. The maid who called her said that a friend was waiting. Mrs. Moffat hurried back to the house where Mrs. Samuel Gill told her of the death of Mr. Moffat.

Some time today the body will be started to Denver. Mr. Evans will accompany it. He will probably arrive in Denver on Wednesday, at which time funeral arrangements will be announced. Mr. Moffat's only daughter, Mrs. Marcia McClurg, is abroad.

David H. Moffat was a figure in the financial world. He was born with a genius for money making. He did not discover this talent until he was grown to manhood, but the years he had lost were atoned for by subsequent decades of strenuous effort at capitalistic achievements.

No one man in Denver had the vast business affairs that rested on the shoulders of Mr. Moffat. He was closely affiliated with the public utility corporations, and carried on affairs of a semi-private nature with the same sagacity that he gave to his successful enterprises of a public character.

As president of the First National bank, as president of the Denver Union Water company, a large stockholder of the Denver City Tramway company, the International Trust company; the Denver & Northwestern Railway company—which is the holding corporation for the tramway—Mr. Moffat had the really vital financial interests of Denver well in hand. But when his hand became enfeebled he was quick to realize its impending incapacity, and steadily he shifted to younger and stronger hands the reins with which he had driven to financial heights.

While Mr. Evans will directly succeed Mr. Moffat, in all probability, in nominally guiding the destinies of the "Moffat

(Continued on Page 3—Col. 1.)

Mines Made Him Millionaire

Mines first made Mr. Moffat a millionaire. He was already known as a banker of steady head and clear judgment, and had financed one railroad and was busy with another, and in all probability would have become a rich man if he had never owned a mine. But when the Leadville boom started he invested heavily while he was building the South Park railroad into the district, and when the road was completed it hauled much of his own ore. It was the Little Pittsburg which made him really a rich man; and besides, he was interested in the Louisville, the Maid & Henriette and the Resurrection group.

He repeated this success when the gold camp of Cripple Creek was discovered. While with one hand he was building the Florence & Cripple Creek railroad, with the other he was investing in promising prospects. The result was that vast wealth poured into his pockets from the Victor mine, the Anaconda group and the immense ore bodies of the Golden Cycle—to this day one of the richest mines in the district.

BORN JULY 22, 1839

David Holliday Moffat

DIED MAR. 18, 1911

THE COMRADE OF '60—"WE'LL MISS YOU, DAVE!"

SO THE PEOPLE MAY KNOW

The death of David H. Moffat marks an epoch in the history of Colorado.

He was in all respects an extraordinary man. Essentially a builder, he did things on a large scale. He exemplified the ruling and vital spirit of the gigantic West. He had a dominating personality, and became by his own unaided exertions the most important man in Colorado.

But he always kept his house in order, and his death, unexpected by the people at large, will not create any financial disturbance, or interfere with the onward march of this commonwealth.

Perhaps no higher tribute could be paid to the perspicuity and the commanding character of this most remarkable Empire builder than the simple characterization of this eminent citizen who this morning lies cold in death, leaving behind him a heritage for the state he loved, and continuously toiled for. His works, the things he has accomplished, will be a blessing not only to his own, but to future generations.

The circle of Colorado pioneers is constantly narrowing.

Mr. Moffat was its most distinguished member. His mind was always on large enterprises. His hope was to make Colorado the greatest of the Western states, and to be at the head of the safest and largest financial institution in the Rocky mountain country.

They used to say he took his bank to bed with him, so deeply was he interested in its welfare.

At any rate there was nothing half-hearted in anything David H. Moffat did or started to do. And there was always much manna in the fields he garnered.

Born in the conservative East he came, in early life, to Colorado and soon became prominent in the history of the territory and later the state.

Perhaps the rugged majesty of our mountains, the tremendous grandeur of our vast plains and deserts of those days proved an inspiration to this remarkable man, who both lived and died Colorado's most notable citizen.

The Post believes that Mr. Moffat was one of those men whose wealth has a tendency to enlarge their sympathies, to fill them with good will, particularly toward all those whom they have known in less prosperous years. To such generous natures the loss of sympathy and friendship is a grievous deprivation. For the neglect of the rich on the part of the poor is quite as unjust and quite as hard to bear as the reverse condition.

There was certainly no insolence of riches in the make up of Mr. Moffat, no pride and superciliousness of wealth.

He had his failings, doubtless, as we all have, but he was a man possessed of sterling qualities, and his death will be deeply deplored by many who knew the numerous acts of unostentatious generosity he performed.

There were many things most splendidly unusual in his personal composition, among them, perhaps, the strange character of his enemies. To some natures the successful man has committed no sin except that of being successful.

Mr. Moffat demonstrated, personally, the truth of Carlyle's dictum, "the king is the man who can." He had faith in himself and his powers. He builded and bettered great enterprises. He wrote his name large in the history of the West and in the financial pages of the nation.

He was a most unusual citizen, a man of extraordinary acumen, and Colorado has reason to mourn him deeply and sincerely.

ODD LITTLE TALES OF DAVID H. MOFFAT RELATED BY FRIENDS

Wonderful Luck, Generosit and Keen Insight Into Business Recalled.

He Made $4,000,000 From a Tract Bough for Dumping Ground--Woman Once Saved Him From Assassination.

Many are the anecdotes that are related concerning David Mo fat. From the old-timers in Denver come varied and seemingly i exhaustible stories concerning his traits of character, his busin methods, his friendships, or ones dealing with incidents in his rise position and wealth.

Mr. Moffat was always exceedingly democratic in his ways. Th was one of his chief sources of popularity all through his care From this trait many anecdotes have arisen. But the man's chara ter afforded a fruitful field for the weaving together of odd litt tales. Some of these, as told by the dead financier's friends, follo

PAID $20,000 FOR A SEEMINGLY BAD CLAIM; MAKES $3,000,00

"THE luck of Dave Moffat," was a proverb among old-timers, many of whom had seen his Midas touch quicken into productive life enterprises that had been abandoned or forced to lie idle from one cause or another.

Nine-tenths of the old prospectors of a generation ago went first to Moffat with their finds. He knew them personally, the good and the bad, and they knew that if their prospects were good they would have no difficulty in getting a "stake" from him.

"Old Bill" Campbell was a familiar figure in the early days of Leadville, a prospector who tramped the hills with hammer and pan looking for "color." He located a group of claims that looked good to him and was able to convince Mr. Moffat that they were worth development. The banker advanced $20,000 to Campbell and waited for the returns which surface indications promised.

They failed, and finally Campbell c fessed failure. He went to Mr. Mof and explained that he was broken in sp and in pocket. His health was gone a he had no means of paying back the $20 that had been advanced to him. He fered Mr. Moffat the claims, which h been patented.

It was either that or nothing, and Moffat took over the claims, menta condemning the judgment that had p suaded him to give the $20,000 in the fi place.

Mr. Moffat put a shift to work on t claims and almost the first load of r taken out of the shaft showed phenome values. Development work was prosecu with double shifts and the Louisville mi the name Campbell had given his clai produced more than $3,000,000. It is c sidered even now one of the rich mi of Leadville, late development uncover mammoth bodies of zinc ore.

HIS LIFE SAVED BY WOMAN WHO LEARNED OF A PLOT TO KILL HI

"I ONCE saved David Moffat's life," stated Mrs. Caroline E. Downing, whose husband, the late Major Jacob Downing, knew the financier since boyhood days in the state of New York.

"It was many years ago, back when Davis H. Waite was governor of Colorado," continued Mrs. Downing, with a reminiscent shake of the head. "The miners at Leadville were clamoring for better conditions, the mine owners refused to come to their terms, and everybody who lived in the state at that time knows of the riots that kept that town in an uproar for a long time.

"David Moffat was one of the biggest mine owners, as was James J. Hagerman, for whom Hagerman Pass, on the Colorado Midland road, is named. Both these men refused to enter into any sort of agreement with the miners, and feeling against them ran high. At that time, my husband and I took our meals at the same hotel, and at the same table in a private dining room with Governor Waite and his wife, both of whom we knew very well. The conversation often was upon the subject of the situation at Leadville.

"Mrs. Waite grew somewhat confidential with me, and one day she sa 'Dave Moffat is going to be kille they're going to get him! He refuses make any move toward arbitration, he's going to be killed.' Her air of c viction convinced me that she had lear of some plan against his life, and wh I listened to her further remarks cha pioning the labor cause, I decided to w Moffat. I went to his daughter, M Marcia McClurg, and told her what had learned without telling her how had learned it. She said she made i point never to interfere in her fathe business.

"'But, Marcia,' I exclaimed, 'Do y understand that I am telling you y father is to be killed—to lose his li Do you consider that it would be interf ing to tell him that much? I know wh I say is the truth. He must see governor at once!'

"Well, the thing dawned on her, a she told her father that he must Governor Waite immediately. Mof found Hagerman and together they cal on the governor that night. Next d Moffat left for New York, where as mained for a number of weeks, until danger had passed."

LIFELONG FRIEND ASSERTS HE WAS ONE OF KINDEST HEARTED ME

IN THE death of David H. Moffat, Mrs. George W. Wigginton, who belongs to one of Denver's oldest families, mourns the loss of a life-long friend. Mrs. Wigginton's father, George T. Clark, was a Denver pioneer, and the cashier of the First National bank even before Mr. Moffat was interested in the concern.

When Mrs. Wigginton's mother—then Miss Kate Goss—married George T. Clark, the Moffats, then married only a few months, came to the wedding, and for many years the two families lived neighbors when the residence portion of Denver was what is now the heart of the business section.

"I cannot remember when I did not know Mr. Moffat," said Mrs. Wigginton, "for our families were the closest friends, and Marcia Moffat, Mrs. M Clurg and I were reared together.

Many people, who never saw Mr. M fat except on his way to the bank fr his home, said he was cold and unfrie ly. He was not cold at all. In his he there was never a kinder, more war hearted or generous man than Da Moffat.

"I remember when my brother, Fra Clark, was a little fellow of 9 or 10, a Mr. Moffat came to the house and h pened to ask the boy what he would l to have more than anything else—if wouldn't like to have a better gun th any boy in Denver.

"Frank was delighted, of course,

(Continued on Page 3—Col. 3)

Wealth Estimated $25,000,000

Mr. Moffat's wealth has been variously estimated all the way from $8,000,000 to $25,000,000. This latter figure is given in the Cosmopolitan magazine of a few years ago in its series, "Captains of Industry." Some of his closest friends think this figure overestimates his riches; others are sure he had at least that much.

Comparatively little of the Moffat wealth came from real estate. His holdings, aside from the First National bank and the International Trust company, are chiefly in the "Moffat Road," the Denver Union Water company, and his mining properties. He was formerly a heavy owner of Denver City Tramway property, but of late years had disposed of much of this and kindred interests.

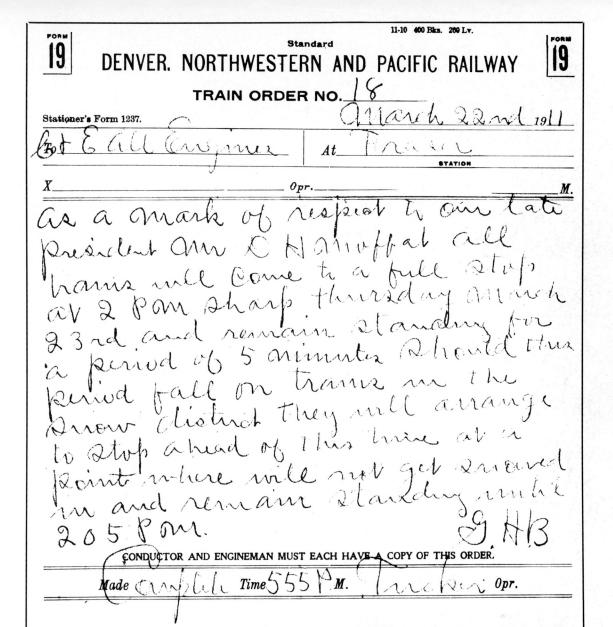

Form 19 Standard
DENVER. NORTHWESTERN AND PACIFIC RAILWAY
Form 19

11-10 400 Bks. 200 Lv.

TRAIN ORDER NO. 18

Stationer's Form 1237.

March 22nd 1911

To E All Engineer | At Tolland
STATION

X_____ Opr._____ M.

As a mark of respect to our late
president Mr D H Moffat all
trains will come to a full stop
at 2 PM sharp thursday March
23rd and remain standing for
a period of 5 minutes Should this
period fall on trains in the
Snow district they will arrange
to stop ahead of this time at a
point where will not get snowed
in and remain standing until
2.05 Pm.

G H B

CONDUCTOR AND ENGINEMAN MUST EACH HAVE A COPY OF THIS ORDER.

Made Complete Time 5.55 P.M. Tucker Opr.

The Denver Post tells the news, David Moffat is dead! Another Colorado pioneer is gone; an era in western railroading is closed but the Moffat Road will live on. The honors, the eulogies, the kind words were spoken far and wide but of these surely none could have been more fitting than the honor accorded David Moffat in the simple words of this train order (above) under which at exactly 2:00 PM, March 22, 1911, not a wheel turned anywhere on the Moffat Road as the men and women of his railroad paid their respects and said good-bye to Uncle Dave.

One of Moffat's favorite charities was the Oakes Home for T.B. patients. In his memory this plaque (right) was placed in the home. Half a century later Hugh Turpin found it stored in the organ blower room of St. John's Episcopal Cathedral of which Moffat was a vestryman. It is now preserved at the Colorado Railroad Museum thru efforts of Louisa Arps.—*left, Denver Post; right, DPL; above, Mrs. Louis Larsen, CRRM*

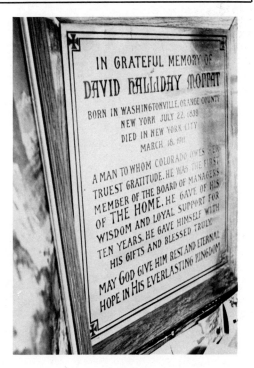

IN GRATEFUL MEMORY OF
DAVID HALLIDAY MOFFAT
BORN IN WASHINGTONVILLE, ORANGE COUNTY
NEW YORK JULY 22, 1839
DIED IN NEW YORK CITY
MARCH 18, 1911
A MAN TO WHOM COLORADO OWES HER
TRUEST GRATITUDE. HE WAS THE FIRST
MEMBER OF THE BOARD OF MANAGERS
OF THE HOME. HE GAVE OF HIS
WISDOM AND LOYAL SUPPORT FOR
TEN YEARS. HE GAVE HIMSELF WITH
HIS GIFTS AND BLESSED TRULY.
MAY GOD GIVE HIM REST AND ETERNAL
HOPE IN HIS EVERLASTING KINGDOM

171

1910
Denver, Northwestern & Pacific Railway.

Pass --:Mr. H. W. Conard:--
Chf.Clerk to Gen.Mgr.,Colo.Midland.

UNTIL DECEMBER 31ST 1910, UNLESS OTHERWISE ORDERED

N? B 139

W. H. Drul
GENERAL MANAGER

1915 N? C 658
Denver and Salt Lake Railroad Company

Pass - Mr. H. W. Conard & Wife
C. C. to Rec'r.,
ACCOUNT Colorado Midland Ry.

GOOD UNTIL DECEMBER 31ST 1915 UNLESS OTHERWISE ORDERED
NOT GOOD UNLESS COUNTERSIGNED BY

COUNTERSIGNED

W E Morse
VICE PRES. & GENERAL MGR.

Morning in Craig! "Zimms's Sacred Ox" as No. 11 was locally known, sits on the wye with a reefer — probably loaded with fresh beef and other perishables — the mail and express car and the unique coach-Pullman car *David Moffat*. In the station No. 2 is loaded and ready to depart for Denver, while a 200 class engine stands with tender towards the photographer, near the gilsonite storage sheds. The gilsonite was often shipped out on No. 12 in the evening. Sheeps wool is piled on the right awaiting loading.

A pair of passes (top) reflect the changed corporate structure of the Moffat Road with its new name and different officials. The passes are issued to Mr. Conrad of the Colorado Midland which by 1915 was only four years from abandonment. — *above, DPL; passes, CRRM*

172

13

The Road Ends at Craig

The Denver, Northwestern and Pacific Railway was never to build west of Craig. David Moffat died on March 20, 1911, trying to finance an extension from Steamboat to Craig and also the big tunnel. W. G. Evans took his place as president, having been vice-president since the organization of the road.

The death of Moffat shook D. C. Dodge and all of Moffat's friends who had come to his aid to complete the line to Steamboat. None had more to lose than Evans who had been the right hand of Moffat. He took over courageously and could now be seen as the great man he was.

H. A. Sumner, Chief Engineer, left at this time and this was also when George Barnes became superintendent.

It was not easy to get investors for the coal business when the Rollins Pass line could not give any better account in winter than it did, for this is when the coal companies had to have dependable service.

The Goulds were fighting for their lives with their own enemies and could not tolerate the new competitor that a tunnel might make of the Moffat.

Who would want to take sides and invest in the Moffat when the big dogs had one another by their throats? In fifteen months, with no investors in sight for the tunnel including the still reluctant Denver capital, the line went bankrupt.

D. C. Dodge and S. M. Perry became receivers. W. G. Evans now began a search for public funds for the tunnel. His faith in the line was never to end. He wanted the tunnel and as chairman of the Republican Party he would use his influence time

and again, though he was losing everything he had except some land holdings.

The receivership of Dodge and Perry ended in a reorganization eleven months later. The line was now the Denver and Salt Lake Railroad with Newman Erb as president.

There were three things Erb promised to do: to build the tunnel, to get the line started toward Craig, and to build the cutoff between Phippsburg and Hayden as proposed by H. A. Sumner. The cutoff would shorten the line by many miles and in effect, eliminate two legs of the triangle which the line forms as viewed on a map. This would mean a great deal when through trains were running to Salt Lake City. Erb challenged Denver to come up with two thirds of the needed funding and he would secure the last third.

Meanwhile Blauvelt, Sumner's assistant from the beginning, took over construction of the 41 miles of line to Craig. Of course the right-of-way had to be secured, but on the whole people cooperated and the line soon reached Mt. Harris where coal mines were opened.

Hayden was a well established community and received with gusto the coming of the first train. On Railroad Day the recently formed new county of Moffat sent a baseball team from the little town of Craig. They tied with Hayden but vowed to get even at Craig's Railroad Day.

In October, 1913, the rails passed the Cary Ranch with its 2700 acres of irrigated land and 11,700 acres of pasture.

John S. Cary and Robert Cary of the Mine and Smelter Supply Company used this ranch as a dude ranch and show place to entertain their guests and prospective customers for mining supplies.

Harry Farrington Carpenter as a college lad came out to spend his summers working on this ranch and worked his way up to ownership of a near-by ranch and leadership in the life of the state.

Hayden became the postoffice for Carpenter. This town had been laid out with the promise of the half-way division point between Denver and Salt Lake being located here.

It was November 19 at 3:00 p.m. when the rails touched the W. H. Rose place. For thirty-one years he had been expecting the railroad "the next year". All the school children of Craig had been let out and the business houses closed. Many old timers were on hand as the rails were laid. The engineer was obliging by letting the children, many of which had never seen a locomotive, into his cab. It was almost dark when the construction cars were empty and only one box-car left as the first train arrived at the site where the station, simply a box car, would be located.

This country had been too far from a railroad to develop. It was W. G. Evans and his sister Anne who thirteen years before had been so highly impressed with northwestern Colorado that they urged Moffat not to let Colorado down, but open this country with a railroad. How else could the country be developed? So we must understand all the excitement of this day.

The celebration was set for Saturday, November 22nd, but late in the afternoon on Thursday the biggest storm of the winter set in. Earlier in the afternoon snow would fall, then melt, turning the railroad area into a sea of mud. Friday night it began snowing again. Saturday morning the sun came out, melted the snow and increased the size of the mud puddle.

The four car train picked up passengers in Phippsburg, Steamboat Springs and Hayden, arriving late, but little Craig had its band there to welcome them in the mud. Since it was meal time, the guests (1600 of them) were assembled and fed in a remarkably short time. Pioneering was not dead here. People had stuck it out by careful planning and long hours of hard work.

Since the floats could not be dragged through the mud, shots were fired by the cowboys and all proceeded to the baseball game. The field was in a terrible condition, and in short time the players were as muddy as the field. Craig's star player sprained an ankle, but Dr. Wheeler, himself a great

ball player, was off on an emergency and unable to help out. Because most of the Craig players were working in the coal mines where a strike was taking place, they lost the game 33 to 0.

Late in the afternoon Number 1 arrived with the Marcia carrying railroad officials and a few Denver people.

Ada Honnold Jones writes of this era,

After the railroad came a homestead rush into the new County. People from many states and all walks of life in cities wanted 160 acres. They shipped livestock, horses, cattle, chickens and furniture. That first spring, many of them encountered their first hindrances of Homesteading and Pioneering.

When we had one of those late cold snowy springs, feed was scarce and very hard to get. Many were camped down by the railroad tracks. Everywhere was a sea of mud, and they were late that spring getting out to their claims. But as hard as life was for the homesteaders, there was a homesteader in every gulch.

Craig would some day find Ed Johnson running a grain elevator. The railroad men would move in the freight cars for the elevator and chat with the former railroad operator of the defunct Colorado Midland.

We will let United States Senator Edwin C. Johnson tell this himself:

"While I was manager of the Craig Milling and Elevator Company, Bill Freeman, the president, told me that outside of the coal companies at Oak Creek, Wadge, and Mt. Harris, that I was the heaviest shipper on the line. You will recall that I operated a farmers' cooperative and handled most of the shipments for Moffat County farmers.

"I recall that once I had a shipment of four cars of hogs stuck in a blizzard just outside a snowshed near Arrow or Corona for four days. When they reached Denver, many of them were dead and the balance in very bad condition. The loss was very heavy. The tunnel overcame that shipping hazard.

"The Moffat crews were good customers of the Co-op. I supplied them with flour, bran, grain, beans, eggs, chickens, honey, vegetables and all kinds of fruit from Vernal, Utah, and the Grand Valley country. I regret that I do not have a snapshot of those good old days.

"One day a tramp came down the railroad track with his bundle on the end of the traditional stick. He asked me how far it was to Salt Lake. I said, 'two hundred thirty-one miles,' but I didn't tell him that the rails only extended one mile west of the mill. He trudged on. In an hour he was back, mad as a hornet. I kept out of a fight by giving him a sack of apples and peaches and a nice ripe cantaloupe."

174

At the same time that all this was taking place in Craig, the railroad division point was moved from Fraser past Klondike siding to Tabernash. Here the railroad people found a cold reception. Tabernash, four miles north and down grade, was seven to ten degrees colder than Fraser. The confluence of Crooked Creek, Fraser River, and Ranch Creek made this spot the low area, where all the cold air of the mountains dropped. Freight trains were literally to freeze to the rails in Tabernash, when the thermometer dropped from forty to sixty degrees below zero.

Trains froze to the rails because of the frost fogs that hung over the community. The grease in the journals got too cold, when for some reason or other there was a tie-up on the pass and a freight would be left standing a few hours at night. The mallets would shove and tug and pull the train to pieces trying to get it loose from the rails. According to J. B. Culbertson, when it got to 65 or 70 degrees below zero, a train would freeze up while the mallets were being cut in.

But it was not too cold for Pastor A. A. Fonken to come down to serve the railroad men that he knew in Fraser or to go up to Western Box Sawmill out of Tabernash. He was as welcome to preach at the bar in Tabernash as he had been in Fraser. He was a firm believer in prohibition, but the men all knew that he loved them although he hated liquor. His saddle might be stolen from his horse; he might be too conscientious to accept an annual pass from the railroad because he did not want to be stopped from speaking in favor of labor, if the occasion demanded; but he did not stop his trips to lumber camps, the new town of Granby and the older town of Hot Sulphur, pedaling his bicycle down the wagon roads and pushing it up the hills.

The characteristic stories of Tabernash were like this one: Number Two had been held two days in Tabernash while the railroaders were trying to open a blockade. A prominent Eastern clergyman was on the train. When Sunday evening came, he approached with a suggestion that they hold a church service in the coach. As the railroad car had only very feeble oil lights, the word was passed around Tabernash to bring your hymn books and hay-burners (lanterns). With a rancher or two, railroaders and passengers crowded in that coach with lanterns hung from the baggage racks, a service was held. The people thumbed the indices of their different hymnals finding the hymns common to most of the song books. A quartette, composed of Conductor Charlie Clark, Bob Parrott, the black porter from the Pullman car, and one other man,

whose name is forgotten, led the singing. After the clergyman had preached the sermon and the lanterns had burned dim from the lengthy singing, a Negro spiritual was begun by the black porter.

"Some folks say that a preacher don't steal, but I found one in my corn field." The eastern clergyman held his sides as he laughed. The benediction was sung. The first religious service had been held in Tabernash in a railroad coach.

That night Number One got down the hill. Holladay was brakeman and also acted as baggageman. He left on the platform of Arrow the mail sack, not knowing that $55,000 was in it. It lay there all night. It was not stolen. This was the payroll for some lumber camps near by.

Another threat to the Moffat Road, although one which never materialized, is described by Art Weston who was a member of the locating party for the line.

I will now shift the scene to Wyoming and another railroad which I think could conceivably have ruined the fortune of the Moffat. In September, 1907, I went from Raton to Laramie where I secured a job as draftsman with the Laramie, Hahn's Peak and Pacific Railroad Company. This company had a track built thirty miles westerly across the Laramie Plains to Centennial. Their plans were to build across the Medicine Bow mountains into North Park, thence through Walden to a coal field at what is now Coalmont. This was finally accomplished about January 1, 1912. I remained with this company until the spring of 1913.

This line was being promoted by a Jew named Van Horn of Boston, Massachusetts. The president of the road was Fred A. Miller, who resided in Laramie. In 1910 they had Mr. J. J. Argo run a "preliminary" survey across the Continental Divide from the vicinity of Cowdrey via Pearl into the Encampment Creek drainage and across the Continental Divide between the Encampment Creek and the headwaters of Elkhead Creek, thence down this stream to Steamboat Springs. The idea was to tap the very high quality coal field on Deep Creek, north of Steamboat.

It would have been possible to build a two per cent grade line over this route and to cross the Divide at 10,500 feet above sea level. The length of this line from Laramie to Steamboat was one hundred eighty-seven miles. The Moffat was then operating over Corona Pass at an elevation of 11,666 feet, and the length over this route was two hundred fourteen miles. This indicates that the Wyoming road had by far the best route and had also the best coal market. Denver was not a good coal market, as it was already supplied by nearby mines. But the territory along the Union Pacific to

175

Omaha had no coal and was a good coal market.

It has always been my idea that if the promoters of the Laramie road had been able to finance and build this road, it might have been the last straw that broke the Moffat. At that time and for many years thereafter the Moffat was just barely kept alive under a receivership, and a strong competitor could have been the end of it. However, the Laramie road went into a receivership about the time it reached Coalmont and eventually it passed under the control of the Union Pacific. There were times in the years I am referring to that it looked as though the Moffat would be junked and probably it would not have stood the strain of a rival. But this is now all water over the dam; just another case of 'It might have been.'

But the rails did not reach Salt Lake except on the surveyor's map. Craig was the end of the line. The subsequent drilling of oil wells around Craig and later in the development of the Rangely Field, the hauling in of sheep's wool, and trucking in of gilsonite, spoke the truth of this great empire that would have had a railroad, but for the "kings" who did not want the competition for their resources or their lines.

Newman Erb held the presidency until September 16, 1915, when the stockholders became restless because of his inability to secure more capital to go further west. Erb had been backed by Dr. G. S. Pearson of London, England, who was president of the board, until he lost his life in the sinking of the Lusitania.

W. I. Hoklas recalls Pearson's visit:

"In 1915 I was in Mt. Harris, with an engineer friend—Crawford, when the passenger from Denver came into town with the Marcia (formerly Dave Moffat's private car) attached. My friend called my attention to it — said to me, 'George Pearson of London is in that car, he is looking the road over, is going to sell his interests in the Mexican Central and build this road on to Salt Lake.' George Pearson returned to New York, sailed on the ill-fated Lusitania, and was lost at sea. His son George came over — wound up all interests and took the money back to England."

Charles Boettcher became the new president. His loyalty as a bondholder who would not sell the line to any other interest is a story of reflected admiration of David Moffat's dream.

Gerald Hughes had refused the presidency saying he knew nothing about running a railroad. Lawrence C. Phipps, Sr., and Lawrence C. Phipps, Jr., joined these men in a pact not to sell Moffat stock or bonds, until the Moffat road was part of a transcontinental line. Bill Freeman was in the pact but near the end did not keep the pact. These men had caught the vision of Dave Moffat and realized there was only one way to build Denver, and that was to finish this road. Too much cannot be said for the loyal, hard-bitten tenacity of these men in the dark years that followed.

Bankers and financiers are frequently classified as hard-boiled men who see only dollars. As to how much sentiment for their friendship with Moffat played in this deal will never be known. Perhaps sentiment became a faith in a man that amazed them, a man who they knew must be right in his dream of building this road and an empire.

But bankruptcy followed with Boettcher and Wm. Freeman becoming trustees.

Moffat's friends had a trump that Bill Freeman would hold, until the day arrived when they would threaten to build a cut-off to connect with the Rio Grande.

176

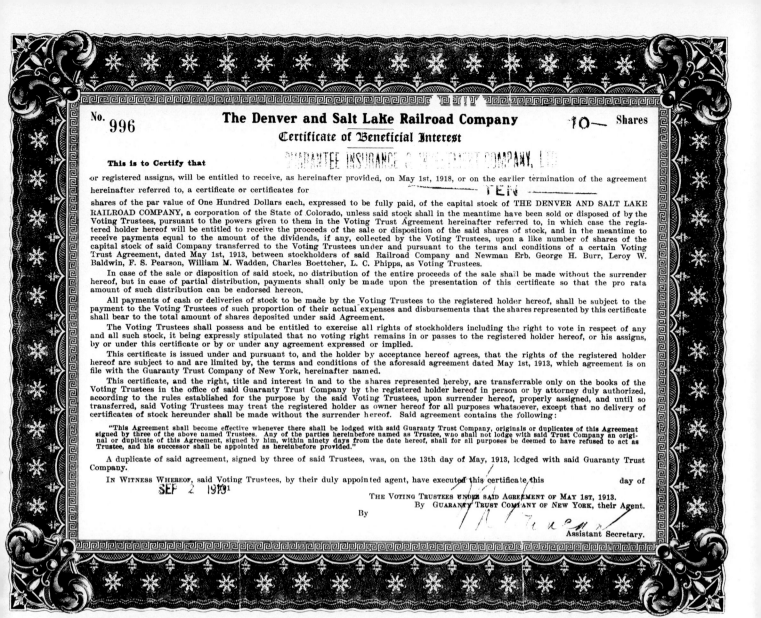

On May 1, 1913, the Denver, Northwestern & Pacific was reorganized as the Denver & Salt Lake Railroad and these certificates (above) were issued, later to be exchanged for stock in the new company. While the financial maneuvering took place, the rails continued westward and are seen (left and below) at the Bear River — now the Yampa — east of Hayden in the summer of 1913. Engine 21, pushing the track laying train, should soon be re-lettered with the new initials D. & S.L. — *above, CRRM; others, Chester Otis Bennett. DPL*

RAILROAD DAY IN HAYDEN! The cooks are busy preparing a hardy western meal while the crowd enjoys watching a good basketball game (left-center and bottom) and everyone waits for the train to come. The moment arrives (top-left to right) and the first train steams into town with three cars of ties, a caboose and two coaches bringing passengers from towns to the east. A few months later we see Hayden (below) with the passenger train passing in the distance. The high spring waters around some poorly constructed fills forced the use of the lightweight 390 and 391 as power on this end of the line. —*above-right, Farrington R. Carpenter: below, L. C. McClure: others Chester Otis Bennett: all, DPL*

CRAIG . . . at last!

Once again the Moffat Road was building west. The work train with the track laying machine is seen in these two photos (left) just west of Hayden. On November 19, 1913, the first train (left-bottom) crossed Fortification Creek and entered Craig. A Railroad Day celebration was set for November 22nd with a special train to bring celebrants from Yampa, Steamboat and Hayden. Its arrival (right-center photos) came in the midst of the first big snow of the year but nothing could dampen the festive mood of the day. The steel rails of the Moffat Road now linked northwestern Colorado with the rest of the nation and from the temporary box-car station at Craig (top-right) it suddenly seemed a much shorter distance to the business center of Denver with its warehouses (below) and markets for the goods of mine, farm and ranch. Uncle Dave would be happy today! — *below, Cullie Biggs Welch: right, right-top and opposite-bottom, Earl Blevins: left-center and top, Chester Otis Bennett: all, DPL; R.P.O., Mobile Post Office Society*

DENVER & CRAIG.
TR. 2
24
OCT
1914
R.P.O.

Business is good! A long train struggles up Rollins Pass near Loop, with borrowed Burlington & Missouri River engine 179 assisting on the point, evidence of the need to borrow power to handle the business. But the Moffat Road was plagued by the over-riding problem of Rollins Pass. The heavy grade, snow in winter and run-off from snow and springs causing heaving and mud slides the rest of the year. The workman is digging a ditch to help drainage and loads of cinders have been dumped to stabilize the track. — *L. C. McClure, CRRM*

14
Warning!
More Business Means Greater Loss

Charles Boettcher became president in September, 1915. Coal traffic was growing steadily now but Boettcher was concerned about the railroad's ability to handle this business. He asked W. E. Morse, a proven railroad general manager, to prepare a report relative to the necessity of building a main range tunnel. Mr. Morse submitted this data on January 21, 1916.

The report provided insight as far as wages were concerned. The idea of moving the terminal point to Granby was found to save nothing, for wage contracts were based on at least one hundred miles. The same applied to anything being gained through a longer tunnel because the wages would be the same from Denver to Tabernash.

The abbreviated report is presented here but a single statement by Mr. Morse offers dramatic proof of the problem the railroad faced. "It is clearly evident that as the density of traffic increases, the increased ratio of expense will essentially increase at a greater ratio than that of income."

REPORT OF W. E. MORSE
(Excerpts)
Traffic Development Necessitating Tunnel

From the foregoing statement of facts it is apparent that it will be impossible to develop the traffic beyond 20 to 25% and handle at any cost during the seven months of more or less adverse climatic conditions, and not more than 50 to 60% during the remaining most favorable five months of the year.

During the past twelve months six additional coal mines (with a present capacity of 3000 net tons and within another six months of 4000 net tons per day output) have been opened. Three additional mines will be opened in the next six months and in addition several of the oldest large mines have added to their faculty of production within the past year so that the capacity of the coal mines already open and in active operation is now 7500 tons and by September 1st, next will be conservatively 9000 net tons per day, which would mean to handle over 14,000 gross tons eastbound per day of coal alone, or an increase of 211% over the total business now being handled. It is not intended to convey that it is probable that the railroad will be called upon to handle an increased traffic of 211% per year for the next two years, but it is believed that if the railroad is prepared to provide reliable service throughout all periods of the year that the coal tonnage can be increased 150% within the next three years.

Inasmuch as the coal traffic is the predominating one and the advantageous market for the same is at the period when the railroad is contending with severe climatic conditions over the divide, it is clear that the larger percentage of development in coal traffic could be made in those seven months of coal consumption period provided the railroad could handle it.

Our coal operators at this writing are several thousand tons behind their orders and are not, and never have been, in position to actively solicit business except in summer months when practically all the business is storage business taken at reduced prices more or less unremunerative. I mention these facts only to indicate the encouragement to future investors and the possible avenue for increased investment and increased activity of the coal operators already located upon the line if instead of the busines soliciting them they could solicit the business and at a time when people wanted coal and were willing to pay a good price for it.

We cannot in reason anticipate increased investment or expect greater activity in commercial development of any substantial sort along the line of the railroad *unless a tunnel is provided and facilities* afforded to *insure reliable service 12 months of the year. . .*

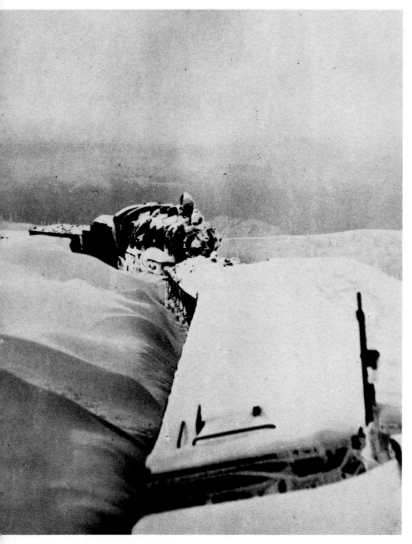

The Moffat Road's Archilles heel was the line over Rollins Pass. Snow often delayed traffic and on occasion completely blocked the line as in this scene during a 1918 tie-up. The line's future lay with coal traffic from mines such as the McGregor at Milnor (right) where a gondola shortage has forced the use of box cars for coal loading. — *right, L. C. McClure: both, CRRM*

Estimated Tunnel Expense
2.6 Mile Tunnel

As per report of Chief Engineer Blauvelt attached, the estimated expense of the above tunnel proper based upon bid already received from reputable and reliable contractors is,
.... $1,345,113.00
Construction approaches
to tunnel   1,159,255.00
TOTAL   2,504,368.00

Details of above expenditure contained in Chief Engineer's report. This tunnel eliminates all 4% grade, all curvature in excess of 10°, and all the serious snow and adverse climatic conditions at present encountered. Eliminates all present snow sheds and would require only short snow sheds, if any; reduce the mileage 8.42 miles between Tolland and Tabernash.

This tunnel can be successfully operated with steam power by transfer of the present ventilating plant from Corona to the tunnel, estimated length of time to construct tunnel and approaches 22 months.

For the period January 1st, 1917, to January 1st, 1918, the gross tonnage is estimated at 2,438,000 provided the railroad *could handle* over present line which is doubtful, but if handled would be at almost prohibitive expense, but for the purpose of comparison is estimated to cost to handle over present line ....$826,500.00 or $8.07 per 1000 gross ton miles.
Estimated cost to handle through 2.6 mile tunnel
....$225,300.00
or $2.72 per 1000 gross ton miles.
An aggregate saving of ....$601,200.00.

Estimated Tunnel Expense
4 Mile Tunnel

No reliable estimate of time to construct can be made account excessive tunnel length but at any reasonable cost would consume at least 42 months. It is probably unsafe to estimate the expense of this tunnel and approaches at less than
....$4,250,000.00
as the excavation of tunnel without mishap would likely increase the cost to this aggregate.

Economics of Tunnel Operation

Based upon present costs of labor and material facilities and appliances for the calendar year January 1st, 1915 to January 1st, 1916, there was handled 1,696,000 gross tons between Tolland and Tabernash at an expense of $487,000.00, or $6.84 per 1000 gross ton miles, all costs included. With the 2.6 mile tunnel this gross tonnage is estimated to be handled at an expense of $171,300.00 or per 1000 gross ton miles of $2.97, indicating a net saving of $315,700.00.

Estimated expense to handle with 4 miles tunnel ....$142,400.00 or $3.23 per 1000 gross ton miles, indicating an aggregate saving over present line ....$344,600.00 and over the 2.6 mile tunnel of $29,900.00

This computation has been made from actual operation and are not theoretical or estimated as concerns any important features, or that would materially influence the result. Indeed the figures are regarded if anything ultra conservative.

The results indicated assuredly warrant tunnel construction not only as an economic proposition applied to the present mileage and the present traffic, but become increasingly attractive considering the future possibilities regarded in the most conservative manner.

It would be my recommendation to construct the four mile tunnel provided the same can be financed and construction started within 60 days. In fact it is seemingly imperative that *some* tunnel be started at once if the development of this property is to continue and if it's financial status is to be maintained or improved. Competition is keen and is likely at any time to become more acute as concerns revenue per ton mile upon the commodity which represents our principal tonnage. Prices of material of all classes are constantly and rapidly increasing. Wages gradually being forced upwards and rates in adverse direction, and no railroad can hope to indicate satisfactory results and operate 4% grades and 16° curvature even with favorable climate, much less so when those adverse conditions are augmented by the most serious snows, gales, and slides, almost continuous for seven months of the year. The more tonnage undertaken to handle under these unfavorable conditions the less net revenue will result after such tonnage reaches a reasonable amount, and that limit has in our opinion been nearly or quite attained for the seven month period named.

The property has a wonderful future if provided with reasonable facilities to expand its revenue and handle the same with proper regularity and expense. Without such provision I cannot predict a satisfactory outcome.

Yours respectfully,
(SGD) W. E. Morse
Vice-Pres. & Gen'l. Mgr.

Charles Boettcher was in the working shoes of David Moffat. Did he see the fortune that would soon be made in meeting the demand for oil and coal in Routt County? Boettcher had seen coal train after coal train being added.

At this time Boettcher must have had all his cash invested in good securities as well as all those men and their sons who had been with David Moffat. They never once thought of selling their securities to prove their faith in this coal road as a war approached. If they would not risk their investments, how could they expect ordinary or out-of-state investors to do so? Or were they just realists to the unscrupulous power of Jay Gould and Harriman?

186

Coal and Oil, New Business for the Moffat

That the future of the Moffat Road lay in hauling the rich energy resources along its line, has been proven by the energy boom of the 1970's. The beginning of this traffic can be seen in photos of the Oak Creek Mine (below) and the Colorado-Utah Coal Mine (left-bottom) at Mt. Harris with rows of miners homes visible in the background. Some of the larger mines had their own locomotives to switch at the mine, such as this 0-6-0 (right) of the Edna Coal Co. While oil traffic never developed near the extent of the coal business, it has been steady traffic as in this photo (left) of an almost solid train of tankers en route from Craig to Denver. — *left, L. J. Daly, DPL; right, Richard Kindig; others, L. C. McClure: all, CRRM*

The battle to keep traffic moving over Rollins Pass strained the railroad to the breaking point. It was an operation costly in equipment, men and the endless delays to traffic. It was a good day on the hill when a plow could lead a train without delay (right) to the shed at Corona, but the brakemen on the train in this scene (below) are signalling a "break in two" which may mean a long delay and while the rotary has recently cleared the line, the wind can come up at any time and quickly drift around the stalled train. Another train (bottom) is led by a rotary with five engines for power as it inches upward near Ranch Creek in 1924. If they reach the safety of Corona snowshed they then must contend with the terrible gas from the smoke of five engines. — *right, A. L. Johnson: below, Joe Preiss: both, CRRM; bottom, Joe Preiss, DPL*

Forest products have been important business for the Moffat from the start with much traffic coming from Middle Park. However, a somewhat unusual contributor of lumber traffic was the Jenkins Lumber Co. which built a narrow gauge line from Newcomb (bottom) which is just east of the present site of East Portal, to the Jenkins Saw Mill, a few miles southwest up South Boulder Creek. A homemade, upright boiler locomotive (right) provided power up this rickety track with the return run mostly downhill with the loaded cars. The gentleman seated along the track is Professor Ramaley, a long-time summer resident of the area and teacher at the University of Colorado, Botany Department's Mountain Laboratory which meet at Tolland. — *all, DPL*

The interior of Corona snowshed on a fine day in Indian summer after a light snowfall. Winter winds will soon drive snow thru every crack to build a wall of snow between the shed and the path cut by passing trains. This left little room for a man in the shed to avoid a passing train and when several engines occupied the shed at once, the gas and smoke could become deadly. — *Joe Preiss, DPL*

15

Cheating Death on the Moffat

Railroading on the Moffat was dangerous and only quick thinking allowed men to cheat and stay alive.

George Barnes told the author this story in the home of W. W. Rush with Bob Bishop listening and offering suggestions and corrections. The story is also varified by the diary of the General Manager and the letter press of H. A. Sumner.

After the first winter the short snowshed at Corona had grown to cover the wye, the long passing track, as well as the main line. In fact, the shed had been extended a half mile further west of the passing track.

The terrible winters had borne out the prediction of a man by the name of Marsh, who had said that it was against God Almighty to build a road over Rollins Pass. It was nothing unusual for the entire pass to be drifted twenty feet deep leaving Corona inundated with snow, as some valley community is during a flood.

But no shed could keep the wind-driven snow from sifting through the cracks and nail holes. Plenty of snow had to be removed by the section men and rotary. The shed was so big and the storms so frequent that the western half mile of the single track shed was cleaned only wide enough for the trains with no clearance on the sides for a man to stand.

This snow froze solid on the sides of the track in the shed leaving a ledge on top of it, which on the day of this story was seven feet above the track.

George Barnes, as conductor of Number Two, was bringing his passenger train up the west side of the pass.

The train had been coupled in behind a three-engine freight, which had a rotary plow. They lost so much time in the snow, that Barnes was worried because of a second freight train, which was following them by fifteen minutes.

As they entered the Corona shed, Barnes prayed that the head engines would pull them through to the east end of the shed before stopping, lest the second train plow into his frail wooden passenger cars in the blinding smoke of the shed.

But the rotary crew signaled a stop at the first water plug and coaling station, though provisions were made for water and coal further ahead.

Barnes sent his flagman into the gas filled shed.

Ventilators (smoke stacks) had been built every few feet to carry the smoke out, but when a half dozen engines got in there belching forth gas and smoke, the shed was an inferno. Men passed out in the gas, and it became a dreaded place.

Section men were warned and ordered not to walk through the sheds even during storms, for fear they would get caught in the meat grinder blades of a rotary plow coming in the sheds. But who wants to walk out in a howling blizzard? Men would gamble, take chances, and lose. They have been known to be caught by the cylinder of some engine, as they crouched on the side of the wall. The remains would be picked up in apple boxes.

Now the flagman was Jim Baker a new man, whom Barnes immediately realized was unfamiliar with this shed. So Barnes dashed out with lantern and fuzee.

As Barnes raced down the snowhed, the gas was

so bad that his lantern went out. He passed the brakeman standing on the track without seeing him.

Barnes could hear the second freight train coming in the rear of the shed. He lit a fuzee and stopped under a ventilator. There the air was better, and there he was able to see the snow bank on the sides above him on which he could stand, if he could get up there. He made a jump for the place and fell back. He spied a bridge spike on the wall of the shed. If he could somehow make a lunge for the spike and grab it, he would not be ground up. He could hold on and brace himself on the snow and attempt to throw the fuzee into the cab of the freight engine as it passed.

Panting in the high altitude air and coughing from the gas, Barnes made a second desperate lunge, grabbed the bridge spike, and pulled himself up on the ledge of snow, just as the engine came up on him. The smoke from the passing engine caused him to cough violently, so that he could not throw the fuzee, but he did yell, as only a desperate man can yell. He heard the engine stop puffing, for Ernest Anthony, the engineer, had closed the throttle. As the cab passed, he could hear the fireman ask, "What's the matter?"

Anthony replied, "I thought I heard a man yell."

Barnes was now opposite the first freight car. He climbed from the snow to the top of the car, crawled over the top to the front, and felt his way down the car's ladder. Coughing in the gas of Anthony's engine, he climbed up the ladder of the tender, crawled over the tank up the coal pile, and slid down the coal to the floor of the cab. He yelled, "For God's sake, don't move. I don't think you have run over my flagman." Coughing and gasping for breath, he told Ernest Anthony of the new flagman standing out there protecting his train.

"Now, don't move, no matter who tells you to move, until I come back."

Barnes crawled out the forward window of the cab of the 115 and walked ahead on the runway to the front of the engine. What this gas must have been, we can only guess, for down on the track it had been heavy enough to put out his lantern. He climbed down the front of the engine and fumbled his way back. He literally bumped into his flagman, who was faithfully standing on the track, as Barnes had ordered. Jim Baker could not have been seen or heard by the engineer, and he would have had no escape from the meat grinder.

Barnes and Jim Baker walked back to the pay car which was the last car of the passenger. They sat down and rested. Barnes knew that between the train of coal ahead with the brakes set, and a three-engine train behind, that the wooden coaches of his train would have collapsed, and a fire would have burned alive the passengers that had not been killed in the rear-end collision. The passenger train could not have been bumped ahead by the crash, for the coal train would have held it immovable.

Both of the men were black from smoke and soot, their lanterns out, when they passed through the coaches. The passengers were innocent of the danger from which they had miraculously been saved.

Barnes was so done up, when he reached the baggage car, that he had to rest again. Opening the door in the far end of the baggage car, he crawled up over the tender of his engine to tell his crew what had happened. From there he crawled out the cab window along the side of the boiler on the running board of the engine, which is above the drive wheels. Then he went in the caboose ahead and blew up about what had happened. He proceeded out the far door of the caboose and crawled over the coal and freight cars to the center malley. We need not repeat the story of gas, the fumbling, the trembling of nervous hands, the panting for breath, and his opinion of the idiots up ahead.

He finally reached the snowplow mallet, where he exploded to the snowplow conductor, whom he had trained as a brakeman. There were no words left in all of hell, when Barnes got through, and God Almighty must have wished there had been more such words.

He looked up the conductor of the freight, whom he had trained as a brakeman under him. The man said the snowplow needed coal. Barnes replied, "You could have pulled ahead as usual, cut off, and got your coal from the dock on the passing track ahead. Or you could have pulled on the passing track and let our train run around you. You could have come to stop right at the coal dock and water plug in that case."

Barnes said he would go to the Big Boss with this. The plow conductor mumbled that he just wanted enough coal and water, so that they could get down the other side and back. There is no question that by this time everyone was scared. For who had ever heard Barnes pour out all hell before?

Now Barnes had to repeat his performance of

getting back to Ernest Anthony's engine. He wanted Anthony to back his train up enough so that it could go in on the siding. But Anthony said that the blizzard was so bad that they would be helplessly stuck, if that were attempted.

The mess was untangled, but Barnes did not recover easily from his narrow escape from the meat grinder wheels of the 115. It was weeks until he was calmed down. After this Barnes would never take his train over the pass between two freight trains. He no longer cared if he lost hours; he was not going through that experience again.

"This," Barnes says, "was my most miraculous escape from death." This was devotion, clear mindedness, quick action, and an all out dash that kept the Moffat road intact, with "no passengers killed, no passengers seriously injured." Brakemen broken in under Barnes, as with Clark, Holladay and Pierson, inherited the fear of blockades and snowsheds, and they too were trained to take all precautions.

On August 16, 1917, the name of W. R. Freeman appeared with Charles Boettcher as receivers. Freeman was the General Manager but the men quickly found no hope in his management as conditions worsened decidedly.

Not all men were as lucky as Barnes had been as we see in this tragic report of the death of R. H. May. It begins with the account of hard riding engines that burned too much coal which was back-breaking to the fireman. The crews of the early days that had not fled to conditions of better lines wondered if they were fools. New men, willing to go through hell rather than be without a job, worked under these conditions.

The following account was written by M. McGlone, the Secretary-Treasurer of the Brotherhood of Locomotive Firemen and Engineers. He wrote this in a letter to Timothy Shea, Acting President of the Brotherhood on August 26, 1919, from Tabernash.

Conditions on the Denver end of the line are not so bad. But there are a few hard-steaming engines and a few hard riders. Firemen will burn from 16 to 20 tons on a train from Denver to Corona, a distance of 65 miles through 32 tunnels and 6 snow sheds. The condition of the sheds are bad and the one at Corona in particular. There have been a number of Brothers gassed and burnt in this shed and one of them died.

As I was on the Engine that Fireman R. H. May died on I can give you exact facts of the case which are as follows:

Called at Tabernash for 2 p.m. left at 3:05 p.m. and arrived at Corona at 11:20 p.m. We had fol-lowed a train into the shed, both trains consisted of three engines each. Train that we were helping was stopped so that our engine was just at the end of the double track and the narrow part of the shed without ventilation. We had stood ther [sic] about 15 mins. when the gas and smoke beacme [sic] so thick that it extingushed the oil troch [sic] that I had burning on the oil tray also putting out the lanterens. [sic] The fireman said that it was sure getting thick and that he was getting weak. I gave him a cup of Coffee that I had made before going into the shed. He was then so weak that he could not take the cup from me. I held him so that he could drink it, he getting weaker all the time. I picked him up and laid him with his head out the gangway. So that I could fan what fresh air I could to him. I felt myself getting weak so I laid him back against the coal gate and started to get to my side of the cab and whislte [sic] for help. And so place myself that if I did go under I would not fall against the fire box or doors.

Instead of getting to my side of the cab I fell out of the gangway. So that I lay with one of my legs under the tank hose and the other one over it. This was the condition that I found myself when coming to. When I got back in the cab Fireman was still breathing a little but still out. I look at my watch it was 1:55 a.m. So you can see that I was out about 2 hours. The fireman from the rear helper had walked over the train. I called to him to get me some help.

While he was walking to the head of the train. Train started to pull up so that they could out [sic] the helper. Which takes about 20 minutes. As it is impossible to see or walk except between the rails when there are any trains in the shed and there were three trains this night.

This shed has always been considered not safe to make meets in. The former Management agreed that only in extreme cases of emergency would any meets be made there. But even after this case had happened present dispatchers continued to make meets at this point.

(Note that J. B. Culbertson had been fired at this time but would come back at a later date.)

The helper firemen are required to run their own engines at this point. Which is very unsafe. As the snow and ice will pile up so that man has to stand on the rear tank sill as snow and ice will not clear him on the [sic] so has to ride on sill to keep from being drug of tank. They are not clothed to get down and dig out switches and ride around this shed after firing an engine up the hill which means anywhere from 10 to 16 hours without anything to eat. So you can see that it is very easy for them to be overcome while in this condition.

On the second district out of Tabernash Every [sic] train is a local and men can not get anything to eat after 10:00 p.m. at any point between

Phippsburg and Tabernash. There are two engines that are burning 25 to 30 tons of coal, 408, 409. The Coal chutes at Kremmling are not safe as the men above shovle [sic] from 8 to 6 tons of coal off the chute aprons. Chutes not high enough. To let coal roll on the tank. There are not any conditions here where men can wash or change Clothes.

These were the men as well as those on the front who were to win a war. The guise of war has often been an excuse to cut back on safety and comfort for employees. Don't say these men would rather live in the poor house or take up a life of crime. These were the true red-blooded Americans that made this country.

The Moffat Road constantly faced the problem of braking trains on the terrible four percent grades on Rollins Pass. A typical case was one which occurred on Arpil 24, 1917, when eastbound freight Extra 118 ran out of control after the train had made a stop at Yankee Doodle Lake. A short way down the hill the train crashed.

The report of the Interstate Commerce Commission states, "It is therefore believed this accident was due to the error in judgment on the part of the engineman Dittman in failing to apply the air brakes soon enough after his train started from the place where it was stalled. He stated that he made the first application when the speed was from two to four miles an hour. Student engineer Morse, however, stated that the speed was about eight miles an hour when the engineman first applied the brakes. The testimony of all the employees of Extra 118 who were interviewed was to the effect that engineman Dittman controlled the speed of the train very well up to the point where it stalled. But as he immediately lost control after starting the train from that place, it is apparent that he permitted the speed to become too great before applying the brakes. The margin of braking power for the weight of this train was entirely too small to permit its safe control on a four percent grade."

There had been considerable progress made in air brake technology during the early years of the century and especially important to mountain railroads was the development of the tripple valve in 1909. This permitted the use of retainers, meaning that the brakes are retained or prevented from releasing completely.

Even with such improvements accidents continued to be frequent and took the lives of countless men and also caused much property damage. In view of this President Freeman agreed to cooperate with the Westinghouse Air Brake Company in conducting tests on Rollins Pass, using an ex-

194

perimental Automatic Straight Air Brake.

On August 10, 1921, what was considered a very heavy train on the Moffat — 2431 tons — was made up to test the new brakes. The train moved from Idlewild with seven locomotives and or course, no end of time was lost at Ranch Creek tank as each had to take water. The train arrived at Rollins Pass in the Vorona snowsheds where six of the locomotives were removed. One engine, a Consolidation (locomotive with 2-8-0 wheel arrangement), then brought the train down. The first problem occurred after the train slipped through Needle's Eye Tunnel at milepost 62.5 which was in a reverse curve just west of Dixie Lake. But the problem was only that there had been too heavy a reduction of air brakes. As soon as the air brakes were pumped up, about three minutes, the train proceeded down to Dixie Lake siding where the usual brake inspection was made. The crew carefully went over the train, feeling the temperatures of every wheel. They found that even with their fingers they could touch the wheels without discomfort. This was in contrast to the usual experience in which the wheels would become cherry red and the train would stand at Dixie Lake to cool the brakes.

The train proceeded to Antelope where another inspection stop was made. The brakes on two cars were then cut out, leaving thirty two cars with brakes to handle thirty five cars, since the brakes on the caboose also were not working. It was found in the inspection that after twenty seven minutes all of the wheels were uniformly warm without discomfort to the touch, a distance of three inches in from the tread. An emergency brake application was made on the two percent grade after the train left Ladora. It was very smooth and without the usual slack action bumping between the cars. The train then continued to Denver with two more stops en route to inspect the wheels.

As far as the Moffat Road was concerned, this test proved that such a brake was quite practical. However, little is known of this proposed system today and it seems very likely that the cost of changing the brakes on the entire fleet of American railroad cars was simply too great to permit serious consideration of such a change. All records of the tests and development of these brakes were ruined when water from fighting a fire leaked into the basement where they were stored at Purdue University.

When we consider the tragic accidents that occurred on the Moffat and many other mountain railroads, we realize how important these improved brakes might have been if the tests made that summer day had only been carried forth to develop the new system.

Loose rocks might crash down to the track at any time and this was the case when engine 115 (above) was caught and derailed. In this 1906 photo (left) engine 302 has hit a slide and is too close to the edge for the comfort of the train's passengers. Egeria Cañon was the location of this massive slide (far left) caused by spring rains. Powder kegs wait on the flat car as officials discuss their plans with a ''powder man'' before starting the cleanup. — *above, Billy Rush: others, Joe Preiss: all, CRRM*

Brotherhood of Locomotive
Tabernash Lodge, No. 859
Firemen and Enginemen

EQUIPMENT ON ENGINES

1 Pair Wrecking Frogs
1 Bull Chain
1 Scoop Shovel
1 Coal Pick
1 Broom
1 Clinker Hook
1 Ash Hoe
1 Water Bucket
1 Shaker Bar
1 Red Lantern
1 White Lantern
2 Tallow Pots
1 Hand Oiler
2 Pair Wrecking Frogs on Mallet Engines

TOOLS FOR ENGINEERS' TOOL BOXES

1 Hand Hammer
1 Soft Hammer
1 12-inch Monkey Wrench
1 15-inch Monkey Wrench
1 No. 2 Alligator Wrench
1 No. 4 Alligator Wrench
1 9½-inch Air Pump Wrench
1 8½-inch Cross Compound Wrench
1 Loose Nose Spanner Wrench
1 Packing Iron
1 Packing Hook
1 Lubricator Wrench, Bull's Eye
1 Flat Chisel
1 Cape Chisel
1 Torch

EQUIPMENT ON CABOOSES

1 Axe
1 Bar, Claw
1 Bar, Pinch
2 Brasses, 4¼ x 8
2 Brasses, 5 x 9
1 Bucket, Water
1 Bucket, Dope
4 Burners, Lantern
2 Burners, Blizzard
1 Burner, Lamp
1 Broom
1 Can H.L. Oil (2 gal)
1 Can Sig. Oil (2 gal.)
1 Can Car Oil (5 gal.)
1 Chain Switch
1 Chest, Medical
1 Chisel, Cold
1 Cup, Tin
1 Coupling, 3 Link
1 Extinguisher, Fire
2 Flags, Green
2 Flags, Red
1 Funnel
12 Fusees
1 Globe, Red (extra)
2 Globes, White (extra)
6 Gaskets, Air Hose
1 Hammer
1 Hatchet
2 Hose, Air
2 Hose, Air, Dummy

1 Hose, Air, Tail
1 Hook, Packing
1 Iron, Packing
1 Jack, Journal and Bar
4 Keys, Brake Shoe
1 Knuckle, Tower
1 Knuckle, Climax
1 Knuckle, R.E. Janney
1 Knuckle, Trojan
1 Knuckle, Emergency
1 Lamp Cupola
4 Lanterns, White
2 Lanterns, Red
2 Lamps, Blizzard
1 Oiler, Car
2 Picks, Track
2 Pins, Knuckle
2 Replacers, Car
1 Saw, Hand
4 Shoes, Brake
1 Shovel, Fire
6 Shovels, Track
6 Shovels, Snow (in winter)
1 Sledge (10 lb.)
1 Spike Maul
10 Lbs. Spikes, Track
24 Torpedoes
2 Wedges, Journal, 4¼ x 8
2 Wedges, Journal, 5 x 9
5 Lbs Waste
1 Wrench, Track
1 Wrench, 18-in. Monkey

ARTICLE 1.

Section 1.—Engine Classification.

Class 1. Simple engines of 137,000 pounds or less on drivers.

Class 2. Simple engines over 137,000 pounds on drivers.

Class 3. Mallet Articulated Compound engines.

Section 2.—Rates of Pay.

FIRST DISTRICT.

Class 1. Engineers, $5.10 per day, 5.10 cents per mile; Firemen, $3.55 per day, 3.55 cents per mile.

Class 2. Engineers, $5.70 per day, 5.70 cents per mile; Firemen $3.90 per day, 3.90 cents per mile.

Class 3. Engineers, $6.50 per day, 6.50 cents per mile; Firemen $4.18 per day, 4.18 cents per mile.

To many of the men the union was their hope for better working conditions. Life was tough on the Moffat Road as evidenced by the low pay scale, the list of very necessary tools for the engine and caboose, and the primitive facilities such as the bath house (bottom-left) at Tolland where we see — from left to right — Louis Larsen, his fireman Walt Smith and an unidentified gent after finishing their run. In winter the worst problem was the smoke and gas trapped in the sheds as in these scenes at Corona with only the pole tops visible and smoke curling from the sheds. We share the view that Moffat men saw (bottom) as they entered and left the sheds. — *above, DPL; below-right and bottom-opposite, Mrs. Louis Larsen: below and bottom, Joe Preiss and all others, CRRM*

World's Best Brakes

The Westinghouse Air Brake Co. arranged to use the Moffat Road to conduct tests using an experimental Automatic Straight Air Brake system. On August 10, 1921, a test train of over 2400 tons was made up with five engines and is seen (opposite-center) ready to start up the 2% grade to Irving. There, two mallets were added and the entire train stopped (opposite-bottom) to take water at Ranch Creek. Upon reaching Corona all engines except 2-8-0 No. 117 were removed. This one locomotive then took the train down the pass safely and with complete control. Moffat officials pose with their inspection car (right) alongside the test train at Jenny Lake; left to right are Airbrake Inspector Ainsworth, President Freeman and General Supt. M. L. Phelps. The train is seen again at Newcomb (below) as the tests were nearing completion. While highly successful, the system never went into general use. The Moffat, however made considerable use of a "water brake", seen in operation (opposite) on engine 300. Saturated steam piped out just above the water line lubricated the cylinders which in reverse operation were provided a steady compression of power against the drivers. — *opposite-top and center, CRRM: others, State Historical Society of Colo.*

This is how a mallet looked to the engine crew! Stokers were eventually added but until then it was sometimes necessary to have two firemen to feed the double fireboxes. — *CRRM*

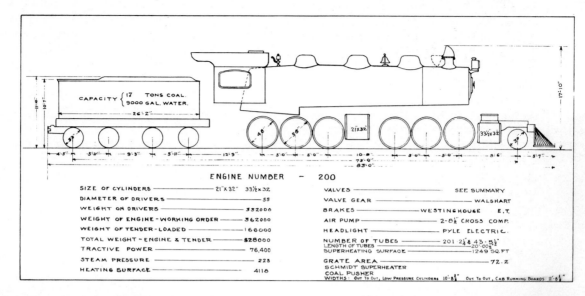

ENGINE NUMBER — 200

SIZE OF CYLINDERS	21"x32" 33½x32	VALVES	SEE SUMMARY
DIAMETER OF DRIVERS	55	VALVE GEAR	WALSHART
WEIGHT ON DRIVERS	332000	BRAKES	WESTINGHOUSE E.T.
WEIGHT OF ENGINE-WORKING ORDER	362000	AIR PUMP	2-8½ CROSS COMP.
WEIGHT OF TENDER-LOADED	166000	HEADLIGHT	PYLE ELECTRIC.
TOTAL WEIGHT ~ ENGINE & TENDER	528000	NUMBER OF TUBES	201 2¼ & 43 - 5½
TRACTIVE POWER	76,400	LENGTH OF TUBES	20'-00½
STEAM PRESSURE	225	SUPERHEATING SURFACE	1249 SQ. FT
HEATING SURFACE	4118	GRATE AREA	72.2

SCHMIDT SUPERHEATER
COAL PUSHER
WIDTHS : OUT TO OUT, LOW PRESSURE CYLINDERS 10'-8½" OUT TO OUT, CAB RUNNING BOARDS 11'-8½"

16

Pranks and Miracles of the Famous 200's

It is part of our American ballyhoo and way of doing things to have the longest bridges, the tallest buildings, and the most powerful engines.

No one thing is more characteristic of the Moffat than the two-engines-in-one, 200 class mallets, (Mallet is the correct word but Moffat boys said "Malley") built by American Locomotive Works after the style of "Old Maud" on the Baltimore and Ohio.

The first 200 engine was ordered in November of 1908, as the rails were being pushed by Colonel Dodge into Steamboat. Enthusiasm was running strong among the railroad men so that when these engines, the most powerful in Colorado, arrived the boys took great pride in them. A mallet has two sets of drive wheels. The first set can swing under the boiler to enable the engine to go around curves.

The Moffat had plenty of sharp, sixteen-degree curves on the branch line over the hill, with plenty of heavy four per cent grades.

When the Moffat was built, she had in fact, modern engines. The little six-wheel switch engines were described by a Union Pacific official on the first run as "most powerful mogul." The eight-wheel consolidations were in keeping with that type of power all over the country. Even the much-joked-about four-year-old Chesapeake Beach, re-numbered 390 and 391, compared favorably to the Pennsylvania Railroad passenger engines of that day.

Engine 200 immediately replaced the six-wheeled switch engine and the consolidation eight-wheeled engine which had been used to push the rotary.

Men could say one hundred and one hundred makes two hundred. The mallets were not quite that powerful, but they did turn out 76,400 pounds tractive effort, having been delivered at a cost of $33,045 and weighing 363,000 pounds.

The first 200 was very satisfactory, except that it needed a pony truck placed ahead of the front set of drive wheels. The following year three more engines came out as sisters made from the same plans and patterns costing $29,805. The lower cost likely came from the fact that blueprints were at hand.

But with the increased size of engines came the increased difficulty in re-railing them. The Moffat had hesitated to buy a wrecking crane because of financial difficulties. The much-feared jam came on a February day, when Engine 201 got out of control above Antelope and turned over on her side with the tender and three freight cars shooting through the air like sky rockets, trimming the tops off the trees.

For several days freight was carried around the wrecked 201 and passengers had to walk around the monster that lay helplessly on its side.

George Thompson was the master mechanic for the road. He was a good mechanic and designed the road's only specially designed engine, Engine 303. But George Thompson did not have nerve to think about setting the 201 on her feet again without a wrecker.

Although aware that a feud existed between Thompson and Barnes, Superintendent Deuel sent Trainmaster Barnes up to get the mallet on the track, making it clear that every man, tool, and engine on the railroad would be at the command of George Barnes.

The February morning that Barnes arrived on the hill was bitter cold. The temperature was as far below zero as men wished it above.

Barnes first observed that the holes dug for the anchors and deadmen were not properly located. So he had to begin by crossing the roadmaster in having these holes re-located. The section men got busy, cursing the frozen ground, as they swung their picks with the occasional flash of spark warming the air.

The plan was to place pulleys between the anchors and the engine with heavy chains running through the pulleys from the wrecked engine up the track to Locomotive 200. Charlie Peterson was at the throttle. Another chain was similarly run from the engine through a pulley to a hog (consolidation engine) down the track. Louis Larsen was at the throttle of this engine.

Barnes had informed both engineers to pay no attention to anyone else. When he was ready to make a try at lifting the overturned giant to her feet, he cautiously signaled the two engineers to proceed. The bridge foreman at this moment hollered that they should stop as some of the links in the heavy chains were cracked. Barnes paid no attention at all, neither did the engineers, who cracked their throttles open and gradually pulled the 201 to its feet.

The impossible was accomplished without a wrecker. Deuel said, "Barnes, you have re-railed the largest locomotive in the state." Barnes confessed that he might have done the job better if he had cut a rail. There was a tradition, long before established by an earlier roadmaster, that no rail would be cut before they got to Salt Lake City. Barnes accomplished the feat of re-railing the giant without breaking the tradition.

The frame of this engine was broken in nine places. Barnes supervised the dropping the 201 down to Antelope siding, where she waited for Number One and Number Two to pass. Meanwhile, Barnes burned up George Thompson by supervising the chaining of the frame together by two mechanics. Charlie Peterson was ordered to haul four cars and the 201 down the hill with Engine 200. The trip was made without further mishap.

The Thompson-Barnes feud continued. Thompson refused to allow Barnes to run the engines after they were put across the turntable. This is, technically speaking, the boundary line between master mechanic and trainmaster.

One day a 200 was ordered for a run. It was put across the turntable, but Thompson would not let it leave.

The crew had been called and stood there, while Thompson and Barnes argued over the engine. Barnes said finally, "There goes the company's money. I don't give a G— D— for you. When those engines are across the turntable, they are mine. But you better mind your own business, and know when I am boss, and stop this getting in other men's way, or I am going to tear into you."

Deuel's clerk, Simmons, stood there petrified, for no one dared to talk back to Thompson, who was a terrible bully.

Barnes concluded with these words, "I am going to Deuel and tell him I am resigning and why."

Deuel immediately rang for his clerk, Simmons, who came in and was told to go get Thompson, "right away." As Barnes left Simmons could see that something was wrong. He asked him, therefore, what the trouble was.

Barnes boarded the street car swearing to himself that he would never do anything else than run passenger trains.

The next morning Barnes' telephone rang, and he was told that Deuel wanted to see him.

Kissing his wife goodbye, Barnes walked to the car line and rode down to the office.

When he arrived, Deuel called Simmons in. "I want you to hear this, also. Barnes is boss. Call Thompson."

Thompson came in, looking as tough as ever, but no doubt hiding his own fears. Deuel had just nine words to say.

"Barnes is boss. You are subject to his orders."

They were both good men, but each got under the other fellow's skin. This order should have settled the matter, but Thompson "died hard" as was discovered when a hog derailed at Tunnel Fourteen, and Barnes called up a Colorado and Southern wrecker to re-rail her.

All day long Barnes and Thompson fought like cat and dog, until in disgust the Colorado and Southern wrecker foreman said, "You can fight all you want to, but I am going to lift this engine just as I see fit."

Barnes replied, "Yes, that is right, as long as

you don't do something that I consider wrong."

At dinner time, Thompson and Barnes sat glowering at one another like a tough old tom cat and bull dog. Barnes said finally, "You are your own worst enemy. You'd give a lot to have your own words back. No reason on earth the two of us can't get along."

Thompson answered, "You are right, George. When they are over the turntable, they are yours."

George Thompson was as splendid a mechanic as Barnes was a trainmaster, else Deuel would have fired Thompson long before.

Some time later a new superintendent took over. He was a booze fighter and had been let out of his last job for that reason. On the Moffat he used to go out in his private car to sober up. This man was tipped off by a friend of his, the general manager of the Santa Fe, that he had better listen to Barnes. This was evidence of the respect in which Barnes was held. Colonel Dodge, however, had other ideas. He felt that no man could ever rise from the ranks to become a good official.

On one occasion, a superintendent was warned that the easiest way for him to get all the men on the line down on him was to fire Barnes.

Indeed, those old 200 mallets could tell many a story about George Barnes and all the things they had to do under his orders out on the line.

The mallets caused a great deal of trouble when they got off the track. Engine 208, for example derailed going down the four per cent after having gone through Needle's Eye Tunnel (Number Thirty-two) on the east side. It would have been simple pulling her back on the rails if she could have been pulled down hill.

Unfortunately, she had taken off at too severe an angle to do this. The only thing left was to set blocks that were as high as the rails on the ties and then drag the 200 mallet up the four per cent across the frogs that were spiked down.

Several mallets were brought down from Corona to pull the 208 back on the rails. But since the 208 was on the ballast and ties, she seemed permanently anchored. The mallets could only spin their wheels.

More engines were called out of Tabernash and run up to Corona and on down to the derailment. When eight engines had finally been coupled behind the 208 she gave up her stubborn fight to stay off the rails and block the line.

On another occasion Engine 208 derailed in a wrestling match with a snowslide at the sharp curve below the loop. Sid Kane was at the throttle with fireman Tom Conway. As they were running low on water, the only thing that could be done was to shovel snow into her tank. Roadmaster Paul Paulson ordered his section men to go into the tank and shovel the snow back in the tender away from the manhole. It got stifling hot in there from the heating pipes that were provided to keep the tanks from freezing solid. The section boys claimed that Sid Kane and his fireman, Tom Conway, were having it entirely too easy shoveling the snow in the manhole, so the engine crew traded places and got into the tank.

It was about midnight. Nels Johnson came off the Loop with another 200 engine and pulled in behind the 208. Nels and his fireman, Pinky Lewis of Phippsburg, started setting frogs under the derailed engine. The safety valves of Nels' engine were popping on and off so that when Pinky and Nels turned around the side of their engine to pick up another frog, they did not hear any unusual noise. It was midnight. As they returned with the frog, the 208 was gone. She was seven hundred feet down the mountainside, having been swept by a second snow slide of treacherous wet March snow that had piled up in the form of a cone on the cliffs above.

Tom Conway described what happened inside the tank for a Denver Post story.

I was a fireman, staying at Arrow, 11 miles west of the summit of Corona Pass. The morning of Feb. 18, 1922, Sid Cane, an engineer and I were called to man engine No. 208 for snowplow duty. We plowed away, reached the top of the pass, ate lunch, and started back down the west side.

This day there was another locomotive ahead of us. As we dropped down the hill he hit a drift and stalled. We came up behind him, coupled on, and tried to pull him out, just as you might try to tow another car out of a drift. Right then a small snowslide ran into the side of our engine, the 208, and we were stalled too.

A third engine following us tried to pull us free, but couldn't. The engineer of that engine then pulled back a short distance.

We knew we were stuck for a while, and we knew what this meant. We had to keep the engines "alive" — that is, with fire going and steam up. The 208 had lots of coal, but little water. There was nothing else to do but shovel snow into the water tank under the coal pile in the tender. There steam from the boiler would melt it into water to be converted in turn into steam.

Old 208 used more water than most locomotives because of leaky flues, and the two other crews had to pitch in and help us shovel snow. About 8 p.m. Paul Paulson of Denver, the roadmaster, and a crew of fresh men arrived to help.

The snow began to pile up around the tender's manhole, so I went down inside the tank to shovel the snow forward and make more room.

It was pitch dark down in there, so I had to use a torch. In just a few minutes the torch went out and I yelled up for somebody to give me a light.

"I'm coming down!" someone yelled. It was Cane. He dropped into the tank, lit the torch, and started to help me shovel the snow forward.

It was hard, exhausting work, and we didn't talk, just grunted, shoveling as hard as we could.

Cane and I had been working together about five minutes when we heard a strange sound.

It was dead of winter, but it sounded like thunder!

I stopped to listen. In that second or so I had time to notice that the crew outside had quit shoveling snow down to us. I heard one man shout and another man yell in fear.

Then came a roar like somebody had whacked the steel of the car with a giant mallet. I felt the tender give a great heave.

"Snowslide!" I yelled at Cane. The next instant the torch was out and we were in darkness, rolling and pitching in that steel dungeon.

One minute I was under water, the next I was out of it. I was hurled from side to side, and tried to protect myself from hitting the steel walls with my hands, but I never knew which way I was going to fly.

There was a continuous roar and clatter and clang. I realized we were sliding and rolling down the mountainside.

I kept waiting for a drop off, a sudden quiet fall, and then crashing, mangling death.

How long did we drop and roll? I don't know. But suddenly we were motionless.

"Cane!" I yelled as loud as I could.

"I'm here," he gasped. But I could not see him in the dark.

"Cane!" I yelled again. "Are you all right?"

He groaned. "I guess," he said then. "I can move."

"We've got to find the manhole," I told him. "Look around. Feel around. We've got to get out of here!"

I could hear him scrambling around.

"Please God," he said, more to himself than to me, although I could hear him, "let the manhole be up."

I knew why he prayed. If we were upside down and the manhole faced into the snow, we might die inside before they could get to us, either from lack of air or freezing. We were drenched through with icy water. My teeth chattered. Still I kept running my hands over the steel walls.

Suddenly Cane called out.

"I've found it!" he yelled. "Over this way, Tom!"

I crawled and scrambled toward his voice, and suddenly his hand grabbed mine and pulled it up and put it on the edge of the manhole. In another second we were crawling into the night.

About this time Nels and Pinky, together with George Schryer and his fireman, from still another engine that had arrived about this time, started hollering down, just in case a miracle had happened and someone would be alive.

Tom Conway and Sid Kane climbed out of the engine tank, which had fortunately landed right side up. Risking their lives in the spot where two slides had occurred that night, Nels Johnson and Pinky Lewis slid down the very steep mountainside to help shove the two engineers up the very slippery wall.

Nels acknowledged that if it had not been for the fact that the boys had suffered only slight scratches, as they slushed around in the two feet of snow and water inside the tank, they would never have been able to have gotten the men up, a difficult task even in the summer time.

Roadmaster Paul Paulson and the section men could not be found. They were apparently buried under the snow at the bottom of the slide. One man was found dead two hours later. Nels Johnson went back to the Loop telephone to call in the news of the disaster. The rescued engine crew, meanwhile, had been put in the caboose of the freight train that had come down off the hill. Here they thawed out and rested.

That night the men attempted to shove slim poles down through the snow to locate the bodies. By morning the search for the men was taken up in earnest, with reinforcements arriving. The men on hand were exhausted from exposure and the altitude. Charlie Johnson was among those who had arrived. He had been caught in a similar slide and rescued only through the stunt of shoving a long two-man wood-saw through the snow, for the saw's teeth would catch on the clothing of the men.

A telephone call was sent to Fraser for all the saws that could be found. An engine rushed these

This is where engine 208 ended her journey after being caught in an avalanche. Sid Kane and his fireman, Tom Conway, were inside the tender of their engine shoveling snow to obtain water to keep their engine alive when the slide carried them 700 feet down — soaked but unhurt. Track was built down to the engine and by means of block and tackle and a mallet headed down grade for counterbalance, the 208 was pulled back up and soon returned to service. — *Joe Preiss, DPL*

saws up to the spot, while valuable time passed. When the engine arrived, one handle of each saw was taken off. That end was shoved through the deep snow and the men carefully sawed through the snow. Several bodies were revealed. It was, however, a week later before the last body was secured. The pet dog of one of the men had been brought out of Denver, in hope that it could smell his master.

With this story in the papers of the nation, you can imagine how the tale that I will now relate got started. A Middle Park woman had taken Number Two out of Grand County for Denver. The train was running on a night schedule at that time. The lights within the Pullman were out. This good woman awakened just as the train crawled by the spot where the disaster had occurred. The spring moonlight of Easter season illuminated the scene, and she beheld coffins lined along the right-of-way for the bodies they hoped to find. The combination of moonlight, fresh snow, and a sudden awakening produced the story, though the coffins were only railroad ties.

There is a story that is told sometimes in connection with this incident, though it may have happened on some other occasion. One of the section men killed was found to have on his person a money belt containing from two to seven thousand dollars — how much depends on who tells the story. It seems that no one claimed the body, until the discovery of money was made. Then, even the city of Denver claimed the body. This man was buried in Hot Sulphur. No sooner was the body interred than someone would show up, claiming to be a relative. The body would be dug up and the coffin opened. The story goes that the Sulphur Springs grave-digger had to re-dig that grave several times that winter.

Engine 208 was left for many months where she had fallen. As the engine and tender had landed right side up, she appeared to have just run to her resting place. A ramp was therefore built down to her on a thirty-degree grade. Rails were spiked down the ramp and piles driven at the top with anchors placed. Jess Spohr was the superintendent in charge of bringing 208 up the ramp. George Schryer was at the throttle of the mallet that pulled her up by the aid of block-and-tackle arrangements. George simply had to pinch off the air and let the weight of his mallet raise the 208 inch by inch. When she had reached the top, she was blocked and a switch spiked in. The job was over. The 208 surely had lost the round with that snow slide, but she had not had her shoulders pinned to the mat by the fall. Those who drive up on the west side of the old right-of-way to Corona today can still see the ramp.

It seemed that the 200 engines were trying to out-do one another in the pranks that they pulled. Once the 210 had helped a freight up the hill and was sent back to Tabernash following ten minutes behind two other mallets, the 206 with George Schryer at the throttle and the 204 with Bert Clark at the throttle. When Schryer looked back as he dropped over the Loop Trestle and saw the 210 was gaining on them, he opened up his throttle and came off the hill a little faster. He was running quite fast when he passed Loop siding. He dashed into the Loop tunnel and sped on down to Ranch Creek, where he had a wait order for another train. As the 210 was included in the wait order, the line was tied up, until the 210 showed up. They waited and waited.

Finally, they went to the telephone to talk to the dispatcher. About this time Tom Carr, who was the engineer of the 210, came on the phone. His story was that near Sunnyside, the 210 had stripped herself as a drive rod broke and cleaned off all the air pipes, so that there were no air brakes or air reverse gear to control the monster. He and his fireman immediately unloaded while she was still moving slowly at ten miles an hour. The 210 soon ran wild. George Schryer knew immediately that that was why he had observed her gaining on him. Tom Carr said he ran on down beyond Sunnyside until he could see both tracks of the Loop, and

there below both of them lay the 210, which had hurled itself from the upper level, bounced on the right-of-way at the lower level, and then gone on over the cliff to her final resting place.

George Schryer fully believed that the 210 must have almost jumped on top of his engine. He figured that the noise of their driving rods had prevented him from hearing the 210 jump. It is self-evident that George and Bert could not have been more than two minutes away from disaster.

With this accident it seems that the 210 was content to call off the track meet. The 210 was scrapped, the parts most useful being run up on a ramp and taken to the shops to become part of other engines. Some say the boiler blew up when she did this marvelous broad jump. Others violently disagree. Anyway you can pick yourself a souvenir today, for some of her junk is still there.

The 200 mallets did a great service for their country in World War One and World War Two. The Rio Grande leased some for a time at the beginning of the second World War.

When the first Rio Grande Prospector (two-car streamliner) had motor trouble at Fraser before the war, it was a Moffat mallet that came to the rescue and pulled her up to Moffat Tunnel.

The 200's are a legend of slow-moving, bull-dog power that rarely slips her drive wheels. They were built to run twenty miles per hour and could not do more than thrity-five. According to Master Mechanic Fisher they were not excessive in repair work.

A pair of 200's at work! Engines 216 and 208 approach Coal Creek heading west with a long freight on February 14, 1946, just fourteen months before the Moffat would become part of the Rio Grande. Almost four decades earlier, in October, 1908, L. C. McClure photographed engine 200 (left) just after this first Moffat mallet had arrived in Denver. — *above, John W. Maxwell; left, CRRM*

The 200's had many adventures as seen on these pages. No. 210 (right) was rolled by a boulder and lies with her stack almost inside the Japanese section boss' front door. Later she waits (below) to enter the Tabernash shows with A. F. Norbury, the Moffat's No. 1 engineer, -on the right- posed with her. No. 208 and plow 10200 (left) rolled over near Tunnel 32 in 1918, after being hit by an avalanche and the engine is seen (left-center) awaiting repairs. On another day, No. 207 (bottom) ran away when George Shryer was unable to build up air pressure below Ranch Creek because the helper engine had not been cut into the train line and the train had broken in two. For a real show of power, it is hard to match this scene near Needles Eye Tunnel where an unidentified mallet has gone on the ground and five engines are attempting to pull her back onto the rails. Eventually another mallet arrived and the task was accomplished. — *left-center and bottom, —DPL; right and below, Joe Preiss: others, Mrs. Louis Larsen: all CRRM*

PLOW TRAIN AT RANCH CREEK — Robert E. Jensen

In the winter of 1912-13, plow 10200 still sported her "Red Devil" paint scheme, said to be able to melt any snow it couldn't plow. But by next year the rotary would be repainted plain black and lettered for the reorganized Denver & Salt Lake RR. After moving ahead to clear the east switch, the rotary will back unto engine 200 and be ready to move ahead as soon as the mid-train helpers finish taking water. Now that the 200, first of the Moffat mallets and built as an 0-6-6-0, has had a well weighted pilot truck added, she can handle the point on freights; her power will be welcome today for the report from the Sunnyside weather station is of heavy snow on the hill with the wind rising. It'll be a long, hard run to the shelter of Corona snowshed and a hot meal!

210

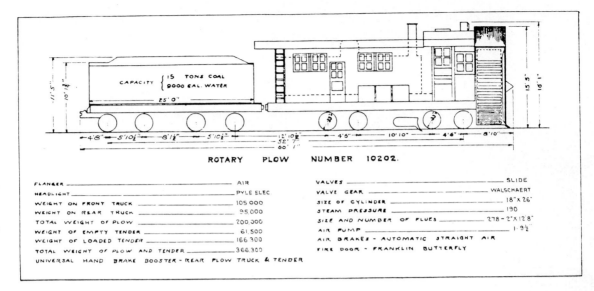

ROTARY PLOW NUMBER 10202.

FLANGER — AIR	VALVES — SLIDE
HEADLIGHT — PYLE ELEC	VALVE GEAR — WALSCHAERT
WEIGHT ON FRONT TRUCK — 105,000	SIZE OF CYLINDER — 18"x 26"
WEIGHT ON REAR TRUCK — 95,000	STEAM PRESSURE — 190
TOTAL WEIGHT OF PLOW — 200,000	SIZE AND NUMBER OF FLUES — 278-2"X 12'8"
WEIGHT OF EMPTY TENDER — 61,500	AIR PUMP — 1-9½
WEIGHT OF LOADED TENDER — 166,300	AIR BRAKES - AUTOMATIC STRAIGHT AIR
TOTAL WEIGHT OF PLOW AND TENDER — 366,300	FIRE DOOR - FRANKLIN BUTTERFLY
UNIVERSAL HAND BRAKE BOOSTER - REAR PLOW TRUCK & TENDER	

17

Fighting Snow
With the World's Biggest Ice Pick

Back in the days of Vice-President and General Manager W. E. Morse a method had been found to untangle the blockades that developed when the hill got snowed under. Morse had asked Barnes to take over the hill as dispatcher. Barnes had replied, "Now, Morse, you and I will clash. For I will run the whole railroad and not listen to you or anyone."

Several days later the line was tied up when Barnes was in a card game with some boys in a caboose at Arrowhead. The operator brought into Barnes a new bulletin announcing that he was "dispatcher extraordinary" in complete charge of everything west of Tolland. Barnes turned to his friends and said, "Just hand over everything you have. I am your new boss."

Barnes recognized that one of the worst problems in keeping traffic moving over the hill was that Tabernash, the west division point, would run out of crews. By the time the line was open, there would not be a crew left to operate. For trains sent east of Tabernash would have lost so much time that the crews would all be exhausted when they got to Denver. Then another snowslide or blizzard would strike and block the line, the crews being in Denver on one side of the blockade and the need for crews being in Tabernash, on the other side of the blockade.

Barnes immediately began sending the crews east out of Tabernash over the worst part of the

Hill to Ladora or some other siding. Here the engine and caboose were uncoupled and quickly run back over the hill and down to Tabernash. In this manner the sidings beyond the worst part of the hill were filled with trains, which could be picked up by crews originating out of Denver.

Barnes had refused, however, to allow the stockmen's special of seven cars west of Tolland. Morse had wanted this train run up the hill and side-tracked at some place like Ladora, where it could wait until the blockade was cleared. This would have given the seven-car special filled with men returning from the stock show a chance to move quickly. Barnes had refused this request because there was no water or food at Ladora. If a sudden turn of worse weather developed, Barnes did not want to organize a rescue for the passengers. It was bad enough keeping the crews fed, not to mention three hundred fifty passengers. The special was returned to Denver, while over at the tie-up between Loop and Sunnyside men worked feverishly to open the line. No further trouble developed. The slide was removed by the rotaries and eleven trains were moved east.

Then it was that Barnes said to Morse, "Now you can send up your special." It made a good trip without any further delay.

The road had three rotaries. Normally the battles with rocks and tree trunks and derailments on ice kept one of the three in the shops, leaving two to keep the upper part of the hill open.

It was during one of these battles with snow that a boomer brakeman in disgust at the Moffat said, "The only reason they made the line standard gauge was to enable them to borrow cars from other roads." The Moffat was short on cars but under Freeman and his master mechanic, Charlie Peterson, she became the best equipped road in the world to fight snow.

Freeman was afraid to cross Peterson to whom the credit for the excellent condition of the motive power and snow fighting equipment goes.

The severity of the storms, the length of the blockades necessitated the best snow fighting equipment. The Moffat's entire security was tied up in its ability to battle snow.

To get any coherent story of these great blockades, which cut Middle Park and the northwestern part of Colorado entirely off from the rest of the world, is not easy. The battles were so hard on the men that a typical reaction might be that expressed by Van Vrankan. He came to the Moffat in 1906, from a Colorado Fuel and Iron short line. Unlike the many men who left because of the uncertainties of the future, the low wages and the terrible conditions, Vrankan stayed more than 40 years and rose to first on the seniority list of conductors. His answer when asked about snow fighting . . . "I don't want to remember it. I want to forget it."

To better understand such feelings and to get the blizzard-blown picture, we have the memory of Joe Preiss, a rotary fireman in 1918. To this twenty-five year old man this account was chiselled in his memory by the blast that swept out of the Fraser River Valley that day.

The rotary powered by a mallet was sent down from Corona to Ranch Creek wye where it took on water, turned and pulled ahead a short distance up the hill to be ready to tie ahead of the two freights and a passenger train which would be coupled together after taking water.

Naturally the line was clean until above Loop where they approached Sunnyside, as a storm swept all the snow it had dumped into the valley below with such force that the eight engine train found every fireman swinging heroically to keep up steam. The enginemen were unable to see ahead. In less than an hour they rounded Ptarmigan Point and finally had to work their mallets simply to keep moving. Then the train died. In time Joe fought his way back to the mallet behind him finding both fireman and engineer unable to get water into the boiler with either injector. It

seemed uncanny that in less than an hour they had emptied their water tanks.

The decision was made in the white cold hell to kill the engine and to attempt to get the passenger train disconnected immediately and backed down before the track drifted in. The latter was quickly accomplished while Joe crawled under the low pressure cylinders to unscrew the cocks and let the water out. In fifteen minutes or so the men called to him, "Come out or you will be buried alive."

Joe answered, "I will be through in three minutes."

When he got back into the cab, he asked the engine crew if they had looked at the strainers of their water hoses that brought water from the tender, for fine cinders could blow in as they took water through the large manhole at the tank.

The strainers were clogged, but the water was less than a foot deep which meant that they could not have made the mile into the safety of the snow sheds.

Joe determined that he would keep his plow alive so that when they would receive help from the top, they would be able to throw some of their own snow out, when the rotary coming down would shove a pile of snow into their two hoods.

Now for such emergencies in this desolate country the engine crew carried a commissary in the tender locker. The commissary was a foot wide, fourteen inches deep and about thirty inches long. It always carried two pounds of coffee, eggs, potatoes and ham or steaks. Usually at the beginning of a trip the fireman would place the potatoes in the warm sand dome to bake slowly. By mealtime the fireman had also thrown a small piece of boiler plate into the fire to get hot. A wire tied to the boiler plate allowed him to retrieve it and place it on the deck of the cab. There the coffee would be cooked and later put on the oil shelf to keep warm. Then the potatoes were retrieved and the steaks fried.

But on the rotary there were three men to be fed including the pilot for the big rotary wheel that cut the snow and hurled it out. This was a general storm that had struck the entire state and Wyoming. Help would not arrive promptly, in fact it did not come until thirty days later.

How did the men sleep? All the engine crews carried "hay boards" which were planks. Since mattress ticks were filled with hay or straw, the expression "hitting the hay" came into existence. These hay boards were planks six feet long, and a foot wide on which the crew (in all of their clothing) lay down across the cab.

The Moffat's other rotary got a train with the Japanese extra gang and all the help and food needed into the Corona shed from the east. On its return to Tolland it must have chewed its way into some rocks and trees with the crew unable to see the slide. This meant the rotary had to go back to Denver's Utah Junction shop for new blades. Both the Colorado Midland and the Colorado and Southern were asked for help.

Meanwhile the "fit-to-be-tied" Bill Freeman sent Art Pearson, the roadmaster, to the west end by the only route available which was on the Rio Grande south to Pueblo and then west to the town of Wolcott where wagons were carrying mail over the wagon road to State Bridge. This was a time consuming trip of 319 miles plus the wagon road to State Bridge and then back east to Tabernash on the mixed train operating in the emergency.

Section men brought Art Pearson as far as their motor cars could climb. Then in the cold high altitude he struggled past all the abandoned engines to the rotary to waken Joe Preiss about midnight by knocking on the rotary cab door. He was welcomed in by Joe who made coffee and a sandwich for him. Seeing that Pearson was utterly exhausted, Joe put him to bed on his hay board. Joe would not let Pearson attempt the last mile in the morning, but he went ahead to the shed and phoned Joe Culbertson, the chief dispatcher, that Art would come up when he had had more rest.

Through the following weeks some of the train was dug loose by men and pulled down to Tabernash on the west end. However, during the last week Joe had to carry coal in a gunny sack eight car lengths to his rotary to keep her warm. Snow was also shoveled into the tender tank to make water. Of course, their food was gone long since, and they had gone time and again to Corona to eat in the beanery.

Thirty days later the rotary got down that mile. Joe was proud to see his engineer crack the throttle of the big wheel and throw out the snow that was in the scoop. With chains through the grab irons, the helpless rotary was cut loose from the dead mallet and pulled up to the Corona shed where another crew took over. Then Joe and his men went back to Denver for a good sleep in a comfortable bed.

The management did everything possible to keep the line open. In bad weather the rotaries would work out of Tolland on the east side and Arrowhead on the west side, but most of the time was spent running between Ranch Creek wye and Spruce wye, for above this elevation the snow drifted badly. From Corona to Arrow was eleven and three-tenths miles. The rotary was not to make this faster than one hour and seven minutes.

Any delay that would tie up the line so that the rotaries could not make their rounds for eight hours during a storm was almost certain to precipitate a blockade. If the snow got over twelve feet deep, the rotary was unable to handle a drift until it had been lowered by dynamiting and shoveling to that depth.

The sudden changes in temperature between a sunny spring afternoon, when the sun blistered through the thin high-altitude air, and the low temperature to which the thermometer plummetted a degree a minute after sunset caused rails to snap. Inasmuch as the rails would be surrounded by ice leaving only a groove for the flange of the wheels, the ball (top of the rail) would break off, when the warm morning sun struck the exposed part of the rail, while the lower part was buried in twenty to forty below zero ice. The fact that trains moved only ten miles an hour saved many a serious wreck. When a new rail had to go in, the rail would be tied behind an engine and dragged to the place, the section crew walking in the light of the rear headlight, which was left on. Oh, what a life the section men put in on the hill! Shoveling snow, crawling under derailed cars, picking ice out to put in a new rail, freezing as they worked, huddling by a fire made of kindling and kerosene. Yes, Bill Freeman's gandy dancers led a terrible life on a twenty per cent cut in wages.

A tie-up could occur from misjudgment on the part of an engineer. One man passed up the Ranch Creek water tank thinking he had plenty of water. Getting into deeper snow than was expected he used up his water and tied up the line with a dead engine and a stalled train.

The worst thing that could happen would be for the rotary to derail.

If the derailment required the big hook, it would be hours before it arrived. Then how could the wrecker get over a line full enough of snow to need the use of a rotary unless another rotary was on the right side of the derailed rotary?

The derailment of a car necessitating a wrecker was certain to cause a long delay that would turn into a blockade if heavy snow continued to fall. If we are to picture the Divide, we picture continuous snow, not just one storm but continuous winds that kept the track full.

During a two weeks long blockade one March, Tabernash was about eaten out of food. L. C. Hinds tells a humorous story of how, when his stock of groceries was low, he had received two cases of eggs. He rationed eggs to all his good customers. One lady came in and asked, "Just how fresh are these eggs?" Mr. Hinds said, "They are eggs from Steamboat, and that is all I know. Do you wish your two dozen or not?"

The woman was undecided and stood by watching Mr. Hinds sell one case in a few minutes. When he was half way through the second case of eggs, he turned to her and said, "You better make up your mind." Finally when the last two dozen were in sight she handed her money over.

Some of the stranded train crews living in their cabooses realized how desperate the situation was. They had been wrapping their vegetables carefully in newspapers, so that at night the vegetables would not be frozen. The water in the caboose was in a beer keg and though they took their turns keeping the fire up there was always some ice on the water in the morning.

To relieve this situation some of the men walked ten miles south to Bill Wood's commissary at his sawmill camp at Idlewild or Irving Spur (Winter Park). Nearly all railroad men could depend on Bill Wood giving them a ham, sack of flour, potatoes or anything he had. Money was no consideration at all. These men, unless they caught a ride back on some engine returning off the hill, would have a long tramp of ten miles the next day through the deep snow or down the right-of-way, which was the only space plowed open for travel.

Tri-weekly train service with the west end was established whenever blockades developed. The mail would be dropped off at State Bridge and carried over on sleds or wagons to Wolcott. This was the only contact with the outside world except by telegraph and telephone.

Medicine could be brought in by first class mail. Some men walked out from State Bridge to Wolcott and took the Rio Grande back to Denver.

This March F. A. Van Vranken determined to try hiking over Berthoud Pass from Tabernash with several others, including Charlie Foy. The first day they walked the ten miles to Irving Spur. Here they stayed overnight with Bill Wood, who fed them at his saw mill dining room. Next morning they tried to make skis out of fence boards and wire the skis on their feet with baling wire. But these homemade skis were a failure. The men next tried to make sled runners of these boards and became human sleds. But this did not work. So they gave up in desperation and walked out dragging their feet every few steps out of the drifts so deep they sank in to their hips.

They only knew where the highway was by the lane cut through the trees. (This highway was shorter and over a different route than the present one.)

Charlie Foy got tired as he went down in the soft snow and said to Van, "Come and help me." Van in all seriousness answered, "That is all right. They will find you in the spring." Van and the other men started walking away. Foy's heart sank thinking he was left behind. With a grin such as only Van has, he returned to Foy, who was pulled out of the snow. Not far ahead they discovered a shack almost buried in the snow. They made their entrance after pulling the shingles loose from the roof to start a fire. Then they melted snow and icicles, which they had gathered from the roof's edge and to which they added coffee grounds.

With good strong hot coffee they ate their lunch, which had been graciously packed by Bill Wood's cook. After this rest it was not so difficult to make the last assault on Berthoud Pass. When they had reached Berthoud, they had climbed over three thousand four hundred feet since they left Tabernash and two thousand four hundred feet since they left Idlewild that very morning. Besides climbing that height they had traveled twenty-five miles in deep snow.

It was down hill to Empire where clean beds, hot restaurant food and the promise of train service were at hand to get them back to Denver and their loved ones.

During a one week blockade not only was Corona isolated, but so were the Sunnyside weather report station and block office two miles below the pass. At that time two men kept the road informed about the weather. One man was an Irishman by the name of Chancy McCrow. His partner was an Englishman by the name of Albert Lee. These men worked twelve hour shifts. During this blockade the Irishman died. Albert Lee phoned off the hill, "What shall I do? We have only one bed, and Chancey is dead in it." The dispatcher told him that they would have been up before, if they possibly could. He was advised to dig a hole in the snow outside and place the body in it. Then secure it against coyotes with ties and rocks, until the line was opened.

Now the coroner was Willard, who lived in Tabernash. Naturally he had to go up on the first engine that reached there to make his investigation. But no sooner did Willard get up there than the line was plugged with snow again. The county commissioners almost went crazy, for each day Willard was up in the blockade, it cost the county

Engine 206 and a rotary plow emerge from the snowshed at Yankee Doodle Lake. This shed was found to trap more snow than it avoided and was soon removed. Far above is visible the long shed at Needles Eye Tunnel. — *DPL*

six dollars. As some men can raise an awful tempest in a teapot, so the story went around Sulphur that the county would go broke paying Willard. Finally the plows got through to Sunnyside and rescued Willard and the body. Willard rode in the cab of an engine dispatched down the hill, while the body was left to ride on the engine tank. Jim Quinn, for years a resident of Hideaway Park and a county commissioner, declares he will never forget the day the engine came down with that body on the tank. The body was buried in the Fraser cemetery.

In 1917 a forty-one day blockade of the line began on the west side, when a train ran into deeper snow than expected and floundered for lack of power. The train was brought back off the hill in pieces. This process took several days. In such trying moments with the rotary unable to back out, engine after engnie that was sent to clear up the blockade went dead.

If you had lived in Northwestern Colorado, you would not have held the railroad in too high esteem at such times, for you might have gone to Denver on business and been stranded there, while your ranch and family needed you in Middle Park.

The railroad could not help leaving a feeling of exasperation in the minds of people who suffered so many inconveniences from the delays. Business life was jeopardized and bottle necks in crucial items developed.

From Fraser to Tabernash field glasses and telescopes were turned towards the hill, when the clouds lifted. Wives, mothers, and sweethearts watched the smoke of plow trains trying to break through. Prayers were said and uttered with groanings for safety of the men, who were exposed to rock slides, privations, and sickness.

At home in Tabernash Mrs. Lyman Mills knew when it must be cold on the hill for one morning she had brought in a saucer of milk to warm three times before a stray cat could drink the freezing milk. The news of what the pony telephone line over the hill reported, was carried quickly all over town.

The normal running time of freights from Tabernash to Tolland was five hours, but one time it was six weeks before a freight got through. Daisy Jenne's scrapbooks, now preserved in the Grand County Museum, provide details on the tie-up. The men at Corona lived in fearful memory of that March tenth wind of 1916, which unroofed the snowsheds by its one hundred-mile-an-hour hand and completely paralyzed the Moffat.

The Corona sheds were a smoky nightmare.

One day a train switching in the sheds came out with Brakeman Bill Barringer missing. Every one went around asking "Have you seen Bill?" They finally found that he had been brushed off but not hurt. Bill left the Moffat when Engine 100 blew up but later landed a real job on the Southern Pacific.

When engines were caught between places in blizzards, the men used to fry their steaks on their scoop shovels. Billy Rush conceived an idea of cooking meat in a pail under the petcock of the water gauge, with just a little thin spray of steam over the meat. Another method used to cook meat was under the ashpan of the engine. As to sleeping, that was one of the worse problems during these battles on the great white desert.

The most serious problem was ice forming on the rails. By the time the winter was half over the ice had formed solid between the rails, leaving a groove next to the rail which the section men kept picked open. The track looked like city paving around a streetcar line. Then a warm spring day would come and the water would run. This line had been built only as a temporary line. The culverts were plank affairs not more than eight inches square. These soon froze full of ice.

Thus with the poor drainage provided for the line and the enormous quantities of water that would run, we see the ice filling the groove for the flanger, and an engine derailing.

So it would come about that during a blockade, while men were hand picking the rails clean around the Loop, the track nearer the pass drifted deep with ten-foot or more of snow and the ice would form under the snow over the rails as high as ten inches, as it built up day after day.

All the men that could be coaxed off Larimer street in Denver would be gotten on the hill to pick snow in great extra gangs. A rotary plow was helpless on ice. One simply had a derailment to handle beside the ice to pick.

The most disastrous of such blockades lasted for forty-three days in April and May of 1920. Late spring snows had inundated Middle Park and northwestern Colorado with tremendous drifts of snow. Ranchers ran out of hay to feed their cattle as each day brought more snow. Then the snow stopped and the sun melted it in the day time and the nights froze the water.

Cattle began to starve as the road was tied up with new blizzards sweeping in. The coal mines in Routt County were closed down. One mining superintendent sent up a carload of miners, who began chopping their way over the hill. But since Bill Freeman and this superintendent clashed, the miners went home.

Since Berthoud Pass highway had not been opened for the spring, tractors were fitted with plows and volunteer crews of men from Middle Park began a desperate effort to open the highway. Dynamite and shovels were used. Each town sent up food, quarters of beef. Men fried their steaks on their snow shovels. It was an epic battle. The highway was being opened, while Chairman E. E. Sommers gathered relief supplies at Empire.

Freeman gave this statement to the press regarding the railroad's battle to open its clogged line. "It has settled down to be a dogged fight. The men report tough progress. Ice six to ten inches on the rails threaten to derail the plows. Snow is generally ten feet deep. The plow can drive ahead only for its length and then the ice must be picked out. No one can even guess just when we will get through, but with continued good weather we will have track open in a few days."

The battle of the Moffat went on. Cattle thinned out; ranchers went broke. Then the line was opened up.

The first train was a solid train with hay. The second train, so they say, was snuff for the Swedes. And the third train was the long overdue Number One with mail, express, and passengers.

Perhaps no one thing did more to raise a cry for the Main Range Tunnel than this terrible experience.

Then came Master Mechanic Charlie Peterson and the world's largest ice picks. Engines 211 and 216, both mallets, were equipped with hydraulic ice picks, which could be raised when going over switches. The picks were big thirty-inch chisels, six inches wide, and two inches thick. These mallets would start at the top of the pass and shove these ice picks down inside the rails, ripping out the ice as the mallets snorted and spun their wheels. Then the mallet would back up and the rotary would slip down and pick up the ice and hurl it out of the cuts. The ice pick engine would return and root up more ice, while the rotary waited its turn to come down, pick up the ice, and hurl out the ten feet of snow drifted over the ice.

For five years Master Mechanic Charlie Peterson kept the motive power in such perfect shape that Interstate Commerce Commission inspectors gave the Moffat a one hundred per cent record at Utah Junction. Can any road in the country beat that record?

Thus equipment for snow and ice fighting was developed that was second to none with every efficient mallet kept in the best of shape so that the years while Moffat Tunnel was being built the blockades were reduced to a minimum, and it could be said that "the hill was well nigh licked" mechanically speaking, though the financial drain mounted in maintaining this superb snow fighting equipment.

To the lasting credit of Freeman is the fact he kept Charlie Pearson as master mechanic.

After one disastrous tie up, a five-engine coal train was started east out of Tabernash to climb the pass. George Schryer, one of the engineers who had helped open the pass, had warned an official that a snow cone overhanging the track below the Loop ought to be shot. I guess the officials were afraid Freeman would fire them for wasting time and powder. The coal train was composed of a rotary plow, two mallets, twenty cars of coal, George Schryer's mallet followed by the fourth mallet and fifteen cars of coal, the caboose, and the fifth mallet.

Their orders were to wait at Ranch Creek for the passenger out of Denver. It was to have pulled in the wye. But when the freight went through Arrow, it received new orders changing the meeting place to Loop.

When the coal drag got to Ranch Creek, the five engines took on water one after another as well as the rotary. When all were ready, the plow whistled its two long blasts, which rang shrill through the cold night air. The mountains echoed the call, which was answered by the locomotives. The first engines lunged ahead, the rumble of cars running

Master Mechanic Peterson fitted these hydraulically operated chisels on two mallets to gouge ice from alongside the rails. They could be lifted to pass over switches and were of great help in fighting ice problems on Rollins Pass. — *Ben Stone, DPL*

down the line. Soon the other engines pushed the slack ahead, and the train was moving with the slack shifting back and forth between the engines.

They moved around the hill on up past the old log loading benches and headed east and then south ever upward. Schryer had a hunch about the snow cone. When he was under it, he turned on his headlight, which reflected against the coal car ahead. His fireman asked, "What did you turn the headlight on for?"

George replied that he had a hunch the slide was going to let loose on them from the snow cone. He said he wanted to see it hit.

Hardly five seconds followed until the slide hit and Schryer cried, "prepare yourself."

The fireman said, "Prepare yourself for what?"

George did not need to answer. Boulders, tons and tons of snow came with tree trunks, and still more snow and boulders ringing against the bell and steam domes with terrible thuds. The win-

dows of the cab on George's side were crushed in, as the snow piled in the gangway and windows, filling the cab. Coal cars could be heard rolling hundreds of feet down the steep mountain side. They sounded to the fearful ears of the men like dynamite explosions.

More of the slide struck, the engine started to turn over. It settled back down on the rails again, as more snow came in the cab from the back curtain. Gas and smoke belched out the fire door. The snow was over the stack. George and his fireman tried wildly to stamp the snow down to keep above it.

The engine started tipping over again. A boulder cracked on the bell making a sound like the toll of death. Another car rattled on down hundreds and hundreds of feet below. But the engine settled back to the rails. The men still frantically jumped up and down to keep above the snow. Their heads were against the cab roof, the gas was terrible, the engine was buried under the slide.

While the Irish fireman thinks of his little ones at home and the Canadian engineer thinks of his wife, a third onslaught of the slide strikes with terrible force, and it seems an eternity before the engine settles back for the third time.

The engine is buried under snow, the gas and smoke choking the men. The fireman used the entire Moffat vocabulary of curses and foul language on the disaster. The men are spared being hurled seven hundred feet to their death.

Schryer hands the Irishman his extra handkerchief. An explosion of gas occurs in the engine. The men dig with their finger nails to crawl out of the lower side of the cab to get to air. Finally the snow must have melted at the engine stack, as the gas was relieved. The men were out in the air. The

ledge the engines stood on was so filled with snow that they almost slipped over the embankment.

They beheld the second mallet was on the track. Its crew crawled out. Seven cars went over the cliff behind that mallet and eight ahead of George's mallet.

Both fireman refuse to stick to their engines. The Irishman said, "You can. You don't have a family of kids." There was eminent danger of more snow slipping any moment. So George and the other engineer took over shoveling their ways back in the cabs.

Fourteen hours later the remainder of the train was backed to Tabernash and George began to remove the snow from the engine with a pick. It was piled six feet higher than the cab roof.

The passenger train, which had fallen down

George Schryer, in the second of two mallets, wondered if the snow cones on top of the ridge would hold; his fears came true as an avalanche caught the train and sweep several cars far down the slope. In these two photos we see the result of such avalanches; the plow has been rescued and taken to Tabernash from where it will soon again be doing battle. — *DPL*

somewhere in its run from Denver, was saved by the delay. Otherwise it would have been caught in the slide and the Moffat would have lost its record of no casualties to passengers.

After the slide, Blaine Markle, the conductor in charge of the train telephoned the report in to Freeman, who asked with great worry, "Did any of the mallets go over?" "No. And neither did any of the men!" came the burning sarcastic answer of indignation.

During these grueling battles a close fraternity was established between the men. Management highly respected the moves the men on the top of the world resorted to in fighting these epic battles. There was no rigid rule book play for every move as has grown up on many railroads. If the men devised some idea or felt that they by common consent had a better idea, management kept hands off the men who fought the battles. Perhaps this liberty in part appeased their scalping from low wages. Larsen, intimate friend of President Bill Freeman, testifies to this spirit.

Not only was a fraternity formed among the railroad men but with many non-rail who had interests in the men. Frank Carlson was most gracious and accommodating to men who lost mittens, or wore out shoes and galoshes, or needed warmer caps. Notes were sent down on engines for the needed supplies. The men never forgot these friendships even after the hill was abandoned for the Moffat Tunnel. The fraternity included Frank Carlson, Sr., Bill Wood, Sr., and L. C. Hinds.

I wish that it were possible to give a day by day picture of a blockade. But the minds of men tried to blot out the memory of those battles for there were so many. It was like the war. It was best forgotten. But what we have written is representative of the piercing cold, the panting for air in working above timberline, the curses that seemed to help warm the air and cut the ice, and the loyalty of men who were good and not so good, as all men are.

The finest tribute to these men is given by General Manager W. A. Deuel in his journal which he kept from day to day for the better part of the years 1907, 1908, and 1909.

Thursday, April 8th, 1909: Rotary 10201 Engs. 109 and 105 arrived Jenny Lake 10:30 a.m. and waited there as has been custom for Extra 103 and 102 and Number One Engine 302 and 110 following. Extra 103 hung up in snow about one eighth mile east of Jenny Lake and plow train backed down to help them, in starting, they pulled draft rigging out and went back for balance of train, and

this time pulled draft rigging from another car; while delayed trying to chain up this damage the rotary with her two engines got snowed in so could not move. Passenger train was backed down to Tolland and returned to Denver. Extra west with all her engines and caboose of plow train backed down to Tolland for coal, water and to pick up section men to dig out rotary and her two engines; they then endeavored to release plow train but storm was so severe with wind from forty to sixty miles per hour that they only got far as Yankee Doodle shed where they remained for the night, keeping plow and her engines in water with snow. Train Number Two was turned back from Sulphur Springs as Number One.

Friday, April 9th, 1909: Extra 200 started from Utah Junction picking up all available men to go to relief. This train got to within three-fourths mile of plow train and walked the men the rest of the way, train backing down out of danger line. Storm and wind still so severe that only way could make progress was by tunneling under engines and plow and leaving crust on high side to prevent drifting in. This equipment was completely buried under snow; got dug out and brought the two sections together at 8:30 p.m. arriving at Jenny Lake 9:20 p.m., where all took water and started west but snow was from ten to twenty feet deep and so hard that four consolidation engines could not keep plow against it and as they were running short of coal came back to Jenny Lake and tied up for the night at 12:45 p.m. 10th. In meantime had Rotary 10200 coming from Sulphur Springs to Arrow to start east from there.

Saturday, April 10th: Storm abated. Started extra 200 and 103 with two cars of coal from Tolland for relief train at Jenny Lake; men in meantime trenching snow from below Yankee Doodle Lake to enable relief train to get through, and reached there 1:00 p.m. and took Rotary 10201 one and one-half miles west of Jenny Lake where they met Rotary 10200 which had started east from Arrow, and the 10201 backed down to Jenny Lake to let east bound rotary pass them; then went to Arrow and tied up.

Easter Sunday, April 11th, 1909: Rotary 10200 with engines 103, 105, and 111, while working in snow eighteen to twenty-three feet deep were derailed at 2:20 p.m. 1,000 feet west of Corona Shed; after making several efforts to re-rail it was deemed best to get the Pass and freight trains with the three engines from Rotary back into Shed for safety as storm was so severe with usual high wind that they would all have been snowed in. All tied up in shed leaving Rotary 10200 in snow until storm would permit men to work.

Owing to danger of getting passenger train stuck it was not considered safe to turn that train east, all passengers were well cared for.

Train Two and Rotary 10201 were held at Arrow pending storm going down. This storm put all the wires out of service between Tolland and Corona, and our only means of communication was via Colorado telephone to Sulphur Springs, thence by telegraph to Corona. At 7:20 p.m. arranged for Engine 20 to bring Jap gang of fifty-two men to Arrow to have available when advisable to start relief train east.

Monday, April 12th: Storm still bad. Started relief train with Rotary 10200 and eighty men with diner from Arrow 8:00 a.m. but account of severity of storm sent them back from Loop. Wind at Corona fifty-two miles per hour.

At 12 noon channel between Shed and derailed rotary had filled to depth of ten feet, for distance of 1,000 feet and storm so bad men could not work.

Tied up at Corona giving men rest and had everything in readiness to make early start in morning should conditions warrant.

Tuesday, April 13th: Started Rotary relief train at 6:00 a.m. with men and got far as Sunnyside basin when had to get back for coal and water; men walked up from that point, but unable to transfer passengers account of severity of storm. Did not make another attempt on account of danger of getting relief train stuck.

They were unable to make better than ten feet progress in thirty minutes with the mallet and two helper engines. Still storming and wind twenty-four to forty-six miles. All tied up for the night at Corona after shoveling one third distance west of Shed. Run a provision supply train from Steamboat to Arrow to protect needs of people at intermediate points.

Wednesday, April 14th: 5:30 a.m. Wind dropped to fifteen miles, snowing hard, got relief train with Rotary 10201 out of Arrow 6:40 a.m. with wind then twenty-four miles; they got within one and one-half miles of derailed Rotary and effected transfer of all but six passengers, but as Eng. 20 had been damaged in the hard work going through snow ten to twenty feet deep, they returned at once to Arrow for coal and water and to change engine. 4:00 p.m. arranged to get thirty men from the Utah Junction west as far as they could be taken by train then to walk balance of way to Corona, but on account of slide at Tunnel twenty-seven worked there all night and returned to Utah Junction early Thursday morning. At 6:30 p.m. Relief train got to within one mile of Corona, but had to return for coal and water and tied up at Arrow.

As coal supply was getting low at Arrow, we ran a coal train from Yampa; this train brought all available men from Yampa east to assist at blockade. All tied up for the night.

Thursday, April 15th: Started relief train from Arrow 5:50 a.m. and got within one-fourth mile of blockade, when had to return to avoid being blocked in behind them. Came east again at 12 noon within two hundred fifty yards of blockade. Wind thirty-four to thirty-six miles, went back again to avoid blocking. Wind at 1:00 p.m. forty miles and drifting badly; ten to eighteen feet snow in channel. Men at Corona wet and worn out tied up for rest.

Sunday, April 18th: 2:30 a.m. Rear trucks of Rotary and all of engine 110 except rear tank truck derailed by ice in 'Little Bogan Cut,' men wore out, tied up for rest.

Made pull 8:15 a.m. and got wheels of 110 close to rail, but damaged front draft gear of Engine 102, and as all were short of coal and water, Engines 300, 200, 102, and 105 with passenger equipment returned to Corona. Coaled and watered all and turned Engine 102 and started back 11:30 a.m. Were there at 12:15 p.m.

Snow in cuts was fifteen feet deep and so hard that blades of rotary would only rasp against it like a piece of sandpaper, making it necessary to work steam on all five engines on descending four per cent grade to do any cutting.

Rotary 10200 with four engines and Jap gang being held at Arrow to meet emergency.

2:10 p.m. Rotary 10201 and Engine 110 re-railed and moving; at 3:55 p.m. were again derailed by ice and had several subsequent derailments up to 11:30 p.m., at which time they reached Jenny Lake and tied up for the night.

Monday, April 19th: Weather still favorable and following program lined up: Extra west Engine 21 to leave Arrow 1:00 a.m. with Mdse. train and Jap gang; Plow train, Rotary 10200 with two cars engine coal for Corona to leave Arrow 4:00 a.m. for Tolland to protect train No. One and Extra west — and Rotary 10201 with delayed passenger train to leave Jenny Lake 7:00 a.m., resuming regular service, which plan was carried out.

It is notable that during this period of eleven days almost continuous blockade, involving two rotary plows, eleven locomotives and various other equipment, operating under what was unquestionably the most severe weather conditions to which men and machinery have ever been subjected in work of this kind, there was no physical suffering to any one of passengers or employees, nor was there other than slight damage to power and equipment. This may well be ascribed to the unremitting vigilance of the employees involved, who responded without a protest to each call, and put forth their best effort at all times.

We see here a panorama of snow fighting scenes on the Moffat Road. Prior to delivery of the mallets or when a mallet was unavailable, the 100's were used as (above) we see a team of three behind rotary 10200 and (left) two 100's are at work near Sunnyside; both photos date to the winter of 1905-06. Roatry 10201 is seen (below) powered by a mallet as they turn at Spruce wye before heading back up the hill. Ranch Creek wye was the usual turnaround point on the west side of Rollins Pass and we see (right-top) a plow train making a water stop during the winter of 1919, while that same winter the wrecker is found at work (right) after the plow derailed leaving Ranch Creek. At Sunnyside (far right) two twelve hour shifts of storm watchers kept alert to sudden weather changes that might mean trouble on the hill. But on what appears to have been a good day on the hill, this rotary (right-bottom) leads this day a long freight toward Corona shed; this day men and machines kept the line open but what will tomorrow bring? — *right and right-top, Joe Preiss: far right, Mr. Louis Larsen: right-bottom: A. L. Johnson: left, L. C. McClure: above, Colonel George Pappas: all, CRRM*

In these photos we see typical scenes of snow duty on Rollins Pass. The rotary (above) has run out of coal near Sunnyside, while (below) a plow waits at Loop Bridge for a meet with a freight during the busy years of World War I. As this plow train (top) approaches Corona shed the men are probably turning thoughts to a good hot meal that awaits them. The general manager noted in his diary when he felt it safe to lay off the rotary crews and we see (right) it sometimes was not until well into June. For a few brief weeks in summer Corona was bare of snow (below-right) but it would be a short intermission. — *above-opposite and right-bottom, DPL; top, Mrs. Louis Larsen: others, Joe Preiss: all, CRRM*

ACK Denver J J Chgo
" Meeting Mohler, Trumbull Brown
Palace Hotel 4 pm
Clear & partly Cloudy

June 12 - 1905
WAD. on No 1 to Arrow, back on 2.
Pt Cldy & light wind.
DHM. & WFJ. in N.Y.

June 12 - 1906
WAD in Grand Co. -
Cloudy & Calm.

Rotary Crew laid Off - for Summer.

Friday June 5 - 1908.
Car Marcia Ke aves McCoy
Spl. about 8 pm today for
Denver, FGM & party,
Pulled off Rotary Crew
today.
DHM N.Y.
WAD. west of Steamboat Spg.

In a massive show of power a rotary heads toward Corona powered by two mallets and trailing a caboose with section men, a tool car full of picks and shovels and bringing up the rear a 100 class engine running in reverse to make possible a retreat should the plow train be disabled. The attack is the final assault against a lengthy blockade during the spring of 1920, when the Moffat Tunnel was still a dream. — *Bert Clarke, DPL*

18

The War Without the Tunnel

World War One caused an unprecedented demand for coal that was in part met by the Yampa coal fields. This gave the Moffat a tremendous increase in traffic. The continued drain on finances from snow fighting over Rollins Pass had taken forty per cent of the entire income of the railroad, so that bond holders were becoming more and more restless.

With the demand for coal no one dared think of scrapping the line during the war except the regional U. S. director of railroads. Thus the Yampa coal fields were expanded after the fashion that Moffat and Dodge had hoped for eight years previously. But without a Main Range Tunnel, the road continued to go in the red. The men went on strike tying up the line. They had $180,000 coming in back wages. The cost of living had skyrocketed. The terrible privations that the men suffered over the hill in winter did not leave them in a good mood to receive only part pay for their work. Bondholders resented that their money was hopelessly tied up in the road. For men with money were making the enormous profits of war time speculation.

July 13, 1918, the Denver papers carried headlines announcing — "U.S. Comes to Aid of Moffat Road With $1,300,000." Sub headlines read, "Rail Administration to Take First Line Receivers Certificates to Advance Cash, to Wipe Out Bills, and Leave Million for Betterments."

Denver was awakening to the danger of the Moffat being torn up immediately following the war emergency, when the roads were expected to be returned to the owners.

Businessmen and civic leaders formed a committee headed by W. G. Evans, that reported to the Federal Rail Board in Washington. Again the papers carried such headlines as "Report Filed Shows Great Rail Need in Northwest Colorado." The article contained a statement Moffat had made many times. "Vast resources that could be tapped by extending Moffat Railroad are declared in statement." The present development of Rangely oil field is delayed proof of this truth.

The war ended. The Moffat had business that she never had before. But the deficit in 1918 had been $1,067,057.11. Bill Freeman, co-receiver, had "hung the road together with bailing wire," as the boys said, so that this deficit was cut to $956,282.96 in 1919, and to $670,519.19 the following year. During those three years, the deficit incurred through Rollins Pass alone could have almost paid for the orignally planned main range two and six-tenths-mile tunnel at the 9,930 feet elevation. In fact, the cost of snow removal in the first ten years of the road's operation would have built the originally planned Main Range Tunnel. The coal bill during the war to pull trains over Rollins Pass was $2,000 a day.

All kinds of rumors got into the press, as the Bankers Trust Company of New York got restless.

January 1, 1920, Denver citizens read this headline — "Consolidation of Line Makes Nation Cross Roads Center. Burlington Main Factor With Tunnel Either Under James Peak or Berthoud." The Berthoud Pass route was considered the shortest. It necessitated either the rebuilding of the Colorado and Southern Narrow Gauge through Idaho Springs, or a complete relocation to the three and five-tenth-mile site under Berthoud.

Any one with an idea was able to find some newspaper reporter who could make copy out of it. One story that made headlines was a far fetched tale about how the Georgetown Loop line was to be extended beyond Silver Plume connecting with the Breckenridge and Dillon line. A new line was to be built down the Blue to Kremmling. This most outlandish line would have necessitated not only the straightening out of a most crooked narrow gauge, rebuilding every bridge as well as laying all new ties and heavy rails in making it standard gauge.

Moffat men and counties supported by the Moffat had their hopes kept up, but most of it was only newspaper talk as Leckenby later proved. The last serious attempt to complete the Moffat had been by the Rock Island, which in 1910 had caused extensive estimates to be made.

> The Moffat, as far as Steamboat Springs, had cost $12,544,573.55 including equipment and betterments to September 30, 1909. To complete the line to Salt Lake it was expected to cost $15,238,060. When we recall that H. A. Sumner constructed things cheaper than he estimated, these figures are of great value. If traffic rights over the Rio Grande-Provo branch and the main line on into Salt Lake from Provo could be secured, it would cut down the cost of construction a million or more. Shops at Salt Lake were expected to cost one million and terminals the same sum. They estimated the building of the six-mile tunnel would take six years making the Rock Island venture total the entire sum of $49,000,000. This would buy out the Moffat, complete the line, and motive power and necessary rolling stock, and build the tunnel.

Moffat men were beginning to wonder, if A. C. Ridgway had not been right, when he said in leaving the road that, "it is going to be a graveyard for railroad men." Many men left the line, seeking jobs elsewhere. Such headlines as came out October 26, 1921, encouraged this. "Moffat Road Again Menaced in New Move to Junk Line." November fourth, the men were made restless by this announcement in headlines — "System Faces $2,500,000 Deficit. High Wages Responsible — According to Freeman and Others Involved in Suit."

But high wages were not responsible. It was the money that should have gone into a two and six-tenth-mile Main Range Tunnel that was putting the line in the red.

October 26, 1921, the Denver Post carried an article announcing that "the Bankers Trust Company of New York, trustee for the bondholders, petitioned District Judge Samuel W. Johnson of Brighton to shut down the road at once, unless wage scales and operating costs are reduced to 'a basis adequately remunerative for the proper conservation and upbuilding of property'." The story was continued that "the line was losing about a million a year."

The court answered that it "is not going to say the wages paid are unreasonable, until evidence has been introduced. . . . The Moffat Road ought to pay as good wages as any other road similarly situated."

November twenty-fifth, 1921, the morning papers announced in Denver that the Moffat road was to close her shops in an effort to reduce expenses.

The court case went on and news came that the receiver may ask for the right to cut wages twenty per cent, as the receiver had only a few days to make a showing to the court that the line could be operated without a loss.

Freeman further asked the right to reduce passenger train service to tri-weekly.

The fall was mild, so that little coal was ordered by Moffat company patrons cutting down the amount mined and shipped out of the Routt County fields over the Moffat. It seemed the very gods were against the Moffat continuing any longer.

You did not have to be a $25,000-a-year man to figure out, that though the road was saving $2,000 a day with the shops closed, that a payoff was coming when the line would be crippled from run-down equipment. As evidence of where the road would soon be, Friday morning's paper told that three engines were smashed in a collision in Corona snowsheds between a freight train and helper engine. How long the line could operate with closed shops was a question.

The Denver News carried a challenging article on December 18, 1921, by the editor of the Steamboat Pilot of Steamboat Springs. Charles Leckenby wrote that "the matter that has worried the northwest part of the state is the evident fact that there is something on foot, apparently something agreed upon affecting our interests, of which we are not informed and can obtain no information.

"Wages were reduced approximately twenty per cent, time and a half for overtime was abrogated, as likewise the double time service for operation over the twenty-seven miles of excessive grade on the hill.

"Arbitrary closing of coal mines of the Moffat road territory amounting practically to a lockout has prevented the receiver from showing during the limitation of time allowed him for showing a balance on the right side of the ledger. This may be taken advantage of to show the court, that the Moffat road is an insolvent and impossible utility."

In these statements are held the fears and thinking and pondering of the rancher, coalminer, and merchant of northwest Colorado.

December twenty-first the Post carried the headline "Moffat Railway Granted a New Lease on Life at Brighton Court Hearing. Freeman and Boettcher Given Another Chance to Operate as Conditions Better."

Eight days later Chas. H. Leckenby sent out a striking call. "If Colorado and especially Denver permit the junking or the passing of the Moffat road, this catastrophe will mark the rise and fall of the great city and the greater state.

"It will mean that the pioneer spirit which, though surrounded by every obstacle, built up the empire has decayed and passed and is no more. . . .

". . . Are there no more David Moffat's, Walter Cheesman's, or John Evans' among us any more?

"Did the Empire building spirit of former days die with the pioneers? And is Denver and the state to fall with decay now.

"Have we degenerated into such a lot of cowardly profiteers that we now even refuse to use our own money to maintain one of the greatest arteries that bring our wealth to us. . .?"

"From seventy-five million to one hundred million dollars every year go out of Colorado into securities of distant places at small rates of interest because it seems that the patriotic spirit of Colorado is dead, and we are too cowardly and too niggardly and parsimonious and miserly to take a chance on our own values and to protect our own state.

"Is not there one real unselfish, courageous hero left among us?

"If there be, let him step forward and we will follow. And we will not desert, and we will not run away. Who is the man of the hour?"

The Moffat road may have been a bottomless pit to financiers for only one reason. That the sacrifices of those who began a line were not backed up with adequate capital, which we see existed within the state. It is my opinion, that if the three or four million needed to construct the Main Range Tunnel had been provided in the days of Colonel Dodge, when Moffat had a heavy heart because of business acquaintances who refused to back him in Denver, we would have seen in the Moffat a financially sound road, even though it had never been completed to Salt Lake.

The originally surveyed Main Range Tunnel was reached by a continuation of the two per cent grade to an elevation of 9,930 feet. There were no curves over ten degrees except possibly one or two twelve-degree curves. This two and six-tenth-mile tunnel was below the elevation where terrible winds and drifting snows tied up the line.

The twenty years' fight against the grades, curves, and blizzards of Rollins Pass proved that the blockades occurred higher than this tunnel. (The Ranch Creek wye (10,200 feet) and the Spruce wye (10,990 feet) were well above 10,000 feet and it was between these two wyes that the rotaries chewed their way continuously in bad storms. It must also be remembered that the temporary branch line was not provided with ample drainage to handle water freezing in culverts, running over the tracks, as would have been provided by the line to the proposed tunnel.

H. A. Sumner himself recommended that this tunnel be built considering the density of traffic expected. Had such a tunnel been in operation as late as 1910, the Moffat would have weathered the financial storms without the loss of the average fifty days a winter. Neither would the Moffat Tunnel district have been taxed for the terribly expensive Moffat Tunnel route. Neither would the railroad have had such high Moffat Tunnel taxes to pay. With the road paying dividends, it is entirely conceivable that capital might have been interested in completing the line. Modern steam, or diesel, or, better yet, electric power would have handled that elevation through the tunnel just as satisfactorily as Soldier Summit is fought and Tennessee Pass (10,240 feet) operated on the Rio Grande today. The money to accomplish all of this went out in useless snow fighting.

The Moffat was saved by the wage cuts. Freeman was given a chance to hold the road together. Leckenby came back from the court case to tell the inside story that no railroad was seriously considering buying the Moffat and that every one should back Freeman, as there had been entirely too little cooperation by every one in any way involved with the Moffat.

So the men took their cut. A little more buying power was taken out of the hands of the public. With the same thing happening all over the country, the inevitable 1929 would happen when the ability of the working man to buy could not keep up with the manufacturer's production.

There was coal to haul, and there was oil. Oil had long been known to exist in this territory. It was brought into production in 1918 and shipped over the lines, until the completion of an oil line years later. Coal and oil saved the Moffat. Freeman juggled the repairs and improvements to the paper edge thinness to keep the road going. The men paid for the snow fighting, out of their low wages.

As an example of the cost men were paying for this, let us consider two stories of Criss Lomax.

The place is Corona. We do not think of the beautiful little lakes or the water falls across Middle Boulder Cañon. We think of gassed men in the Rollins Pass snowshed, the endless poker game that went on and on, and the rule that no wives were allowed to be brought to the top of the world. But there was a woman there, the wife of an operator. It was her first day. Her husband had been given special permission to have her come up.

Criss Lomax was the operator on duty when the daily occurrence of a gassed man being carried into the office happened. It was the custom to lay such men on the floor until they came to.

This man was a strapping big fireman by the name of Gallagher. As he moaned and groaned on the floor, the operator's wife came into the room. She knew nothing about this being a daily occurrence and cried out, "Do something. This is terrible." But no one paid attention. After they had attempted to make the usual explanation that this was the usual thing and that he was surely all right or he would not have been groaning so terribly, no one paid any attention to the woman.

But she was not so easily pacified. She went back to her room to get some ammonia. She hurried back to the operator's shanty, turned the fireman over on his back and with trembling hands attempted to give him a whiff of the ammonia. But instead of a whiff, he got some of the genuine liquid down his nose. Gallagher came to life like three madmen. The woman fled as the train crew found themselves unable to hold him to the floor. The maddened man smashed furniture, tore the phones from the walls, and wrecked the office and instruments. Lomax and the train crew fled out of the office down the little hall into the smoky train shed. As the liquid ammonia all turned to vapor, the fireman calmed down, becoming a normal man. The work of restoring the wrecked office became the emergency task.

As humorous as this story may be, it tells the terrible conditions that the men worked under and explains why so many Moffat men had such high doctor bills.

Nels Johnson confirms the above story regarding the terrible conditions of gas with the story of several helper engines waiting on a siding in the shed. Johnson discovered that all the men were gassed but he and Conway. Jack Russell and Bill Miller were gassed in their engines. Miller was lying against an engine pipe with his face burned to the bone.

Engine men and fireman tried all kinds of smoke masks, and often presented a very ugly picture wearing their smoke snout and hog snout.

George Schryer recalls the time five helper engines were coupled together on the Corona siding waiting for a freight that was coming up the hill. George was in the cab of his engine, which was near the middle of the line up. Since the snow was high over the snowshed, the gas from the engines was slow in getting out of the few ventilators that were not buried under the snow.

Suddenly George was aware that the engines were running wild down the cañon cut by the rotary through the twenty-foot snow west of the shed. He immediately guessed that he and all the other men had been gassed. His fireman was out, but now in the semi-dazed condition was coming to in the bitter cold air, which had aroused Schryer.

George cut his engine's air into the air line, which had been under the first engineer's control. Working his brake valve, cycling it back and forth to build up the air line, George began restoring the braking power of the heavy engines on the four per cent.

He held on to his whistle cord warning the freight, which would be coming around Ptarmigan Point any moment. His fireman by now was recovering enough that, when he beheld the freight coming round the bend, he attempted to jump. George caught him knowing he would be ground into hamburger under the wheels of the engine, for the cut in the snow was a hopeless wall over which no one could jump.

It seemed impossible to stop the five mallets, but the freight ahead could be easily stopped, for it was coming up the four per cent. Schryer kept working his brake valve back and forth building up the line pressure, so that the engines slowly came to a stop — thirty feet from the freight train.

The next problem was to render first aid to the men, several of whom were burned from collaps-

230

ing against steam pipes.

Chris Lomax tells what he calls a humorous story:

A five-engine train had pulled in from the west and was waiting on the siding for a two-engine train from the east. This siding was long enough to accommodate a five-engine train, which pulled into the snowshed and crept up behind the first train. But the head engineer could not see in the smoke and gas. Van Vranken says that though you could not see a fuzee, you could sometimes smell them. Apparently no one was flagging behind the first train. The second train crept up behind and coupled into the caboose, which was behind the last engine on the first train. In fact, the snow was drifted over the tops of the snowshed leaving few of the ventilators open, so that the second train's engineer feeling his way in the darkness realized that he had coupled into the caboose. It so happened that the roadmaster was sleeping in this caboose. Roadmasters and trackmen had to grab a ride any way they could, to get over the line. This roadmaster awakened with the shock of the second train coupling in and beheld the caboose folding up. He dashed ahead, jerked open the door, attempted to climb the ladder on the rear of the helper engine's tender. But the caboose caught up with him and reached up with a board and nail, which snagged him in the pants and lifted him high over the engine tender.

The roadmaster hoped against hope that the nail would hold, and that the engineers on the second train would close their throttles. But the hoggers thought the rail was just a little slippery, when they met the resistance of folding up the caboose, so they just opened their throttles a little more.

The roadmaster's pants gave way, and he tumbled over the side of the engine sliding down the icy side of the packed snow in the snowshed landing on his back under the engine. Here he was uanble to turn over or crawl out. He dared not move less he be scraped by the engine.

Well, anyway the air was better where he lay. The man wondered how long it would be until he was discovered, for the noise of the crash and the hissing of steam from the engine drowned out his voice.

As he looked up, a red hot coal from the fire box dropped on his chest. The helpless roadmaster could not even get his hand free to shove the clinker away. It burned through the man's clothes burning a space on his chest the size of his fist, until the man's blood cooled the clinker.

This is a humorous story, because a man lived and was able to go to work again after hospital treatment. But there were stories that were not humorous.

Therefore, when we say that the road was saved from scrap by the increase of the coal business and the discovery of oil, we add the ability of President Freeman "to take food out of the bellies of the men by the low wages he paid." These men gave up

Just in time for the rush of wartime business, the Moffat purchased ten 2-8-2's for heavy freight service. The engines proved too rigid for the tight curves on Rollins Pass so saw little service running over the hill. —*L.C. McClure, CRRM*

twenty per cent of their wages, time and a half for overtime and double time for working on the hill. Thus their pay dropped far below the money other mountain railroads paid.

The sixteen-hour law was not observed on the Moffat until a much later date. Men have worked without relief as long as ninety hours at a time. The high altitude caused a man to be in agony for his breath, if he ran a hundred feet. The severe weather caused frost bites and the expense of extra clothing. The poor health of many men in later years is laid to these terrible conditions.

These men were indeed unsung heroes who contributed their part to the saving of the Moffat.

Under David Moffat as president and under W. A. Deuel as general manager from 1910 to 1913 a devotion was built up by the men for the road. Joe Culbertson said the feeling of the men was that they would go to hell for Colonel Deuel. No wages ever paid a gandy dancer could get them out in the storms, but Colonel Deuel could, for he was just one of his men. Now with Bill Freeman as president and general manager, the men were driven and their devotion began to ebb.

Much of the credit for the Moffat's ability to continue through these years must fall on a big Swede by the name of A. L. Johnson. When Freeman had needed a new clerk, Johnson applied for the job and brought along a very high recommendation from Emily Griffith, founder of the famed night school which still bears her name. Coming to Denver from a poor Texas cotton farm, Johnson began attending the night classes and was soon spotted by Miss Griffith as a young man with great potential.

Johnson read and observed the best in railroad-ing, learned quickly and gradually moved up to become assistant superintendent and eventually general superintendent. As the "Jekyll-Hyde" Freeman began spending more of his time log rolling and conniving with his board regarding the moves and counter moves in railroad politics, it seemed often that Johnson was running the railroad.

The Moffat was in the blood of its men as steel rails and engines rarely were, for the road was Dave Moffat and Colonel Deuel and Northwest Colorado.

The board of directors never seriously questioned Freeman's ability and held him in high esteem. So also did the press picture him when he retired. The unfortunate fact is that the Moffat boys took a loss that they never gained back in the prosperous years or even in better jobs when the merger took place. Knowing the price they paid in low wages and devotion to duty in terrible conditions, it is easy to understand the deep resentment of the Moffat men toward Rio Grande men running red ball and in streamliner service.

Many men sought other railroads. Their places were taken by "boomers", some of whom had been fired for inefficiency on other lines and could no longer secure a job on a decent line. But with Johnson as superintendent, Joe Culbertson the chief dispatcher, Bill Jones, chief engineer, L.J. Daly the trainmaster, Charlie Peterson, master mechanic, George Barnes, conductor extraordinary, and Louie Larson, the veteran hill man, the road accomplished miracles with the little cash it received. The Moffat served faithfully as the nation was at war.

In December, 1918, a fire at Tunnel 16 forced passengers, including newlyweds Mr. & Mrs. Joe Preiss, to walk (left) between trains on either side of the tunnel. By World War I, Tolland (top) had changed from the tourist town it was when the railroad arrived in 1904, but it was still a lively town with lumber mills working nearby. We see the rotary (right) carefully working to clear the yard near the coal pocket in 1918, while we have a view of the new coal pocket just after a slight mishap. Joe Preiss was called for a run at 4:00 AM on Easter morning in 1920, and while waiting he took this shot of the car pushed a bit too hard up the coal pocket track. That same day the lengthy spring blockade began up on Rollins Pass. — *left and right, Joe Hewitt; all DPL*

The Moffat Road was not alone in having snow troubles as evidenced by this Union Pacific train during a tie-up across Wyoming in 1917, but for the Moffat such conditions were common rather than unusual. During the lengthy blockade of 1918, this mallet (above) was allowed to go dead while the other two engines managed to back the passenger train down to Arrow. After two weeks a rotary plow finally reached this stranded coal train (left) as the crew shovels snow drifted around their engine and caboose. Fabian Smith is the first man to the right of the engine. In 1918, the U.S. Railroad Administration purchased a plow from the Colorado, Wyoming and Eastern Ry to insure that the Moffat was kept open to vital traffic. The plow became the Moffat's No. 10202 and is seen (right-bottom and far right) along with a C.W. & E Ry. locomotive borrowed for use on the Moffat. As work progressed on the Moffat Tunnel the battle of Rollins Pass must be continued as in this massive show of power (right-top) as five mallets and a 2-8-0 head up the hill to assist a plow train. A typical day on the hill can be visualized by this train order (right) issued in October, 1925. — *below, University of Wyoming; above, Fabian Smith, DPL; right-top, Mrs. Louis Larsen; others, Fabian Smith: all, CRRM*

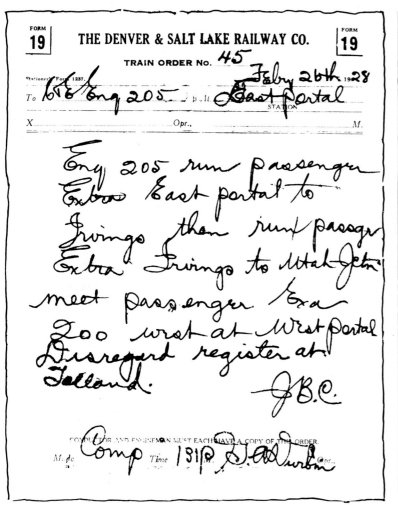

THE DENVER & SALT LAKE RAILWAY CO.

FORM 19

FORM 19

TRAIN ORDER No. 45

To Eng 205 _____ East Portal _____ STATION

Feby 26th 28

Eng 205 run passenger
Extra East portal to
Irvings then run passgr
Extra Irvings to Utah Jctn
meet passenger Extra
200 west at West Portal
Disregard register at
Tolland.
J.B.C.

CONDUCTOR AND ENGINEMAN MUST EACH HAVE A COPY OF THIS ORDER.

Made Comp Time 131P J. A. Wurbon Opr.,

This is the train order issued to Louis Larsen by long time Dispatcher J. B. Culbertson giving authority for the first train to officially run through the Moffat Tunnel; (of course, work trains and test runs of freight trains had gone through the past few days). This photo (above) captures the exact moment that engine 205 entered the tunnel, while (below) the train is seen emerging at West Portal less than 15 minutes later. The spirit of Uncle Dave must surely have been proud that day! — *Train order, Mrs. Louis Larsen, CRRM; others, DPL*

19
Building the Moffat Tunnel

Dave Moffat's insight in building the Moffat Road has as its monument, the Moffat Division of the Rio Grande, which served as an invaluable one hundred seventy-five mile cutoff for the Rio Grande during World War Two carrying all the traffic the line could handle. According to a statement by Gerald Hughes, one-third of the business of the Rio Grand would be lost today, if the Moffat division were removed from the Rio Grande railroad.

When Moffat started building his Denver, Northwestern and Pacific, Jay Gould controlled the Rio Grande and fed it through the Pueblo gateway by the Missouri Pacific.

Gould's fear was that the Missouri Pacific business from Kansas City, St. Louis, and the East would be lost to the Rock Island and Burlington, which were his competitors, if Denver became the gateway for David Moffat's road.

Gould never realized that it would be profitable to use the Moffat as a cutoff to pick up Burlington and Rio Grande originated traffic for the Rio Grande without hurting the Missouri Pacific substantially.

From St. Louis to Salt Lake by Missouri Pacific and the Pueblo gateway the distance is 1,530 miles. Before the Dotsero cutoff the Burlington hook-up with the Rio Grande was 1,673 miles and the Rock Island was 1,603 miles. In other words, shipments were likely to go Missouri Pacific. But with the Dotsero cutoff built and the Moffat Tunnel open the Burlington had 1,498 miles, Rock Island 1,503 miles and the Missouri Pacific remained 1,530 miles. This is

why Gould and his successors feared the Moffat Tunnel route. But what happened was that all three roads made inroads on the Union Pacific, so that the Missouri Pacific held its business and the Burlington and Rock Island added Chicago and Eastern business, which otherwise went Union Pacific for their shipping route was 175 miles nearer competing with the Union Pacific.

If Gould had not fought the Moffat and had allowed Moffat to build his own Dotsero Cutoff and exchange business at Dotsero, Moffat could have secured money to build the originally planned two and six-tenths mile Main Range Tunnel, and Gould's Rio Grande would have had a great increase of business.

Denver could have been on a transcontinental trunk line twenty years earlier. Northwestern Colorado's valuable coal and mining business would have been developed by capital which was afraid the Moffat would be scrapped as it struggled over Rollins Pass.

Denver could have become a manufacturing center during World War One instead of having to wait until World War Two. The war, of course, was not in the Pacific in 1915, but Denver would have grown substantially, as would all of Northwestern Colorado with a two and six-tenths mile tunnel well under the bad storms keeping traffic moving on a financially sound road.

To Colorado investors the grass was naturally much greener outside of its own state. There is no question that many times the money needed to build the original tunnel was invested out of

237

the state. But Harriman's and Gould's war against Moffat successors did not make the investment look good.

The year Dave Moffat and U.S. Senator Hughes died, a bill was introduced in the legislature by Gaines M. Allen of Denver. It was known as State Tunnel Construction Bill Number 402. The idea proposed had to be taken to the voters and though it was lost in 1912 at the election, the bill had served one excellent purpose. It had given Moffat men a shot of adrenalin.

W. J. Evans was Republican political boss of the state at this time and lead the fight for the Moffat.

It was only natural for men to turn to the state to accomplish what they were unable to do by themselves. That is what our governments have always existed for. Almost a century before New York and Pennsylvania had built a canal system. No sooner was the Erie Canal open than the first railroads in New York state began to receive direct financial help from the legislature, when they floundered in financial difficulties.

This first look towards the state for help brought a series of moves. An effort was made in February 1913 to get the tunnel built with Denver funds. April 14, 1914, the Supreme Court considered this move unconstitutional.

Meanwhile another effort was made to finance privately the building of the tunnel under the Erb regime of the Moffat. Erb had promised to raise half the funds if Moffat men secured the other half. Colonel Dodge, S. M. Perry, Henry M. Porter, Phipps, Boettcher, and Gerald Hughes were among the largest subscribers who brought the list up to two and one-half million. The Denver Clearing House broke precedent and subscribed a million dollars, but Erb failed to secure his half.

The state help idea gained favor in the months that followed and the Tri-Tunnel Plan was introduced, proposing not only a Moffat Tunnel but a Monarch Pass Tunnel and a Cumbres Hill Tunnel. Pueblo, however, defeated this bill by a very narrow margin of votes November 2, 1920. Pueblo had always been ill-advised by interests which tried to make it appear that Pueblo would become a first cousin to a ghost city if the Moffat Road became a main line. In contrast we find the growth of Denver making Pueblo a stronger city by reason of the need for steel and other industries.

Enthusiasm was gone for the building of a

Moffat Tunnel except in the hearts of a few practical visionaries, who knew Dave Moffat had been right.

Then came an act of providence. A flood swept down the Arkansas River drowning out all of Pueblo's opposition to Moffat Tunnel. For Pueblo citizens were afraid Northwestern Colorado and Denver would have the memory of an elephant and would not be interested in an emergency session of the legislature to build a dyke to prevent another such catastrophe.

This flood really did bring a change of heart, though it was a wet trail and not a saw dust trail that led the Pueblo members of the legislature to the Capitol building to pass, without one vote of opposition, the Moffat Tunnel District Bill and the organization of the Tunnel Commission. Of course, there followed legislation helpful to Pueblo's flood control. The Tunnel Commission did not have to be spurred to action. The need for the tunnel was critical. When the first plans, however, were announced, they included drafts for a pioneer bore seventy-five feet east of the main tunnel. The reason given for this added tunnel was that a pioneer bore was necessary to speed the construction of such a tremendously long tunnel.

Engineers, however, immediately saw that every foot of rock removed was added expense which would be paid for in taxes. Art Weston, therefore, wrote an article in the December 1922 Colorado Engineers' Bulletin entitled "Why Two Tunnels." Weston summarizes today his purpose in writing that article.

I wrote an article which was published in the December, 1922, Bulletin of the Colorado Society of Engineers, under the caption 'Why Two Tunnels.' The bill as passed by the legislature called for a tunnel and nowhere referred to it in the plural. My article was a criticism of the plan to construct a 'pioneer' tunnel parallel to and seventy-five feet from the main tunnel. It was proposed to use this as a means of working the main tunnel through 'cross-cuts' and the propaganda used was that this would speed up the work. Such a pioneer or supplemental tunnel had never been used in the United States, but had in some of the very long tunnels in the European Alps. (It was also being used in the tunnel through the Cascade Mountains in British Columbia.)

Of course I knew that this 'pioneer' tunnel was intended to be used to bring water from the western slope to Denver for domestic purposes, but they did not come out in the open and say so. At that time David W. Brunton, a famous mining engineer, (also the inventor of the Brunton Pocket Transit) was consulting engineer for the Moffat Tunnel Commission. In my article I told how some long and large section water tunnels were then being built in California without any 'pioneer' bore, and being built very rapidly. They were driving their 'heading,' that is, the top part of the tunnel, by using a new development in fuses, known as 'delay fuse.' They would drill some holes four feet, some eight, some twelve, and some eighteen feet. Then, by the use of delay fuse, they shot each depth in succession. This threw most of the muck over the bench and down on the floor of the main bore. From there it was loaded into mine cars by mechanical loaders and hauled out, using two parallel tracks. The tunnels were wide enough for this as the mine cars used a two-foot gauge track.

In a few days after the Bulletin containing my article was published the daily papers stated that Mr. Brunton had gone to California to investigate the methods being used in the tunnels there. In other words, I started him off, but, of course, they persisted in building two tunnels, as they had intended. About this time I had a conversation with my old friend, L. W. Blauveldt, who had made an estimate of the probable cost of the tunnel.

As I remember his estimate was $6,720,000. I said to him, 'If we were going to build this for a railroad probably we could do it for your estimate, but it is going to be built by some politicians, and it will cost twice or more what you estimate.' He did not agree with me, in fact, he became somewhat angry with me for criticizing his estimate. I wasn't so far wrong, but I had underestimated what politicians can do in spending money. It actually cost over eighteen million dollars.

The tunnel was 'holed-through' on February 18, 1927, with appropriate ceremonies being broadcast over the radio. The first train through was February 26, 1928. There was a good deal of delay in driving due to soft rock that they could not hold with the usual tunnel timbering.

But why was a six-mile tunnel needed at all? Moffat's first and most famous chief engineer had recommended a two and six-tenths mile tunnel unless the traffic became very heavy. President Freeman was satisfied with a short tunnel at this location. Senator Phipps was not particular as to which location was used for his main determination was to get Denver on a transcontinental line. Gerald Hughes, however, saw Denver's need for water. He had been on the Denver Water Board in the days when you were allowed to water your lawns only on certain days each week. Gerald Hughes argued that a transcontinental line could not build a city unless it had water. Further he knew the taxpayers of Denver would not hear to the boring of a water tunnel through the Divide to bring western slope snow water to the city.

In an interview with Lawrence C. Phipps, Jr. he suggested that with the popularity of the railroad tunnel at hand Gerald Hughes saw an opportunity to get a water tunnel, if the railroad tunnel was located at the 9,000 foot level and constructed with the aid of a pioneer bore. The people might be fooled, but it would be for their own good.

If the cost of the tunnel could have been hidden in a general tax such as the cost of war, people would take for granted their tunnel. But unfortunately the tax had to be special, ever to remind the taxpayer of the tunnel cost and to become sand in their shoes.

The Tunnel Commission got busy, first, by constructing living quarters, baths where the men could shower after work, recreation halls, and eating houses. Private business enterprises pulled strings, sought political influence to secure these concessions. But to the great credit of the Tunnel Commission, they were not granted. The entire income from this adventure was $600,000 clear. This was applied on the cost of the tunnel construction. Indeed an engineer like H. A. Sumner would have been pleased with the wholesome atmosphere for the men and the use put to these profits.

Next came the opening of the tunnel from both ends. The first electric engines for the narrow gauge construction cars were hauled by sleds from Irving Spur to West Portal. The pioneer bore was under construction midst great fan fare of newspapers and magazines. Difficult conditions were soon found at the west bore. Hearts sank for this meant increased cost Immense twelve by twelve timbers were crushed by the heavy pressure in the tunnel. In time the adverse conditions made it very evident that the cost would be much more than estimated. The mountain challenged the men with streams of water that poured in from lakes above. It soon began to look as though a fortune would go into the construction of the tunnel. Annoyed by the problem of the rotten condition of the rock, which had been broken in some prehistoric upheaval before, George Lewis, one of the engineers, could not sleep at his West Portal headquarters one night. In this restless state he conceived the idea of a traveling cantilever needle bar to hold the ceiling up while the tunnel was being dug. He awakened some of his companions and they discussed the idea. He rushed into Denver and had some difficulty getting his idea across, but out of this idea came the Lewis Cantilever Bar. It might be described as consisting of "two sixty-five foot steel beams three and one-half feet thick tied together by rigid struts and braces and supported on enormous one foot square Oregon fir. This rested on the bench of the tunnel heading and with a third of its length projected to the rear the girder carrying the supporting timbers that held up the roof, while the muck was carried away and permanent timbering put in place." Endless belt conveyors and electric shovels filled the cars that removed the muck.

As the East Portal entrance was not in such difficult rock, the work progressed faster from that end. The center of the tunnel was reached by the East Portal crews, while the West Portal crews were some distance away. This center was called the apex of the tunnel, for it was higher than either end to facilitate drainage during construction. Immediately a new problem arose. From this spot west a descending grade would be followed in the digging of the tunnel. Water would have to be pumped up to the apex, until the West Portal crews were reached. Having learned that anything might happen, the men installed enormous pumps. Then Crater Lake above let loose a stream that defied the pumps. One man, as he walked in hip boots, was electrocuted by the current of the electric trolley wire. The death toll was to climb to nineteen men actually killed while working in the tunnel. But when we compare this to the 2,000 who lost their lives years before in the construction of the Simplon tunnel, we see that safety was on the conscience of man.

As the East and West Portal crews neared one another, great excitement prevailed. On February 12, the graveyard shift of West Portal, under C.M. Paul, drove a forty-foot bar through to the East Portal crew who grabbed the bar and tusseled with it.

It makes a good story to say that the survey was straight for this tunnel. However, when W. C. Jones prepared the tunnel for guniting and concrete reinforcement some time later, he found that it had thirteen angles which were from one to nine minutes off.

The Denver papers had a field day of excite-

Newcomb (top) became the station stop for East Portal and a spur was built to bring supplies to the tunnel site. On the west side Irving was the nearest station and on Feb. 22, 1925, four teams were used to haul this sled (above) from the railroad to West Portal, with the Lewis Traveling Cantilever Girder, used in the west side of the tunnel. Winters were harsh as in this scene of the officials dorm at East Portal. — *below, Arthur F. Hewitt, all, DPL*

ment bringing the news to the public. The winning crew from West Portal was treated like the royal house of England by a celebration thrown in Denver. No doubt they deserved the honor more than any king.

A ceremony, of course, had to be provided for the next day. Distinguished guests from Utah and Colorado were taken by President Freeman over the hill to West Portal. But this special train battled the wrath of Old Man Winter, who made the Moffat use two rotaries to keep the hill open.

It has not been my purpose to tell the story of the Moffat Tunnel construction. For, it is an engineering feat that would be insulted by anything less than a book-length story. Edgar Carlisle McMechen has done that well in his two-volume work "THE MOFFAT TUNNEL OF COLORADO."

Suffice it to say that no popular scholarly scientific magazine ignored its construction. Such headlines for articles were coined as "Colorado Tears Down Her Mountains," by A. Chapman and "How Railbuilder's Dream Came True," by Theodore Fisher in *Popular Mechanics*.

Denver was kept posted faithfully by her two rival papers, who ran such big headlines that a century from now some one might think Denver had built the tunnel.

Among the tunnel workers were some men who liked Middle Park well enough to adopt it as their home. To this day they will tell you stories of how tools were wasted by the contractor, because he was paid on a cost plus basis. This makes interesting talk. A little of it is no doubt fact for in business the same occurs. The disease of waste is not a government disease alone; it is part of the American way of doing things. But to understand what happened we must remember that the unexpected broke loose time and again flooding machinery with fractured granite or water and that in such emergencies the loss of tools was very secondary to getting pumps going and the emergency met.

To the credit of the Tunnel Commission this great undertaking was carried out when it looked as if the impossible was ahead.

In my mind, however, the greatest increase in cost over estimate came from unforeseen rock formations. H. A. Sumner in October 1909 had advised the management of the railroad, "There is always an uncertainty as to conditions to be found in a long tunnel, the material changes in character, the water conditions are unknown, the amount of lining cannot be determined, and there are a number of doubtful questions, which only actual construction can determine."

Very apparently L. D. Blauveldt made little lee-way in his estimate for conditions that could be expected for fear a more likely estimate of the cost would frighten the public support of the tunnel idea. The fractured condition of the rock encountered in almost all of the short tunnels the road had constructed previously, the terrible pressures found in two tunnels which caused abandonments of them, and shoo-fly built around them, are well established in the letters of H. A. Sumner. All of the first thirty tunnels were in L. D. Blauveldt's district as field engineer during the construction of the road and were well known to him. Blauveldt should have listed a warning if nothing else about the probable higher cost.

H.A. Sumner had estimated the cost of the road including fifty-four tunnels and had built it at less cost than estimated. I am firmly convinced Sumner would have estimated closer and have not undershot his estimate so far.

It is very illuminating for Arthur Ridgway, former chief engineer of the Rio Grande, to say that though it would be adverse to his company, a much fairer way of renting the tunnel would have been on a wheel basis, which could have paid for the tunnel at no great hurt to the Rio Grande.

Denver Post on February 1, 1929, carried an editorial saying, "Taxpayers left holding the sack on Moffat Tunnel." Such a feeling was aggravated by a statement to the press by J. A. M'Ilwee who told how he had offered to build the tunnel for six million and stated that he had $300,000 in bond, which he would have posted. I am afraid he would have lost his bond. Nothing was ever built without gossip. The gossip this time was very ugly.

But the agreement being what it is, the tunnel district can consider this as their World War Two contribution. For without Moffat Tunnel one highway never would have been opened to handle the jam of Pacific coast materials. When an unfortunate fire in the timbering of Tunnel Ten made this route useless for three months, the old main line through the Royal Gorge could not begin to move the troops or war materials. It was simply a case of other roads already overtaxed being worked harder and the entire west coast jam increased in intensity.

As to how favorable Denver would have been for an industrial city without the Moffat is

We see here a panorama of life and work at the tunnel sites. The Lewis Traveling Cantilever Girder (top-left) supports the roof while the Osgood Compressed Air Shovel mucks out the debris to be dumped from the West Portal trestle (above-left) which is today the site of Winter Park ski area. The West Portal office is seen (above-right) to be a rough, uninsulated structure that must have been cold in winter. The dining hall (top-right) was known for its good food. A cross cut (below-left) connected the railroad tunnel to the pioneer bore and to be sure stress was not causing dangerous movement, engineers (below-right) made constant checks. —*below-right, DPL; others, Moffat Tunnel Commission.*

further questioned, for Denver is what she is because she is the hub of communications and the competition of this Moffat Tunnel gateway has made, to a great extent, it such.

The real complaint returns to the citizens, who as small investors prior to World War One saw the green grass outside of Colorado to the tune of many times the cost of the originally proposed two and six-tenths mile tunnel. There were few great men of wealth in Denver but there were millions being invested outside of the state by the rank and file. Probably enough money was lost in useless investments, in wildcat oil schemes, to have built the tunnel through the main range, which H. A. Sumner recommended in the early days.

The two and six-tenths mile tunnel would have lengthened the route fourteen miles and added five and seven-tenths miles of two per cent grade in comparison to the present six and twenty-three hundredths mile tunnel. This lengthened route, however, would not have been too serious. To get a more beautiful route a new railroad will have to be located for the Rio Grande's two routes go through the most rugged part of the Rockies, not around them. So incomparable is this route in beauty to any other route that the Rio Grande's passenger future is insured.

When H. A. Sumner recommended the two and six-tenths mile tunnel, he recommended it on the expected 8,200 tons of traffic. Even before the Rio Grande had a hook-up to use this route, the Moffat had exceeded this tonnage in hauling coal. "Joe" Culbertson smiles when he tells us of the 47,000 to 49,000 tons of freight handled daily through this tunnel, not including passenger trains, of course.

In fact, the tonnage handled today would have caused in time a second bore to have been put through the Divide, likely at the 9,470-foot elevation. This survey would have made a four and one-tenth mile tunnel with the original tunnel as a relief tunnel for returning helper engines and a guard against bottlenecks, as well as a second route in case of derailments or other blocks in the longer tunnel. The point still is that both of these tunnels could have been paid for by traffic carried and snow removal saved by the years that preceded the opening of Moffat Tunnel.

Does this not eloquently bespeak the realistic vision of Dave Moffat in battling to open up Northwestern Colorado and this route?

It is further true that with modern steam and diesel power all present traffic could have been handled through the one two and six-tenths mile tunnel. With a financially sound road it is likely that the line would have been electrified at an early date from Tabernash to Denver. This would have been an economic answer to the problem with electro-generative breaking cutting power costs up to forty per cent. Arthur Ridgway, as chief engineer of the Rio Grande, urged the company to begin setting aside money for the electrification soon after the Rio Grande began operating over the line. Engineer departments of two major electric companies have worked on plans for the electrification and it may yet be the final answer for the Moffat division.

Now, having weighed most of the factors regarding Moffat Tunnel, we continue with the story of the official opening of Moffat Tunnel on February 26, 1928.

Both Denver papers seized the opportunity, presented, and magnificently told the story letting the entire nation know that Faith had removed the mountains.

One smiles today when we read of the bombs exploded on the Rocky Mountain News roof at the opening of the tunnel. One laughs heartily as each paper tried to out-do the other paper in bringing this big scoop to its readers, as their own exclusive story. It is all part of the romance of the way Denver does things. It was a privilege to live in Colorado and read the Denver Post.

If the parsons said prayers for the lost souls who cut out church-going that Sunday, I do not know, but four trains sold out all their tickets and Rocky Mountain Statesmen and railroaders from all lines accepted the invitation of Bill Freeman.

Dave Moffat would have been very proud of his men that day. They handled the motive power well. No oversight occurred to embarrass the little road. Old Man Winter's stronghold was conquered on a typical blustery day high above the tunnel.

Those who attempted to drive to East Portal on the narrow county road found the snow too deep. Cars stalled and men became a fraternity of brothers chaining car to car and pushing and shoveling. The Tunnel Commission sent down teams to extract the helpless cars and though the worshippers of the gas buggy arrived too late for the best of the celebration, coffee and sandwiches were waiting for them.

The veteran conductor, George Barnes, was not the first conductor through the tunnel. He claims Bill Freeman, the president, was angered by the probable line-up of trains the papers had printed, and had side-tracked his train out of spite. Joe Culbertson, chief dispatcher and very loyal friend of George, differs thinking that the engine pulling Barnes' train fell down causing the delay.

Four trains of ten cars each had merrily followed the proud 200 engines up the two per cent grade to East Portal. Regular Number One was in the rear of the parade with Engine 303 and Chester Foltz at the throttle. The trains were combined into two twenty-car trains and pulled through the tunnel after the spike driving ceremony was over. Louis A. Larsen, engineer; T. F. Garr, fireman; Frank Spaulding, conductor; F. A. Van Vranken, brakeman; and R. E. Dunlap, flagman, made up the crew of the first official train through the tunnel. Of course, work trains had preceded this train as well as several test-run trains.

But, the most humorous incident of the day occurred when the first train quietly drifted out of the West Portal of the Tunnel. There stood a sign with these words: "WE BUILT THE TUNNEL. THE POST DIDN'T."

Superintendent A. L. Johnson ordered the sign torn down by section men, but he never knew whose idea it was until twenty years later.

The residents of Middle Park had been denied the right to walk through Moffat Tunnel, even though it was not in use, before the celebration.

Among these people were the constructin workers, who with Doc Susie Anderson of Fraser would have had to take the night train over the pass and spend at East Portal nine cold hours waiting for the celebration. The soft-spoken, kindly Doc Susie blew up, and with the help of bystanders took an old broom and dipped in some tar and painted the sign with the same hands she had cared for the injured.

The venom was taken out on the Denver Post, which had ballyhooed the celebration to such an extent that these hard working people wanted it to be known who built the tunnel.

The sun blistered the eyes of those gathered at West Portal to see the 205 come through the tunnel with her twenty-car train.

Miles away in a Pennsylvania Dutch town of Selinsgrove, a Susquehanna University sophomore read the story of the opening of Moffat Tunnel in "Popular Science." This lad had read everything he could get on the subject of Dave Moffat's exploits and had plotted on geodetic maps the proposed western extension of the line. Twenty years later he dug through the actual survey maps and engineers letters to write this book.

Yes, Dave Moffat's victory was headline news in New York, where men had said "No" to his idea twenty years before.

The Rio Grande Railroad was on hand to use this tunnel by contract only.

On Ocotber 8, 1927, Arthur Hewitt took this photo as the tunnel neared completion. Engine 303 is furnishing compressed air for work in the tunnel but already the air-operated shovel is parked, waiting for shipment and clean-up is starting. Weeks before the official opening, engine 120 became the first locomotive (other than mining and construction engines) to enter the Moffat Tunnel (below) as it pushed in flats loaded with ties and rail. —*DPL*

February 26, 1928, was a clear day with the ground at East Portal bare of snow, as 2500 passengers arrived aboard four special trains to join hundreds who drove to the site, some becoming stuck on the snow blocked county roads. Otto Perry took this historic photo (above) of the third section near Rollinsville with mallets 207 and 200. The ceremonies began at 12:15 PM and included the driving of a gold spike provided by the *Denver Post*. This honor went to ex-Governor William H. Adams and Governor Oliver H. Shoup who is standing at the center of the photo. We see a general view (below) of the event with engine 205 standing ready after having coupled to the second section as the four trains were made into two for the run through the tunnel. The program included remarks by Mayor Bowman of Salt Lake, ex-Mayor Bailey and Mayor Stapleton of Denver, Moffat Tunnel Commission President Robinson and D&SL President Freeman. — *all DPL*

UNITED STATES OF AMERICA

NUMBER 7314   NUMBER 7314

STATE OF COLORADO

$1000   **$1000**

THE MOFFAT TUNNEL IMPROVEMENT DISTRICT
INCLUDING THE
City and County of Denver
COUNTIES OF GRAND, MOFFAT, ROUTT AND CERTAIN PORTIONS OF THE COUNTIES
OF EAGLE, GILPIN, BOULDER, ADAMS AND JEFFERSON

MOFFAT TUNNEL SUPPLEMENTAL BOND

The Moffat Tunnel Improvement District *(hereinafter called the district), a public corporation organized and existing under and pursuant to the laws of the State of Colorado, for value received, hereby acknowledges itself to be indebted and promises to pay to the bearer hereof, or, if registered, to the registered holder of this bond* **ONE THOUSAND DOLLARS**

in gold coin of the United States of America, of or equal to the present standard of weight and fineness, on the first day of January, A. D. 1978, as hereinafter provided, and to pay interest thereon, as hereinafter provided from the first day of January, A. D. 1927, in like gold coin, at the rate of five per centum per annum, semi-annually, on the first days of July and January in each year, upon presentation and surrender of this bond and the interest coupons hereto attached as they severally mature; both the principal of and the interest upon this bond being payable at the American Exchange Irving Trust Company of New York, in the City of New York, U.S.A., (or at such other bank in the City of New York, as may hereafter be designated as the fiscal agent of the district), which bank is hereby ordered to pay the same without further authority out of any moneys in the Moffat Tunnel Supplemental Bond Fund, created by said district and by it deposited with said bank for such purpose.

This supplemental bond is issued by the Moffat Tunnel Commission in the name and on behalf of The Moffat Tunnel Improvement District, for the purpose of supplementing the fund derived from the issue of the Moffat Tunnel Bonds bearing date July 1, 1923, and to pay valid indebtedness contracted for the construction of the Moffat Tunnel, its appurtenances and equipment, by virtue of and in full conformity with the Constitution of the State of Colorado, and Chapter 2 of the Session Laws of the State of Colorado, 1922, approved the 12th day of May, A. D. 1922, and a resolution of the Moffat Tunnel Commission adopted the ninth day of June, A. D. 1927.

This supplemental bond is payable out of the Moffat Tunnel Supplemental Bond Fund created by the Moffat Tunnel Commission and derived from the proceeds of levies made upon the real estate situated within the county limits of the City and County of Denver, County of Grand, County of Moffat, County of Routt and portions of Eagle, Gilpin, Boulder, Adams and Jefferson Counties comprising The Moffat Tunnel Improvement District, which levies constitute a perpetual lien on a parity with the tax lien for general state, county, city, town or school taxes, and no sale of such property to enforce any general state, county, city, town or school tax, or other lien, shall extinguish the perpetual lien of such levies.

IT IS HEREBY CERTIFIED, RECITED AND DECLARED that all acts, conditions and things required to be done, to have happened or to exist, precedent to and in the issuance of this supplement bond, have been legally and properly done, have happened and been performed and do exist in regular and due time, form and manner as required by law and in full and strict compliance with the Constitution and laws of the State of Colorado, and that the obligation hereby created exceeds no limitation imposed by law.

This supplemental bond may be registered in the holder's name on the books of the Treasurer of The Moffat Tunnel Improvement District, at Denver, Colorado, such registration being noted upon the bond by said Treasurer, after which no transfer shall be valid unless made on the Treasurer's books by the registered holder and similarly noted on the bond; but this bond may be discharged from registration by being transferred to bearer, after which it shall be transferable by delivery, but it may be again registered as before. The registration of this supplemental bond shall not restrain the negotiability of the coupons by delivery merely, but the coupons may be surrendered and the principal and interest made payable thereafter to the registered holder of the bond.

In Testimony Whereof, *the Moffat Tunnel Commission has caused this supplemental bond to be executed in the name and on behalf of The Moffat Tunnel Improvement District and signed by the President of the Commission, sealed with the seal of said district and attested by the Secretary of said Commission, and has caused the interest coupons hereto attached to be signed with the facsimile signature of the President of the Commission, as of this first day of January, A. D. 1927.*

20

Moffat Tunnel Scalping Party

On January 18, 1929, less than a year after the Moffat Tunnel had opened, an unheard of youthful attorney, Farrington Carpenter of Hayden, startled Denver and northwestern Colorado with a law suit that he took to the Colorado District Court in Steamboat Springs, county seat of Moffat County.

Carpenter asked that the lease between the Moffat Tunnel Commission and the Denver and Salt Lake Ry. be set aside as illegal and collusively obtained.

We must consider the events which led to this accusation and which would result in the residents of the Moffat Tunnel District being scalped to the extent of $25,258,191 which they would be required to repay over the next half century.

If the cost of the tunnel had been anywhere near to the original estimates there might have been no such problem but the original authorization of bonds in the amount of $6,720,000, proved to be less than half the total cost. Unexpected difficulties were encountered including great amounts of underground water on the east end and unstable rock for almost the entire west half of the bore. To meet these increases a third bond issue was sold in January, 1926; this one in the amount of $3,500,000.

It was now obvious to the railroad that they could face a huge debt and must therefore take action to protect their interests. To this end the Denver and Salt Lake Railway Company was incorporated in Delaware with the principle owners being F. H. Prince of Boston, Alex Berger of Martin, Virginia, and the following men of Denver; Charles Boettcher, Gerald Hughes, Senator L. C. Phipps and L. C. Phipps, Jr. This company was organized for the purpose of taking over the Denver and Salt Lake Railroad which at that time was in receivership.

On January 6, 1926, the new company entered into a contract with the Moffat Tunnel Commission which made the railroad responsible for repaying two-thirds of the cost of the first two issues of bonds including the interest. It should be remembered that one-third of the cost was considered to be accountable to the water tunnel and not the responsibility of the railroad. A critical point in the agreement went unnoticed by almost everyone including the press. A front page story in the *Rocky Mountain News* of January 7, 1926, indicates their unawareness by the statement that ". . . the reorganized Moffat road, will accept immediately the terms of the tunnel commission for rental of the railroad bore at an annual rental sufficient to retire and pay two-thirds of the tunnel bonds under a contract involving payment of $16,736,310 in the next forty-six years." No mention is made in the contract, nor was the general public or the press seemingly aware, that the third and fourth bond issues were not part of the agreement and must be repaid by someone. The residents of the counties in the Tunnel District would be shocked to learn they would repay those unmentioned bonds.

247

The basis for Carpenter's suit was in the fact that the attorney for the Moffat Tunnel Commission, Norton Montgomery, was also with the law firm of Hughes and Dorsey. Gerald Hughes was, of course, Chairman of the Board and a major stockholder in the Denver and Salt Lake Railway which now leased the tunnel. What was the propriety of such a relationship?

The case was immediately complicated when on January 28, 1929, the Moffat Tunnel Commission filed suit in Federal Court in Denver to collect the rentals already overdue from the Moffat Road for the first year of tunnel operation. That same day the Denver and Salt Lake Railway filed its own suit in Federal Court denying that it owed any rental and asking that its title to its leasehold on the Moffat Tunnel be quieted. The railway then asked that Carpenter's suit be removed from the Moffat County Court to the Federal Court which it was. There then began a lengthy battle which went from Federal Court to the U.S. Circuit Court of Appeals. At that point Gerald Hughes himself pleaded the case for the Moffat Road. When Carpenter attempted to argue the matter of fraud in the procurement of the lease, on the basis that one lawyer had rep-

resented the opposing parties, Judge Robert E. Lewis refused to allow Carpenter to argue that point before his court.

Carpenter later stated, "I wish now I had argued it in defiance and gone to jail for contempt, for it is established law that "fraud" can be raised at any stage of a proceeding and there is not much doubt but what the Supreme Court of the U.S. would have thrown the lease out when it was shown to them the circumstances under which it was made." It was felt at the time that had Carpetner actually been put in prison for contempt, the National Bar Association would have come to his defense.

The court upheld the lease agreement and the entire matter was quieted and the final financial arrangements determined as shown here.

THE MOFFAT TUNNEL BOND ISSUES
Four Bond issues were made as follows:
1-$6,720,000; 2- $2,500,000; 3-$4,500,000;4-$2,750,000
Total Principal of four bond issues $15,470,000
Total Interest payments over 50 years 28,765,901
Total cost of bonds $44,235,901
Repayment from rentals as follows:
Rentals on Railroad Tunnel over 50 years $18,252,710
*Rentals on Water Tunnel over 50 years 700,000
Rentals on telegraph lines over 50 yeras 25,000
Total rentals over 50 years $18,977,710
Estimated tax requirements over 50 years $25,258,191
Total rentals and taxes $44,235,901
*The Water Tunnel rental will be increased to 25ᶜ per acre foot for water brought through the Tunnel in excess of 56,000 acre feet in any one year.

All Moffat Tunnel bonds will be paid by 1983.

It is difficult to calculate the benefits of the tunnel to Denver, the counties along the railroad and to the vast area which depends on the vital transcontinental link made possible by the tunnel and the Dotsero cutoff. Perhaps the tunnel simply suffered from all the disadvantages of public enterprise. By contrast, the Cascade Tunnel was built quickly and effectively by a railroad without public assistance. Yet today it would be difficult to argue the tunnel is not now right and necessary for without question it meets a vital need in our transportation network.

Likewise it is of questionable merit to be still accessing blame for the shortcomings of the men who undertook and managed the enterprise that resulted in today's railroad and tunnel. The board of the Moffat Road no doubt felt as pious as angels on the proper side of the throne, for

FARRINGTON R. CARPENTER — *DPL*

this was their just reward for holding on to the bonds. The Rio Grande can certainly not be made the culprit; they paid dearly for the Moffat. Stock which was next to worthless when the line was in receivership, later sold for $155 a share when the tunnel lease was signed. The cost to the Rio Grande to gain complete control of the Moffat eventually was five million dollars.

Sadly forgotten were the real pioneers who, after fighting the hill for years, found themselves laid off when the tunnel reduced the need for the many crews required for hill operation. The increase in business, seemingly as near as the long delayed cutoff, would someday give the line new life but the question was often asked, "did it pay grandpa to be a pioneer?"

And finally, what of the residents of the Moffat Tunnel District? Obviously the Moffat Road could not have paid the entire cost of the tunnel but some more equitable division of the costs was possible. Arthur Ridgway did not hesitate to say that though it would be adverse to his company, the Rio Grande, a much fairer way of renting the tunnel would have been on a wheel basis, and it would have been of no great hurt to the Rio Grande. If indeed the public was expected to repay a part of the bonds, the facts should have been made clear and the misconception never perpetrated, that the rentals would cover the repayment of the bonds.

The idea of a main range tunnel began with a noble and honorable businessman, David Moffat. He too was scalped but the soldiers of the Interstate Commerce Commission eventually drove the scalpers off to a reservation and today the road West is clear. The tunnel bonds are all but paid and the district's residents are free from any further assessments.

Perhaps now there can be peace among the tribes and the salute of victory given to the real heroes, the men of the Moffat Road.

In this view from behind East Portal can be seen the ventilation plant and the adjoining water tunnel. A portion of the legislation establishing the Moffat Tunnel Improvement District is reproduced here, including references to construction and use of the tunnel as well as issuance of bonds; sections upon which controversy later arose. — *above , L. J. Daly, DPL; right, Moffat Tunnel of Colorado, Edgar C. McMechen*

SECTION 9. The Board shall have the power to enter into a contract or contracts for the use of said tunnel, its approaches and equipment, with persons and with private and public corporations, and by said contracts to give such persons or corporations the right to use said tunnel, its approaches and equipment for the transmission of power, for telephone and telegraph lines, for the transportation of water, for railroad and railway purposes, and for any other purpose to which the same may be adapted, no such contract to be for a longer period than ninety-nine (99) years, and the tunnel shall be put to the largest possible number of uses consistent with the purposes for which such improvements are constructed. In making such contract or contracts and providing for payments and rentals thereunder, the Board shall determine the value of the separate and different uses to which the tunnel is to be put, and shall apportion the annual rentals and charges as nearly as possible according to the respective values of such uses. No such contract shall be made with any person or corporation unless and until such person or corporation shall bind himself or itself to pay as rental therefor an amount determined by the Board and specified in the contract, which shall be a fair and just proportion of the total amount required to pay interest on the bonds provided for in this Act, plus a just proportion of the amount necessary for their retirement, and plus the cost of maintenance of the tunnel, its approaches and equipment. The Board may require any of such contracts to be entered into before beginning the construction of said tunnel or before the expenditure of funds under the provisions of this Act, if in its judgment it is deemed expedient.

There shall be no monopoly of the use of said tunnel and its approaches by any one use, or by any person or corporation, private or public, in respect to the several uses, and the Board may continue to make separate and additional and supplemental contracts for one or more uses until, in the judgment of said Board, the capacity of the tunnel and approaches for any such use has been reached. When such capacity has been reached contracts for the use of said tunnel shall be given preference in regard to such uses according to their priority, and subsequent contracts shall be subject to all existing and prior contracts. The Board shall have the power to prescribe regulations for the use of such tunnel by the parties to contracts for such use, or any of them, and to hear and determine all controversies which may arise between such parties, under such rules as the Board may from time to time promulgate; and all contracts shall expressly reserve such power to the Board. All contracts may be assigned or sub-leased, provided that the original contracting party shall not be thereby relieved of any obligations under said contract or lease. Subsequent leases or contracts for the same use must provide for the reimbursement to the prior users of an equitable proportionate amount theretofore paid for the retirement of bonds, including interest thereon, said amount to be determined by the Board, and the judgment and action of the Board on all matters referred to in this section shall be final except as specifically in this Act limited.

SECTION 10. (a). To pay for the construction of said tunnel, its approaches, equipment and expenses preliminary and incidental thereto, and to pay interest on bonds issued as hereinafter provided for during the period of construction, the Board is hereby authorized to issue the negotiable bonds, of said District in an amount not exceeding Six Million Seven Hundred Twenty Thousand Dollars ($6,720,000), to bear interest at a rate not exceeding Six per cent. (6%) per annum, payable semi-annually. Said bonds shall be due and payable not less than ten (10) nor more than fifty (50) years from their date, and shall be known as "Moffat Tunnel Bonds."

ROLLINS PASS BECOMES HISTORY!

Suddenly the battle of Rollins Pass was over and scenes like this (above) were history. But the hill had the last word; it was discovered that plow 10201 was on the west side of the Moffat Tunnel and was two wide to go through. The next summer it was taken over the hill but just as the trip started (below) it derailed on the deteriorated track. —*above, L. J. Daly: below, A. Clarke, DPL*

The first train through the Moffat Tunnel has turned at Irving Spur and the crew pose before the return run — left to right — engineer Louis Larsen, fireman T. F. Carr and conductor Frank Spaulding. At far right is Dr. Susan Anderson who devoted her life to caring for the health of those living along the Moffat. The arrival of the first train marked the closing of the Rollins Pass branch which a quarter of a century earlier David Moffat had planned to replace in a year or two. The hill line was not abandoned but simply allowed to stand idle. On two occasions trains again operated over Rollins Pass, one being the plow special (opposite) and the other following a minor cave-in when timber failed in the Moffat Tunnel forcing use of the hill for a few days. On that occasion Ed Harrison's section crew was called to re-open the line and are seen at Corona where Ed's fifteen year old son John, recorded the date "July 8" (1928) by placing pieces of coal in the snow bank. The night before a fire struck Corona causing extensive damage and this was the scene (lower right) after that destruction. The line remained in place as a guard against any more problems in the tunnel but permission was finally requested and granted by the I.C.C. to abandon on May 14, 1935. The track was in too poor a condition to operate a work train so scrapping was done by private contractors using trucks, starting July 18, 1936 with all rail removed by late fall. — *right, John Harrison: below, Frank Spaulding, DPL; lower right, CRRM*

Train Crew of First Train Through The Moffat Tunnel, Feb. 26-1928

251

COLORADO RAILWAY CO.

LOCATION SURVEY

July 1886.

between

DOTSERO *and* GLENWOOD SPRINGS,

VIA

Grand River (north side) running westward.

JUNE 16, 1934 — Crowds are gathering at Bond, special trains have arrived from Grand Junction and Salt Lake City and all is in readiness for the opening of the Dotsero Cut-off. However, the specials from Denver are running late and by the time they arrive the ceremony will have to be held under rainy skies. But the idea of this line is not new; nearly half a century earlier the Colorado Railway planned this route as indicated by the survey (top) with a date stamp of when acquired by the Denver, Northwestern & Pacific, shortly after the Moffat Road was organized — *photo, DPL; map, CRRM*

Now . . .

The Denver & Rio Grande Western Railroad
offers
FAST, DEPENDABLE FREIGHT SERVICE
Via **TWO** Routes
between **Colorado, Utah and the Pacific Coast**

A New and Shorter Route *via* Denver, the Moffat Tunnel and the Dotsero Cut-off	An Established Fast Route *via* Colorado Springs, Pueblo and the Royal Gorge

CRRM

21
Dotsero Cut-off

Part Two of Moffat History is over. The boys Uncle Dave left to salvage his dream, however, are growing mature and grey in the continued uprising of the Missouri Pacific control of the Rio Grande.

Part Three begins in February 1928 with the opening of Moffat Tunnel and the continued game of delay for no good purpose by the remnants of the Gould dynasty who delay and delay the building of the cutoff. Rio Grande President J. S. Pyeatt, while aware of the need to build and operate the cutoff, was bitterly opposed by his superiors.

It is true Denver is sure of plenty of water so she can grow, thanks to the insistence of Gerald Hughes in building the six-mile tunnel with its pioneer bore. Senator Lawrence C. Phipps, Sr. is still growling "Denver must be on a transcontinental line." His son, Lawrence C. Phipps, Jr. has taken over the active battle to make the Moffat dream come true as "Dad is busy in Washington." Gerald Hughes stands staunch to the vision of David Moffat, knowing that the temptations to sell for profit must not take place until the new through route is assured. Charles Boettcher gives the last energy of his fleeting years to the compact these men formed by which they bound themselves by their own words of honor to stand by one another and not sell stock or bonds before the Moffat reached Salt Lake.

Part Three can not be written with cold unrelated dates, but in a mosaic of different colors which bring out the pattern that paved the road and opened it for traffic in 1934. The latter part of this legend finds Uncle Sam at the throttle through the Reconstruction Finance Corporation. The Rio Grande has the Moffat, but Uncle Sam has a debt against the Rio Grande, so Uncle Sam takes over the Moffat as security that the Rio Grande will made her loan good. Receivership comes to the Rio Grande and the appointees of the New Deal, McCarthy and Swan, take over the Rio Grande as well. These men see the reality of Dave Moffat's vision, which they bring out in the merger of 1947.

Having finished our explanation of Part Three we turn to the subject of the chapter — Dotsero Cutoff.

Though Moffat Tunnel was open, the railroad was still only half completed and the Rio Grande's Van Swearingan owners had no intention of building a cutoff or allowing one to be built.

Gerald Hughes, chairman of the Moffat directors, knew this and would not trust the Rio Grande under its ownership at that time. Moffat men had conceived the idea of building the cutoff themselves and securing from the Interstate Commerce Commission a high portion of the rate on the interchange business they would have with the Rio Grande at Dotsero. If the Moffat had succeeded in building the cutoff it is conceivable that the Moffat would have eventually taken over the Rio Grande instead of the opposite occurring.

The dickering continued for seemingly endless years but eventually the Interstate Commerce Commission ruled in favor of the Rio Grande. This very involved struggle is perhaps most coherently described by Robert G. Athern in his history *Rebel of the Rockies*.

All through these manuevers the Denver papers and Chamber of Commerce were diligent in seeing that the Rio Grande did not get some agreement by which they would bottle up the Moffat Road and refuse to use it as a transcontinental line.

From the beginning the Moffat Road had been making headlines, and she was going to keep on making headlines for her battle was that of getting Denver on a transcontinental railroad.

The earliest surveys for this Dotsero cutoff had been made by the Denver Utah and Pacific engineers. Union Pacific and Rio Grande fathers, as we have mentioned, had at least considered a route through Gore Cañon on down the Colorado River to Glenwood Springs. The Colorado Railway ran a survey down and made filings. H. A. Sumner saw that a route survey was run down the river mainly to get the drop in elevation. H. A. Sumner had included in his arguments for the use of Gore Cañon the need for a connection with the Rio Grande at Dotsero to offer a western outlet for Routt County coal. The letters of Sumner find that the early construction of this thirty-eight mile line was considered, but advised against it because it was considered that cattle shipments from the Glenwood Springs area would go via Moffat without the branch being built, as the route and rate were so much cheaper. (One hundred fifty miles less via Rollins Pass.) So hostile was the Rio Grande under Gould that it could be seen that no interchange in traffic could be expected.

In 1913 Edward Cowden, a locating engineer of long standing in the State Highway Department, made a survey.

In 1924 during the construction of Moffat Tunnel a former Rio Grande engineer, Lee Furman, ran a survey for the Moffat. For it was the intention of the Moffat owners to build this cutoff. Later they bought up the right-of-way rights and incorporated the Denver and Salt Lake Western Railroad Company. The Rio Grande fought the Moffat ownership of this cutoff, as we have said, and won the control of it through the Interstate Commerce Commission. The Rio Grande finally got around in 1931, three years after the opening of Moffat Tunnel, to run its own survey which was superior in distance by three miles and with less curvature. J. C. Gwyn and Lee Furman ran the line.

The many delays by the Van Swearingan ownership of the Rio Grande in beginning construction of this link was considered evidence of their desires to find a way to hold the Moffat without using it as a transcontinental line.

The Hughes-Phipps-Freeman-Boettcher con-

trol of the Moffat prevented this disaster by their untiring efforts and by their agreement not to sell Moffat stock to the Rio Grande until the cutoff and the trunk line was in operation. The Rio Grande offered these men $155.00 a share, which was four times the market value for the Moffat stock.

It was 1932 when the Rio Grande secured a R.F.C. loan to build the Dotsero Cutoff. The hearts of Moffat employees, who had frozen atop Rollins Pass, sank, for they had longed to run the transcontinental trains. The cutoff was in actual construction in November of '32. Arthur Ridgway, the chief engineer of the Rio Grande, had years of experience and was indeed the most able man in the country to supervise this modern piece of construction. The field engineer in charge of the work was a former chief engineer, J. G. Gwyn. Lee Furman was his assistant and Art Weston was office engineer.

In the fall of 1932 the contract had been let to three companies who had been among the six firms building Hoover Dam, Utah Construction Co., Morrison-Knutson Co., and Bechtol Co. The winter was a severe one with low temperatures and little snow to stop the frost line sinking deep. It was June 15, 1934 before the line was completed. The maximum grade was less than one per cent (seven-tenths per cent) and maximum curvature was six degrees. Two tunnels were bored and ten bridges thrown across the Colorado River with one across the Eagle near Dotsero.

It is a good story in itself of how Bill Freeman needled the Rio Grande during the construction of the cut off, for the old animosity in denying the Moffat the right to build this cutoff lingered. While in New York, Freeman wired chief engineer, Bill Jones, of the Moffat to investigate the progress of construction on the cutoff. Jones got the wire when he was in that territory. Naturally the rails were being laid from the Rio Grande to the Moffat, so Jones had to find himself a ride from Orestod over to the point where the rails had reached. When Jones reached this point and saw the construction train, he took for granted it was not necessary to go over the newly laid track as it was obvious the construction train could not have gotten in unless all the track were laid. Mr. Jones had asked the construction engineers if he could be extended the courtesy of seeing their reports of construction. They were very obliging. It was easy to take a liking to the Virginia gentleman. He was always reasonable. His smile was just part of him. His jokes may have been "corny" once in a while but in the wilds of this part of the Rockies they were very welcome.

When the Moffat chief had poured over their reports and turned back to Orstod the boys on the job smiled and hoped to meet him again. "Nice fellow." "He's got brains." But it was not what men said about him; it was what men felt after having been with him that counted. The world needed the punch he put into life.

At Orestod W. C. Jones made out a report and wired it to New York as requested. The only thing the telegram lacked was the sparkle in his eyes. Cost of wire $125.00.

Some months later Freeman flew into Jones unmercifully for not having covered the last seven miles. Freeman had an espionage system by which he could get men unknowingly to tell on one another. By this he was able to break up the unions and to earn the dislike of most of his men who lived in fear and trembling of every move they made.

But, if Freeman worried his men, he scared the mighty men of the Rio Grande, who were carrying out orders from the Van Swearingans. President J. S. Pyeatt was afraid of Freeman and would not deal directly with him or go to Freeman's office. Arthur Ridgway, chief engineer, was on occasion sent over to deal with Freeman.

As the cutoff was near completion, Freeman refused to cut in a switch to hook up the cutoff to his line at Orestod. George Berry, an engineer of the Rio Grande, finally cut the line and built the switch. The newspapers again buzzed, as a tie was chained across the cutoff by George Berry for fear some Rio Grande car would mysteriously run on the Moffat track and start a wreck, if not a war.

Bill Freeman surely helped the newspaper reporters with spicy news. As the day approached for the grand celebration for the opening of the transcontinental service over the cutoff and through Moffat Tunnel, Bill Freeman found an opportunity to collect an outstanding bill the Moffat held against the Rio Grande for repairs and a portion of the tunnel rent, which the Van Swearingan Brothers had seen unwise to pay to the Moffat, until the line was opened, in spite of statement after statement sent them.

The Rio Grande was staggering under the bad weather of the depression while the Moffat was faring considerably better.

It was June 13, 1934, and Bill Freeman was feeling very good. A Rio Grande official came over to Freeman's office to say something about the running of the first trains over to the celebration. Bill Freeman quietly asked how they expected to get over to the Moffat. The official answered that they had a contract allowing them to do so. Freeman roared back, "Yes, but you do not have a contract to get over the Northwestern Terminal switch from the interchange track. Unless you have every cent of the $388,000 the Rio Grande owes us, I will not let you over the road. You will have to have it in the bank before closing time so the bank has time to find out if the check is good."

The Rocky Mountain News came out with a headline MOFFAT ROAD ASKS $320,000 OF RIO GRANDE.

June fourteenth the headlines read "$388,000 Asked For" and carried the story that the debt amounted to a million for three years.

When newspaper reporters asked Freeman about what would happen to the ceremony planned, Freeman replied, "The celebration is the Rio Grande's show."

The switch was spiked shut and Rio Grande officials knew they had overlooked in the contract a small item which Bill Freeman had gleefully discovered; that the contract did not include Rio Grande access to the Moffat Road's subsidiary, the Northwestern Terminal, which provided connections between the two roads.

To the joy of the directors of the Moffat and the laughter of the Moffat men, Bill Freeman announced he had every cent on the barrel head. Investigation proves the Rio Grande paid cash immediately for most of the sum and the rest was held in escrow by the First National Bank so that the evaluation committee could adjust any items over which there was a dispute. Some adjustment was later made in this figure.

The same evening the cash was put on the barrel head, as the hands of the clock yawned, the first freight of the Rio Grande crossed over the much disputed switch. Louie Larson climbed into the cab to pilot the first run of the now famous freight, "The Flying Ute," which was to give the Union Pacific competition into San Francisco.

Bill Freeman, who had seen to it that everything worked perfectly for the opening of Moffat Tunnel, handicapped the Rio Grande by allowing nothing larger than the 1170 class consolidation engines and 3400 class mallet over the Moffat.

FIRST TRAINS RUN OVER DOTSERO CUTOFF, MARKING NEW ERA IN PROSPERITY OF WEST

The Post Telephone MAin 2121

THE WEATHER

'Tis a Privilege to Live in Colorado.
Sunday—Sun rose in Denver at 4:30 a. m. Sun sets in Denver at 7:31 p. m. There are 15 hours and 1 minute of sunlight in Denver Sunday, the same amount as on Saturday.
Highest temperature in Denver on Saturday, 71; lowest temperature on Friday night, 51.
Denver and Vicinity (radius 20 miles) — Partly cloudy and somewhat warmer Sunday; Monday generally fair.
Colorado—Partly cloudy Sunday; warmer in north and east; Monday generally fair.

HOME EDITION

Paid circulation of The Sunday Post over 190,000 greater than total paid circulation of all other 12 Sunday papers printed in Denver and Colorado, Wyoming and New Mexico combined.
Average Paid Sunday Circulation for May 301,202

PRICE TEN CENTS

Paid Circulation of THE DENVER POST Last Sunday Was 301,027

THE BEST NEWSPAPER IN THE U. S. A.

NRA

THE DENVER POST

84 PAGES   DENVER, COLO., SUNDAY MORNING, JUNE 17, 1934   VOL. 42—NO. 319

HIGH OFFICIALS OF TWO STATES DEDICATE LINE

GALA THRONGS GATHER FOR TRAIL-BLAZING DOTSERO CUTOFF TRIP ON POST SPECIALS

Thru the Denver Union station, Saturday morning, poured a stream of individuals of high and low degree, all moved with the excitement of participating in an event which already is marked for the history books. They formed the throng of 2,250 people who left here to participate in the ceremonies attendant to the opening of the Dotsero cutoff. This picture shows part of the gay spirited crowd which boarded the chamber of commerce special, the last of three Denver & Rio Grande Western special trains to clear the Denver yards and pull the grades upward to the Moffat tunnel and thru the very heart rock of the continental divide.

THOUSANDS CHEER AS DOTSERO CUTOFF IS OPENED

Now the Rio Grande paid the cost of its delaying tactics on upgrading the joint trackage despite the efforts of Chief Engineer Jones. Two curves that could have been straightened out were the reason for limiting passenger service to the consolidation engines and one weak trestle had caused Freeman to refuse to allow the Rio Grande's 3600's. It should be remembered that even the Moffat 400 series McArthur engines were hard on the several remaining sixteen degree curves and thus the fear of allowing the Rio Grande's 1200's with their larger drive wheels.

Several months later the Rio Grande 1200 McArthurs were allowed over the Moffat. But even these did not represent the heavy power of the Rio Grande, which could not come over for years until trestles were filled in and several curves straightened. For the Rio Grande had at that time as fine mountain type passenger engines and as fine 2-8-8-2 mallets as there were in the country.

Everything was against the Rio Grande that day. Bill Freeman had raved and ranted, threatening to fire any operator who failed to hand up an order hoop and delay the specials or the regular passenger service of Five and Six. So the men were shaking like aspen trees in Indian summer, thinking they might disappear in the frosty breath of Freeman.

June 16th dawned over Denver with officials still wondering what new invention or discovery of cussed contrariness Freeman might concoct. The first train to leave Denver Union Station for the celebration was the now famous Pioneer Zephyr of the Burlington, which President Budd had brought out to honor the occasion when the Burlington secured a direct west coast connection. Zephyr 9900 picked up at Utah Junction two Moffat men to pilot her at 6:47 a.m., Conductor F. H. Van Vranken and Engineer W. L. Smith. The Zephyr reached Orestod at 11:50 a.m. The three twelve-car trains following on thirty minute intervals, however, did not have an uneventful run. Veteran Rio Grande train crews handled these trains.

Moffat engineers and conductors were their pilots. Not having run a test train, the Rio Grande found that her consolidation engines lost time in dragging the twelve-car Pullman trains up the two per cent.

The crews fumed and the officials cussed Freeman, who was blamed for everything, while the passengers sang "Sweet Adeline" and "How Dry I Am." One reporter said the passengers in his train cheered when they went across the switch on which Freeman had collected the back money. But the real hard luck struck the third section, which had the president's private car on it. In Denver a drawhead was pulled. Time was lost as cars were switched around. This delay was serious, as the time set for the ceremonies was determined by the hour of the national radio hook up. The time was short now.

The consolidation engines, having been worked hard and carrying no auxiliary water car, ran out of water at Coal Creek water tank. When they attempted to start on the two per cent, another drawbar came out. Drawbars come out every once in a while, but why they had to on this day no one knows. The most humorous version told about the incident is that Freeman had insisted that Moffat men handle the throttles of the engines and that since the Moffat boys were not used to the big power, they yanked the trains in two. The men who handled the throttles, however, were one hundred per cent Rio Grande men with plenty of two per cent grade experience going up to Palmer Lake. Most embarrassing of all incidents was the dumping into the lap of Governor Johnson's wife the entire contents of a dinner table when the coupler went out . . . This was in Pyeatt's car.

The air was charged with trouble from the spiking of the switch and the law of averages came to bat that day against the Rio Grande. At Plainview an operator, filled with the fear of Freeman, pulled a boner and delayed one train.

On ahead, the operator at Kremmling put out an order with the date 1914 and Conductor Allen asked the officials what they should do? The officials cussed and said, "We might as well keep on running." They did.

Meanwhile Bill Freeman's special ran to Orestod and on up around the curve, where he could look down upon the ceremonies at Bond.

At Bond Rio Grande dining car chefs had barbecued beef over the pits of the future engine house. Thousands of people could sit down to the fine food. But the trains were arriving late. The first section had been an hour late. Reports on the last section, which was short on time to begin with, showed that she was one hour and twenty-five minutes late. The president of the railroad was on this section and could not possibly make Bond in time to deliver his radio speech.

The vice president of the road said to G. F. Dodge, "What shall we do?" G. F. Dodge was in charge of public relations. He had fought for years for a good advertising department and he was not going to give up this national hook-up because the brass hats were on a late train. This likeably courteous and yet determined man was prepared for this emergency. He pulled out of one pocket the speech his clerk Carlton Sills had written for the president and gave that to the vice president. He pulled out of his other pocket the speech he had written for the Governor of the state, Edwin C. Johnson, who was riding in President Pyeatt's private car. The newspaper reporters looked up into the heavens and saw the rain coming. Dodge had an umbrella to cover his head. The clock said it was time to begin. The Governor of Utah, Henry H. Blood, spoke first and then the carbon copy speeches were read. The world knew little about the trouble down in the out-of-the-way spot, where autos had gone crosswise of the trails leading in, and where trains were late. The president of the railroad was relieved to hear from his private car the delivery of his speech. Edwin C. Johnson later congratulated Dodge on making the best speech he had ever made. The speakers huddled under umbrellas. A shot rang out from a cowboy, who added his touch to the occasion. Some one, who was so lucky as to have ridden on the Zephyr, told how their train had scared a deer. In the midst of it all the third section of the train with the business men of Denver and the railroad presidents pulled in.

The special trains from the west had been on time. High school and veterans' bands were striking up their tunes. Western Colorado would now have a cheaper freight rate to Denver.

The Rio Grande, which had been unable to parade her magnificent million pound mallet over the Moffat, was ready to parade her before the speakers stand. The fine equipment had come in from the west. The Zephyr took her turn and every one cheered as all the trains paraded by in review.

The honor of Master of Ceremonies had been shared by Chancellor Frederick M. Hunter of Denver University and Herber J. Grant of Salt Lake City, who was president of the Mormon Church.

The public, who had never found out how muddy the trails could get around Bond and who had not missed the best of the show by being passengers on the specials that were late, read all about the occasion in the Denver papers that had room for little else.

You could read in these papers how eight hundred fifty men had worked on the construction of this important link from November '32 to June '34. There was room, of course, in the Post for Orphan Annie who was startling some genius by her knowledge. Believe it or not, you read that prosperity was coming around the corner through the NRA and PWA, which claimed to have given five million people jobs.

Yes, the depression was on, and the Rio Grande was launched on a new adventure. In this adventure President J. S. Pyeatt had been bitterly opposed by the Rio Grande chief own-

258

The third section of the Dotsero specials (top) races out of Denver behind D&RGW 802 and 1177, while the Burlington's famed *Pioneer Zephyr,* first train to leave for the ceremonies, pauses at Hot Sulphur Springs. D&SL President Freeman's special (left) meets the *Zephyr* enroute; he had his train parked on the line to Craig, overlooking Bond. The new through route was soon handling Rio Grande freights (above) and the *Panoramic* (right) seen at Winter Park on March 10, 1935. — *left, Leda Reed; top, right and above, Otto Perry, DPL*

ers. It was an unfortunate time to prove he was right.

Gerald Hughes and the rest of the Moffat trustees relaxed, for the cause they had fought for was now secure. David Moffat's dream had come true. Denver was on a transcontinental line.

These men began to sell their stock and bonds at a good price. Gerald Hughes, who had invested with Dave Moffat and his father from the beginning, found that his investment had never borne any interest. But he was not sorry. Denver was on the main line, for which Uncle Dave had fought.

By December the Rio Grande was in the same condition dozens of other railroads were in the United States — IN NEED OF A LOAN FROM THE RFC. So the costly Moffat stock had to be turned over to the RFC as security. Wilson McCarthy and Henry Swan were appointed trustees, McCarthy becoming president.

Headlines told how democracy was threatened by the RFC's owning the Moffat. Labor was likely to run wild. Would the United States Government have to pay taxes to the State of Colorado and the counties? If she did not, schools would close and Middle Park would be bankrupt, so men talked, like old gossipers.

Wilson McCarthy took a sane course. The Moffat paid taxes, though she would not have had to, for she was the United States of America. School districts continued to receive their forty per cent hand-outs to keep them going, and instead of the Democrats running off with the road, some Republicans, who held positions above, pinned Wilkie buttons on section men, who answered, "We will wear the buttons, but vote as we please."

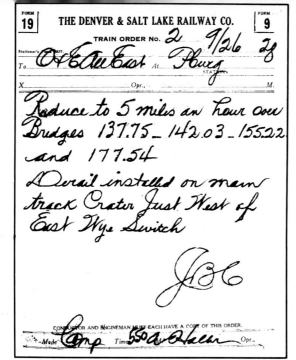

THE DENVER & SALT LAKE RAILWAY CO.

TRAIN ORDER No. 2   9/26   28

To O&E&E East At Pburg

Reduce to 5 miles an hour over Bridges 137.75 – 142.03 – 155.22 and 177.54

Derail installed on main track Crater Just West of East Wye Switch

The Moffat Road was in dire need of heavy maintenance after years of bare bones budgets. Chief Engineer W.C. Jones was quick to begin work when the money became available, using work trains such as this one with a crane, gravel dump cars, water cars and a Jordan spreader. One of the most pressing problems was the deteriorated condition of the line's many bridges as evidenced by this train order (top) giving a five mile an hour speed restriction on four bridges. —*photo, Otto Perry, DPL; train order, Joe Preiss, CRRM*

22

Rebuilding the Moffat

The grand scale of railroad construction, which Sumner had had to exchange for the most expedient way possible to get to the coal fields, now had a yellow light. West of Sulphur line changes could soon be made. Neglected maintenance could be carried out. All because the building of Moffat Tunnel had ended the costly snow removal and disastrous blockades.

President Freeman had guided the road in a period when some men would have been happy to make a fortune junking the line. He, however, had discovered the way to make a fortune by hanging on to the road, buying its bonds cheap, knowing that in the not too far distant future there would be a good market for this little indispensible cutoff. So he determined to hold maintenance to nothing as long as that was possible.

A. L. Johnson, Joe Culbertson, and in fact the entire Moffat staff knew that the line had kept going on such slender repairs more by miracle than by wisdom. If the many trestles were not filled, the tunnels gunited or concrete lined, disaster would overcome the line.

The man to whom the fun of rebuilding the Moffat fell was W. C. Jones. Of course, he had the task of converting Freeman or licking him. There were men who had the patience to win the president. If they could have won him is an open question with the odds against them. But the fact that master mechanic Charlie Peterson had maintained the locomotives in first class shape down these years is proof that an indispensable man could handle Freeman. But what a terrible cost

any one paid in doing this. "Bill" Jones was an exceptionally determined man. When too many things got in his path, his safety valves popped. Unfortunately some of these explosions landed on his subordinates for small failures when the other Bill (Freeman) was the cause. Jones came west a very sick man with little energy to pamper Freeman but with an enviable professional record. He had held such positions as Chief Engineer of Appalachian Electric Power Company, the Roanoke Railway and Electric Company and of the Lynchburg Light and Traction Company. He would never have come to the Moffat, if he had not been taken down with Hymertic Malaria Fever. In five years he dropped in weight from one hundred sixty-eight to one hundred twelve pounds and was making the rounds of the best hospitals. At Johns Hopkins he was given ninety days to live. He ran into a friend who asked, "Bill, what's wrong with you?" When Jones told his story, the friend extolled the wonders of Colorado's climate, saying, "I went out to Colorado with T.B."

Five days later Bill Jones was working for the Moffat as an assistant engineer at Tolland, where some re-alignment and surfacing of track was in progress. It was not easy, when you had not eaten any solid food in five years, and when you had to sneak off to suck the juice of oranges and eat raw eggs with a half teaspoon of vinegar. But six weeks later he had an appetite for the first time in five years and was eating at Mrs. Sinclair's boarding house. In two months he had gained twenty pounds.

Jones found that the right-of-way of the Moffat was strewn with junk that had been left from wrecks or had fallen off the equipment. Some effort had to be speedily made to get the line in shape for the through trains of the Rio Grande. A small amount of work had been done in the year preceding — 1926, but this is how the Moffat appeared to the new engineer. Jones prepared this description for a report to the *Engineering News Record,* September 2, 1937.

> . . .The D&SL was threatened with extinction as high costs and physical difficulties of operation created never-ending deficits and sorely tried the hearts of operating and administration officers. Maintenance was non-existent, for there were no funds for roadway upkeep. Somehow trains crawled over loose rails resting on rotten ties, eased around sixteen degree curves, poked their way through fifty-five tunnels whose old timbers had not been touched since installed thirty-five years ago and crept over creaking light timber bridges. Sometimes the neglected track or structure failed and spilled trains into a cañon or down a mountain side. Short sidings of less length than most freight trains and all too infrequent intervals complicated the task of doubling up on steep grades and caused exasperating delays in train meets. Passenger trains had a schedule running time of fifteen miles per hour and were never on time. With no schedule freights wormed along from station to station. No wonder that in 1922 when the road was blocked by a rock fall in a tunnel, there were grave doubts whether operations would ever be resumed.

In 1928 a heavy program of ballasting and rail replacement was begun. The program, however, waned for a time as the building of Dotsero cutoff was delayed by Gould interests in the Rio Grande. The rebuilding was resumed when the cutoff was under construction and a gravel pit was opened one hundred forty-three miles out of Denver beyond Congre Mesa, where a mountain of volcanic ash crowded the main line so that it could be easily loaded.

The pit was worked with a two hundred-foot face opened by blasting. Bill Jones accomplished the remarkable when one blast brought down 125,000 cubic yards of material by a single blow of 29,000 pounds of powder in twelve well holes forty feet deep and two hundred feet of four by five foot coyote tunnels. This was a yield of four and three-tenths cubic yards per pound of explosive. By such methods the chief engineer dug, crushed, and loaded the gravel for twenty-five

cents a cubic yard. The ballast was of exceptionally high quality. Its porous, yet hard nature weighed from 1,850 to 2,250 pounds per cubic yard. In the track it provided perfect drainage and stood up sufficiently to permit tie replacement without disturbing the ballast under adjacent ties.

President Freeman particularly fought tie renewal. The worst ties, however, were renewed with creosoted ties and out of these old ties the section men split 12,000 fence posts during the winter months and used them in the construction of the first fence most of the right-of-way ever had.

The original eighty-pound rails had been laid in 1903 to 1909 as far west as Steamboat and eighty-five-pound rails in 1911 to Craig. In 1927 one hundred-pound rails had been laid for twenty-five miles. By 1930 the heavier rails reached mile post sixty-six and by 1935 they were in Orestod, where the Rio Grande joined the Moffat.

These changes are related as facts, but each move was fought with the Rio Grande's refusing to pay its share until Bill Freeman blocked the movement of the first transcontinental trains.

Line changes were necessary, for we recall Moffat had to give up his grand scale of building for an effort to get into the coal fields the cheapest way possible.

At Pallas Summit a line change was made for two and a half miles improving the curve and grade. Characteristic of these changes was the work at mile post ninety-four and ninety-six where four hundred twenty-one degrees of curvature shortened the line eight hundred twenty-five feet, cut out several sharp curves, and increased the speed limit from twenty miles per hour to sixty.

Naturally the sidings were too short for the increased tonnage the long trains hauled. Frequently these extensions involved some heavy grading in cañons. But perhaps worst of all was the condition of the one hundred seventy-five wooden bridges, which had a total length of two and five-tenths miles and were entirely eliminated by fills and line changes. The next most serious problem was the condition of the timbering in the fifty-two tunnels which totaled ten and seventy-two hundredths miles in length.

For years "The Chief" had been conspiring to correct this defect. Forms that could be easily removed had to be made. Pressure from fractured conditions of the rock had to be met, for these pressures varied in the direction from which they came. Moisture, the many curves in the tunnels, plus the narrow confines of the sunless cañons, all added to their problems. Very rarely was a tunnel located where a man could drive to the location by car or bring supplies in by trucks. By this time a heavy procession of time freights and transcontinental passenger trains was added to the Moffat coal drags and cattle trains. Helper engines had to get back to the terminals. It was not an easy job.

If one is to understand the man who rebuilt the Moffat, one must remember that he was away from home more than at home — a home he loved. Sleet, snow, cold winds, and the blasts of President Freeman, he had to fight. To understand Jones was to see him arguing, battling with the other "Bill." The battle of these two was epic.

But to change the policy of replacing the timber with timber was a job requiring the conversion of President Freeman. Hardly had the first tunnel been bored when engineers began crying for something more permanent than timber. But even in the days when money was at hand, that money was wanted for bonds by President Freeman. So Jones had to convert or lick the president.

Worst of all tunnels was the newly built Moffat Tunnel. Here timbering disintegrated under the terrible pressure of the mountain and the water that poured through the tunnel from the lakes above. The air which was blown by the ventilating fans from East Portal through to West Portal to clear the smoke out during the movement of trains and afterward force dry air intermittently through this wet hole did not add to the life of the timbering, which was being replaced by more timbering at the cost of $133,000 a year. Jones said the tunnel could be concreted for $875,000. The plans for the concreting were prepared literally under cover by Jones, who had to hide the paper and maps every moment some one came to the door, for fear it would be Freeman.

When it was discovered, Freeman said, "Jones, you're crazy. It can't be done."

Jones would not be licked. He argued. He planned. He conspired, and though every item in the entire estimate, was fought over, the plan was accepted. The tunnel was concreted for the estimate, and $1,190,000 in maintenance was saved, as not one cent of repairs was made until the line was absorbed by the Rio Grande.

In 1937 this program was in full swing. Moffat tunnel was concreted and gunited and other tunnels were attacked, so that 14,567 feet of guniting and 18,233 feet of reinforced concrete became the new lining replacing the rotting timber.

In these hectic days Jones never dreamed of the time he would be a Kiwanian and attend the Wednesday luncheons of the Denver club week after week and year after year, nor did his wife dream that a night would ever come when the telephone would not ring telling him of some new prank Nature had contrived against the Moffat which needed his mind. Jones might have been a brother in the same fraternity with the president but he was not proud of the fact. Like the majority of Moffat men, Jones was a Mason of the thirty-second degree. Jones loved all the Irishmen more than one certain brother of his fraternal order.

If the walls of the offices in the Denver National Building could talk, they would tell many stories:

Bill Jones comes in and greets President Freeman cordially. Freeman snarls: "Who in the h— asked you what kind of a morning it was?"

A few minutes later Ed Sunergren comes in ignoring the president. Fifteen minutes later Freeman comes around to the desk where Sunergren is sweating over his work and asks, "What are you doing?"

Ed explains. Freeman wants to know why he is doing it that way. Ed explains as only Ed can explain, and Freeman argues until he is convinced he is wrong. Ed has to go to the library to borrow some books. Freeman wants to know why the office does not have them. Ed patiently explains there is no money in the budget for the fifty dollars worth of books needed and Freeman tells him to get them.

Today it is humorous to see Freeman trying to spite Jones. But there will never be enough paint over those walls to stop the plaster from seeing that. Jones would never have stayed to be chief engineer, if he had not long before discovered that Freeman was a bluffer.

The engineering department was used to such situations. When Ed Sunergren was hired by Bill Freeman to test Moffat Tunnel's cement during the lining of the tunnel some time after its construction, many problems developed. The meanest one was a chemistry lesson that shot out of the smoke stacks of the engines. The soot and the steam formed sulphuric acid, which began to eat up the rail joints and cut the life of

The collapse of this bridge in Egeria Cañon made the Moffat management aware that the road's bridges must receive immediate attention after years of deferred maintenance. Two major projects involved building fills over the Coal Creek bridge (below) and the giant wooden trestle at Rock Creek, seen (bottom) as work began in 1929. The Moffat designed forms on rollers to be used in lining tunnels including eventually the Moffat Tunnel. —*above, L. J. Daley: bottom, Joe Preiss, CRRM; others, Ed Sunergren, DPL*

the rails to a fraction.

For some reason or other the Moffat's chief engineers have always been considered indispensable to the wrecking crews, so that Bill Jones was going and coming day and night. The office engineer, who stayed behind to keep the office going, did a great deal of thinking. One thing he thought about was this acid. Ed Sunergren made quite a study of the electric precipitator, which is used in cement plants to remove the dust and foreign matter. Los Angeles used the principle to remove from its sewers, dangerous gases which would otherwise explode. So Ed dreamed and worked until he had several ideas for the use of the same, in the smoke boxes of engines or in the refuse places in Moffat Tunnel.

The idea was never tested, but it is characteristic of the engineering that went on on the line that had problems that some of the world's largest railroads never had to face. To a great extent the diesel has solved the smoke nuisance in Moffat Tunnel. Electricity will be the answer, and perhaps that is why the electric precipitor was never tried.

The finest tribute Jones could pay to Sunergren was paid years later, when some old timers were gathered in the engineering department for a picture. The arrangement of the men did not suit Bill, who said, "Let me get here between my two old friends, Turner and Ed Sunergren, who taught me railroad engineering."

The rebuilding of a railroad is first of all men, and second, materials.

On one occasion the chief's wife met him at the station. Number Two had pulled in. From the wire Mrs. Jones thought there would be an ambulance for her husband. Everyone was off the train but "the chief." She was gravely concerned, for she had found out that he had been terribly sick. Then he crawled off the rear of the last car, all doubled up with the pain from a rupture.

They went by taxi to the railroad doctor. The seriously ruptured chief had to climb the stairs. The astonished doctors said, "We must operate right away."

All night long the gallant rebuilder of the Moffat hung between life and death. His wife was rightly furious that he had not been sent down the day before in the caboose of a train and had not been met by an ambulance.

Mrs. Jones called the Moffat offices demanding to talk to the president. Mr. Freeman knew

that a storm was coming. He would not talk. So Mrs. Jones said, "You tell Freeman, if my husband dies, he will have no railroad."

The president's office knew just what that meant — a law suit that she could win.

To say the least, railroad officials were at the hospital and everything humanly possible was done to save "the chief's" life. He came out of it, but was in bed for many weeks, too weak to lift his head.

Meanwhile the usual humor of nature tied the line up and "the chief" was needed on the hill. So Freeman sent Superintendent A. L. Johnson to visit Jones and tell Jones, if he did not get dressed and out on the line, he would be fired.

Jones said to Superintendent Johnson, "You see how weak I am, I cannot raise my head. You tell that blankety-blank man to go to hell."

Many weeks later the sick engineer crawled to his office to gather up his personal effects, expecting to be fired. Freeman called him to his office and greeted his chief with such words, "Say, is it true that you told me to go to hell?"

"I sure did."

The president laughed and laughed, saying that was the best joke he had ever heard.

Bill Freeman, the self-styled "Savior of the Moffat", was a man of contrasts. He had much to his credit; he encouraged the A.S.A. brake tests and the development and use of flange oilers. His deeds of kindness to children of Moffat men were widely known. Above all he did manage to keep the railroad running through difficult times. In balance, however, he continued to be the object of distrust, disgust and ill will to employees, shippers and even to Rio Grande officials.

In December, 1934, Wilson McCarthy became the last president of the Denver and Salt Lake Railway. This event followed when the Rio Grande found it necessary to make another loan from the Reconstruction Finance Corporation and to do so pledged its Moffat stock as the collateral. McCarthy was a native of Utah where he had been a successful cattleman and eventually a judge. While not a railroader he proved to be very able in his task of setting the future course of the Rio Grande and the Moffat Road. He made friends rapidly among the employees and shippers. He decided to keep Freeman on in an advisory capacity but the arrangement did not last very long.

A board of directors meeting was in progress to discuss Jones' proposal to fill the trestle with material that needed to be removed from the right of way. One of these trestles was the famous steel one at Coal Creek. "The Chief" having presented his material, was interrogated by the one-time president. His questions were carefully answered. Then a cross examination began with the same questions asked over and over again, until the temperature of the chief engineer flashed and he replied he had answered those questions several times.

President McCarthy immediately excused Jones, who went down to his office for a second time to gather his personal effects. Some time later he was summoned to the Holy of Holies expecting to be fired.

"Sit down, Jones. That man Freeman made me so mad that I lost control of myself most shamefully. I closed the Board of Directors meeting and told Freeman he was fired. He started crying. I said, 'Cut out the tears. You don't have a heart. You never thought a kind thing. In fact, cracked ice pumps through your veins!'"

The Moffat staff breathed easier with Freeman gone. The light was green for the work of rebuilding the Moffat. A. L. Johnson and every old time Moffat official and man knew what was needed from the experience of the years. The only question now was which method would prove the best in making these changes. For example, should the big trestle in Rock Creek Cañon be replaced with a steel trestle? Or was a fill the proper move? Jones was in his glory and not as sympathetic to old ideas as A. L. Johnson who was open to the suggestions of most men. No one would run over Culbertson. He stood his grounds — come what may. The little Moffat family get-togethers, in which these plans were discussed, found Johnson giving every one a chance to speak his opinion and reasons. Then "A. L." weighed the problem and made his decision. In time these conferences were naturally held over at the Rio Grande office, for the Rio Grande was renting the right-of-way for its transcontinental business. Here the same pattern of conference was held. Even safety men and roadmasters were being called in to listen and make comments on plans. A vote would be taken in a very democratic fashion and a report made to the board.

So it came about that General Superintendent A. L. Johnson saw the Moffat become a first class road. The Rio Grande in the last hours exerted more and more influence in Moffat affairs which was natural and right, for they owned the Moffat. The Moffat was rebuilt according to the wisdom of Johnson, Culbertson, Daly, Schneitman, Turner, Sunergren, Duncon, and a host of others whose suggestions were heard and considered. W. C. Jones was chief engineer, proud of his accomplishments in carrying this out. His determination at times exploded. But in these battles with Nature, who never would call quit to her pranks, it took some very determined men. The Moffat men might fight among themselves, but just let an outsider step in and say a word and how the Moffat boys stuck together. All the strength and frailties of the human soul were in these boys. They were truly men as we know men. They received bruises in their disagreements. They at times gossiped but not "A. L." He was even above revealing some of the feuds that he was under for years, feuds that hurt his memories.

The story of rebuilding the Moffat is over. We must go back in history to pick up the story of the men who never lost a passenger's life, and the spirit that possessed presidents as well as gandy dancers.

President William R. Freeman, a man of great ability but often unable to deal reasonably with employees or customers, retired in Dec. 1934, after a colorful career described in this *Denver Post* story. Much of the responsibility for rebuilding the Moffat fell to these officials seen with their inspection car at Tolland on June 5, 1935; from left to right, R. S. Gardner, an I.C.C. inspector, Master Mechanic Charles Peterson, Chief Engineer W. C. Jones and General Superintendent A. L. Johnson. The Burlington was keenly interested in using the new Moffat-Rio Grande route for connections and thus loaned their dynometer car (right) for tests before the Dotsero cut-off opened. — *left, A. L. Johnson: right-above, Denver Post, all DPL*

W. R. FREEMAN, WIZARD WHO SALVAGED MOFFAT LINE, RETIRES

Colorful Figure. Goes Out of Railroad Business.

With the retirement of William R. Freeman, president of the Moffat road, as operation and control of that line were being taken over Friday by the RFC, railroading loses one of its most picturesque and colorful figures.

You won't find the name of William R. Freeman in "Who's Who." But every railroad man and big financier in the country knows "Bill" Freeman as the man whose wizardry as an operating executive saved the Moffat road from the junk pile and turned a 232-mile streak of rust into a live and vital railroad link which now stands valued, on the basis of its bonds and stocks, at 21 and one-fourth million dollars.

On Oct. 17, 1917, Freeman took charge of the bankrupt Moffat road as coreceiver with Charles Boettcher, Denver capitalist. At that time, the road had about $35 in its treasury. Against this was a mass of debts. The creditors encamped upon the doorstep of the Moffat road were only a small part of the worries of the receiver. His big bugaboo—and never was there one more real—was the "hill," as Moffat roadmen called the section of the Continental divide over which the line was trying to operate.

By Jan. 1, 1927, Receiver Freeman, with a skill that smacked of magic, had rehabilitated the Moffat road, dragged it "out of the red," converted it into a moneymaker and had piled up one million dollars in its treasury.

PUT DOWN LABOR TROUBLES WITH IRON HAND.

The story of how "Bill" Freeman licked the "hill," while he was staving off creditors, put down labor troubles with an iron hand, overcame financial, physical and human obstacles, and achieved for what some big railroad men regarded as a little "one-horse line" the distinction of having the lowest operating ratio of any comparable road in the country, is one of the most stimulating chapters in American railroad history.

As a receiver, Freeman became a living, integral part of the road he had been called upon to salvage and save. Its existence became his existence. The situation called for a strong hand. He was a martinet. He not only personally directed every operation on the Moffat road, but he knew everything that was going on on that line at every hour of the day or night.

In his younger days Freeman had been a railroad telegrapher and dispatcher. His ability as a telegrapher was one thing in which he took particular pride.

'Railroading Wizard' is the title which William R. Freeman had won before he retired Friday as president of the Denver & Salt Lake (Moffat) railroad. Because of his management, the 232-mile road underwent a phenomenal rehabilitation, achieved a 21-million-dollar sale value and now is going under RFC control until the Denver & Rio Grande Western repays its RFC loans for purchase of the system. Freeman is shown here in a happy mood at his desk Friday just before he stepped out of the road's active affairs.

HEARD EVERY MESSAGE SENT OVER LINE.

There was one telegraph line along the Moffat road. In his office as receiver, Freeman had installed a muted telegraph key which was connected with the line. Every message that went over the Moffat road wire was heard by him in his office. He knew where every train was, what it was doing, how it was powered and how it was being operated.

It was nothing unusual for Freeman to stop in the middle of a conversation with a caller, pick up his telephone, call a subordinate and demand to know why two engines had been put on a certain train when it consisted of only a certain number of cars which engine No. so-and-so could handle by itself. Thru such careful attention to the most minute details, Freeman slashed operating costs and at the same time built up operating efficiency.

While he was operating the Moffat road mechanical perfection was one of Freeman's hobbies. At Utah junction he created a shops plant which for its size was unexcelled in the country. When his doors were closed to all other callers the salesman of a new piece of shop machinery which would increase the efficiency of the shops and help to reduce expenses always could gain admittance.

SHOPS REBUILT SPECIAL LOCOMOTIVES.

Out in the Moffat shops at Utah junction, they rebuilt locomotives when the road could not afford to buy new ones and later on they continued this rebuilding because they could build the kind of engines which were required for the peculiar operating conditions of the road.

During the early years of the receivership, the Moffat road time and again was threatened with being consigned to the junk pile. Freeman, with a resourcefulness which bordered on the phenomenal and a ruthlessness that won him enemies, staved off these attempts. And while keeping the road alive with his own individual determination, he conquered the dreaded "hill."

Winter and spring snows meant blockades on Corona pass where the Moffat road crawled over the Continental divide. Snow along the rails packed and froze so hard that locomotives could not stay on the rails. It was nothing unusual for an engine and snowplow to pile up on this packed snow, jump the track and roll down the side of the mountain.

ICE PICK SYSTEM CONQUERED "HILL."

Freeman and his men devised a system of "ice picks." These were fingers of steel which were attached to the pilot of the locomotive just in front of the front wheels and close up to the rails of the track. These picks tore the packed snow and ice loose from the tracks and insured keeping the engine on the rails. That licked the "hill." From that time on, the only winter blockade occurred when an engine crew permitted their water supply to run low and they were snowed in before the boiler could be replenished.

Freeman, who started his railroad career as a call boy and worked for the Union Pacific, Santa Fe, Pullman company, Colorado Midland and the old Denver & Rio Grande before becoming receiver of the Moffat road, was made president of the Moffat when it was reorganized and returned to its owners on Jan. 1, 1927. Today he is rated as being better than a millionaire.

During the dark days of the receivership bonds of the Moffat road dropped to as low as $4.85 per $100. Stock which the Rio Grande and RFC have purchased at $155 a share then was worth virtually nothing.

INVESTED HEAVILY IN MOFFAT BONDS.

Every dollar that Freeman could get was invested in Moffat road bonds. He had confidence in his ability to resurrect the Moffat road. When the road was returned to private ownership he was one of the large stock and bondholders. He had gambled on his conviction that stocks and bonds which had been kicking around and which were considered in the "cats and dogs" class would be valuable. And he won.

Freeman sold his stock at $155 a share. He is still said to be a substantial bondholder.

From many parts of the country Freeman was deluged with offers to rehabilitate ailing railroads or take charge of roads which were barely getting along. But because of his loyalty to Gerald Hughes, chairman of the Moffat board, and the Phipps interests, who had stood with him thru the dark days of the receivership, he remained at the executive helm of the road until construction of the Dotsero cutoff had been forced and David H. Moffat's dream of the Moffat road as a link in a new transcontinental route thru Denver had been realized.

With construction of the Moffat tunnel and the Dotsero cutoff, and the rehabilitation of the Moffat road, this dream became a reality.

Station Numbers	Ruling Grade Ascending Per Cent	TIME-TABLE No. 49 JANUARY 16, 1944 STATIONS	FIRST CLASS					SECOND CLASS			
			D. & S. L. 12 Mixed	D. & R.G.W. 20 Mountaineer	D. & R.G.W. 8 Advance Six	D. & R.G.W. 6 Exposition Flyer	D. & S. L. 2 Passenger Mail & Exp.	82 Freight	74 Freight	72 Freight	78 Freight
			Arrive Daily	Arrive Daily	Arrive Daily	Arrive Daily	Arrive Daily	Arrive Daily	Arrive Daily	Arrive Daily	Arrive Daily
0	0.0	DENVER (D&SL)	6 30 AM				3 00 PM				
1		PROSPECT (D&RGW)		6 38 AM	9 44 AM	12 44 PM					
2	0.5 0.3	FOX JCT.	6 11	6 36	9 42	12 42	2 45				
3	0.91 0.4	ENDO	6 05	6 33	9 39	12 39	2 41				
4	1.84 0.3	ZUNI	5 52	6 30	9 36	12 36	f 2 38	5 10 AM	9 45 AM	3 35 PM	10 20 PM
7	2.90 0.0	RALSTON	5 47	6 26	9 32	12 32	f 2 34	5 01	9 38	3 27	10 13
12	4.82	LEYDEN	5 32	6 17	9 25	12 25	f 2 27	4 48	9 25	3 14	10 00

The war brought a tremendous increase of business to both the Moffat and the Rio Grande as indicated by this employee timetable (top) listing five passenger and four scheduled freight trains daily in each direction. The Rio Grande's famed *Exposition Flyer*, operated jointly with the Burlington and Western Pacific on the Chicago-San Francisco route, is seen about one hour out of Denver behind 4-8-4 engine 1711. — *above, Otto Perry: both DPL*

23

On Advice of Al Perlman

Wilson McCarthy and Henry Swan took over the management of the Rio Grande and the Moffat in 1934. They were faced with the constant complaining of Rio Grande bondholders that too much money was being spent in bringing the railroad up to standard practice, so that heavy locomotive power could be used.

One of the first jobs was the blasting out of the sharp curves beyond Tunnel 16 where the line bypassed the never completed Tunnel 17. In World War II extensive work began on the establishment of Centralized Train Control which was begun over the block signal section from Denver to East Portal prior to the war. Beyond the West Portal of Moffat Tunnel it was impossible at that time to run satisfactory communication lines to control block signals or to send train orders for the line from Dotsero to Craig, because of the wet conditions in the tunnel.

To make possible the establishment of CTC beyond West Portal, a dispatching office was built in a modern brick building at Hot Sulphur Springs, at the wye, about a mile east of the station. Here a modern coal facility had been built as well as water tanks. Also a diner-parlor car which had come from the old Chesapeake Beach railroad, was removed from its trucks and set in between the wye as an eating place for the crews.

Some sidings were eliminated between Winter Park and Dotsero and others were extended to accommodate the longest freights that were expected at that time or the foreseeable future.

All of this work was accomplished under the restrictions and expenses of wartime emergency contracts and under the direct supervision of Al Perlman from his Denver office of the Rio Grande.

Perlman came from the Burlington to be chief engineer of the Rio Grande and special assistant on engineering to Wilson McCarthy of the Moffat. Perlman moved almost with vengeance in preparing the Moffat lines after the belated maintenance of Bill Freeman's bailing wire policy. He often clashed with Moffat men such as when Jones wanted to use volcanic ash instead of slag to which Perlman was accustomed. However, Perlman had one very special ability, that of making some wise choices including one which was to determine the future of the Rio Grande.

On advice of Al Perlman, a tall, lanky engineering college graduate, Gus Aydelott, came to the Rio Grande with a desire to learn the actual working of a railroad from the practical side. He was a graduate engineer who saw the importance of leaving books to see how the classroom measured up. The very fact he did not want to work under his father, General Manager of the Burlington, showed he had his father's determination.

The most serious problem facing the railroad was the condition of rail in Moffat Tunnel. The welded rail was now failing because of the sulphuric acid produced from the steam and smoke of the engine stacks. After two V.I.P. sons of shippers had taken their turns getting fired as Roadmasters, Gus Aydelott was appointed to that position. He accepted the challenge of laying new welded rail in lengths of 1,000 feet through the Moffat Tunnel during war time, when up to fifty one trains were dispatched over the line in a single day.

One of the first actions necessary was to remove the accumulation of soot that rose from the top of the rail to the wall of the tunnel. This was dangerous for the laying of new rail because along the sides of the tunnel were water channels covered by heavy blocks more than two inches thick. But not all of these blocks had been replaced over the tunnel ditches when the section men had opened them after stopping to get water for their motorcar engines. This created a dangerous situation for men at work.

Half the old time gandy dancers had left for better jobs at 65ᶜ an hour rather than the 44ᶜ paid here. Many sawmill operators and lumber jacks hired out at Tabernash and Fraser to help on the tunnel rerail job. Gus would drive up from Hot Sulphur to watch the confusion that the office-prepared plans got into. The lights used to illuminate the Tunnel were a Christmas tree-like line, held by men recruited on Denver's Larimer Street skid row. Each man held a section of the line with four 100 watt bulbs. The electricity was furnished by power plants on motor cars. Ed Bollinger operated two plants with thirty men to hold the line and nineteen year old Eddie Berquist operated the other line using twenty men. Both groups came in from the West Portal side on motor cars after the 4:00 a.m. passenger train had passed. A wait of twenty minutes was needed to clean the tunnel of smoke but not for these men; they rushed in to work, never knowing if they would spill over a broken rail or other hazard.

Many of the men had no idea when hired, of the winter conditions that existed on the Moffat and came unprepared for temperatures of 35 to 40 degrees below zero. They kept warm at Winter Park station but even the short trip to the tunnel could spell agony. Many local men also worked on the project including two school principals who were so over-paid that though they had master's degrees, it was profitable for them to work weekends and during Christmas vacation.

The old rail had to be loosened and replaced by a thousand foot section lying along the side in the soot. A mechanical spike puller was brought in that had been a failure elsewhere but Gus made it work. In doing so he got cut by it

dangerously close to his left temple. From his motorcar's first aid kit, Ed Bollinger patched him up and from that day on the first aid kit was miraculously replenished.

Can you imagine a filthier place than this 60° degree tunnel which served as the sewage disposal for every troop train going through? That the pioneer spirit was alive in many of these men was evident. Getting up at three in the morning in mid-winter was hard on wives and children. Time and again the Fairmount motor car refused to work in the 30 degree below zero morning air, so a cover was put on Eddie Berquist's pick-up and used to transport the workers from Fraser to the Tunnel. In a day of gasoline rationing there was always a filled tank to get these men to work. Those in authority always turned their backs when it was necessary to fill the tanks of those providing transportation.

The longest tunnel block would be about four hours. Two thousand foot sections could be secured, then out went the men to wait around, hoping for two or four hour blocks during the fifteen hours and fifty-five minutes the law allowed men to work. When the men would go back into the tunnel usually one or two of the strings of lights would blink off. Fuses in the power plant would be checked and then the line; one hundred men would be stopped working. The fault was always that a light connection to a bulb had been pulled off. The problem was that the supervisors would yell at the men "quickly get your light up" and in attempting to hurry, the skid row outcasts would accidently rush and break off connections. This situation was uncovered by Ed Bollinger after the first time he went back in the tunnel and his string of lights went out.

Eddie Berquist had the same problem and began to think it was plain nonsense not to stop this continual ripping off of light connections but the bosses had their own idea of how to hurry the men and the problem continued. One evening as Roadmaster Gus Aydelott and several other officials stood outside the tunnel, Eddie told them just where the railroad should be stuck, in language that the Fraser parson would not dare to have spoken.

Everyone expected that Eddie would be fired the next morning but not so. Section boss Ed Harrison had been quietly instructed by the roadmaster to make the statement that nobody, including the General Manager or the President of the railroad would tell Eddie Berquist or Ed Bollinger what to do with their powerplant and the men who were holding the light lines. They were in complete charge from that time on and of course, there was no problem from that day on.

Wages remained tragically low and one Saturday evening instead of going to bed early, the gandy-dancer preacher took a carload of section men to a union meeting in Denver. All the wives were happy for they knew that their husbands would come home sober. The men in the lodge hall reminded Bollinger of a presbytery meeting. The men voted to strike!

The following Monday morning Gus asked Ed Harrison, "Well, what did you boys vote to do Saturday night?" "We voted to strike."

If you will realize that strikes were considered as conspirator-contrived acts that should not occur in wartime, you have the atmosphere the country was being fed by the press. Gus Aydelott, who was not in the inner circle of the railroad men at that time, simply said: "You men deserve everything you've asked for and more, too. I hope you get it." That evening the parson hammered out on his typewriter the experiences of the day saying, "Gus will either be fired or become railroad president." Of course he was not fired and he eventually became the president. Al Perlman and the rest of the men recognized that Ed Harrison and the others had done what was right.

Now that same week Ed Bollinger attended the Denver Presbytery meeting which was held in the North Presbyterian Church in Denver. He proposed near the end of the meeting, during the Social Education and Action report, that presbytery go on record as backing the maintenance of way employees of the Moffat railroad. He explained that these men were working at low wages under live steam locomotives that were derailed time and again at 40 below zero and in impossible smoke conditions in the Moffat Tunnel. They deserved a raise.

An elder got up and moved that the motion be immediately tabled, and a tabling motion cannot be discussed. Then the pastor of Central Presbyterian Church got up and moved that insasmuch as his father had been a railroader, and so many of them knew the truth of what had been said, that the Committee on Social Education and Action be given the power to make a statement. He explained that the tabling of this motion was to prevent the Denver Post and its irresponsible reporters from blackening the name of the Church. Ed Bollinger was so disgusted that he never reported to his section men how the Church had failed them.

Wartime conditions on the railroad were very trying for train operators and agents. There were two operators and one agent at Winter Park and there were no block signals further west until the Centralized Traffic Control was installed. Let us examine a typical situation at Winter Park. A helper engine on the east end of the siding is standing and waiting for train orders. A freight which had its double-header cut off, has moved ahead so the passengers from Number Two can get on and off and so the mail and express can be loaded. On the far end of the siding another freight has pulled in and received orders to proceed as soon as Number Two arrives. Add to this the fact that forty section men are waiting for another tunnel block to open so they can get in to lay rail and several officials are in the operators room, all adding to the nervous tension under which the agent and operator must work.

The career and sometimes the life of an agent or operator could end prematurely because of conditions like these. In one case a woman operator at Radium, standing between the passing and main tracks, was struck and killed by an open door on a refrigerator.

As many as twenty-five men lost their lives on section cars because no orders were required to give block protection to these men in the heavy traffic of returning helper engines, work trains, and the passenger *mainliners* as they were called. But it's a miracle that no passenger on the Moffat was even injured during the war. One night, however, after a broken rail had been replaced on the fill back of Hideaway Park near Woods Spur, that rail broke because it was already fractured when relaid. The coach-Pullman almost turned over; as it settled back on the track, the frightened passengers heard the conductor say, "Everything's all right now; we're still on the rails." And the next day Ed Bollinger remembers putting another fractured rail that had been removed earlier, back into the track because there were no good rails left to use. This is how serious track conditions had become.

The worst tragedy that came to the line occurred when Tunnel 10 caught on fire on September 20, 1943. Of course a tunnel cannot burn but the timber lining can. That day, veteran conductor J. A. Pierson was informed by engineer Vaughan that he smelled smoke as he went through the tunnel. Conductor Pierson called the dispatcher:

THREE DENVER FIREMEN KILLED
BATTLING RAIL TUNNEL BLAZE

Meet Death in Bore on Moffat Road, Probably From Suffocation; Body of Only One Is Recovered.

"This is Pierson on First Number One, Engine 302. We are at Quartz. My engineer smelled smoke in the tunnel from creosoted timber burning." The dispatcher answered, "Do you know where Bert Schneitman is with the bridge and building gang at Crescent?" "Yes, indeed, that's only two miles west of here." "Would you get in touch with him?" So the train stopped at the B. & B. cars at Crescent and reported the conditions.

When Bert Schneitman, a man of practical experience very worthy of his job, found what had happened, he asked permission to dynamite both ends of the tunnel to seal it off so that the fire would be extinguished. General Superintendent, A. L. Johnson, was immediately informed of the situation but he did not realize how serious the fire had become and said, "No! What do you want to do, shut the line down!" Now no sane man is going to hold this against Johnson because Al Perlman later said the same thing.

Two engines with fire hoses were quickly sent to the tunnel followed by a train of water cars. The intense heat of the fire prevented the men approaching close enough to make much headway and occasionally the wind would change direction, forcing the men to quickly retreat.

Again Schneitman asked permission to close the tunnel; this time he wanted to hook a chain to a locomotive and use it to pull down timber 1200 feet in and hopefully save that much of the tunnel. But Perlman thought it all could be saved and refused.

An appeal was then made to the Denver Fire Department which reluctantly cooperated by sending Captain William R. Perry of Engine Company Eight along with three other firemen. Included were Chief Driver Jim Williams, selected because of his considerable experience with mines, Doug Parrish, a machinist and expert with pumps and John Kennedy who volunteered because he was a former Moffat employee. He had been fired in a row with Bill Freeman over the union.

The four Denver firemen and their pumper truck were loaded on a special train with Fabian Smith the engineer and Andrew D. Pitt the fireman. Andy Pitt still remembers what happened. "I was called that evening and was glad because being pretty new I did not get called for the road too often. One of the Denver firemen had worked on the Moffat (John Kennedy) and knew the engineer. He asked if he could ride the cab

The Denver Fire Dept. sent this engine (above) and a crew of men to attempt to control the tunnel fire but three of the crew lost their lives in the line of duty. With the fire finally out, work went on around the clock in an attempt to reopen the line. Rio Grande Chief Engineer Al Perlman supervised the work and we see him (seated) with Section Boss Chris Kusulas on their motor car during the blockade; the car Marcia is visible in the background. During these years it was necessary to lay new rail in Moffat Tunnel (right-top) and during the tunnel blockade great amounts of cinders were removed from the tunnel. The doors seen in this 1936 photo (far right) were found of no use and soon removed.
— *below and right, D&RGW courtesy Jackson C. Thode; top, Denver Post, CRRM; others, DPL*

and help fire. I was kinda annoyed because I was young and liked to fire but I figured if he wanted to work I would have an easy trip. When we got to the tunnel it was just filled with smoke and fire. I had to stay on the engine because we were going to start making trips back to the Coal Creek tank to refill the water cars. We only made one trip because by then the firemen were dead.''

When they arrived the firemen donned smoke masks and penetrated the tunnel about seven hundred feet. The wind shifted; the two men on the hose were courageous and didn't come out. Captain Perry found his respirator was leaking and came stumbling out of the tunnel. G. E. Hamilton, D. & S. L. roadmaster, then took a mask and went in search of Parrish. He found him a hundred feet from the end of the tunnel and attempted to bring him out but collapsed as he left the tunnel. Hamilton was revived but all efforts to save Parrish were unsuccessful. The other two men, Williams and Kennedy, could not be reached and remained in the tunnel until it was cleared many days later.

Within hours the full impact of the blockade was being felt. All Rio Grande traffic had to be sent via the Royal Gorge route and Moffat freight was sent via the cutoff or trucked from Rollinsville to Denver as was done with both passengers and mail. In normal times the blockade would have been serious; in the middle of World War II it was an emergency.

Work equipment from both the Rio Grande and the Moffat was gathered at the tunnel but by now the tunnel had caved in for much of its length. This was a job for tunnel workers and so arrangements were made with the War Manpower Commission to bring workers from the Big Thompson Water Diversion Tunnel. For more than two months the tunnel workers and railroad crews battled the terrible heat of the still smoldering fire, the continual danger of monoxide gas and the now badly deteriorated rock. Finally a completely rebuilt Tunnel Ten opened to traffic with the passage of D. & S. L. Train Number 1, at 4:53 P.M. on December 1, 1943. Nine weeks had passed and with it perhaps the worst crisis in the history of the line.

One old problem was finally handled as a result of the tunnel fire. During the blockade a crew was sent to the Moffat Tunnel and cleared out fifteen years worth of soot which almost covered the track.

The war years told a story of an ill-prepared line valiantly attempting to serve the public; most of the time doing so with success.

On April 23, 1942, engine 3600 (above) managed to trap herself. Derailed by a large boulder, she tore into the props in tunnel 38, causing the tunnel roof to fall and bury the locomotive. Otto Perry photographed this scene (below-left) on Nov. 16, 1935, as 16 cars derailed near Rollinsville after the train got out of control and reached speeds believed up to 65 mph. A constant problem before the installation of electric warning fences, was of falling rocks such as derailed this train (below-right) leaving a tough clean-up job for men and machines. — *below-right, G.S.D. McCall: all, DPL*

Life for dispatchers and operators could be nerve wracking as in this photo (above) at Winter Park with passenger and freight trains as well as helpers crowded on the main and passing tracks. On Sept. 27, 1938, this head-on wreck occurred at Lowell Blvd. just a short distance west of Utah Junction, between D&SL 201 heading east and D&RGW 1201. As this shiny new diesel passed Plainview on April 5, 1942, few people would believe that a decade later steam would be nearing the end of the line on the Rio Grande. — *below, R. H. Kindig, CRRM; right, Otto Perry and above, both DPL*

On April 13, 1947, just two days after the Moffat Road officially became part of the Rio Grande, Richard Kindig took this superb photo of engines 406 and 209 heading west with 53 cars at Coal Creek. The short girder span and fill replaced the long steel bridge in use since the line was built. Kindig caught another historic event on film as we see freshly painted Rio Grande 3366 in Utah Jct. shops on Nov. 29, 1947. The former D&SL 206 become the first of the Moffat Road locomotives to be renumbered and in a few days would be back in service with its new identity. — *CRRM*

276

24

"Denver & Salt Lake" — Should be the Name

The modern Rio Grande was born early on the spring morning of April 11. 1947. A long series of court battles over the Interstate Commerce Commission's reorganization plan was brought to final settlement in February, 1947, when the United States Supreme Court upheld the I.C.C. plan by a vote of eight to one. As Trustees McCarthy and Swan concluded their duties they could point to a record of considerable accomplishment in the rebuilding of the railroad.

At 12:01 a.m. on April 11th, the Rio Grande emerged from trusteeship and at the same time merged with the Denver and Salt Lake. George Dodge, Director of Public Relations for the Rio Grande, made a profound statement in discussing the merger; "Denver and Salt Lake should be the name". Dodge felt that a modern corporation's best advertisement was a name that described what it had to sell.

Only northwestern Colorado and to a lesser extent Denver had suffered from the defeat of the direct Moffat line to Salt Lake City. In the state's northwest, the name "Moffat Road" meant the dreams of W. G. Evans and David Moffat for the undeveloped potentials of their area and that of neighboring Utah. As the region was opened by the coming of the railroad the ranchers, businessmen, oil men and miners saw their dreams being fulfilled. The name of David Moffat and the ideas he stood for represented their hope and brought their appreciation.

Unfortunately Colorado had fallen prey and become a pawn in a high stakes game on Wall Street. The Rio Grande, in spite of its nearly wrecked physical condition had developed the state's timber business, mines of all kinds, industries,

potato fields, fruit orchards and you name it! Up into the 1920's, railroads had been the lifeline of the people; they appreciated the dreams of Palmer, Dodge and Moffat, for their dreams had also been those of the people. The sentiment attached to the name Rio Grande was great.

The employees of both lines were one with their shippers and passengers. William Freeman was his own worst enemy but served his board's interest loyally. He had the wrong temperament to be involved so intimately with the Rio Grande management the last years. If a firm but conciliatory man had been president of the Moffat at this hour, the personal vindictiveness between the two managements could have been eased.

Every age has its foibles and so it was with efforts to bring the managements of the two railroads together. Al Perlman determined to standardize the index systems of the two engineering departments. The Moffat's, being much smaller, was to be renumbered and indexed with the Rio Grande file. Perlman suggested to Ed Sunergren, office engineer for the Moffat, that he empty the files on the floor and get busy. Following these instructions the staff labored painstakingly but the work seemed endless; the cost grew and then came the order to dump everything back in the files. These records were later found in the back of the new garage built for the Pueblo superintendent's rail and highway cars.

Next all the Moffat locomotives were renumbered according to the Rio Grande system. This was but a waste of money as there was no conflict in operable engine numbers. This had been proven during the war when Moffat mallets were leased to the Rio Grande. Last and most counter-productive

Near the time of the merger we see engine 208 (above) in typical Moffat Road condition during the later years — dirty but working hard. The great blizzard of 1949 brought a massive blockade to the Union Pacific line across Wyoming (below) and for several days much of their traffic was re-routed via the Rio Grande including (left) U.P. Train 106, the *City of Portland* seen near Plainview on Feb. 19, 1949. Although the merger was effective on April 11, 1947, actual operations were little changed until issuance of D&RGW MOFFAT DIVISION TIME-TABLE NO. 1 on June 8, 1947, replacing the last D&SL Time-Table. The steam era was fast closing on the Rio Grande when on Oct. 27, 1956, engines 3609 and 3619 (right) completed their helper duties and headed for Denver on the last steam engines to pass thru the Moffat Tunnel. They are seen during a meet at Tolland on the return run.
— *left, Richard Kindig and timetable, CRRM; right and above, Otto Perry: below, all DPL.*

was the painting out of all signs that read "Denver and Salt Lake". This action ground into the bruises of northwestern Colorado.

The most serious error of Rio Grande management was the way in which Moffat officials were treated. Under consolidaton rules they had to be retained at the salary level of their former position. A. L. Johnson was given a menial job of handling reports of shipments. Lost in this job, not knowing how to type and forced to write out tedious reports, his spirit was crushed. The whole idea was to break him so he would give up and save the railroad his salary. To a man who had been previously offered a much finer position by the Union Pacific and who had given himself so wholeheartedly for years to running the Moffat for Freeman, this was dastardly cruel.

In contrast, the hot-tempered W. C. Jones was placed at a desk for safe keeping, away from his arch enemy Al Perlman. Fighting intelligently, Jones made himself invaluable to General Manager West and thus found an important place with the Rio Grande.

Al Perlman was the corporation man out to make use of every modern insight and technology so he could pay high dividends. But it was Gus Aydelott who was understanding of the fine men of both companies and steadied the keel to end inner fears and fightings. It was given to "Gus" to take the progressive Moffat that Al Perlman found and integrate it into the "Rebel of the Rockies".

Gus Aydelott perceives the new place of the railroad in our fast changing American way of life and has guided the Rio Grande on a course to insure it a vital transportation role. The old Moffat Road stands clearly as a vital part of this modern railroad, a fact which is no small tribute to those who planned, built and struggled to keep the line in operation through so many lean years.

The Denver and Rio Grande Western Railroad Company

MOFFAT DIVISION

TIME-TABLE
No. 1

Takes Effect Sunday, June 8, 1947
12.01 A. M.
Mountain Standard Time
Superseding D&SL Time-Table No. 52

NOTE IMPORTANT CHANGES IN TIME-TABLE RULES

For the Exclusive Guidance of Employes;
Not for the Information of the Public

E. A. WEST
Vice President and
General Manager

L. F. WILSON
Assistant General
Manager

W. R. McPHERSON
Superintendent Transportation

A. L. JOHNSON
Superintendent

Following minor cave-ins at tunnel 41, the decision was made in 1952, to completely remove the tunnel which was located about 1¾ miles east of Radium in Black Tail Canon. With section boss Jerry McCall's crews standing by and everything in readiness, the *California Zephyr* (above) passed thru on its westbound morning run and minutes later a massive explosion literally removed the tunnel. Crews quickly moved in and the line was open in time for the eastbound evening *C. Z.* to pass without delay. Al Perlman and Gus Aydelott recognized McCall's ability and in spite of having no college training, promoted him to Pueblo Division Roadmaster and handed him the task of planning the relaying of rail in Moffat Tunnel. The rail was welded at Tabernash (below-right) and McCall brought section men from all over the Rio Grande to handle the job expeditiously.— *all, G.S.D. McCall*

281

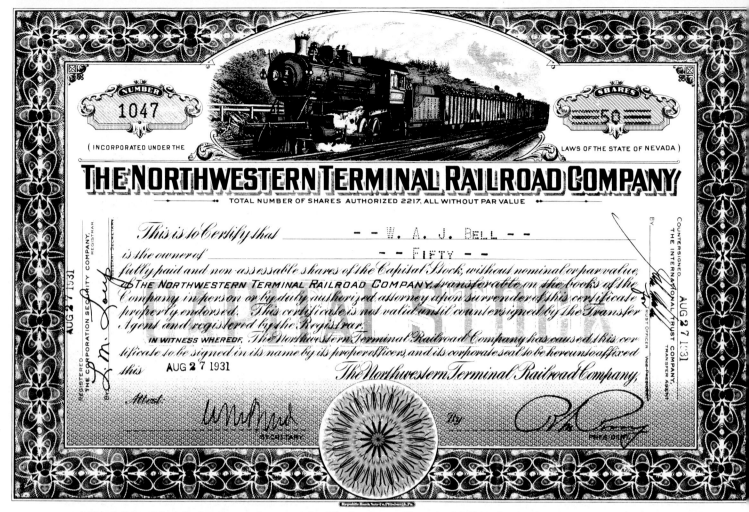

A Rock Island freight heads southeast on the Northwestern Terminal RR at Sandown, about to leave the line which provides its connection to the Rio Grande's North Yard. This is part of the network of industrial and connecting trackage which made the little known railroad's stock valuable to Joel Fisher (right) and enabled him to challenge the Rio Grande for a premium price on his shares. — *below, Ronald C. Hill; right, Yale University Alumni Club; and above, both, CRRM*

25
Joel Fisher
and The Northwestern Terminal Railroad

By the early 1950's, David Moffat's railroad was indeed a fully integrated part of the modern Rio Grande but one more act remained to be played out and the plot centered around one-time Denver and Salt Lake subsidiary, the Northwestern Terminal Railroad. The line had been built to provide access for Moffat Road trains to the Denver yards and included trackage from the depot to Utah Junction. The Northwestern Terminal was not included in the merger with the Rio Grande but instead leased its trackage to the Rio Grande which did own some of the stock and bonds.

The Rio Grande's sometimes rough-shod dealings ended in the middle of April, 1958, when a soft-spoken man of exceptional finesse received justice in full for his stock and bonds in the Northwestern Terminal.

The man was Joel E. Fisher, whose appearance at the old Stout Street headquarters of the Rio Grande shook her directors, officers and attorneys into realizing they were no longer almighty.

Joel Fisher had graduated from Yale University magna cum laude in only three years, at the age of eighteen. In the Yale class record he had written about the Swede who had to sleep a quarter-mile away from everyone else because of his snoring. Later on, in 1913, he worked with such Swedes on the construction of a rugged piece of railroad in British Columbia. He never forgot their names — Louis Vellander, Oscar Kihlstrom, Alec Johnson, Carl Carlsen. By chance these men had all once worked for Dave Moffat in Colorado, and told Joel Fisher about their former boss.

When Fisher was 21, World War I broke out. He returned home from Canada, gave his private yacht to the U.S. Navy, and enlisted in the Army. After training with a broomstick instead of a rifle on Governors Island, he sailed to France as an officer in the first contingent of soldiers.

In the early 1920's, as a result of his memories of the Moffat men he had met, Joel Fisher purchased odd amounts of the bonds of both the old Denver and Salt Lake and of the former Northwestern Terminal.

Three decades later, on March 2, 1951, Joel Fisher wrote to the stockholders of the Northwestern Terminal:

This is the first annual report ever given you by the company, and it may well be that some of you do not even know where your property is located.

Your company owns about 250 acres in Denver and Adams Counties, Colorado (subject to lease to the Denver and Rio Grande Western Railway, expiring January 1, 1977), including:

1. Some 30 acres of industrial property, reaching right up into the heart of the City of Denver.

2. The property which has been featured by the Rio Grande as part of its new "North Yard", just outside of Denver.

3. Approximately 2 miles of the Rio Grande's transcontinental main line.

4. The Belt Line, including approximately 2 miles of the freight cut-off by which the Chicago, Rock Island and Pacific Railway obtains direct access to this same North Yard.

5. Direct connections to the Denver Union Stock Yards, constituting another mile of track.

Historically, your property was assembled some 50 years ago, by David H. Moffat, that far-sighted citizen who sought to place Denver on a transcontinental railway . . . Some small part of Moffat's faith in his railroad system had been transmitted to me by a small group of ordinary laborers. . .

In the late 20's, as many of you know, the Denver and Rio Grande began to buy in Denver and Salt Lake stock, which rose from 10 to 155; eventually, in the 30's, notwithstanding the depression, it offered to buy in all remaining shares of D.&.S.L. at 155, and, with the help of the R.F.C., it went through with the deal. More recently, it retired, at par, a substantial part of the same D. & S.L. income bonds.

Still later (March 1949), it offered to buy, at 67, all outstanding income bonds of the Northwestern Terminal. Approximately 90% of them were so purchased. At that time, having privately bought some 10% of the stock of the Terminal, it urged all remaining stockholders to sell to it, at $1.00 per share, along with approval of an amendment to the Terminal's lease, by which ceiling interest on the 5% bonds would be limited to 3½%.

. . .I somehow could not see my way to selling out, for so minute a figure, an investment which to me represented a moral claim of $450 per share on former unpaid interest. I recalled that each unit of two shares of D. & S.L. stock had been valued at $310 per unit; nor did there seem any reason why shares of the Terminal, representing an equally strategic property, and undiluted by reorganization costs, should be sold at any such price as $1.00 per share.

Finding that many other stockholders felt the same way, but, weary, were willing to see me take hold, I purchased enough additional stock to give me control. I then arranged to have my personal attorney(now one of your directors) intervene in this matter and in the rent dispute, at my expense, in order that my views might be presented. Shortly thereafter, without additional costs to the company, interest on the Terminal bonds was raised to 5%. The conflicting interests of the Rio Grande, at once holder of 90% of your bonds, and lessee of your property, was underlined by their vigorous opposition to increasing the interest rate on those very bonds which they held.

But this defeat for the Rio Grande at Fisher's hands did not compare with the vindication he wrested from them in April 1958. Fisher insisted the railroad make a fair settlement with him for his bonds and stock, under threat of denying them use of a crucial thousand feet of track for access to Denver.

The Rio Grande reluctantly agreed, also fearing Joel Fisher might sell out to the Rock Island — and the Union Pacific was far too interested in the Rock Island to leave the Rio Grande comfortable. For his 10% of the Terminal bonds, Fisher received $133,321, and from his stock $731,650, for a tidy total of $864,971.

Fisher had never been a Coloradoan; though he was a mountain climber most of his life. From 1933 until his death in 1966 he was a vestryman of the Church of Heavenly Rest on Long Island, New York. He also served as president of the Samaritan Home for the final 10 years of his life. His widow, now 85 years old, is a delightful person with whom to correspond, as the author can attest.

The mighty little railroad outlived its savior by only two years. On December 30, 1968, the Northwestern Terminal was granted its own petition for dissolution.

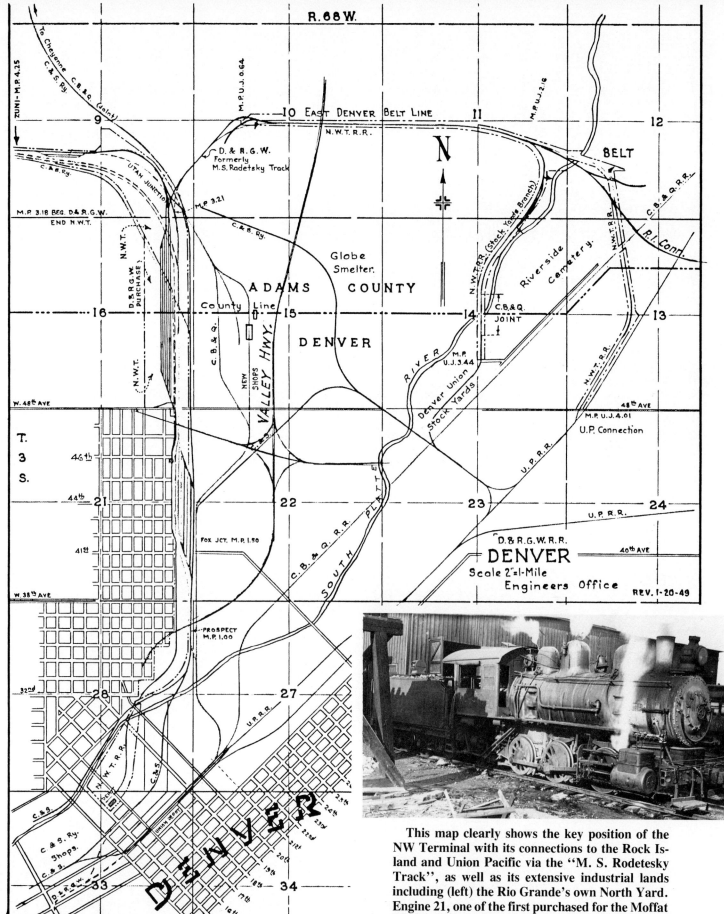

This map clearly shows the key position of the NW Terminal with its connections to the Rock Island and Union Pacific via the "M. S. Rodetesky Track", as well as its extensive industrial lands including (left) the Rio Grande's own North Yard. Engine 21, one of the first purchased for the Moffat Road, ended its career (above) as a NW Terminal switcher. — *left, Ronald C. Hill; above, Robert A. LeMassena*

Over the span of years Moffat Road passenger service really changed little, the usual consist being two or three cars except for tourist and other excursion trains. For a comparison we see engine 300 heading west with Train No. 1 near Rollinsville on May 26, 1940, and two decades later the diesel powered *Yampa Valley Mail* is seen in Rock Creek Cañon on Jan. 28, 1962; the usual consist has been increased with addition of observation-lounge car Glenwood Cañon for members of the Intermountain Chapter, National Railway Historical Society. — *top, Richard Kindig; above, William C. Jones.*

26

We Have Never Lost a Passenger's Life

No greater tribute can be paid to the men of the Moffat — from gandy dancers to president and board members — than to say that no passenger was ever seriously hurt on their line. When we recall the dangers of rock slides, tunnel fires, blizzards and gassy snowsheds at Corona, this is indeed a high tribute.

From the day the first passenger train was dispatched in 1904, through the merger with the Rio Grande in 1947, this record was held true. In the more than thirty years since then, this honor has been preserved by a clear record of Rio Grande passenger operations over the former Moffat line. In total this means a record of seventy five years that these railroaders can honestly state, "We have never lost a passenger's life." Without question this is among the finest safety records in American railroad history. There are few railroads in this country that operated through the hazards that the Moffat Road dealt with and until recent years did so without block signals. Today the Rio Grande operates with electric fences to warn of the fall of rocks in cañons and with the safety of centralized train control and the most modern signals.

The story of the safety record of passengers is not a story of luck alone. It is the story of narrow escapes, boners that some loyal Moffat man saved from becoming a tragedy. It is the story of taking no chances with the lives of passengers. It is the story of officials urging safety, veterans preaching it to their brakemen and firemen. It is the story of dispatchers ever watchful of their operators.

It is also, however, the story of every mile post being a cross marking the grave of some engineer, fireman, or gandy dancer who lost his life through

carelessness or the unforesseen in the performance of his duties.

The safety record for passengers is in contrast to the high death rate among personnel. The first death came in the days of the surveyors' work.

A fine young man by the name of Riddle from Colorado Springs was working in the party of M. H. Rogers in South Boulder Cañon. On their return from Spring Gulch Riddle took a short cut down a snow bank using a survey stake as a brake. But as he daringly went down the bank fully under control, he struck a spot where the crust of the melting snow had turned to ice, and he was dashed two hundred feet below on the rocks in one second flat. He died before a cot could be brought to him.

The character of H. A. Sumner now comes out as we find him going out of his way to relate to the general manager in a letter the kind of man Riddle was. "Mr. Riddle was an exceptionally bright young man entirely devoted to the work he had to do and had all the qualities necessary to make him a very competent engineer, if his life had been spared," wrote Mr. Sumner.

Accidents don't just happen.

They may come from a veteran employee getting careless because he brushes close to death every day. It comes from the unforeseen happening when it might have been foreseen at another time.

One "brass hat" official was judged by those working under him as having caused serious accidents simply because of his refusal to heed the advice of men who knew their jobs. In one instance he forced sick men to leave their beds to assist during a wreck; soon after two of these men died as their condition grew worse. That "brass hat" was in great contrast to Dave Moffat, who was so worried about a train stalled on the pass that he stayed all night in his office to hear word of his men. Likewise, General Manager A. C. Ridgway attempted to walk eighteen miles up the mountain with Bob Bishop carrying food to some men stalled over the pass at Ptarmigan Point. Ridgway gave out and had to take refuge in some outfit cars, but Bishop made it.

This would not be history, if we wrote that all Moffat men were angels, nor would it be fact to say all the devils were beyond good deeds, as lazy and indifferent as they might have been. For as rough and apparently little good for anyting they might appear, when the occasion arose and the need was clear, these men crawled under engines, froze on top of box cars they decorated, or dashed blindly through smoke on section cars through tunnels hunting a broken rail that might derail and kill them.

This was the road that never lost a passenger's life. And don't fool yourself, luck could not hold out forty-four years unless men had been awake and loyal in watching other people's lives.

While the trains were operated over Rollins Pass, one day George Barnes' train, Number Two, the daily passenger, was coupled behind a freight during a terrible blizzard.

The train consisted of a rotary and a mallet; then came the coal drag with a mallet in its center and a mallet behind the caboose with George Schryer in charge. The passenger train followed, being coupled directly behind the last mallet.

When the train reached the Corona Shed, the first mallet cut-off and ran on into the shed, the engineer failing to whistle back through the storm to the other engineers to cut in their air pumps.

Now a four per cent grade is a very steep grade on a railroad. George Schryer kept his eye on his air gauge as hc dozed off and on in his rear mallet cab. All of a sudden he discovered the train was slipping. He glanced at the gauge and the air line was low. So he cut in, having no idea through the blizzard that the head engine had cut off. George began using his water brake in the cylinders and cycling the brakes off and on so that he could build up the line.

Back on his passenger train George Barnes began setting hand brakes and crawling ahead from car to car setting the retainers up only to discover that the brakeman on the freight was too green to know what to do in an emergency. But what could you expect of brakemen on a road that had cut their pay twenty per cent in days of prosperity?

Schryer deftly continued to coax the air pressure up and was able to stop the runaway freight train with the passenger train in the reverse lead, by the time they had run two miles down to Sunnyside.

Barnes says that he blew his top in anger at the freight brakeman, who did not know how to set up retainers. Barnes refused to accept that man as brakeman on his train at any time.

It was the resourcefulness of Schryer that saved that day as many an engineer and conductor or brakeman had done down the years. This was how the "no injury" record was maintained.

Perhaps you will laugh and say that the Moffat operated only a two-car jerk-water train. This may have been true sometimes over the years but there were also summer days filled with long trains of tourists, fishermen's week-end specials and countless picnic trains. In more recent times hundreds of skiers would ride each weekend to Winter Park or Steamboat Springs.

After the Dotsero Cutoff opened, a parade of Rio Grande trains rolled over Moffat rails. The *Exposition Flyer* was inaugurated jointly with the Burlington and Western Pacific and soon the first class scenery began to draw a share of the Chicago — San Francisco business which had usually gone to the Santa Fe or the Union Pacific and Southern Pacific route. By running over the Moffat the distance to the Pacific was cut 175 miles for Denver passengers as compared to the trip via the Royal Gorge route.

After World War II, an entire fleet of new trains was placed in service, utilizing the most modern streamlined cars and powerful diesel locomotives. The *Mountaineer* offered overnight service between Denver, Grand Junction and Montrose, the famed *Prospector* ran overnight between Denver and Salt Lake City and America's most famous train, the *California Zephyr,* replaced the *Exposition Flyer* on the jointly operated Chicago - San Francisco run. One other train, while the least ballyhooed, became the most fondly remembered; the *Yampa Valley Mail.* It remains a fond memory in the social life of northwestern Colorado.

Originally the Denver, Northwestern and Pacific offered passenger, mail and express service on Numbers 1 and 2. Meals were served at Arrow in a fine station restaurant but a parlor-diner was soon purchased from the Chesapeake Beach line and added to the train. As the line built west new cars were purchased including Pullmans and diners and soon the Moffat passenger trains became a way of life for the area's residents and a delight to tourists who appreciated seeing the mountain flowers and rightly prided themselves in the beauty of their country. Local folk were happy to hear the occasional remarks of world travelers describing the scenery of Rock Creek Cañon or Egeria Cañon as being equal to what they had seen in Switzerland.

When sons or daughters went off to college and later to war, their parents knew that the "George Barnes" of the railroad would deal firmly and fairly with their young and someday they would return home aboard a Moffat train. The best in American home life and neighborliness was planted, cultivated and harvested on these trains. Friends regularly met when going to Denver for the National Western Stock Show, to the doctor or on business. These were pioneer spirited men, women and children who were grateful for what "Uncle Dave" had brought them. The train also handled local needs: a trip to lodge meeting or church in a nearby town or just to visit with friends or share family gossip. During this era life in much of northwestern Colorado centered around the comings and goings of Trains 1 and 2.

When Wilson McCarthy took over the Moffat, Superintendent A. L. Johnson lent an ear to the needs of passengers and shippers because the company was already losing business now that highways were being kept open all year round. The result was that Numbers 11 and 12 were added to provide over-night mixed passenger and freight service. The new train was referred to in jest as the "Hog and Human". Railroaders, however, called it "Zim's Sacred Ox", Zim being the dispatcher on duty at night when the train operated. He was determined not to delay the train and gave it right-of-way over everything until World War II when the Rio Grande's business became of first concern.

When the Pullman began to lose patronage, management found a unique answer by rebuilding two cars to a combination arrangement with forty coach seats and four Pullman sections. The cars were named *David Moffat* and *Winter Park* and just fit the road's need to continue offering good passenger service while holding costs down so that the l. c. l. (less than carload lot) freight and gilsonite shipments could keep the train making money. With the usual Moffat pride, the crews handled the mixed runs better than many famous streamliners on other roads.

Numbers 11 and 12 offered a special kind of service known only on mixed trains. Everyone between Denver and Craig could count on supplies of fresh meat, bread and groceries at local stores because of the handy schedule of these trains. Walter Wood, son of Bill Wood, was the Texaco oil dealer in Granby. He remembers that when a sudden jump in tourist business left his gas tanks low, he could call the Craig refinery in the middle of the afternoon and at three o'clock the next morning a tank car of gasoline was delivered. In Fraser the section men voluntarily carried the l. c. l. groceries to the town's two grocery stores. And so it was all along the line; the train was a part of the good life of these people.

With the end of World War II and the merger with the Rio Grande, many things changed. General Manager Perlman proposed to remove all Moffat passenger service and instead provide truck and bus service. A storm of protest broke forth with a loud and clear public outcry, reminding the Rio Grande that the people paid taxes for the tunnel. The sentiment was that the train belonged to the people, the company was only a lessee and the train was still needed, especially in winter.

Perlman would have had little trouble removing these trains, much as hundreds of passenger trains all across America were then being discontinued as the public forsook them, except for the fact of the tunnel being property of the tunnel district for which the residents had long paid taxes.

A quick compromise was reached and a new schedule developed which combined a coach and Pullman bound for Craig, with the Rio Grande's *Mountaineer* on the run between Denver and Bond. Beyond Bond the two trains operated separately. The new schedule was somewhat longer and only a scant few rode this less convenient service and did so in bitter disgust.

There had often been interest expressed in having an early morning train from Craig to allow a few hours for business in Denver, then return in the evening. With this in mind the schedule was changed and Trains 9 and 10 inaugurated as the *Yampa Valley Mail.* Despite the fastest schedule in the road's history, the rail route could not compete with the two hour shorter bus route and once more the people failed to use the train service.

Finally the old day schedule was resumed but planned so as to connect with streamliners in and out of Denver. Patronage was light at first but to the surprise of most everyone, the train began to capture the interest of rail buffs, tourists and skiers. Tour groups began to charter an occasional extra car and on weekends the usual consist of baggage-mail car and one coach often grew to two or three coaches. Much to the Rio Grande's credit, top quality passenger rolling stock was used including a dome car and for a short time a buffet-lounge.

Unfortunately, while the weekend trains often carried a respectable load, the weekday count sometimes was no more than the crew count. After a long series of train-off hearings before the Colorado Public Utilities Commission, the ruling called for the train to be dropped. Only Commissioner Henry Zarlengo voted in favor of retaining the run and proposals to go to a tri-weekly schedule or convert the train to a mixed passenger and freight train gained little support. When the date for the last run was announced for April 7, 1968, a literal pilgrimage of the faithful came to make the final round trip from Denver to Craig. The Rio Grande found it necessary to use almost all its spare passenger equipment to run what proved to be the longest passenger train to Craig in recent memory.

The people of northwestern Colorado did not give up their train without a fight although they had given up utilizing it many years earlier. James Moffat Pughe, representing the Craig Chamber of Commerce, made a last ditch effort to save the *Yampa Valley Mail* by a law suit filed in February, 1969. Part of his brief contended that the number of passengers carried by the Rio Grande increased from 16,914 in 1961, to 39,073 in 1965 and to a projected rate of 39,970 for 1967; and that the railroad failed to prove there would be no future public demand for the service.

The brief continued: "The record further discloses that the overall economic health of the railroad is very prosperous, and the savings to it by the discontinuance would amount to less than one percent . . . that the railroad requested the discontinuance of mail service with resultant loss of revenue . . . that the railroad expended practically nothing to advertise the service . . . that the economy of the area gives promise of increased growth".

Pughe concluded that the order of the Public Utilities Commission was unjust and unreasonable under the facts before it, and asked the court to set the order aside.

While Pughe was writing up his case, the Chamber of Commerce withdrew its suit. That which was being hidden by well-paid lawyers remained so and this time there was no champion to lick them.

"To do justly, love mercy, and walk humbly with God", has never been popular when it mixes religion with business.

So the old days of the Moffat's concern for its passengers in northwestern Colorado ended. No more baking of fresh pies in the dinette kitchen. No more thoughtfulness of a steward making a special trip to the grocery in Craig for ice cream so a young couple could have a wedding anniversary surprise on their return trip. No more attention by a conductor to an elderly widow so she had more than an apple for lunch when the train was tied up.

Those who abandoned rail travel for the highway never knew what they were missing.

One by one the other Rio Grande passenger trains were called for their last runs. The *Mountaineer* came first, even before the end of the *Yampa Valley Mail*. To many on the railroad, the loss of the *Prospector* hurt the most; it was the Rio Grande's own streamliner and not a shared train as was the *California Zephyr*. The famed *C. Z.* itself became the subject of prolonged abandonment hearings which resulted in the Western Pacific receiving permission to drop their portion of the train. A short time later Amtrak was established by Congress to assume responsibility for the nation's passenger service. The Rio Grande was faced with the choice of joining Amtrak or remaining independent but with the legal requirement to continue the present level of service over its line. Present service at that time meant a tri-weekly train and unwilling to become involved with a federal agency which could decide to add new trains and perhaps interfere with movement of freight traffic, the company elected not to join Amtrak.

Thus it was that in May, 1971, a new passenger train was inaugurated over the Moffat Tunnel route. *The Rio Grande Zephyr,* using the Rio Grande's share of the former *California Zephyr* passenger cars, began operating three round trips a week between Denver and Salt Lake City. At first the consist was short and the passengers few. Then the train began to gain a reputation for its fine equipment, excellent diner, amiable crews and matchless scenery and the coaches began to fill. Passenger loads have increased each year and it is now common for the train to be sold out most of the summer and on weekends the rest of the year.

The Rio Grande seems wholly amazed at the popularity of its train. Much to their credit they have maintained a first class operation in the face of obviously high operating costs. It seems that they finally have a train that the public will not forsake!

290

Three quarters of a century of passenger service without the loss of a passenger's life! A fine record for any railroad but on the Moffat Road it was accomplished under the toughest possible conditions. For years it meant battling the grades and snows of Rollins Pass as in this photo (left) in 1905, with the Corona snowsheds still under construction. It also meant running thru slide prone cañons such as we see (above-left) with Train No. 1 in Byers Canon in 1938, or hanging on the sheer cliffs of Rock Creek Canyon (above) as in this 1959 scene. Somehow the road managed to provide good service including a Pullman on the evening mixed train seen (below) about to depart Craig as soon as freight cars are added. —*above, Ed Bollinger and below, both, DPL; above-left, Richard Kindig and left, both, CRRM.*

THE DENVER AND RIO GRANDE WESTERN RAILROAD COMPANY

CLEARANCE CARD

Station _Prospect_   Date _Sept 5_, 195_4_

Conductor and Engineman _1509_

Clearance Card No. _____ Authority to run extra from

_____ to _____

I have _3_ Orders for your train

ORDERS { No. _122_ No. _123_ No. _121_ No. ____ No. ____

No. ____ No. ____ No. ____ No. ____ No. ____

No. ____ No. ____ No. ____ No. ____ No. ____

have been delivered and there are no further orders for your train.

Block Restrictions _none_

OK at _413 P_ M ___ _SFo_ _____ _Edwards_

                   Chief Dispatcher   Operator

This Clearance Card does not affect any orders you may have received.

Chief Dispatcher's initials are not required when orders are to be delivered and executed in ABS territory except as required by Rule 210-B.

_____ Conductor _____ Engineman

To be signed by Conductor and Engineman when required by Rules 217 and 219

On Sept. 5, 1954, the first run of the *Yampa Valley Mail* **(above) is about to depart Denver for Craig with - left to right - Ed Bollinger conferring with Fireman Everett Brown and Engineer Nelse Johnson. The train with typical consists is seen (below) about to leave Craig on March 6, 1966 and (right) passing Finger Rock, near Yampa, on Oct. 22, 1967. The folders (right) reflect Moffat Road passenger history which passed a milestone with the last run of the** *Yampa Valley* **as seen (bottom-left to right) with the train ready to leave Denver on April 7, 1968 with extra cars including these of the Intermountain Ch. Nat. Ry. Hist. Society; at Milner where a small slide caused minor damage and about to leave Craig for the last run on Sun. April 8, 1968.** —*right, Bruce Black; below, Ronald C. Hill; bottom, Robert W. Richardson, CRRM; above, Alice Bollinger and clearance card, both, DPL*

CRRM

Aug. 1904 — *CRRM*

April, 1912 — *Michael Davis*

Corrected to October 1, 1930

THE DENVER
& SALT LAKE
RAILWAY CO.

"THE MOFFAT ROAD"
TIME TABLE

✦

MOFFAT STATION
FIFTEENTH AND BASSETT STREETS
PHONE MAIN 5608

CITY TICKET OFFICE
SEVENTEENTH AND TREMONT PLACE
PHONE TABOR 5371

The **DENVER**
NORTHWESTERN
and **PACIFIC**
RAILWAY
"THE MOFFAT ROAD"

PICTORIAL FOLDER

DENVER
NORTHWESTERN
AND
PACIFIC
"THE MOFFAT ROAD"

YANKEE DOODLE LAKE

ILLUSTRATING
ITS MARVELOUS SCENERY
AND
UNEQUALLED ONE DAY TRIPS

COAL ON THE MOFFAT! This unit coal train has left the Edna Mine and is heading for Oak Creek and eventually Denver or beyond. To handle the tremendous increase in business on the Craig line, the Rio Grande is installing C.T.C. (Centralized Traffic Control) along with new and longer sidings to speed traffic. Future plans include construction of a cut-off to the south of Craig to permit the rapidly expanding business on the western coal extensions to avoid congesting the town. The former Moffat Road is today one of the busiest and most profitable segments of the Rio Grande. —*Denver & Rio Grande Western Railroad, courtesy G.A. Bennewitz, Jr.*

27

Coal Uncle Dave, Coal!

Empties heading west near Tunnel One—*Ronald C. Hill*

Memo of Conversation with a Coal Expert: August 29, 1975

The character of mining in Routt County has changed in nature from pit mining to surface. This is a very viable coal field; one of the best coals in the West. It is strictly for steam boilers and domestic fuel, the latter market being primarily Nebraska, Kansas, Idaho and Washington. This field has great potential and only one way to go — up. Basically there is potential for discovery of additional strip mining fields elsewhere.

This coal ships well compared to other western coal. Because the coal bodies are steeply pitched, further development of the field will undoubtedly be by large companies developing underground strips. Certainly over the long run the great majority of tonnage after 10-12 years must be from underground. The field has easily fifty years production.

David Moffat's vision of the future need for energy from the rich coal reserves of Moffat and Routt counties has been proven in the 1970's. That need is making the Rio Grande one of the West's foremost coal haulers.

The story of coal's long, steady decline is well known. By World War II the steam locomotive was already losing its fight for survival against the diesel. At the same time natural gas was coming within the reach of the average home owner and the coal delivery truck seemed to vanish from our cities. Industry too found that gas and fuel oil were clean burning and sometimes cheaper than coal. By 1954, domestic coal production dropped to less than 400 million tons per year and it was difficult to find anyone interested in discussing the future of coal.

The energy crisis of the 1970's brought a dramatic change with the Federal government urging a rapid boost in production. In 1977, domestic coal production reached 684 million tons but this may be only a start toward peak production in the coming decades. Western coal is a highly desirable low-sulphur variety and as such is ideal for America's utilities which are being asked to switch from scarce natural gas or oil to coal. Washington's goal of 1.25 billion tons production yearly by 1985, means almost a doubling of the 1977 rate and a

major share of this must come from western Colorado.

The Rio Grande has prepared for the boom which is already in full swing on the Craig line. Trackage has undergone extensive upgrading and is estimated to be well capable of handling fifty train per day with heavy diesel power and hundred ton capacity cars. In 1978, the line was already seeing passage of an average of fourteen trains a day; this included the empty movements of unit coal trains returning to the mines.

West of Craig! These words spoke of a dream, a plan to tap the mineral wealth to the west and eventually to reach Salt Lake City. Who can say if the rails will ever reach the Mormon capital but rails west of Craig became a reality in 1978.

Vast coal reserves lay waiting in the Axial Basin and to reach new mines being opened there, a line was built approximately twenty three miles southwest in the direction of Meeker. Another line, now in the planning stage and with construction expected in the early 1980's, will extend twenty miles west of Craig to Lay, on the originally projected route of the Denver, Northwestern and Pacific.

There is the prospect of increased gilsonite shipments and also the possibility of oil shale traffic, although the future of shale remains uncertain. However, the future of coal is solidly established

as indicated in these excerpts from the *Environmental Impact Statement for Northwestern Colorado.*

TOTAL EXPECTED COAL-RELATED DEVELOPMENT

	1976-80	1976-85	1976-90
Cumulative tons coal produced	39 million	121	226
Number of mines	4[1]	7[2]	14[3]
Number of power plants—		3[4]	3
Miles new railroad	23	26	85
Miles new road	15[5]	50	90
Population increase	10,750	9,440	11,870

[1]Seneca 2-W, W. R. Grace, Ruby Construction and Coal Fuels.
[2]1980 mines plus Moonlake Electric, American Electric Power, and Consolidation Coal.
[3]1985 mines plus Thomas Woodward, Merchants Petroleum, Midland Coal, and Paul Coupey, plus an estimated additional 3 mines.
[4]Moonlake Electric and Craig 3 and 4.
[5]Includes coal exploration trails, access roads, and haul roads; other roads are included in the acreage requirements for increased population.

Uncle Dave, you were correct! You dared to build and now others are following, lead by Gus Aydelott, a man of courage and pursuance, giving us a Rio Grande that is well able and ready to handle the demands of future traffic.

296

Phippsburg (left) is a busy rail center, its yard crowded with loaded coal trains ready to head east and incoming trains of empties. Stretching out of sight, an empty unit train snakes its way out of Denver approaching Coal Creek, heading west to the mines. Twenty years ago a typical freight on the Craig line looked like this train passing Finger Rock between Yampa and Toponas. Today coal dominates the economy of this area but this was and is also fine ranching country, due in part to the arrival of the Moffat Road which avoided the necessity of long cattle drives to reach a market. — *left and above, D&RGW; below, Ronald C. Hill*

MEN OF THE MOFFAT: No gathering of railroaders could better symbolize the devotion to duty that helped the Moffat Road thru many lean years than in this photo in front of the Rio Grande's C.T.C. board. From left to right are L. J. Daly, who started as a water boy and rose to trainmaster and finally to assistant superintendent; George Barnes, conductor extrordinary and for a brief period the superintendent; J. B. Culbertson, the first and the last chief dispatcher of the Moffat; Nels Johnson, the number one engineer on the line; and Dispatcher Stevenson who was on duty at the time of the photo, some two decades ago. — *Denver & Rio Grande Western Railroad*

28
From President to Gandy Dancer
— Moffat Men All

The Moffat Road was more than ties, rails, and engines. It was the spirit of Dave Moffat haunting men from the president to the humblest gandy dancer.

Whenever the road was threatened with the junkyard dealer, Dave Moffat seemed to come back and to ride the Marcia over the rails. Then Gerald Hughes, president of the board, would look into Senator Lawrence Phipps' face. That glorious old bull dog would growl, "Denver must be placed on a main line."

Hughes would know that the boys were seeing eye to eye with Uncle Dave. For those men loved Moffat not only because he was a prince of men, but because his vision had been like a searchlight. It had reached further than the short-sighted business insight of others.

Dave Moffat had become a legend among the men. Deuel's regime as general superintendent had brought the best out of the men. Thus among a good number of the men the Moffat had become a cause greater than the pay check.

From president to gandy dancer emotions boiled through men during the trying situations of the years. For the Moffat was more than a road; it was a cause. President Bill Freeman barked out his orders, which insured the increase in value of the bonds he and the rest of his supporters held. Brakemen crawled in his office to be met with a boisterous bluff which would settle down, when

the thunderstorm had passed, to settling some grievances.

Almost every man on the Moffat was some time or other fired by Bill Freeman. He was, however, a big enough man to call some of them back, as they started walking off the job or the next day. Not every man could take such nerve-wracking storms, which came when anything went wrong and landed on men whether they were innocent or guilty.

Bill was known to show consideration for a woman whose husband had been fired for gambling and inefficiency, seeing to it that he was reinstated and his wife received the pay check in the future. On one occasion Freeman heard that the son of one of his brakemen had had a terrible eye injury. Freeman sent his physician and saw that the boy had all the treatment he needed. But he warned the father, "Don't think for a moment that this will stop me from firing you tomorrow if you pull a boner." The story goes that Bill Freeman received fresh mountain trout when that brakeman went fishing. This was not the only time Bill Freeman sent his own doctor. On one other occasion he raised the salary of an employee, a widow, whose little boy hung near death's door in addition to sending his physician.

Bill Freeman was an exceedingly human man, like so many people that walk in the bracing air of Colorado. To the disgust of his successor, Wilson

McCarthy, Freeman said Moffat was just a visionary, who failed, while he (Freeman) had saved the Moffat and had made it a road.

When McCarthy came over to the Moffat office as president, he had Bill Freeman's desk moved out for fear some internal contrivance might make possible Freeman to overhear what went on. McCarthy had no desire to be eavesdropping on his employees, as Freeman did. Out went that desk and back in came a desk which was supposed to be the one Dave Moffat had used.

Master Mechanic Charlie Peterson, Engineer Louie Larsen, and Bill Freeman loved to argue. These arguments waxed furious, for the only way to handle Big Bill was to get as tough and rough as he was and chew right at his ears, if you knew what you were talking about. If you did not have the courage to stand your grounds, Freeman would never respect you.

One day Louie Larsen pulled out of Tabernash a long train of cattle. He was helped over the pass with sufficient power and nothing had gone wrong. Louie handled his air like only a Moffat veteran could, and he had brought the cattle train safely off the mountain. Any small delay would mean feeding the cattle by unloading them at some stockyard. Louie wanted to make a good run. As he hit the two per cent and left the four per cent behind, he realized he was making a good run. Louie's engine, however, was being used as an experimental engine in the use of oil cup flanges on the wheels. Louie had decided that since cattle were such particular freight he would turn the water on the flanges of the wheels that were hot and turn the oil cups off as he did not want his hot flanges from the tortuous curves to break and send the train in the ditch.

By whom should Louie Larsen be flagged down near Tunnel Ten? By President Freeman and Master Mechanic Peterson, who were out inspecting the experimentation with oiled flanges.

Freeman called up to his favorite hogger, "How's this?" as he pointed to water running over the flanges and not oil.

Louie replied that he had made a good run with sixty cars of cattle, and he did not want to put them in a ditch over an experiment. "Experiment on another type of train. I want to get to Denver for this is an important train."

President and Hogger Larsen got in such a heated argument that Master Mechanic Peterson tried to slip away for fear of getting into the inferno.

Freeman spied Peterson sneaking off and hurled a bolt at him. "Won't you stay and stand by your man?"

Having hurled that bolt, Freeman told Larsen to get his train going. Louie whistled in his flagman and released the brakes.

Freeman called up to his hogger, "Wait a minute."

Louie applied the brakes and closed the throttle to hear Bill question him, "Why don't you use water?" To men of another temperament than Larsen, it would have been enough to send them "buggie."

Louie held his ground firmly saying, "Your orders."

Freeman ignored the words and said, "Do you want the water on?"

Louie acknowledged his desire.

Freeman quietly replied, "Then you run the engine, the way you are satisfied. We can work on the oil proposition another time." Eventually the oil experimentation resulted in the installtion of flange oilers on curves. In effect, this brought an energy saving equal to lowering the height of the Moffat Tunnel by two hundred feet.

One of the Moffat's veteran engineers was Layman Mills, who once had a unique experience. He rounded a curve near Craig with the overnight mixed and plowed into a fleecy white snow bank of sheep, which hurled through the air like snow.

The train that Mills pulled in his last years was the famous Number Eleven and Twelve, which carried the hot merchandise between Denver and Craig, making all regular intermediate stops. This train carried not only mail, express, and less than carload freight, but a coach car and a Pullman. Later a combination coach-pullman was built out of a Pullman car for the Moffat at the Rio Grande shops. The coach section of this car was as neat as any Zephyr coach. Two such cars were built. One was named David Moffat and the other one Winter Park. Considerable recognition for this car was given to the Moffat. When A. L. Johnson was asked whose idea it was, he modestly said, "Just say it was developed by the Moffat staff." Trains Number Eleven and Twelve received all kinds of nicknames. Operators spoke of it as "Zim's Sacred Ox" for Dispatcher Zim who fought to keep this train on time like a good warrior. Another name was "Hog and Human". The latest name was applied to it by the Negro porter, who also called it the "Atomic Special."

Layman Mills pulled this train until he wore out like some of the engines. Mills had as near a perfect record as any engineer. One night in the hospital Layman Mills lay waiting for his "Heavenly Express." He turned to the doctor saying, "Going out of this life is as hard as getting out of Denver from Moffat Station."

Perhaps you never pulled out of Denver on the Moffat from her station. It is the case of stopping for a Seventeenth Street crossing, stopping for the Colorado and Southern crossing, stopping to pick up orders at Prospect, stopping as you swing on to the main line at Fox Junction, pulling through the switch and stopping again. You still have a chance to stop at Utah Junction to pick up parts or officials from the stops. You can be held for a meet order at Zuni, which is the far end of the Moffat yards. After you have done all of that you are only four and twenty-five hundredths miles out of Denver, and you have stopped more than the Zephyr did all the way from Lincoln, Nebraska, to Denver.

But the Denver Zephyr will have to go some to have the men behind it like old Number Eleven on the Moffat. When Layman Mills had ceased to pull trains in this world, his widow found W. O. Colwell, treasurer of the road, showing the same kind of interst in Mrs. Mills that Uncle Dave would have shown. Colwell advised her in planning for the future with the money that came to her. That was part of the Moffat family spirit.

The Moffat road like all railroads was its men and women.

George Schryer is said to have taken a fancy for a certain movie star who stood beside him to have her picture taken when Hollywood came to the Moffat. Now George would not trade any gal in the world for his wife, who has watched the hill for years for every move of his trains, and kept meals hot for him. But you know how it is when Hollywood comes to shoot a movie! During filming of Ryley Cooper's *White Desert* in 1925 and *The Trail of '98* in 1927, the boys were likely to wink at the girls and enjoy the good food in the diners where Hollywood was fed together with engineer, conductor and brakeman.

During the filming of *The Trail of '98,* a tragedy happened to the Moffat's third oldest engineer, Bob Bishop, who was respected as a clean cut man. His son, Fayette, stepped out on a snow bank and disappeared under the snow, as he shot down the bank. Thus ended the life of a fine lad and the motion picture world never produce the true tragedy of that setting, though actors played such parts.

Moffat's boys could be lazy, and some were. They could be reckless and gamble with their own lives but never a passenger's life. They could

create humor in the grimmest situation. In the days of W. R. Morse a flood worried the general manager and his section boss at Kremmling. This Irishman was valuable but his reports were filled with tedious details of the movements of the river.

In exasperation, Morse telegraphed, "Be brief. No newspapers."

Night came; the wires were silent. Something was wrong.

Day came and still the service was not restored. Finally the line was repaired and this telegram came through: "River is where track was." Kennedy."

Railroads with such terrible grades that the Moffat had, usually have a run-away or two. Here is a Rocky Mountain News story:

The only one of the four accidents which did not end disastrously took place late in the winter of 1912, according to Conductor F. A. Van Vranken, 2246 Stuart Street, Denver, who was in charge of the train.

The train, carrying twenty-two cars of coal aside from engine, tender and caboose, had pulled out of Corona, the tiny station at the crest of the Divide which claims to be "the top of the world," at a little after 1:00 o'clock in the morning. It started down the eastern slope of Corona pass.

The train began to gather speed as it descended," said Van Vranken, in describing the accident, "and three or four miles out of Corona, the engineer gave a sudden call for brakes — one short, imperative blast of the whistle."

"By the time that my brakeman, Oliver Akers, 3536 Decatur Street, S. S. Cheney and I had set the emergency brakes and got into the caboose, the train was moving fifty or sixty miles an hour."

"About three miles below the spot where the train began to run, there is a tiny siding called Antelope, where there is a half mile of level grade."

"We knew that unless the brakes held tightly enough to stop the train there, it would start down the final sweep of the four per cent grade, leave the tracks and pile up at the bottom of some gully."

"We decided that if the train did not slow down, we would cut the caboose loose, and attempt to save our lives, for by this time the train was going so fast that we dared not jump off."

"The train ran three miles and as it approached the level stretch of road near the siding at Antelope it began to slow down. The emergency brakes held — held strongly enough to stop the train."

When conductor and brakeman found the train at a standstill they climbed out of the caboose and walked up to the engine to find out what accident

301

had caused the runaway. They found the engine empty. It appeared later that as the train started the steep descent, the engineer, who was a new man, suddenly lost his nerve and without attempting to throw on the air brakes, gave the one signal for emergency brakes and jumped, the fireman following him.

"We walked back up the track after we had the train well braced so it would not begin to move until the power was thrown on," continued Van Vranken, "and met the engine men walking in."

"The fireman had a broken collar bone but otherwise neither was seriously hurt. The whole run had taken place in less than five minutes. None of us was frightened at the time of the accident and we got the train started and took it on into Denver. However, for a week afterward the very thought of the run-away made my knees shake."

In the letters of thanks to the train crew by D. C. Dodge, at that time receiver of the road and an old railroad man and pioneer in Colorado, by G. H. Barnes, then superintendent of the railroad, and still a conductor on the Denver and Salt Lake, and W. A. Beerbower, general superintendent of the railroad, only one criticism of the action of conductor and brakemen at the time of run-away was made. The latter were thanked for their courage in staying with the train, but, said the letters, "made one mistake. You should not have gone back to pick up the engine men."

Three other runaways which have occurred on this same stretch of road have ended in the wreck of the trains, and the deaths of some of the trainmen.

The first run-away was caused by the freezing of water in the pipeline of the air brakes. The train ran nine miles below Corona before it left the track to pile up in a mass of wreckage which it took days to clear from the tracks to permit other trains to pass through. In this wreck, Conductor George Briggs, and several of his crew were killed.

In a third similar wreck, Conductor T. D. Shapcott, State Bridge, now a passenger conductor, was one of two members of the crew to escape death. The last runaway occurred about four years ago in nearly the same place. In this wreck, the engineer, Roy Watkins, was the only man killed.

These accidents which have occurred under seemingly unavoidable circumstances, have taken place always on this same bad grade which the tunnel cut out.

"Big Dan" Cunningham, one time superintendent of motive power, was an excellent speechmaker. One of his favorite cracks about his Moffat days was, "it gets so cold and stays that way at Sulphur that the kids learn to ski before they learn to walk."

One of "those kids" was Barney McLean who became a world famous skier.

"Big Dan" worked under W. E. Morse, vice president and general manager who used to tell his enginemen, "I want you to be afraid of this mountain and have respect for it."

On one occasion a very fine engineer, Christianson, overlooked an order and almost had a collision with Number Two at Cliff. Since this was a passenger train it was an offense that could fire a man. "Big Dan" knew how to handle Morse, so he pretended to demand this right in front of the hogger.

The general manager argued, "It takes $25,000 to train an engineer on this road, and he is one of the best men we have."

"Big Dan" remembered Christianson's loyalty beyond duty time and again when he struggled with a sack of coal to reach his engine stuck in a blizzard and keep her warm.

Morse said, "Oh, let him off with thirty demerits." "Big Dan" agreed but forgot to record the demerits.

When Morse left the railroad, Bill Freeman came and the going got very rough. "Big Dan" went to the Rio Grande but burned all demerit records to save the boys he loved.

His tribute to these men was, "The men of the Moffat were the best, most loyal, and efficient men I ever worked with." They had to be, as a man with a yellow streak could not stay with the Moffat.

"They had big loyal hearts. I can say the same of the men on the Rio Grande. I loved them all for they are 'God's children.' "

Big Dam is very worthy of the book written about him by Frank Cunningham, which is called "Big Dan."

No railroad this side of heaven can exist without holding court regularly. A. L. Johnson held court as general superintendent from 1924 to 1947. It's not a popular thing to do. But no road can have discipline without it. The local chairmen of the unions brought their complaints, and Johnson felt he had become the "General Superintendent of Griping."

It has been some years since "A.L." has been out on the road, but he had his fill of the blizzards and blockades as assistant superintendent. The boys can tell jokes about how he overlooked the fact a passenger engine does not have a steam hose on the head end. But they also recall the wintry day he climbed the hill with some Mexicans and slipped fifty or seventy feet so fast that eternity came up with only a tree between him and old Gabriel himself. The Mexicans laughed. Johnson chided them to slide down if they thought it was funny. No one slid. Johnson looked over the cliff on top of which the tree grew that had caught him. He then carefully walked back up the hill not slipping on the icy snow. Johnson remembers the day he lay sleeping exhausted in a cabin with these men. He remembers the lye-like coffee he drank and counted it all right. He recalls a meet order with a rotary in an east side shed, when Lyn Holliday thought he could out-run the rotary in a smoke order.

Perhaps these experiences gave Johnson the tenacity to continue to beg in his letters for safety and more safety. And yet was not too busy to be a church trustee for twenty years.

There was a Greek section boss at Spruce on the east side of the hill. He was called "Doc" by everyone, though his name was Phillip Arvenetta. The year was 1926, and as the opening of Moffat Tunnel was not far away, Bill Freeman held the tie renewals to a minimum. One Sunday several cars were off the track at Boegen Cut Snowshed, which was not in "Doc's" section. This section boss was a remarkable fellow, and as little progress was reported from the derailment, Bill Freeman got on the telephone and disturbed "Doc's" Sunday afternoon snooze.

Phillip answered his ring on the ancient phone and heard the voice of "The Old Man," "Doc, this is Freeman."

The president continued, "They are off up there in Boegen shed. They have been off quite a while. Not going very fast."

The king snipe knew what the president wanted, so he answered, "You bet, I will go up, Old Top."

Only "Doc" could get away with that for "Doc" was the type of king snipe a railroad has to have.

Freeman continued, "You don't have to do anything. Just get them moving."

Doc answered, "Yes, Old Top."

This conversation was overheard by Ed Harrison, who later was my section boss. The "pony line," as the extra wire over the hill was called, was the town newspaper and radio in spite of Bill Freeman's thunder for its use to be strictly company business.

Ed Harrison was another king snipe, who could work miracles in any emergency and had a way with men that gave him one of the largest gangs on the road. Whatever a railroad would do without

gandy dancers and king snipes is an open question. Helper engines running down the hill light drop notes off telling them about holes developing in the track.

The meanest work in the world is done by these boys who grunt and shove and freeze on their open air cars as they "putt-putt" along before sunrise. Believe it or not, on the hill (Rollins Pass) they had to push their cars, for gas motors were not used at that time on the Moffat.

My other section boss was "Dutch" Sothmann. Three college presidents and seven parsons can now say they worked under him either on the Union Pacific or the Denver and Salt Lake. If you pardon the intrusion at this place, I will say that my short time as gandy dancer was under W. C. Jones as chief engineer and Glen Turner as head roadmaster. Then came Ed Hamilton and Gus Aydelott as my superiors with Red Calkins as division engineer. "Bill" Ancell signed my card for the Brotherhood of Maintenance of Way Employes, the boys of the section having dug up the fees as a surprise for me after Kenneth George and Jess Correll had broken me on the Fraser section when Ed Harrison was on vacation. "Chet" Smith taught me how to spike. I was a poor pupil using his shins for spikes. No one would let me spike in Moffat tunnel. They did not want to get hurt, so I ran a light plant, picked up lost spikes as I shoved three section cars. I also carried a first aid kit and patched up every one from a Greek to the future Pueblo division superintendent, Gus Aydelott, who got clipped by a spike puller he was operating.

Now while the gandy dancers were taking the holes out of the road bed that developed, the Moffat passenger and freight agents were rendering a service to large and small shippers that was touched off by a friendly appreciation personally expressed. An old lady in Hideaway Park opened a small grocery store and she was shipping by rail. She received a personal call of thank you from the agent of the Denver office. Time and again the Denver YMCA had a special car for their boys en route to Camp Ouray. Though the number were only eighteen, the management wanted to be sure everyone had a seat and not a crowded car. Normally an extra coach was at the station during the tourist season. If it was needed, it went out. If it was inadequate another coach was added at Utah Junction and even a larger engine. It was unthinkable to tell people they could not get on a train because it was full. If a shipper like Horace Brown at Kremmling had an idea that would improve service, he knew whom to call and his suggestion was appreciated. If Frank Carlson saw that a door on the other side of the station was more convenient for shippers, the bridge and building carpenters were directed to make the change. If Agent Carl Lomax was not getting cars for cattle he knew he could phone and not get a clerk who could do nothing, but he could get the boss who would raise hell so that the mistake did not occur again. No one over the line was afraid to make a move for the good of the passengers or the road. In the office Ed Sunergren knew that Bill Jones would be sure to thank him for what he had done while the boss was out. This spirit existed in spite of all the jealous, envious, spiteful things that happened between the men. The Moffat boys could quarrel and even stab in the back, but like a family of husky teenage sons and daughters, when the crisis came they moved together.

The public growled about everything and the Moffat boys growled back. It was, indeed, a family in which the smallest shipper and the most cantankerous employe had a chance.

The traincrews knew all the old timers, their sons, and grandchildren. They were interested in them. You knew the crews and the crews knew you. Tourists that came back year after year were greeted, "Well, how have you been this year; the boy still in college?" Van Vranken very ably carried on the traditions of senior conductor Barnes when he retired. If your mother or your little boy were on the train and a tie-up occurred, you knew they would not go hungry.

One of the most perceptive commentaries on the Moffat is offered by Errett R. Albritton. His writing is at the same time humorous and enlightening.

The date was July 22, 1937, and I was on a train headed for Denver and a position with the Panama Railroad, a U.S. Government owned railroad operating alongside the Panama Canal in Central America. I had just concluded approximately nineteen years service with the Denver and Salt Lake Railway (Moffat Road) that started with my employment at Craig, Colorado in 1918 as Messenger boy and ended at Steamboat Springs where I had been Agent-Telegrapher for the past nine years. Those were probably the happiest nineteen years of my life, but on that particular train ride I was eagerly looking forward to my new position in the tropics. However, my thoughts also turned to the many good friends that I was leaving in Northwest Colorado. Years later, though, I realized that no matter how far apart good friends may live, they still remain good friends.

My service on the Moffat Road included that of Station Helper at Oak Creek and Craig, Telegrapher at Steamboat Springs (1924), Craig and Denver, Agent-Telegrapher at Kremmling, Rollinsville, West Portal, Hayden, Oak Creek and Steamboat Springs, Agent-Yardmaster Phippsburg and Train Dispatcher — Denver.

While working as Station Helper at Oak Creek in 1919, at age fifteen, the people there tagged me with the nickname of Davie Moffat Jr., due to my reactions toward the derogatory remarks made by some Oak Creek citizens about the Moffat Railroad and its employees. That same year, I started playing semi-pro baseball with the Oak Creek team and I later played with teams at Craig, Granby, Kremmling, Phippsburg, Denver and Steamboat Springs. The nickname stuck with me and by virture of my moving from one end of the railroad to the other and my activities with the various baseball teams, most people in Northwest Colorado knew me as Davie Moffat.

Much has been written about Chief Dispatcher Joe Culbertson. I have known quite a number of Chief Dispatchers and I would rate Culbertson at the top. A railroad, in order to operate at the lowest possible cost per ton mile, must have an efficient train dispatching force. The Moffat Railroad was indeed fortunate that for most of the time it operated as the Denver and Salt Lake Railway, it had Joe Culbertson as Chief Dispatcher and men like A. S. Meldrum, Arthur Durbin and W.C. Patty as Train Dispatchers. Culbertson tried to make a Train Dispatcher out of me, but I lacked the proper experience at the time and possibly did not concentrate enough on my work — anyway, it was nearly twelve years later before I considered myself sufficiently matured and experienced to be a good Train Dispatcher, for Train Dispatching is a very exacting type of work. The only position comparable is the present day Air Traffic Controller at a busy airport and I just recently read an article indicating there is considerable controversy as to which of these two positions cause the most stress and strain mentally. Both positions are unique in that in addition to the stress and strain of maintaining efficient operation, the penalties for mistakes can be catastrophic. Just one mistake by an employee of either category, for instance, could result in death or injury to many people and damage to equipment and property costing millions of dollars. Such an accident, if caused by a Train Dispatcher's error, would result in his dismissal and most likely he would never be permitted to work as a Train Dispatcher on *any* railroad again.

One thing that I did learn from Culbertson was a certain philosophy of his about working your job that helped me in later years and which I have passed on to many young persons who were just starting to earn their way upward in the world. He told me once, "Keep pushing your work — don't let your work push you. Keep ahead of your work,

Judge Wilson McCarthy (top) was president of both the Moffat and Rio Grande when Rev. Ed Bollinger of Fraser went to work as a gandy dancer during W.W. II. One of his jobs was working on the rail bender (above) where - left to right - we see "king snipe" section boss Ed Harrison, Bert "Eddie" Schneitman and Bollinger. Gus Aydelott, then roadmaster, was Rio Grande President when he posed with Bollinger (below) during ceremonies at the opening of the Rio Grande archives in the State Museum. — *top, D&RGW; others, Ed Bollinger*

then, when or if an interruption occurs (like a derailment, collision, etc.) you can absorb it and not get behind with your work, but if you are barely caught up with your work, or are behind, and an interruption occurs, you get further behind and you cannot give proper attention to the interruption or to your normal duties."

Few railroads can say that they enjoyed such a monopoly on transportation as did the Moffat Railroad prior to the advent of the private auto, trucks and busses, followed later on by the airplane. During the monopoly period, a blockade on the railroad due to snow, mud or rock slide, or a tunnel cave-in causing an interruption of traffic for more than a few days was of much concern to the people in Rio Blanco, Grand, Routt and Moffat Counties as in many instances long interruptions would shut down the coal mines and even cause shortages of some food products. More than once the coal mines sent their miners to the trouble spots to assist the railroad men and expedite the reopening of the railroad so the railroad could get back to the business of hauling coal and other freight and so the miners could get back to mining coal. During their monopoly the railroad handled nearly one hundred percent of the coal, livestock and other farm products outbound and practically all of the consumer products inbound and nearly one hundred percent of the mail and passengers both inbound and outbound for the four county area. So in one way, it was an even up arrangement as the people of Northwest Colorado needed the railroad and the railroad needed the people at that time.

The month of February, 1928, holds the record for most cars of coal ever hauled in one month by the Moffat Railroad. During that month, the Moffat Coal Company at Oak Creek ordered one hundred cars each day for each of their two tipples. Victor American (Oak Creek) ordered one hundred cars each day for its one tipple, Haybro Mine fifty cars each day and Routt Coal Company at Routt forty cars per day. The mines at Mt. Harris were also working at the limit of their capacity. The train, yard and engine crews were working nearly sixteen hours each day and although they were making good money — they and all of us working at Phippsburg during that period were sort of glad when business slacked off a bit. Luckily, the railroad had no serious interruptions of service during that month. The empty coal cars were distributed promptly to the mines, based on their need, and the loaded cars were picked up at the mines without any unusual delay, moved to Phippsburg, switched into trains and the coal ordinarily arrived in Denver within twenty hours of departure from Phippsburg.

Although railroading on the Moffat was for the most part a serious and demanding occupation, an occasional humorous situation did crop up.

Many stories could be told about Steve Dwyer, who was employed by the Moffat as a brakeman in the early 1900's, but who had previously worked as a telegraph operator on the Chicago Burlington and Quincy Railroad. Steve liked to smoke cigars and was always bumming them from others — but he was well liked by all and was the victim of numerous pranks because he generally reacted in a blustery way that was funny to his fellow workers. While walking in the snow alongside a moving train up on the "Hill" he slipped and fell, then rolled down the snow bank to the track where his left arm fell across the rail and was severed near the shoulder by the wheels of the moving train. After being released by the hospital, the railroad put him back to work as a telegraph operator and Steve learned to do a real good job with just one arm. However, to illustrate how his friends teased him, Steve's first job as an operator, after the accident, was at Plainview. On his first day on the job, a freight train stopped there to take water on the locomotive. The Conductor of the train walked into the telegraph office, shook hands with Steve, offered him a cigar and told him it sure was good to see him able to work and make a living even though he was handicapped. Steve took the cigar, lit it, and it blew up with a loud bang — it had a firecracker in it.

Prior to Steve's injury, he was working as brakeman on a freight train coming up the west side of the "Hill". It was the day of the fight between Corbett and Fitzsimmons for the Heavyweight Championship of the World, and as most railroad men in those days, Steve and the other crewmen were anxious to learn the outcome of the fight. This, of course, was before the days of radio or T.V. The train stopped at Arrow and although the office was closed, the men knew that the door was locked with a switch lock and, of course, each trainman had a switch lock key. The office had telegraph instruments so the members of the crew asked Steve to contact the Train Dispatcher in Denver and learn the results of the fight. Steve entered the office, called the Moffat Train Dispatcher and after the Moffat Dispatcher answered his call, this conversation took place. Steve — "How did the fight come out?" Train Dispatcher — "What fight." Steve — (somewhat angered) "The fight between Corbett and Fitzsimmons." Train Dispatcher — "I didn't even know they were mad."

President Freeman was an ex-telegrapher. Shortly after he came to the Moffat, he arranged for the telegraph wires to extend to his office and had a receiver and a sending key installed so he could monitor most messages or discussions that passed over the Moffat telegraph lines. He would occasionally call some station along the railroad and when doing so would sign "F". When any of us heard the "F" sign, we immediately started listening as some of his remarks were pretty spicy. On one occasion, I happened to hear him break in on a message being sent by a Western Union telegrapher and which was being copied or received by an operator (telegrapher) at Kremmling who was having a hard time receiving the message. The Kremmling operator had stopped or "broke" the Western Union operator several times and caused several words to be repeated by the time the sender had reached the body of the message. (Good operators rarely "broke" a sending operator even when receiving several messages.) So Freeman, who was a perfectionist, finally became irritated and broke in on the message by calling the Kremmling operator and signing "F". When the operator answered, the following dialogue took place. (To fully appreciate the following you should know that in Morse Code, one dot indicates or stands for the letter E and the sound made by one dot would be short and sharp, comparable to the sound made by striking a piece of steel sharply with another piece of steel.) Freeman — "Why did you break the W. U. operator so often in that message?" Kremmling operator (somewhat shakily) "I didn't think I broke him very often." Freeman — "The Hell you didn't — you broke him on everything he sent you, you even broke him in the middle of the letter E." Silence.

Freeman often swore at his officials and after one such performance when Superintendent Jess Spahr was the recipient, a friend of Spahr's who had overheard the tirade, later told Spahr he didn't see how he could take that sort of thing. Spahr's reply was — "You can take a lot of that for $800.00 per month."

Superintendent A. L. Johnson and Assistant Superintendent Lynn Holliday, in order to eliminate as many confrontations with Freeman as possible, spent a considerable part of their time out along the railroad. One of their favorite retreats was in the Gore Canyon on the Second District. There were no telegraph offices in the canyon, and the canyon's many rock slides and tunnels gave them a good excuse for being there. When Freeman felt he had reason to talk to Johnson or Holliday, he would call Chief Dispatcher Culbertson on the telephone and instruct him to get either or both on the railroad telephone line for him. Too often, as far as Freeman was concerned, Culbertson would later call back and tell Freeman — "They are over on the Second District, in the Gore Canyon and I can't contact them." Freeman finally caught both men and told them he wanted them to come to his office. They did, and Holliday gave me this account of the meeting. When they entered the office, Freeman

306

was seated at his desk. Johnson and Holliday remained standing on the opposite side of the desk from Freeman. Freeman started talking to them in a quiet voice about how lately he had tried to contact them several times and each time had been told they were on the Second District in the Gore Canyon and were not available — then his voice became rather loud as he stood up and started pacing back and forth on his side of the desk, but always looking the two of them square in the eyes (or so it seemed to Holliday and Johnson) and he ended up by shouting — "By God, if I ever commit a crime, I will go over there on the Second District and stand on the main track, in the Gore Canyon, and *nobody* will ever find me."

From president to gandy dancer the spirit of Dave Moffat has run. The spirit has waned, and the spirit has grown. Finally the day came when the RFC took over the Moffat and Wilson McCarthy became president with fellow trustee Henry Swan, vice president of United States National Bank.

The Moffat was on its way to becoming the Rio Grande. Every year the merger was talked about. But the men with debts against the Rio Grande and those who held stocks and bonds could not agree how the line was to be reorganized. Years went by and the Moffat family remained happy never knowing what the merger might mean.

Then came April 11, 1947, and the newspapers almost missed the secret, that the Moffat was no longer a railroad. We don't even know if A. L. Johnson, who had been elected a pallbearer trustee, knew that the road had died. But the night of the tenth the Moffat trains kept on running. The famous "hog and human mixed" with her famous rebuilt coach-Pullman came in from Craig with gilsonite, sheep's wool, oil men and ranchers.

The history of the road was over. A road that had made the headlines all down the years since her conception. She winked out as the Moffat and kept on running as the Pueblo division I-A and I-B of the Rio Grande.

The road that had worried because the government owned her was now part of the Rio Grande, and believe it or not, all the officials were not New Deal Democrats.

April eleventh the Rio Grande brass hats were so tired from fighting for their reorganization and so overcome with the complications of the merger, that they began to have sympathy for the whale that swallowed Jonah.

The Moffat is no more. This is an era, and has been for years, of mergers. The Denver and Salt Lake has ceased to be a family. She has been adopted by the Rio Grande. In her new home there have been and will continue to be changes. And since a railroad is a cause, men's sentiment is part of it all.

By now the smoke of old controversies and from bitter battles has risen enough that certain conclusions are seen.

First, David Moffat secured the only logical route west of Denver through the hog back of the Divide for reaching the western slope of Colorado and a needed trunk line through to Salt Lake and the coast. This honor is shared with H. A. Sumner who conquered the stubborn mountains and located a line that no one has been able to surpass except in refinements which were originally planned.

Second, the absorption of the Moffat by the Rio Grande was to the best interest of the state even though Moffat line patrons have belatedly appreciated the high quality of personal service the Moffat Road had given them.

Third, Harriman and Gould in their war against Moffat tragically delayed the development of the western slope of Colorado and Denver. Their fears, lest their own roads be weakened if the Moffat route was opened, have been completely disproved.

Moffat, in this respect, towered above the greed of Harriman and Gould by never opening a bank, a mine, or a railroad at the expense of competitors but rather caused every one concerned to profit by his adventures.

Engineer Louis Larsen (right) and Fireman Curley Ohren pose by their engine with its large butterfly plow before heading into the storm—*Mrs. Louis Larsen, CRRM*

Fifth, the Hughes, Phipps, Boettchel and Freeman regime had the insight to hang on to the Moffat railroad in the faith that David Moffat's judgment in building the road was sound. In this wisdom they performed a real service to Colorado.

Sixth, the location, construction, and operation of the Moffat were made possible by a high calibre of men devoted to the spirit of David Moffat. This has been the thesis of this book. In spite of all the human frailties of these men they were devoted to their duty far above what could be asked of them and made possible the record of no loss of a passenger's life or even a costly injury. The very existence of the railroad in its most discouraging years was alone made possible by this loyalty when they operated the road with the very food that Bill Freeman denied them due to low wages.

So it came about that the Vista Dome California Zephyr found a short cut through the glories of the Rockies and the Flying Ute brought another excellent high speed trunk line for East and West shippers which would be and will be found open when other routes are delayed and blocked by snow storms. For David Moffat gave us a route under winter storms.

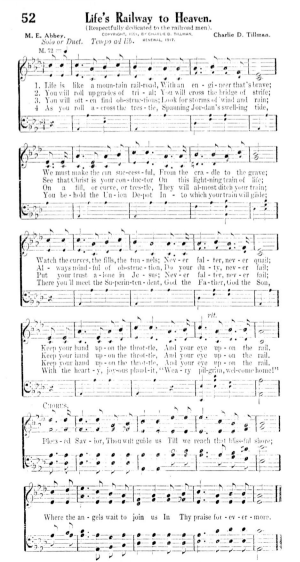

52 Life's Railway to Heaven.
(Respectfully dedicated to the railroad men.)

M. E. Abbey.
Charlie D. Tillman.

CHURCH ON RAILS

For many years the American Baptist Church operated chapel cars to bring worship services to remote areas. One of the finest cars was the *Emmanuel,* meaning "God With Us", built by Barney and Smith and dedicated at the Baptist Convention in Denver on May 26, 1893. The car was used extensively on the Moffat including at Phippsburg, Steamboat and Craig where it is seen (above) in 1930. The interior (top) was like a church with stained glass windows and seating for up to 80 persons. A small organ provided music and the favorite song of most railroaders was *Life's Railway to Heaven,* the words of which were written by Rio Grande engineer M. E. Abbey. The organist's copy from the *Emmanuel* is reproduced here. When lightning struck the car in 1930, engineer and deacon Joe Preiss used his engine's fire hose to fight the fire, after which the car went to Utah Jct. for repairs. — *above, Ernest Kline; top, Jacquie McKeon; left, Mrs. Joe Preiss*

308

MOFFAT MEN ALL!

A few moments in Moffat Road history are preserved in these photos, starting above-left and running clockwise: Blaine Markle poses in front of a work train in Gore Cañon, probably doing track work because of the ballast spreading plow on the engine; Engineer Joe Preiss - right - shares a lifetime of memories with Art Belgin as they relax in their cab after bringing a ski special to Winter Park; On June 22, 1922, with plenty of snow still in sight, the cooks and operators at Corona posed for this picture at the top of the world; Fabian Smith perched himself on his trusty 100 class engine after helping with the rescue of a mallet engine; The mists of time make it difficult to determine names and we have only these identities - left to right - Smith, Fizice, Louie Larsen and Brown for the hardy group enjoying a break in the rigors of winter as they await their runs at Tolland about 1920. — *top, Joe Preiss, DPL; above-right, Fabian Smith: below-right, Mrs. Louis Larsen: others, Blaine Markle, courtesy Neal Miller: all, CRRM*

29

Tunnel of Time

It was springtime in Denver in 1950, when George Barnes signed up for his last run at the age of eighty-nine. It was the author's privilege to deliver the funeral sermon and at the request of many friends it is included here as a tribute to this man of the Moffat.

THE LAST RUN OF GEORGE BARNES

The most loved man of the Moffat Road has been called for the run beyond the end of rails, West of Craig. We are here to wish him Godspeed. We have loved him, admired him, for George Barnes is a two-word definition of a real man.

All over Middle Park and Northwestern Colorado there are ranchers and business men who today look back to the time Conductor Barnes watched them with a hawks-like eye as they rode the Moffat, the life line between their home town and Denver, the stock show, and college. Their parents knew George could handle them and today their hats are off to George Barnes.

His fellow railroaders are both here and at the other end of the line paying tribute to the man who of all men went a long way in building a safety record that can say that no passenger was ever injured in the forty-three years of the Moffat Road. We say Barnes was a man because of his courage and ability to make the right decisions quickly and teach others how to railroad. His character was above reproach. He lived a life that defined his Masonic promises and some how brought the best out of the men he associated with.

To the tourist down the years George Barnes' smile, his stories, his wholesome life was indeed a high point in their travels. They looked forward to seeing him every year.

This afternoon we know why life is good, why the battle is worth waging, for we have seen George Barnes and realize that men can be called blessed even as our Savior said in the Sermon on the Mount.

The Light is green, the hill is open, there are no longer restraining orders, and Uncle Dave stands with a committee of friends at the other end of the run. Farewell.

George H. Barnes was born September 28, 1860, passed away March 27, 1950; buried at Fairmount cemetery, Denver, Colorado, after services by the Rev. E. T. Bollinger. Graveside ceremony by the Rob Morris Lodge No. 92, A.F.&A.M., with an all Moffat crew in charge of the ritualistic service.

THEY WERE FIRST! Engineer A. F. Norbury and Conductor George Barnes began with the Moffat during construction and stayed a lifetime. Posing at Craig, they likely shared memories with Otto L. Fey, the Station Agent for 39 years. His successor, E. G. Deakins, saw the passenger era close with departure of the last *Yampa Valley Mail*. — *above, D. F. Stevens: left, L. C. McClure, DPL*

With each passing year more Moffat men have transferred their seniority to the other side. But who is to deny that they somehow are still riding the Rails That Climb. Join us for just such a venture.

MEET ORDER OF CALIFORNIA ZEPHYR AND EXTRA 210 EAST

It was a moonlight night when the headlight of mallet 210 seemed only a gleam in the shadows and tunnels. A. F. Norburry sat pinching the air on the gleaming black repaint job of the 210 which had been resurrected for this occasion.

A whole string of Pullman and parlor cars rolled behind. They all had been resurrected out of a museum or some one's memory. The extra gangs in fact, had been moved out of several of the cars, but this night they reflected fresh varnish and upholstered interiors as perfect as the Pullman Company had given them forty or more years before.

This ghost train rolled east out of Egeria Cañon down grade towards Rock Creek Cañon. Uncle Dave Moffat sat in the rear of the Marcia. The lights were out as he enjoyed the countryside bathed in moonlight. The fresh snow glistened beautifully but did not hurt his eyes. Others sat with Uncle Dave. The red glow of an occasional cigar or the spluttering of a match revealed others sitting with Uncle Dave.

Uncle Dave seemed in the best of spirits. "Sumner, what did you think of those Texans skiing at Steamboat?"

H. A. Sumner leaned back and chuckled, "Did you ever hear that I would not hire a Texan or a man who smoked a cigarette?"

Uncle Dave answered, "It seems to me I did. And what was that about coloring up a batch of sewer maps for me when I went to New York?"

Sumner chuckled again, "You know the boys got a great kick out of that. I hear that some of them are still tucked away in the files."

A. C. Ridgway leaned over Sumner's shoulder and said, "I wonder when they filled this trestle in Rock Creek Cañon?"

Uncle Dave replied. "Perhaps the fellow will be on the California Zephyr. It's kind of mean holding that new train fourteen hours on a siding to let us by. But I would like to see it."

The ghost special glided out of the Cañon. Norburry, their engineer, blew for a meet with an empty coal train. Uncle Dave went to the back and stood on the platform to wave at the crews of the two engines.

W. G. Evans stepped out with Moffat, and after standing silently for awhile, he asked, "What are

you thinking about?"

Uncle Dave's face was lit up in the moonlight but he remained silent. Evans was about ready to go in the car, when Moffat answered him, "Don't rush. I was just thinking how this country has developed just as we predicted it would if they had a railroad. That is all I wanted."

Evans answered quickly, "I hear Denver is quite a city."

Dave Moffat turned to go back in, saying, "Yes, Denver is on a main line now. In fact, when this road put her on the main line, the Union Pacific had to give her main line service. That's what we wanted for Denver. That is all she needed. When I was a young man, I came out here, hoping to make my grub stake and return."

The cigars continued to glow as the ghost train crawled into Orestod. The men crowded the back platform as they looked at their first diesel pulling to a hot-shot freight towards Bond and the west coast.

Some time later the 210 blew for her meet order with the California Zephyr which answered on her electric horn.

H. A. Sumner said, "Sounded like someone's calf bawling."

The ghost special did not slow down, Norburry was making the 210 do all she could — about

thirty-five miles an hour. "Not bad for a mountain goat."

"She's as good as she ever was," the fireman answered, "and I think this stoker is swell."

This message was picked up by the brakeman who handed it to David H. Moffat, Jr.

"Your vision gave us the only route West of Denver. Your faith in your men shames this age. Your boys never lost a passenger's life. Tell Sumner that his line through the mountains was a difficult job well done."

And as the ghost men sat quietly musing over the past, their special with the Marcia slipped silently into the darkening Tunnel of Time.

Enroute to the Tunnel of Time we pass the lonely remains of mallet 210, lying below the Loop where it landed more than half a century ago. And Middle Park still spreads out majestically as in this 1941 scene from Tabernash. — *above-left, Rocky Mt. News; above, Irving E. Olsen and top, DPL*

Moffat Man Joe Preiss provided data and photos for this book including this scene (above) after abandonment of the Rollins Pass line and (bottom) of Joe taking a sled ride with the lady operator at Corona. Joe was not to see this book completed for on Jan. 5, 1979, he was called for his final run over the hill. His funeral service was given by the author and is included here.

JOSEPH F. PREISS
October 14, 1893 - January 5, 1979

It was my privilege to share in the memories Joe lived with. What an inheritance those memories give us!

I remember others saying, "War! I want to forget it!" But to Joe the difficulties of earning a living in the frozen horrors of the desolate deserts of white drifting snow in a two-mile-high pass were the memories of VICTORY.

For twenty-eight days Northwestern Colorado could not get mail or replenished supplies of medicine, food or repair parts. This great blockade of 1918 was the time Joe Preiss saw the need to keep that rotary snowplow alive, so that when help would come he could get up enough steam to turn its great cutting wheel and be helpful. He and others slept on planks, cooked their meals until their food gave out, then walked a mile through drifting snow in the terror of sub-zero temperatures to get food.

What Joe remembers is the VICTORY of keeping that boiler warm for seven days after carrying coal in sacks from seven train cars away. It was not the hardships, it was the VICTORY that his memory lived with.

Sixty-one years later skiers find a highway open or a tunnel available with no thought of the battles of an earlier day.

What retirement Joe lived with! He saw the good side even of retirement; more time for tomato plants, sprinkling the rose garden or shopping for his wife.

As an admirer said last year to me, "Joe loves life". Our nation is so much richer for Joe having been born. To live with joy in retirement eludes and embitters many of us as we grope our way.

Whenever I approached his door, I did it with expectation of not, "Well, here comes that preacher", but, "Welcome", to share what he had.

In retirement he shared his wisdom lest some hard-working officer in the Mile High Railroad Club would be over-looked. He gave his time sitting at the Rail Fair, but these are only samples of every day.

Joe found that life can be very good in sharing his humor and good spirit. And now that we honor him, our minds may see even further than before, what Joe would long for us to see.

Two thousand years ago a man preached that which Joe experienced. "Blessed are the meek for they shall inherit the earth. Blessed are the merciful for they shall obtain mercy. Blessed are the peacemakers for they shall be called the children of God."

In the scenes the *Rio Grande Zephyr* has stopped for the 50th Anniversary ceremony at East Portal. A crowd estimated at a thousand listened to brief remarks of several speakers and then watched as the time capsule was removed and displayed to the crowd. Several in the audience had been present half a century earlier for the opening event now being celebrated. — *both, Charles Albi*

30
High Green for Tomorrow

The skies and the mountainside were gray, the three locomotives and the entrance to the tunnel were black, and fog and swirling snow dulled the luster of the silver passenger cars.

In this somber setting, the Denver and Rio Grande Western Railroad, the Moffat Tunnel Commission and the National Railway Historical Society on Saturday celebrated the 50th anniversary of rail way service through the historic 6.2 mile tunnel.

—*The Rocky Mountain News,*
Sunday, February 26, 1978

There could be no more appropriate setting for the anniversary celebration than a snowy, blustery winter day. Far above on the narrow ledges of the Giant's Ladder a blizzard raged as if determined to hide every trace of man's brief intrusion as for that moment in time he had flung rails across the crest of Rollins Pass.

Standing among the onlookers was a small remnant of those who knew personally why there had to be a railroad tunnel piercing the front range of the Rockies: hardy pioneers from Middle Park who could recall when the Moffat Road was their lifeline; tunnel construction men who remembered when two cities sprang to life to serve and house the workers but of which hardly a trace remains; the railroaders themselves — section men, trainmen and mechanical crews — part of an ever diminishing band who did battle on the hill those many winters ago. And standing proudly among a lifetime of memories was Mrs. Louis Larsen, whose husband was at the throttle of engine 205 as

it pulled the first train through the tunnel half a century ago.

To the general public absorbed in skiing, orange crush football, busy airline schedules and freeway traffic jams, the occasion went unnoticed or perhaps brought a brief recall of an almost forgotten family member, a grandfather or uncle perhaps, who had been a railroader. To the young people on the ski train the celebration only meant half an hour of lost skiing time while their Saturday ski train waited for the celebration to clear the way into the tunnel and arrival at Winter Park.

However, there were many in the audience who understood the real meaning of the events being commemorated at this desolate railroad tunnel. They knew that this was more akin to a rededication of our faith in the principles set forth by those who had dug and blasted, railroaded and sometimes died to make possible a dream that was a part of the Moffat Railroad. And what of this man named Moffat?

David Halliday Moffat inspired confidence among his workers. They were humble, honest men and women; a guard in his 1st National Bank in Denver or railroad workers be they office secretaries, section laborers, telegraphers or devoted trainmen. He had no labor problems in a day of murderous relations between many companies and their workers.

Moffat seemed to arouse resentment among many of the blue bloods of Colorado society perhaps due in part to his ready acceptance of and by the common working man. Many were there whom he had saved from bankruptcy for he never turned his back on a friend. Gerald Hughes said of Moffat, "He never meant harm for anyone."

His last and truly greatest endeavor was the building of the Moffat Road but in so doing he incurred the wrath of some of the mightest men in America who were already fighting among themselves to control railroad transportation. In his banking business his methods were based not only on the customer's collateral but also on the person's potential ability. As Moffat approached financial defeat he discovered that the one group of men who never forsook him were those who worked on his railroad.

The decision to build a railroad west from Denver to Salt Lake City came only after a most thorough investigation was made into the mineral resources along the route and only after receiving the encouragement of William G. Evans who would stand beside Moffat and replace him after his death.

Moffat placed strong belief in the ability of his men and never was this better seen than when he placed his faith in the route projected by Locating Engineer H. A. Sumner.

The career of David Moffat was rich in accomplishments and the building of the Moffat Road was surely the crowning achievement. To fulfill his dream for this railroad he sacrificed his personal fortune and, like so many great men before him, died a poor man. Poor, that is, if wealth be measured in dollars but if measured in terms of service to his state then he was surely a wealthy man.

As planning for the Fiftieth Anniversary began, it became obvious that it would be necessary to hold the event one day before the actual date. This was due to the limited amount of passenger equipment owned by the Rio Grande, making it impossible to operate a special train to the tunnel. Instead it was decided to schedule the celebration around the regular westbound run of the *Rio Grande Zephyr* which would reach the tunnel at approximately 9:00 a.m. on Saturday morning, February 26th. On its return run the train would pass through the tunnel on the actual anniversary but in the evening, a time obviously not lending itself to a public gathering at a railroad tunnel.

For the opening event in the anniversary celebration the National Railway Historical Society in conjunction with the Colorado Railroad Museum sponsored a rare showing of the Metro-Goldwyn-Mayer silent film *White Desert*. Filmed on Rollins Pass in 1925, the picture portrays the construction of a railroad tunnel and is obviously based on the construction of the Moffat Tunnel then under way. When the workers are snowbound and starving the mighty rotary plow comes to the rescue in a spectacular display of railroading at "the top of the world".

The film was presented in the 2000 seat Paramount Theater, Denver's last downtown movie palace, and was sold out ten days in advance. With accompaniment by the Paramount's twin console Wurlitzer pipe organs, the evening was a resounding success and a perfect salute to the Moffat Road.

On Saturday, February 26, 1978, the Denver and Rio Grande Western placed every one of its passenger cars in service to accommodate almost four hundred passengers on the *Rio Grande Zephyr*. In addition a baggage car was borrowed from the Union Pacific to carry mail and crews from the U.S. Postal Service for a special two-day Railway Post Office. Since there are no longer any regular R.P.O.'s on passenger trains, this unusual event brought requests from every state and around the world from persons wanting the special Moffat Tunnel cachet and R.P.O. cancellation. Over 90,000 pieces of mail were carried on the round trip.

As the train arrived at East Portal it was greeted by a crowd estimated at five hundred persons who had driven to the tunnel site. Alexis McKinney, the retired director of public relations for the Rio Grande, was master of ceremonies at the brief program to eulogize the tunnel and the men of the Moffat Road.

The Invocation was given by the Reverend Edward T. Bollinger:

ETERNAL GOD, You have seen men shiver here for far more than fifty years. You are the one who knows the fall of each sparrow and counts sacred the life of every man who died in this smokey hole. This is sacred ground. You must be amused at us for not remembering the important people who opened this tunnel. Indeed, the first are last.

You remember Andrew Rogers, who first found this tunnel site, H. A. Sumner and Bruce Parker. You saw sixteen year old Nels Johnson digging. You knew Le Claire Daly would be more than a waterboy. You honored George Barnes and little Joe Culbertson. Men like them saw that no passenger in Moffat history was ever injured. You do not see the mile posts, for they are crosses of the men who lost their lives all the way to Craig.

Pity us for feeling important. Amen.

Mr. McKinney then spoke:

Only twenty minutes have been allotted our *Rio*

Grande Zephyr to pause here at the portal of the Moffat Tunnel: Twenty minutes to commemorate a half century of Colorado's most important historical record in transportation!

But that's the way it has been with this fabulous but dramatically practical bore over six miles long through and under the Continental Divide. There's been no time for stopping.

Those who first dreamed of it never stopped striving toward realization of their dreams. Those who engineered it and labored in it didn't stand still. And, since its dedication here fifty years ago its purpose has been to keep trains moving — instead of stalling in snowdrifts yonder on the roof of America.

It is reckoned that nearly 300,000 trains have passed through this tunnel. Coupled together, they'd form a solid string of locomotives and cars reaching nearly three times around the world. People who have passed through it number in the millions.

On an average busy day an estimated 56,000 tons of commerce are carried through — over 20 million tons a year. If anyone can contemplate 10 billion tons of freight, that's somewhere close to the half century's work load of the Moffat Tunnel.

Most of those who gave us this great work are no longer with us. We honor them. The benefits of their contributions have expanded year by year, and will outlast all of us here today.

From among the many who are here, it is fitting that we recognize some of those whose presence gives special significance to this occasion.

Mr. V. Allan Vaughn, President of the National Railway Historical Society, was introduced next and offered these thoughts:

Advertising executives like to tell the story about how there are twenty-five mountains in Colorado higher than Pike's Peak and then ask you to name *one* of them.

The same application could be made to this fabled tunnel we pause in our journey to honour this morning — there are two tunnels in the United States of greater length than Moffat; but can you name either one?

Such is the power in a name, the name of Moffat. In a world of railroad moguls he stood alone in his generation, for he fought an element of danger that, unlike the hostile tribes of plains railroading history, did not show itself until too often it was too late. The quirks of rock, mud, and snow proved well the modern advertising slogan of "It's not nice to fool Mother Nature."

But fool nature the Rio Grande indeed did and the route of the D&RGW is an industrial display of genius and perspiration, of dedicated and talented hands. The gradient out of the Denver valley is a marvel of railroad engineering and consistency and the tunnel we re-dedicate here today is a monument to David Moffat and the Rio Grande leaders who followed.

We cannot see the tons of drill bits used to bore through the rock above and ahead of us, nor can we see the millions of board feet of lumber used to keep the tunnel clear — when we ride through this black hole we lose our sense of direction and seem suspended in motion, and it is only then that we begin to sense the awesome and enormous proportion of this tunnel which brought the nation's edges closer together.

As we ride through the Moffat tunnel today the noises of the camps and saloons are gone, old mining towns are tumbled bits of wooden buildings, and where lived a single generation of man the eternal wind and aspen echo the old tunnel song of "Drill, ye tarriers, drill" and the saga of building this mountain railroading monument is likewise etched in stone. The words are right there for all time — Moffat Tunnel.

Mr. McKinney then introduced Moffat Tunnel Commission President, Rendle Myer:

Today marks the 50th Anniversary of the first passenger train through the Moffat Tunnel. With the Tunnel a proven success, we might take a moment to reflect on Denver as it existed 50 years ago — a quiet tourist community denied the hope of becoming a business and industrial metropolis that could unlock the tremendous mineral and agricultural resources beyond the slopes of the Continental Divide. Colorado's economy and Denver's reputation as the Queen City of the Plains are lasting tributes to the dedicated men who conquered the mighty barrier of the Divide and put the great resources of Northwestern Colorado in touch with the world.

David Moffat's ambition was that Denver should be linked to Salt Lake City on a transcontinental railroad, but he could not raise the money to build the essential link, a tunnel through the Continental Divide. His efforts were thwarted primarily by the stranglehold of Eastern financiers led by Harriman and Gould. The treacherous route over Corona Pass ended at Craig. David Moffat died in 1911.

The political and financial leaders of Colorado persevered led by such men as Gerald Hughes, Senator Lawrence Phipps, Claude Boettcher, W. R. Freeman and Charles H. Leckenby. After several defeats, in 1922 the Colorado Legislature created the Moffat Tunnel Improvement District due in no small measure to the efforts of State Representative George A. Pughe.

From 1923 to 1927 bonds totalling $15,470,000 were issued by the Moffat Tunnel Commission. All but $1,599,000 have been retired. The bonds will be fully paid-off in 1983 as scheduled and the Moffat Tunnel Commission has not levied an assessment on the real estate in the District since 1971.

The Moffat Road had many settings ideal for motion pictures and in 1927, M.G.M. spent several weeks filming the *Trail of '98,* **a story of the Klondike gold rush; unfortunately with no railroad scenes. We see a movie dog team with the Marcia in the background and (right) Glen Spalding with two movie men beside a grave of one of the dogs. Tragically, Fayette Bishop, son of engineer Bob Bishop, was killed during the production.** — *left, Mrs. Louis Larsen, CRRM; right, Glen Spalding, DPL*

The Moffat Tunnel Commission wishes to thank the National Railway Historical Society for its efforts in planning this occasion and the Commission joins all of you in commemorating the Moffat Tunnel which has contributed so greatly to the prosperity of the whole State.

The moment then arrived for which everyone waited; the time capsule was carefully removed and opened. The announcement was made that the contents would be displayed aboard the train for all to inspect. Mr. McKinney then asked the passengers to return to the train as quickly as possible and most needed little urging to seek the warmth of the shining streamliner. Minutes later the giant locomotives came to life and eased the train into the depths of the tunnel. Thus began the second half century of Moffat Tunnel history.

There were those among the throng that day who paused to reflect on the almost forgotten aspects of tunnel history; the fact that this was a celebration for a tunnel that could have been built without public funds, and the shame of Colorado capitalists who through jealousy and a myopic vision had failed to build it and instead forced the creation of the tunnel district. There was another question in the minds of some who knew the tunnel story from its beginning. What if the higher location that H. A. Sumner recommended for a tunnel had been built years earlier?

Yet to all aboard the *Zephyr* as it rolled off the 570 miles to Salt Lake City, far beyond the western peaks, there was a knowledge that men of vision had been forever vindicated in their seemingly impossible dreams. The mountains and the smothering blanket of snow had been formidable foes in a long battle but this day the victory belonged to the Moffat Road.

A CELEBRATION

upon the occasion

of the

FIFTIETH ANNIVERSARY

of the opening of the

MOFFAT TUNNEL

presented by

Intermountain Chapter
National Railway Historical Society

TOUCH O' THE 20'S
Stage Show Starring

KIT ANDRÉE

"THE WHITE DESERT"
accompanied by
ROBERT CASTLE, ORGANIST

Produced by

Vern West

&

William C. Jones

Paramount Theatre
Denver, Colorado
February 23, 1978

"THE WHITE DESERT"

As part of the Moffat Tunnel celebration a showing was arranged of the Metro-Goldwyn movie *White Desert*. Filmed on Rollins Pass in 1925, the story tells of efforts to construct a railroad tunnel high in the Rockies and includes many exciting scenes of Moffat trains in action. The climax is reached as a rotary plow fights to free stranded tunnel workers; this is the only known motion picture film of the Rollins Pass line. The showing was held in Denver's last "movie palace", the famed Paramount with its giant theater organ to accompany the silent film. The showing was sold out several days in advance and this event proved the first in a series leading to the complete remodeling and revival of this historic theater.

A number of Moffat employers were involved in the filming including Louis Larsen who received this message (below) directing him to the filming location with his engine. Fabian Smith was on the plow train for the rescue scenes and took this photo (right) of the action. When the film was released in the summer of 1925, the Moffat Road loaded two refrigerator cars with snow at Corona for this publicity stunt for the Victory Theater. — *bottom, DPL; others, CRRM*

```
Denver 25 March 1925.

Larson, 1:15P.M. Denver.

     Eng 122 to use Denver to Utah Junction; get Eng 105 at Utah Junction which
Mr Howerton says will be all ready and oiled around; take the letter and any
other stuff delivered you here and handle to loop, delivering to Mr Brockman at
Loop.   Mr Brockman may want to hold you at Loop for a time and advises that if
you will come through Corona without eating they will arrange to feed you at the
movie cars at Loop.

                                                          J. B. C.
```

On Saturday, Feb. 26, 1978, the *Rio Grande Zephyr* departed Denver with over 300 passengers. The crew (above-left) included - left to right - on the ground, Conductor George Capan and Head Brakeman Jim Wood while on the engine are Superintendent of Air Brakes Robert Buffalo, Engineer Howard Chandler and Fireman R. L. Andrews; Rear Brakeman Larry Enger is not shown. During the two day round trip over 80,000 pieces of mail were handled on the special Railway Post Office commemorating the anniversary and R.P.O Clerk James Briarton is seen (above) handing mail off to Postmistress Iva C. Seaman at Bond. In the evening the dining car featured this special menu as the *Zephyr* raced off the miles to Salt Lake City, continuing the tradition of comfortable and safe service on the Rails that Climb. — *right, Mel Patrick; others, Ronald C. Hill*

Rio **Grande**
the **ACTION** road

". . . one thing is for certain — the breed of railroader that built this steel highway will be watching from the past and the hardy men of the high iron in your time will be ever watchful and diligent in the art of moving steel over steel — 'through the Rockies, not around them' still the motto of the high country railroaders!"
— *V. A. Vaughn, President National Railway Historical Society, on the occasion of replacement of the time capsule, to be opened in 2028.*

FIFTIETH ANNIVERSARY
OF THE
MOFFAT TUNNEL

MOFFAT
TUNNEL
1923   1927

DINNER
ON BOARD THE
Silver Banquet

FEBRUARY 25-26, 1978

In the heart
Of a man
An idea was born.
Full of desire
To help build the West —
Wanting to share
The treasures of God
Hidden away in the Rockies.
Sowing the seed
In the minds of his friends,
Dave Moffat watched
His Brain Child grow,
"Through the Rockies —
Not around them."
The dream developed
In tunnels and ties and rails.

It was the Moffat Road—
A symbol of brotherhood
Knit in the lives
Of its laborers.
Through snow and hail,
Through gas and slide,
A life was given
For every mile.
And though the dreamer died,
The dream lived on
And today is fulfilled
As the Zephyr rides
Over the Moffat Line
On the D. and R. G.W. West—
Over the Rails That Climb.
—A.S.B.

321

LOCOMOTIVES OF THE DENVER AND SALT LAKE RAILWAY
Compiled by Richard H. Kindig

CLASS 28, 0-6-0

D&SL No.	Builder	Builder's No.	Date Built	Disposition
20	Schenectady	29038	7-1903	Scrapped 10-1939
21	Schenectady	29039	7-1903	Scrapped 10-1939

Drivers Inches	Cylinders Inches	Wt. on Drivers Pounds	Total Wt. Pounds	Tractive Effort Pounds
51	19x26	132,000	132,000	28,160

CLASS 42, 2-8-0

D&SL No.	Builder	Builder's No.	Date Built	Disposition
100	Schenectady	29204	2-1904	Scrapped 5-1937
101	Schenectady	29205	2-1904	Scrapped 5-1937
102	Schenectady	37709	5-1905	Scrapped 5-1937

Drivers Inches	Cylinders Inches	Wt. on Drivers Pounds	Total Wt. Pounds	Tractive Effort Pounds
57	22x28	186,000	209,500	42,420

CLASS 44, 2-8-0

D&SL No.	Builder	Builder's No.	Date Built	D&RGW No. and Date	Disposition
103	Schenectady	39947	5-1906		Sc. 5-1937
104	Schenectady	39948	5-1906		Sc. 5-1937
105	Schenectady	39949	5-1906		Sc. 5-1937
106	Schenectady	41617	11-1906		Sc. 10-1937
107	Schenectady	41618	11-1906		Sc. 5-1937
108	Schenectady	45576	10-1908		Sc. 6-1942
109	Schenectady	45577	10-1908		Sc. 8-1943
110	Schenectady	45578	10-1908		Sc. 10-1947
111	Schenectady	45579	10-1908	1031 5-1949	Sc. 12-1951
112	Schenectady	48148	8-1910	1032 not applied	Sc. 12-1948
113	Schenectady	48149	8-1910	1033 5-1948	Sc. 7-1950
114	Schenectady	48150	8-1910		Sc. 6-1942
115	Schenectady	48242	8-1910		sold to Columbia Steel Corp. 9-1942
116	Schenectady	48243	8-1910		sold to Columbia Steel Corp. 11-1942
117	Schenectady	48244	8-1910		sold to Columbia Steel Corp. 10-1942
118	Schenectady	48245	8-1910	1034 10-1948	Sc. 5-1955
119	Schenectady	48246	8-1910	1035 7-1948	Sc. 5-1955
120	Schenectady	48247	8-1910	1036 3-1948	Sc. 5-1951
121	Schenectady	48248	8-1910	1037 5-1938	Sc. 12-1951
122	Schenectady	48249	8-1910	1038 not applied	Sc. 4-1948
123	Schenectady	48250	8-1910	1039 5-1958	Sc. 3-1951

Drivers Inches	Cylinders Inches	Wt. on Drivers Pounds	Total Wt. Pounds	Tractive Effort Pounds
55	22x28	195,00	219,00	43,980

CLASS 76, 2-6-6-0

Engines 200-209 were built as 0-6-6-0, and rebuilt within a few years to the 2-6-6-0 type; 210-216 built originally as 2-6-6-0's.

D&SL No.	Builder	Builder's No.	Date Built	D&RGW No. and Date	Disposition
200	Schenectady	45604	10-1908	3360 6-1948	Sc. 6-1949
201	Schenectady	46560	10-1909	3361 12-1947	Sc. 6-1952
202	Schenectady	46561	10-1909	3362 not applied	Sc. 12-1947
203	Schenectady	48151	7-1910	3363 5-1948	Sc. 8-1949
204	Schenectady	48230	7-1910	3364 6-1948	Sc. 8-1949
205	Schenectady	48231	7-1910	3365 5-1948	Sc. 8-1949
206	Schenectady	48232	7-1910	3366 12-1947	Sc. 7-1951
207	Schenectady	48233	7-1910	3367 12-1947	Sc. 5-1950
208	Schenectady	48234	7-1910	3368 5-1948	Sc. 8-1950
209	Schenectady	48235	7-1910	3369 3-1948	Sc. 4-1951
210	Schenectady	53292	4-1913		Destroyed 12-5-1924 in derailment
211	Schenectady	53293	4-1913	3370 6-1948	Sc. 7-1951
212	Schenectady	55986	9-1916	3371 7-1948	Sc. 4-1951
213	Schenectady	55987	9-1916	3372 6-1948	Sc. 7-1949
214	Schenectady	55988	9-1916	3373 2-1949	Sc. 7-1950
215	Schenectady	55989	9-1916	3374 5-1948	Sc. 7-1949
216	Schenectady	56296	9-1916	3375 5-1948	Sc. 7-1951

Drivers Inches	Cylinders Inches	Wt. on Drivers Pounds	Total Wt. Pounds	Tractive Effort Pounds
55	21x32 & 33½x32	332,000	362,000	76,400

Note: Weight on drivers of engines 212-216 was 333,500 pounds and total weight was 361,000 pounds.

CLASS 30, 4-6-0

D&SL No.	Builder	Builder's No.	Date Built	Disposition
300	Schenectady	29203	2-1904	Sc. 4-1947

Drivers Inches	Cylinders Inches	Wt. on Drivers Pounds	Total Wt. Pounds	Tractive Effort Pounds
63	20x28	142,000	186,000	30,220

CLASS 33, 4-6-0

D&SL No.	Builder	Builder's No.	Date Built	D&RGW No. and Date	Disposition
301	Schenectady	37708	5-1905		Sc. 6-1942
302	Schenectady	41616	11-1907	795 4-1948	Sc. 7-1948

Drivers Inches	Cylinders Inches	Wt. on Drivers Pounds	Total Wt. Pounds	Tractive Effort Pounds
57	20x28	301—138,500 302—142,000	182,000 189,000	34,405

CLASS 34, 4-6-0

D&SL No.	Builder	Builder's No.	Date Built	D&RGW No. and Date	Disposition
303	Schenectady	48147	7-1910	796 not applied	Sc. 7-1948

Drivers Inches	Cylinders Inches	Wt. on Drivers Pounds	Total Wt. Pounds	Tractive Effort Pounds
63	20x28	165,000	215,000	34,150

CLASS 19, 4-4-0

D&SL No.	Builder	Builder's No.	Date Built	Disposition
390	Pittsburgh	1951	1899	Sc. 7-1937
391	Pittsburgh	1952	1899	Sc. 7-1937

Drivers Inches	Cylinders Inches	Wt. on Drivers Pounds	Total Wt. Pounds	Tractive Effort Pounds
60	18x24	70,000	108,000	19,280

D&SL 390-391 were orginally Chesapeake Beach 3-4.

CLASS 63, 2-8-2

D&SL No.	Builder	Builder's No.	Date Built	D&RGW No. and Date	Disposition
400	Lima	5100	1915	1220 7-1948	Sc. 10-1953
401	Lima	5101	1915	1221 5-1948	Sc. 4-1949
402	Lima	5102	1915	1222 11-1948	Sc. 6-1954
403	Lima	5103	1915	1223 5-1948	Sc. 12-1948
404	Lima	5104	1915	1224 12-1947	Sc. 9-1956
405	Lima	5105	1915	1225 1-1948	Sc. 1-1955
406	Lima	5106	1915	1226 12-1947	Sc. 4-1952
407	Lima	5107	1915	1227 2-1948	Sc. 10-1953
408	Schenectady	55984	8-1916	1228 5-1948	Sc. 5-1952
409	Schenectady	55985	8-1916	1229 3-1948	Sc. 10-1956

Drivers Inches	Cylinders Inches	Wt. on Drivers Pounds	Total Wt. Pounds	Tractive Effort Pounds
55	26x30	232,000	295,000	62,700

Note: Total weight of engines 408 and 409 was 306,000 pounds.

ROTARY SNOW PLOWS OF THE DENVER & SALT LAKE RAILWAY

No. 10200 Built by American Locomotive Co., Cooke Works, December, 1904. Builders No. 30264. All Steel with 13'5'' cut. Length of plow and tender 65'0'', 7000 gallon tender, weight of plow 172,800 lbs., weight of plow and tender 305,200 lbs. Retired by D&RGW April, 1950 and scrapped shortly thereafter.

No. 10201 Built by American Locomotive Co., Cooke Works, November 1906. Builders No. 41454. All Steel with 13'5'' cut. Length of plow and tender 65'0'', 7000 gallon tender, weight of plow 172,000 lbs., weight of plow and tender 305,200 lbs. Sold August 26, 1938 to Northern Pacific Ry. and became their No. 43. Converted to electric drive and became Burlington Northern No. 972550. In service as of 1979.

No. 10202 Built by American Locomotive Co., Schenectady Works, October, 1910. Builder's No. A-4113-B. All steel with 13'5'' cut. Length of plow and tender 66'1'', 9000 gallon tender, weight of plow 200,000 lbs., weight of plow and tender 366,300 lbs. Built for Colorado, Wyoming and Eastern Ry. Purchased by U.S. Railroad Administration for D&SLRR. September, 1918. Sold September 26, 1938 to Western Pacific RR. and became their No. 3. Converted to electric drive 1957. Now scrapped.

BIBLIOGRAPHY AND SOURCES

THE FOLLOWING BOOKS ARE RECOMMENDED FOR ADDITIONAL READING ON THE MOFFAT ROAD.

Albi, Charles and Forrest, Kenton, *The Moffat Tunnel, A Brief History,* Colorado Railroad Museum, Golden, Colorado. 1978

Athearn, Robert G., *Rebel of the Rockies,* Yale University Press, New Haven, 1962. (A new edition is now available under the title *The Denver & Rio Grande Western Railroad,* University of Nebraska Press, Lincoln, 1977.)

Black, Robert A., III, *Island in the Rockies,* Grand County Pioneer Society, Hot Sulphur Springs, Colorado. 1970.

Bollinger, Edward T. and Bauer, Frederick, *The Moffat Road,* Swallow Press, Chicago. 1962.

Boner, Harold A., *The Giant's Ladder,* Kalmbach Publishing Co., Milwaukee. 1962 (out-of-print).

Cunningham, Frank, *Big Dan, A Biography of Dan Cunningham,* Deseret News Press, Salt Lake City. 1946. (out-of-print)

LeMassena, Robert, *Rio Grande to the Pacific,* Sundance Books, Silverton, Colorado. 1974.

McMechen, Edgar C., *The Moffat Tunnel of Colorado,* Wahlgreen Publishing Co., Denver. 1927. (out-of-print)

The following sources provided significant information utilized in both the original edition of *RAILS THAT CLIMB* and this completely revised edition.

CHAPEL CAR *EMMANUEL*
American Baptist Association: Kathy Shirely and Clarrisa E. Kohler.
Green Lake Center, Green Lake, Wisconsin: Lawrence H. Jannssen.
Jacquie McKeon, author of *If That Don't Beat the Devil.*

FILM MAKING ON THE MOFFAT ROAD
Pete Bensen, Howard Dearing, Hazel Howell, Mrs. Louis Larsen and Fabian Smith.

GORE CAÑON CONTROVERSY
W. I. Hoklas: information on Moffat surveys.
Luther Van Buskirk: information on Moffat surveys preserved on tape at State Historical Society of Colorado.

LAST TRAIN OVER ROLLINS PASS
John Harrison.

MAMMOTH - TOLLAND AREA
Mrs. Leda Reed: extensive research on the town and surrounding area as well as first trains to operate over the line.
Mr. and Mrs. David Ramaley: papers and photos of the University of Colorado, Mountain Laboratory for Biology and Botany as well as the Jenkins Sawmill railroad.

MIDDLE PARK LUMBER COMPANY
W. I. Hoklas: survey information as well as photos and papers of surveyor Clay C. Blough.

NORTHWESTERN TERMINAL RAILROAD
John Harrison: map.

ROCKY MOUNTAIN RAILROAD
W. I. Hoklas: notes and information on surveys of the line.
Wolcott Collection: University of Colorado, Western Archives

MUCH ADDITIONAL USEFUL INFORMATION WAS PROVIDED BY THE FOLLOWING PERSONS:
Fred Bauer, E. G. Deakins, T. R. Ellis, A. L. Johnson, Ada Honnald Jones, W. C. Jones, S. D. McCall, Gene Edson Olsen and Irving Edson Olsen.

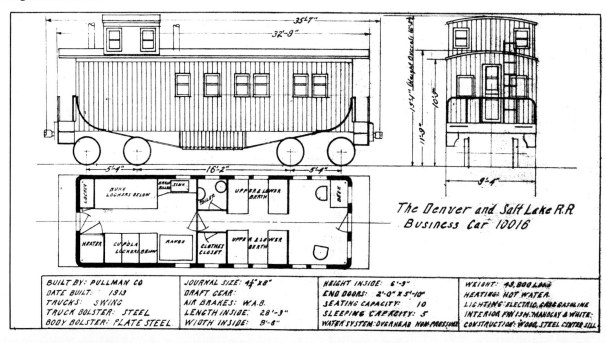

The Denver and Salt Lake R.R.
Business Car 10016

BUILT BY: PULLMAN CO	JOURNAL SIZE: 4¾" X 8"	HEIGHT INSIDE: 6'-9"	WEIGHT: 48,800 LBS
DATE BUILT: 1913	DRAFT GEAR:	END DOORS: 2'-0" X 5'-10"	HEATING: HOT WATER
TRUCKS: SWING	AIR BRAKES: W.A.B.	SEATING CAPACITY: 10	LIGHTING: ELECTRIC, AXLE GASOLINE
TRUCK BOLSTER: STEEL	LENGTH INSIDE: 28'-3"	SLEEPING CAPACITY: 5	INTERIOR FINISH: MAHOGAY & WHITE
BODY BOLSTER: PLATE STEEL	WIDTH INSIDE: 8'-6"	WATER SYSTEM: OVERHEAD NON-PRESSURE	CONSTRUCTION: WOOD, STEEL CENTER SILL

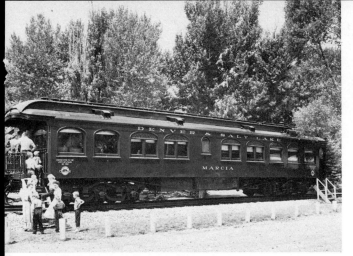

Denver, Colo., June 30th, 1904.

TO DENVER CHAMBER OF COMMERCE:

           Your Merchants Excursion Committee
beg to submit the following report of the excursion "Opening of the
Moffat Road" June 23rd, 1904.

    Tickets $1.50 each.   One-third refunded by R. R. Co. to defray
expense of dinner, music and incidentals.

Tickets received from the R. R. Co. ----------------------- 950
    "   sold by Committee ----------- 640
    "   " " Secy's Office---------- 298
Complimentaries issued--------------- 12
Tickets on hand (Mr. Day) --------- 10
                                    950   950

R. R. Co. carried band free --------- 12
R. R. Co. carried guests of Mr. Moffat free --- 14
R. R. Co. collected cash fares ---------------- 41
R. R. Co. collected tickets ------------------- 905
           Total people carried ----- 972 $972.00
           Less carried free---------------------- 36.00
           Amount due R. R. Co. ---------------- $936.00

Received from Committee for 640 tickets ------------ $960.
Received from Secy's Office sales 288   432.
    "   from cash sales by Secy's first train --- 7   10.50
                 Cash received from Secy.---- $1402.50 $1402.50
                 Cash fares from R. R. Co.   61.50
                                        $1464.00
             Check from John McDonough--------------- 1.50
             Total receipts--------------------- $1465.50

           DISBURSEMENTS PER VOUCHER ATTACHED.

Paid R. R. CO.-- $936.00
  " National Hotel Co. 300 meals at 50¢ -- $150.00)
  "   "   "   503 meals at 40¢ -- 202.20)   351.20
  " Satrianos Band ----------------------62.00)
  "   "   " overtime---------------- 10.00)   72.00
  " C. M. Day Rubber stamp & Cards (Parlor car tickets) .85
  " M. Aldridge for Banner & Carrier $2.50 & .75¢/---- 3.25
                Total disbursements-----------$1363.30

Fares refunded to Committee -------------- None.
Total earnings------------------------- $1465.50
Total cost----------------------------- 1363.30
Net profit for Chamber of Commerce-------- $ 102.20
Herewith my check for $100.70
  " J. McDonough's "   1.50
        Total $102.20

                                      C. M. Day
                                      CHAIRMAN

SO LITTLE SURVIVED!

Of all Moffat Road equipment, the only item to survive in railroad service is rotary plow 10201, which after extensive rebuilding is seen (below) as Burlington Northern rotary plow 972550 in Spiritwood, North Dakota on Jan. 4, 1978.

Business Car *Marcia* was donated by the Rio Grande to the City of Craig (above) where it serves as a fitting memorial to David Moffat whose railroad did much to develop Craig and northwestern Colorado. The Moffat Road's unique caboose-business car 10016, has not survived but is remembered from this plan (left) indicating its unusual design.

Fortunately much of the written record of the line has survived including this report of the Denver Chamber of Commerce concerning their excursion on opening day, June 23, 1904. Leda Reed did extensive research on this topic and notes the event took place just 34 years after arrival of the first train in Denver via the Denver Pacific on June 23, 1870; David Moffat was also involved in that railroad. — *below, David Gasal, F. Hol Wagner collection; others, DPL*

INDEX

This index consists of entries from the body of the text and captions for the photographs and illustrations. Page numbers in italics denote that the subject indexed appears in a photograph or an illustration. The terms "Moffat Road" and "The Moffat" are used interchangeably throughout the book. These terms are not indexed, but the reader is referred to the three corporate entries for "The Moffat": Denver, Northwestern and Pacific Railway; Denver and Salt Lake Railroad; and Denver and Salt Lake Railway. Since it would be difficult to distinguish corporate time periods for certain "Moffat Road" subjects such as locomotives, the reader is first referred to the entry: Denver, Northwestern and Pacific Railway.